Constructing 21st Century U.S. Foreign Policy

Constructing 21st Century U.S. Foreign Policy

Identity, Ideology, and America's World Role in a New Era

Karl K. Schonberg

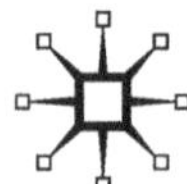

CONSTRUCTING 21ST CENTURY U.S. FOREIGN POLICY

First published in 2009 by PALGRAVE MACMILLAN® in the United States - a division of St. Martin's Press LLC, 175 Fifth Avenue, New York, NY 10010.

Where this book is distributed in the UK, Europe and the rest of the world, this is by Palgrave Macmillan, a division of Macmillan Publishers Limited, registered in England, company number 785998, of Houndmills, Basingstoke, Hampshire RG21 6XS.

Palgrave Macmillan is the global academic imprint of the above companies and has companies and representatives throughout the world.

ISBN: 978-0-230-60776-7

Library of Congress Cataloging-in-Publication Data

Schonberg, Karl K., 1968–
Constructing 21st century U.S. foreign policy : identity, ideology, and america's world role in a new era / Karl K. Schonberg.
p. cm.
Includes bibliographical references.
ISBN-13: 978-0-230-60776-7 (alk. paper)

1. United States—Foreign relations—21st century. I. Title. II. Title: Constructing twenty-first century U.S. foreign policy.

JZ1480.S36 2009
327.73—dc22 2008046844

A catalogue record of the book is available from the British Library.

Design by Macmillan Publishing Solutions

First edition: July 2009

To Kathleen, Ellie, Harry, and Josie

Contents

Preface

I am deeply grateful for the help and support of my family, friends, and colleagues as I worked on this book. Among those who gave me invaluable advice on draft chapters as they were presented as conference papers between 2005 and 2008 were Matthew Baum, Neal Carter, Alex Danchev, Denise Horn, Kenneth McDonagh, Nicholas Onuf, Marc O'Reilly, and James M. Scott. I am deeply indebted to my St. Lawrence University faculty colleagues Margaret Bass, Brian Chezum, Bob Cowser, Traci Fordham-Hernandez, Mike Jenkins, Joe Kling, Val Lehr, Erin McCarthy, and Liz Regosin for their constructive criticism and moral support at every stage of the writing process. Danielle Egan offered me her insight into the work of Michel Foucualt, Alan Draper gave me advice on the publication process, and Michael Greenwald provided me with the benefit of his Talmudic scholarship. There is no finer group of teacher-scholars anywhere, and it is my privilege to call them my colleagues and friends.

This project grew out of the work I began with my previous book, *Pursuing the National Interest: Moments of Transition in Twentieth Century U.S. Foreign Policy* (Praeger, 2003). A few passages from that work are included in the introduction and chapters 1 and 2 of this book in rewritten form.

Without the steadfast support of my family I would never have been able to complete this book. My parents, Cynthia and Jackson Schonberg, encouraged my work on this project with the same selfless generosity that has helped me to learn and grow at every stage of my life. No son could ask for wiser or more loving parents, and any merit in this book is the result of the guidance they gave me as my first and best teachers. Without the patience and support of my wife, Kathleen, and our children, Ellie, Harry, and Josie, this book would not have been possible. Their love was a constant source of inspiration during my work on this project, as it is in everything I do. They are the greatest blessing in my life, and this book is dedicated to them.

Canton, New York
January, 2009

Introduction: International Relations Theory and U.S. Foreign Policy in a New Era

We do not see things as they are; we see things as we are.

—Babylonian Talmud, Berakhot 55b.

The coalition did not act in Iraq because we had discovered dramatic new evidence of Iraq's pursuit of weapons of mass destruction. We acted because we saw the existing evidence in a new light through the prism of our experience on 9/11.

—Donald Rumsfeld, testimony before the Senate Armed Service Committee, July 9, 2003.

Ten days after the terrorist attacks of September 11, 2001, President George W. Bush spoke before a joint session of Congress. After the events of that day, he said, "night fell on a different world." It was a fact so obvious and so often repeated that it became a truism, even a cliché in the months that followed: 9/11 was the day that everything changed.

But it was not true. That al Qaeda had the means and intention to use violence against American interests around the world and that international terrorist organizations might attempt to attack the United States on its own soil were realities well understood long before 9/11. The strategic balance of military forces in the world was not altered. The U.S. economy was damaged, but not permanently or fundamentally—the U.S. stock market recovering its losses in about eight weeks. Compared with the Japanese bombing of Pearl Harbor in the last days of 1941, which did significantly upset the strategic balance of military forces in the world, the material impact of September 11 on world politics was minimal.

At the same time, it is clearly not the case that the 9/11 attacks were unimportant to world history. Their impact was enormous, but the fact that no commensurate change occurred in the global balance of power suggests a critical point for the analysis of international relations (IR) in the contemporary world: perceptions matter, often as much or even more than objective, material power.

What changed after 9/11 was not the world, but the way in which Americans perceived it. In the months after the attacks, millions of Americans struggled to understand what these events should be interpreted to mean about their nation's security and role in global politics. This book is an attempt to understand this process, the means by which a society and its leaders come to comprehend the nature of the international system and their relationship to it, in so doing creating the socio-cognitive basis for action within that system. This study will bring together IR theory and policy analysis to describe the determinants of U.S. foreign policy since 9/11, the assumptions and social processes that gave rise to particular policy choices, and the consequences of these factors for the subsequent course of history.

This book will employ constructivist IR theory to explain U.S. foreign policy in the post-9/11 era. It will argue that to understand the role of America in the world in this period it is necessary to consider not just the relative power relationships between the United States and other actors in the international system, but also the ideational framework through which U.S. leaders have viewed and made sense of the world around them. The first question that it seeks to answer is simple: why has the United States undertaken the policies it has in the years since 9/11? But it will argue that the answer to this question is far more complex than previous generations of IR scholarship, based in the rational-materialist power premises of neorealism, would have conceded. In this era as in every era, the nature of the international environment in which the United States or any state acts can be apprehended by national leaders only through a socio-cognitive structure in which, it will be argued, national identity and ideology are critical variables in determinations of friend and foe, opportunity and threat.

Who the United States is, who its friends and enemies are, and what is possible and desirable in the environment in which they interact are determined not strictly by material, objective power realities but by the social and cognitive process through which state leaders comprehend that reality. In this process, U.S. leaders in every era reach understandings of U.S. interests by appealing to a set of traditional ideals that are to a large extent consistent over time, but interpreted in different ways in each historical era to make sense of and frame a coherent narrative about recent historical events. The administration of George W. Bush in the years since 9/11 behaved in some ways much as every U.S. presidential administration has in the past: it drew conclusions about the nature of the threats and opportunities present within the international system and the appropriate role of the United States in that environment by referencing and interpreting a set of broad, traditional ideas about American identity. It then framed an ideological narrative about the causes, consequences, and meaning of recent events and the appropriate course of future policy on the basis of a set of assertions about the identity of the United States and the international Others with whom it was interacting.

In its emphasis on ideational determinants of foreign policy, this book adds to a body of literature on IR theory that has grown significantly over the last two decades. As Yosef Lapid has written, "Culture and identity are staging a dramatic comeback in social theory and practice at the end of the twentieth century . . . A swing of the pendulum toward culture and identity is strikingly evident in post–Cold War IR theorizing."[1] John Kurt Jacobsen has suggested that "after a long period of indifference, even hostility, toward ideational explanations in political science, the time for ideas has come around once again." The reasons for this revival are "a discontent with the inability of rational interest-based models to explain, let alone predict, policy outcomes (except by resorting to a host of auxiliary assumptions) and the evident onset of another era of profound socioeconomic change." Jacobsen argues that new ideational literature presents a formidable challenge to the "actual softness that hides behind the seeming toughness of rational choice theories which see individuals as calculating interests" and concludes that "beliefs about the connections between interests and policies are at least as important as the nature of the interests themselves."[2]

Collectively known as "constructivism," these theoretical approaches emphasizing the role of shared ideas in international politics have challenged the realist assertion that states have only one essential identity—sovereign, self-interested, competitors for power—by contending that the perspectives of international actors are socially as well as materially determined and that identities and interests are intersubjective and malleable. While for realists the structure of the international system is static and state power determines the course of history, for constructivists the assumptions, beliefs, and values of international actors exert a critical influence on events. As Jack Snyder has suggested,

> Constructivists believe that debates about ideas are the fundamental building blocks of international life . . . People's understanding of their interests depends on the ideas they hold . . . Recent events seem to vindicate the theory's resurgence; a theory that emphasizes the role of ideologies, identities, persuasion, and transnational networks is highly relevant to understanding the post-9/11 world.[3]

This book will employ a variant of constructivism focusing on the intersubjective identities of actors in the international system. Alexander Wendt has argued that such identities constitute "cognitive schemas that enable an actor to determine 'who I am/we are' in a situation, and positions in a social role structure of shared understandings and expectations."[4] Similarly, Ted Hopf has claimed that "a state's own domestic identities constitute a social cognitive structure that makes threats and opportunities, enemies and allies, intelligible, thinkable, and possible."[5] Definitions of identity are thus crucial to understanding the ebb and flow of international politics for constructivists, since actors comprehend their self-interest in large part through their assessment of their identities in relation to those of others in the system.

Foreign policy analysis from an identity-constructivist perspective thus begins by asking how international actors see and define themselves, other actors, and the environment in which they interact, with the assumption that these perceptions tend to determine policy.

The argument of this book will be that foreign policy in the administration of George W. Bush from 2001 to 2007 was rooted in a set of ideological principles derived from particular interpretations of American identity and the identities of other actors in the international system. These ideological and identity premises dominated the administration's discourse about foreign policy both publicly and within the president's circle of advisors and led directly to a specific set of policy choices and consequences, particularly with regard to the war in Iraq. Chapter 1 will examine national identity and ideology as abstract concepts, consider the ways in which they are constituted and affect state foreign policy making, and describe the ways in which these factors have shaped U.S. foreign policy over the course of history. Chapter 2 will examine the ways in which ideas about national identity were shaped into an operative foreign policy ideology in the Bush administration. Chapter 3 will analyze the administration's public use of this ideological framework in its construction of a coherent vision of the identities of the United States and other international actors that served to enable subsequent foreign policy. Chapter 4 will describe the social-psychological and institutional environment within the administration through which these ideological and identity constructions were processed and translated into policy. And Chapter 5 will examine the particular effects in Iraq of these ideationally rooted policies, particularly in regard to the emergence of widespread conflict there in the years after the fall of the Ba'athist government in the spring of 2003.

REALISM AND CONSTRUCTIVISM ACROSS TWO CENTURIES

In his seminal 1953 work, *Ideals and Self Interest in America's Foreign Relations*, the realist scholar Robert Osgood reached the conclusion that there are a variety of factors influencing the way in which the United States defines its foreign policies, national self-interest being only one among them. He suggested, in short, that in the creation of American foreign policy, ideas matter.

While American interests remained relatively consistent throughout history in Osgood's view, they were properly perceived or ignored to varying degrees in different periods due to changes in the dominant intellectual paradigm of each era.[6] He observed that while few national leaders at any moment in history disagreed that there was a "national interest" and that it ought to be pursued, there were often profound disagreements between them about what it was. Every major debate about U.S. foreign policy in the twentieth century, Osgood noted, was about what constituted the national interest and how to pursue it. Definitions of national interest and threat depended on perceptions and judgments that were not based on rational calculation alone. Though Osgood argued that there existed a "national interest" as such, he was forced to conclude that decision makers might not perceive it correctly, define it too narrowly or broadly, ignoring ideals or emphasizing them to excess.

Osgood's observation that there is often conflict over the meaning of the "national interest" suggests that the traditional realist view of states as unitary, rational actors pursuing their self interest defined as power cannot adequately explain the history of U.S. foreign policy.

It is also necessary to contend with the complexity of ideology and identity—the intellectual lenses through which events abroad are perceived, the set of assumptions from which definitions of power and national interest in given situations are extrapolated, the beliefs and values that underlie concrete policy choices.

In practice, definitions of national interest are inevitably shaped by the subjective belief systems of individual decision makers. In this process, the distinction between ideals and interests is false, because in practice human beings, including policy makers, do not tend to make sharp distinctions between these factors but rather to combine and conflate them. Individuals in the same situation may define the terms "national interest" and "power" in very different ways. The realist conception of foreign policy making is not so much inaccurate as incomplete, because nations and national leaders perceive power and national interest through systems of belief that exert a profound influence on their practical understanding of these concepts. As Jeffrey W. Legro puts it, "Models of unitary state behavior depend on collective ideas and under certain conditions require an exogenous theory of the sources of those ideas." Realist arguments that posit the state as a self-interested, rational actor are limited in their explanatory power because, in policy making, rationality is itself bounded by the beliefs, assumptions, and values of decision makers and whole societies. Such approaches are not necessarily in contradiction with ideational approaches, but require ideational framing to fully explain policy outcomes. The subjectivity underlying the "national interest" means that to explain or predict, it is necessary to understand both the ways in which decision makers define the national interest and the process by which these definitions manifest policy.[7]

The realist school from which Osgood emerged had its inception in its modern form in the work of Hans Morgenthau in the late 1940s. In the decades that followed, realism became the dominant philosophy in the study of IR, the standard against which alternative views were measured. The realist school evolved significantly in the second half of the twentieth century, particularly in the late 1970s when Kenneth Waltz's *Theory of International Politics* asserted that it was not the insatiable desire for power inherent in human nature that drove world politics, but the insecurity inherent in an anarchic international system. "Neorealism" still saw competition for power within the system as the primary dynamic of state behavior, but assumed that states' underlying motives were basically defensive, that they typically sought power in response to threats rather than opportunities.[8]

But throughout this evolution, the explanatory power of realism has remained fundamentally dependent on the concept of national self-interest as the goal of state policy. The first generation of realists defined it in terms of power, but conceded that more power would not always serve a nation's interest—if, for instance, it made the nation's neighbors insecure and thus more hostile. But these thinkers never fully acknowledged the imprecision of the notion of power, highlighted by the fact that while the concept could be defined in the abstract, it became less certain when translated into practice; when deciding whether to use force abroad in a given situation, for example, uncertainty and subjectivity overtook the abstract clarity of the idea. Later neorealists often sought to overcome this ambiguity by substituting other notions, such as "security," for power, but these efforts could not make the argument more concrete; if anything, they highlighted its vagueness.

The broad cold war consensus in academic and policy circles may have had the effect of obscuring the subjectivity of national interest during the formative years of the academic study of IR in the wake of World War II. But the end of the cold war suggested very clearly that nonmaterial social and ideational factors are more important than many scholars had previously believed. Realism and later neorealism were the dominant schools of thought in IR theory throughout the cold war because the central theme of global history during that period—intractable conflict between great powers in a bipolar international system that appeared to constrain the behavior of all the actors within that system—seemed to be well explained by their arguments. They were effective theories for their time; the factors they chose to de-emphasize or dismiss (like domestic politics, ideology, culture, and identity) throughout much of the cold war seemed like acceptable sacrifices in the name of theoretical parsimony. That is, until the end of the cold war, a seismic shift in the international system that was entirely unexpected within IR theory because it was a consequence of precisely those factors in the Soviet Union that realist and neorealist theory had neglected. Change in the international system was the effect, not the cause of other changes, and mainstream IR theory did not see it coming.

As Richard Ned Lebow and Thomas Risse-Kappen have written, "Measured by its own standards, the profession's performance was embarrassing. There was little or no debate about the underlying causes of systemic change, the possibility that the Cold War could be peacefully resolved, or the likely consequences of the Soviet Union's visible decline . . . Practitioners remained insensitive to the change after it was well under way."[9] Jutta Weldes, Mark Laffey, and Hugh Gusterson have argued that "the failure of scholars to foresee, predict, or explain the sudden end of what was allegedly the central fact of world politics in the second half of the twentieth century—the superpower conflict itself—suggested an empirical anomaly of gross proportions and raised questions about the adequacy of the basic theoretical presumptions of neorealism." And as Friedrich Kratochwil has put it, neorealism had been "embarrassed" by the changes.[10]

In the wake of the cold war, scholars began turning to "cultural" variables, such as "ideas,"[11] "epistemic communities,"[12] "strategic culture,"[13] and "norms,"[14] to fill the apparent gaps in neorealism's explanatory power. In the 1990s, a school of thought called "constructivism" presented a challenge to the realist paradigm, which attempted to address this issue. Though constructivism was derived from postmodernism and critical theory, the extent to which it applied to IR theory the postmodernist challenge to the underlying material basis of reality depended greatly on the author.[15]

Emmanuel Adler has argued that "constructivism is the view that the manner in which the material world shapes and is shaped by human action and interaction depends on dynamic normative and epistemic interpretations of the material world."[16] Ted Hopf has suggested that constructivism has two defining assumptions that distinguish it as a body of theory: it is interpretivist in that it holds that interests are constructed by human beings as opposed to being a function of some objective reality or assigned by an omniscient observer, and it is structuralist in that it emphasizes the role of intersubjective communities in shaping the interests of their members.[17] Wendt has distinguished the constructivist school from others by noting two basic claims it makes: that "the fundamental structures of international politics are social rather than strictly material . . . and that these structures shape actors' identities and interests." However, he emphasizes that these assertions do not imply any contradiction of most of the traditional assumptions of realism—that international politics are primarily driven by the actions of states, that states can be seen as rational actors, that they are motivated by the desire to survive, that they cannot be certain of each others' intentions, and that the system is anarchic.[18] Constructivists argue that "the structure of the states system contains both material and cultural elements . . . but constructivists give priority to cultural over material structures on the grounds that actors act on the basis of the meanings that objects have for them, and meanings are socially constructed. A gun in the hands of a friend is a different thing from one in the hands of an enemy, and enmity is a social, not material, relationship." Intersubjective definitions of identity are thus crucial to understanding the ebb and flow of international politics, since the ways in which actors identify themselves and others comprise "cognitive schemas that enable an actor to determine 'who I am/we are' in a situation, and positions in a social role structure of shared understandings and expectations." In any given situation, actors derive understandings of their self-interest from their assessment of their identities in relation to those of the actors with whom they have contact.[19]

Whereas all variants of realism assume that states have only one fundamental identity—sovereign, self-interested, competitors for power—constructivists assume that identities are intersubjective. That is, they constitute and define the self of both the observer and observed, and since all actors in the system play both roles, they may be understood very differently by different observers. In all cases, however, constructivists assume that broad identities—capitalist, communist, dictatorship, democracy, Western, Eastern, enemy, friend—will be assumed by observers to imply a much more diverse array of likely attitudes and intentions.[20]

Thus, constructivists differ with realists on the process by which key variables such as "power," "self-interest," and the "system" itself are defined and operationalized by policy makers. Constructivist IR theory asserts that discourse plays a major role in shaping practice; that the ways in which policy makers talk about the world around them tend to define the ways in which they act in that world, prejudicing them toward some options and away from others. Social structures of shared knowledge thus provide a critical background for understanding threats and opportunities in the constructivist view, whereas these are assumed to be self-evident and objectively meaningful by realists. The balance of power in the world should be clear to the leader of any state, realists suggest, but for constructivists "500 British nuclear weapons are less threatening to the United States than 5 North Korean nuclear weapons, because the British are friends of the United States and the North Koreans are not."[21]

David Campbell summarizes this point by noting that "danger is not an objective condition. It (*sic*) is not a thing which exists independently of those to whom it may become a threat."[22] Weldes, Laffey, and Gusterson argue that "insecurities, rather than being natural facts, are social and cultural productions . . . insecurity is itself the product of processes of identity construction in which the self and the other, or multiple others, are constituted."[23] But to say that insecurities are not natural facts is not to suggest that they are unrelated to material realities. If I am walking in the forest and see a wolf, the insecurity I feel is certainly related to the material facts of the situation. But it is still true that I must cognitively construct a meaning for those material facts to produce insecurity; my perspective could be very different if I did not know what wolves were or if I were a biologist seeking to observe their behavior. The subjective context the observer brings to the observed matters to its meaning, which is not innate to material facts but instead must be generated and applied by the observer. The way in which this process occurs is social—minimally, in the sense that an individual's identity, his or her beliefs, values, worldviews, and assumptions, is shaped by the social process of acculturation that is universally part of the human experience. So even if I am alone when I see the wolf, the social process of acquiring culture affects the way in which I understand its meaning to me. But the making and applying of meanings is also a function of immediate and ongoing social dynamics—if I am with other people, my reaction to the wolf will likely be shaped in part by their reactions; if they are not afraid, this fact is likely to mitigate my fear as well. And social structures provide important context in which certain meanings and understandings are entrenched; seeing a wolf in the zoo is of course very different from seeing one in the wild, and this is not simply because of the material fact of fences and cages that keep the wolf away from me. For me to feel safe as I watch a wolf in a zoo, I must understand the meaning of "the zoo" as a concept, and this is a socially constructed and shared idea. I do not worry that the cages might not be strong enough, I do not check each one to be sure it is solid—even though the consequences for me if they are not may be very dire. Instead, I base my actions on the socially shared idea that a zoo is a safe place to observe animals, an idea so deeply entrenched in my psyche that I never think to question it even as I stand just a few feet away from a ferocious animal for whom, in another context, devouring me would be no trouble at all.

Stefan Halper and Jonathan Clarke suggest that this kind of "social reality and the relations, entities, and beliefs within it are not predetermined and fixed but created in and through language."[24] Language is not reality, but it is our only means of apprehending reality so as to make it socially comprehensible and useful. Because human beings are social animals, the reality in which we exist and act every day is largely a social reality and to the extent that it is, it requires language. I can experience the reality of a sunny day without using language, but this kind of firsthand experience represents only a tiny sliver of what we normally consider "reality"—I can't analyze the significance of the experience, can't attach any meaning to it beyond the immediate and visceral, and can't convey any description of it to others without language. While the heat of the sun as it shines on my face is real whether I describe it or not, it has no social meaning unless I describe it and therefore does not exist as a social fact unless I attach words to it, but these necessarily limit and constrain the reality they are intended to convey. Words depict reality in the same way that photographs capture a scene—they make a subjective experience communicable and therefore socially useful, but they are not the thing itself and therefore necessarily alter and corrupt the reality they describe. As Campbell puts it, "The world exists independently of language, but we cannot *know* that (beyond the fact of its assertion), because the existence of the world is literally inconceivable outside of language and our traditions of interpretation."[25]

Thus, for constructivist scholars, discourse analysis tends to be an important means for understanding the ways in which political communities comprehend and act in the world. Hayden White argues that discourse is "intended to *constitute* the ground whereon to decide *what shall count as a fact* in the matter under consideration and to determine *what mode of comprehension* is best suited to understanding of the facts thus constituted."[26] Language enables human beings to communicate, but also traps them within the set of meanings attached to the words they use. Because words only represent or signify reality, they are inherently limiting, shaping reality even as they make it socially useful. Since social understandings of reality are thus shaped by language, control over the specific ways in which they are shaped is a decisive element in the exercise of power within society. As Michel Foucault suggested, "Power produces knowledge," and "power and knowledge directly imply one another." Quoting the French journalist Jean-Jacques Servan, Foucault wrote, "A stupid despot may constrain his slaves with iron chains; but a true politician binds them even more strongly by the chain of their own ideas . . . The link is all the stronger in that we do not know of what it is made and we believe it to be our own work."[27]

International politics and state policy making are not composed of "ideas all the way down." The material reality of the world, of course, has a profound effect on the choices made by actors in the international system and to argue that those actors' perceptions of that reality shape those choices is certainly not to claim that reality is somehow nonexistent or irrelevant. As Legro puts it, the goal of constructivist theory is not necessarily to suggest that ideas trump all other factors in explaining events in international politics, but simply to "make sense of how ideas interact with other factors in specific ways to cause outcomes."[28] Opportunity and threat, friend and foe, are largely subjective categories, constructivists argue, unless threats are understood to be strictly correlated with the capabilities of other actors, which they rarely are. Faced with Osgood's distinction between ideals and self-interest, constructivists would deny the dichotomy and define both as products of social structure. "Power and interest do not have effects," Wendt argues, "apart from the shared knowledge that constitutes them as such." While anarchy remains the overarching fact of the international system for Wendt, it is important to distinguish "an anarchy of friends . . . from one of enemies, one of self-help from one of collective security, and these are all constituted by structures of shared knowledge."[29]

For constructivists, past interactions are important for comprehending the dynamics of the international system since policy makers' memories of past successes and failures and the self-interested or cooperative behavior on the part of other actors are likely to shape understandings of what is possible and desirable in the future. In short, Wendt argues, "*History matters,*" though it would be more accurate to say that *perceptions* of history matter.[30]

"Anarchy" invokes different responses depending on the social-identity relationships of those acting within it.[31] The implications for IR are manifold; consider, for example, the importance of intersubjective identity for Rousseau's stag hunt, in which hunters must decide whether to cooperate to kill a stag, which will feed all of them amply, or to defect when the opportunity arises to kill a hare, which will satisfy only the defector for a short while. The likelihood for Rousseau—and for Waltz, who focused on this allegory to illustrate the dynamics of neorealism—is that anarchy will lead to defection. Constructivism would suggest that the answer is more complex, particularly if we assume that the hunt occurs, as contemporary international relations do, in a state of anarchy but not in a pre-social state of nature. The hunters have some knowledge of each other, and this knowledge must be a critical variable in understanding their responses. How one hunter perceives another will be vital in determining whether he will pursue the hare when he has the chance. Are the other hunters members of his tribe, his brothers, or his friends? Are they enemies? Critically, the answers to these questions and thus to the primary question of whether a hunter will defect do not strictly depend on material factors, but on the hunter's perception and subjective judgment of the others. And this judgment will in turn tend to be derived primarily from his assessment of how like or unlike himself the others are: he will trust and tend to cooperate with those whom he understands as similar to himself and distrust and tend to betray those who are seen as dissimilar. These cognitive schemas do not preclude the possibility of betrayal of a friend or cooperation with a competitor, but they do suggest that very different responses are possible under identical conditions of anarchy, and that specific choices will tend to be determined by perceptions of identity relationships.

Thus, many constructivists view neorealism as not so much inaccurate as incomplete in its encapsulation of the dynamics of the international system. As Henry Nau puts it, constructivism "adds critical missing elements [to neorealism] . . . It does not replace but completes [neorealist theory] . . . National identity organizes and motivates national economic and military power and tells us for what political purposes nations legitimate and use their wealth and power."[32] "Neorealists do not pretend to explain how individual states might behave," Nau continues, "but they issue a stern warning to individual states: if you do not take into account the distribution of relative power and balance against greater power, you will certainly suffer and may fail to survive in an anarchic world."[33] Depicted in this way, neorealism is a far stronger normative theory than it is a descriptive one; it tells states how they should act, but cannot capture or predict in detail how they do act, and while it may be convincing on the first count, its failure on the second should engender some skepticism about its overall usefulness as a theory. If neorealism's emphasis on the national interest as an objective criterion leaves it unable to explain how states define national interest in particular circumstances, it is doomed to failure as both a descriptive and a normative theory of use to policy makers. If, on the other hand, it can be augmented with an understanding of the processes by which national interests are interpreted by states, then it holds the promise of being able to both describe how states do act and generate specific, politically realistic suggestions about how they should act.

Thus it is possible to view neorealism and constructivism as, to some extent, complementary rather than conflicting theories. This conclusion has given rise in recent years to various hybrid forms of "Realist-Constructivsm" that accept many of the core premises of neorealism but seek to augment and expand upon them with elements of constructivist thought.[34] Many leading realists have conceded some merit to constructivism as well, notably Samuel Huntington, who has argued that "national interest derives from national identity . . . the nature of the country whose interests are being defined."[35] Waltz has suggested that states are socialized into certain roles on the basis of their weight in the international system, though this socialization is very limited in its effects in his view.[36] Zbigniew Brzezinski has claimed that "Russia's longer term role in Europe will depend largely on its self-definition." And Henry Kissinger, who experienced firsthand the limits of material power in the closing chapters of the Vietnam War, suggests that "once a nation's image of itself is destroyed, so is its willingness to play a major international role." Kissinger further argues that "a state is by definition the expression of some concept of justice that legitimates its internal arrangements and of a projection of power that determines its ability to fulfill its minimum functions."[37]

The areas of agreement between constructivists and neorealists should not be overstated, but neither should their differences. As Wendt has noted, there is a fundamental divergence between the two perspectives because "neorealists think [structure] is made only of a distribution of material capabilities, whereas constructivists think it is also made of social relationships." Wendt suggests that for constructivists, "social structures include material resources like gold and tanks. In contrast to neorealists' desocialized view of such capabilities, constructivists argue that material resources acquire meaning for human action through the structure of shared knowledge in which they are embedded . . . Material capabilities as such explain nothing; their effects presuppose structures of shared knowledge, which vary and which are not reducible to capabilities."[38] But David Dessler has also described constructivism as positivist social science in that it shares some fundamental underlying assumptions of neorealism: "(1) That we inhabit a world whose nature and existence is neither logically nor causally dependent on any mind; (2) that some of our beliefs about this world are accurate, even if incomplete, descriptions, and thereby qualify as true; and (3) that our methods of inquiry enable us to discover that (at least) some of our beliefs about the world are true.[39]

CHAPTER 1

THEORY AND HISTORY

IDENTITY AND IDEOLOGY IN CONSTRUCTIVIST FOREIGN POLICY ANALYSIS

Left unanswered by previous generations of realist scholarship were, in the view of Ngaire Woods, "questions of which . . . beliefs are most likely to shape the definition of interests in international relations and why and how it is that particular sets of ideas prevail in the international arena."[1] Constructivist theory offers a means to fill this void by asking how interests are defined rather than how they are defended, but constructivists have in turn been subject to calls to "cease and desist their discussion of theory, epistemology, and ontology and get on with demonstrating their comparative advantage in explaining real-world events."[2] This study will seek to advance this agenda by suggesting that two related factors hold critical keys to understanding the process by which leaders and whole societies comprehend and thus act within the world: identity and ideology. This section of this chapter will explore the relationship between these factors and their significance as variables in constructivist foreign policy analysis.

While few constructivists would deny that both ideology and identity can have important effects on state policy, the relationship between them has yet to be fully problematized and its implications for theory and policy fully described. This chapter will argue that there exists an interconstitutive relationship between national ideology and identity. It will contend that ideology is the politically normative element in the cognitive framework of national identity, the set of ideas that explicitly presumes to dictate political behavior, translating philosophical beliefs into instructions for action. It is therefore necessary to analyze both the dominant political ideology in a given society and the broader national identity underpinning it to fully understand the socio-cognitive bases of that society's foreign policy.

Identity

The process of acquiring and employing identity is inherent and automatic for humans, a product of the "human desire to understand the social world and the consequent cognitive need for order, predictability, and certainty."[3] Identity is a cognitive shortcut, a heuristic device that allows the individual to simplify and thus operate effectively within a complex world. As Hopf puts it, "Identities categorize people according to common features, making the other's actions intelligible and an individual's own actions vis-à-vis them intelligible to himself." Identities are thus created to be used, and they are applied within intersubjective social systems, what Peter Berger and Thomas Luckmann call the "social stock of knowledge," Clifford Geertz terms the "web of meaning," and Michel Foucault refers to as "discursive formation": a sociohistorical space in which a given set of meanings hold sway.[4] Individuals assign identities to others that may ascribe broad sets of traits, motives, and intentions on the basis of limited observation of small numbers of such characteristics.[5] Similarly, Charles Taylor has described the "social imaginary" as the set of "ways people imagine their social existence, how they fit together with others, how things go on between them and their fellows, the expectations that are normally met, and the deeper normative notions and images that underlie these expectations."[6] Mark Neufeld has defined intersubjective meanings as "the product of the collective self-interpretations and self-definitions of human communities." Together, social understandings of Self and Other comprise the lens through which actors in the international system view material reality and comprehend threat and opportunity. Neufeld argues that "the practices in which human beings are engaged cannot be studied in isolation from the 'web of meaning,' which is, in a fundamental sense, constitutive of those practices."[7]

Such socio-cognitive structures serve to establish the boundaries of discourse within a society, defining the parameters within which individuals tend to think about themselves and others. They constitute the social framework through which material reality is perceived, understood, and acted upon. They are the environment in which human interactions of all kinds occur and thus the only mechanism through which the real world can be known.[8]

Human beings are social animals. We have evolved to live and function effectively in the long term only in the context of groups. Apart from the very exceptional individual who chooses to live as a hermit, human beings as a species are dependent on social relations with each other for their mental well-being and physical survival (even in prisons, which are by definition places reserved for those who have been removed from society as punishment for transgressions of social norms, the worst punishment is solitary confinement. So deeply is social dependence rooted in the human mind that to exist without it is a form of unendurable torture). Individual identity is created within this milieu—it is intrinsically social.[9] Individual identity is by definition an expression of distinction that therefore requires social interaction with an Other to exist.[10] As Hopf suggests, "Identities can only be understood relationally."[11] Individual or state identities are always and necessarily relative. There can be no meaningful "I" without a "You" or a "We" without a "They." Identities are thus first and foremost instrument of distinction—what defines an individual or a group is not important in and of itself, but rather because of the cognitive space that it allows the individual or the group to perceive between Self and Others.[12]

Whether in individual relationships or international relations, identities are assigned to Self and Other for specific purposes, to make possible an understanding of what the Self is and is not, and to make judgments about the nature of the Other in relation to the Self. As David Berreby states, "Human kinds, then, are not just categories. They're also guides. They tell you what a perception means . . . and so what to expect . . . Once I've classed myself and [a] stranger . . . I know which game to play and which rules apply—how to speak, how to dress, and how to behave toward this other person."[13]

Once social understandings of who We are, are co-constituted with understandings of who They are, our conception of our identity can be interpreted to specify a particular plan for action. It will be argued in this book that such identity-based political agendas are what comprise "Ideologies." The social construction of in-groups and out-groups also serves the purpose of creating expectations about the motives and likely behavior of the Other; once it is known what They are like, it will be possible to make assessments of what They are likely to do.[14]

The relationship between images of Others and the interests of the observer is complex. Positive or negative images do not simply derive from a sense that seeing Others in a positive or negative light will benefit the observer in some material way, nor do understandings of self-interest simply emerge from positive or negative views of the

Other. Social images both reflect and affect international interactions. During World War II, the Soviet Union and its people were depicted in the United States and seen by many Americans in a positive light; these images changed dramatically after the war as entrenched hostility came to define the relationship between the two states. Did social images change because national interest came to be understood differently, or did national interest come to be seen differently because views of the international Other changed? The right answer, unsatisfactory as it might be, is probably "neither" and "both." The human mind seeks cognitive consistency; it strives to create an orderly and comprehensible world, which is only possible if good things tend to correlate with other good things and bad things with other bad things. Thus, if an immigrant population is seen to pose an economic cost to a society ("they're taking our jobs"), that population might also tend to become associated with other negative stereotypes ("they're criminals"). But if I decide that I must buy an expensive home security system because "those people" in my neighborhood have made it unsafe, then it is my stereotyped image of the Other that has dictated a change in my understanding of self-interest, in turn causing me to pay a cost that I would not otherwise have paid. To see either identity images or interests as primary and prior to the other is misguided; each works to instantiate the other in the service of cognitive consistency.[15]

Ascribing identity to individuals or groups is necessary and useful for social life, and those modes of categorization of others that are the most useful will be the ones that people tend to focus on most commonly. "We don't believe in racial and religious and national divisions because we're told to but rather because our daily experiences are organized to make those categories relevant," Berreby claims. "Each of us places himself in whatever human kind feels relevant to the needs of the moment. Understanding human kinds, then, is a matter of seeing how the ever-changing mental dance produces the permanent-feeling human kinds we call tribes, races, religions, and nations."[16]

Rodney Bruce Hall argues that the creation of such distinctions is the fundamental basis of politics. "Our societal self-identifications segment the political realm. When we formulate them we include some and exclude others . . . We cannot formulate an argument regarding who we are without at least implying an argument about who we are not. 'If I am a Pole, then I am not a Czech. If I am a proletarian, then I am not bourgeois. If I am a denizen of Christendom, then I am not a Muslim. If I am a conquistador, then I am not a savage.' . . . We can see in these examples that historically we seem compelled to segment political space."[17] But while there are many in-groups and out-groups working in the lives of most individuals, they are not all coequal in emotional significance or ethical implications; there are some crucial distinctions between them. Perhaps the most significant of these is the moral distinction between fully legitimate human beings, who the ethics of every culture and religion require individuals to protect and not to harm, and those who are not, and thus may legitimately be killed in the interest of the legitimate group.[18] Mark Haas argues that most people see the world divided between "citizens" and others and that "social identity theory predicts that bifurcating the world in this manner will impel people to attribute positive images to one's fellow citizens and negative, even hostile characteristics to all others."[19]

It would be easy to jump to the conclusion that this dividing line is what distinguishes the nation from other kinds of groups, that those outside the nation may legitimately be killed in a specific ethical environment known as war, which the state alone can call into being. Indeed, this might be said to be the central principle of the anarchic international system in which it is assumed that states will from time to time go to war against one another, giving the moral and legal authority to their soldiers to carry out against others what would be considered murder if it were done to their countrymen. But in the contemporary world the reality is more complicated than this, as lines of national identity intersect with and cut across other distinctions, including race, religion, and ideology. Americans find the concept of war with Iraq morally tolerable in part because the U.S. government claims to be fighting on the side of "civilization" against "barbarians," who also happen to be non-Western, Muslim Arabs. It is hard to imagine a situation in which Americans in the aggregate would find the same kind of lethal force a legitimate means in a dispute between the United States and Canada or Great Britain, despite recognizing clear national identity distinctions between the United States and either of those countries. "'We' might not love one another as individuals (we may even hate one another)," Berreby writes, "but there is a sense that 'we' are 'good'; that moral law applies to all of our dealings. The Golden Rule—do unto others as you would have them do unto you—was made for Us. For good or ill, we're supposed to treat one another as people."[20]

By its very nature national identity is and is likely to remain a contested concept.[21] As Benedict Anderson has argued, nations are "imagined communities . . . imagined because the members of even the smallest nation will never know most of their fellow members, meet them, or even hear of them, yet in the minds of each lives the image of their communion."[22] Peter J. Katzenstein claims that national identities come in "two basic forms": that which is intrinsic to the actor and that which is social, able to be constructed only in the intersubjective international environment. But a number of critics have found this distinction problematic because it depends on the subjective judgment of the observer; Katzenstein's claim that "being democratic is an intrinsic feature of the U.S. state relative to the structure of the international system," for example, raises more questions than it answers.[23] Alexander Wendt has distinguished between the "corporate" and "social" identities of states and suggests that four national interests exist outside of the social milieu: physical security, autonomy, economic well-being, and collective self-esteem, though this assertion raises immediate questions about whether and why these concepts also should not be subject to social construction and subjective interpretation.[24] Wendt has argued as well that all past and potential international systems fall into one of three fundamental ideational structures—Hobbesian, Lockean, and Kantian, though various critics have taken issue with this assertion because it severely limits the range of relationships between states, allowing only three: "enemy, friend, and rival—where dozens would be too few."[25] States that may be closely connected socially, economically, ideologically, or otherwise, may nevertheless have serious differences over particular issues at particular times, even to the point of viewing each other as rivals or enemies in a limited sphere within a broader relationship of friendship.[26]

One critical question faced by constructivism as a school of thought is where, how, and by whom is social knowledge created in international politics—the question of "top down" versus "bottom up" constructivism, of where and by whom "national identity" is generated and has its effects on international politics. Some constructivist authors have focused on the international system as a milieu for social interaction in international politics and therefore the place in which intersubjective identities are shaped and operationalized. Systemic constructivists such as Wendt examine the emergence of norms and social structures between states. Wendt argues that international society is built on a body of shared knowledge and to some extent shared norms.[27] He is a "third image" analyst, attempting to refine structural theories that have emphasized the anarchy of the environment in which states interact but suggesting that the meaning of "anarchy" to each of them will depend in part on the way in which each sees and defines others. While starkly distinct from neorealism in their conclusions regarding the motives for state behavior, third-image constructivist approaches share with neorealism a bias toward the international system to the exclusion of other factors—they focus on the relationships between states at the expense of what is occurring within them. The fact that, for example, the "revisionist," "status quo," and "collectivist" state orientations that Wendt identifies are simply given rather than fully interrogated, places state identity at the domestic level "outside analysis" in the view of some critics.[28]

One consequence of this third-image emphasis has been that much constructivist writing "investigates Self and Other as if the only Other for a state were another state," when in fact there is no reason to assume that this is the case. It seems more likely that the full reality of Self and Other must apprehend, in each category, units including but not limited to individuals, families, clans, nations, states, and even the global community as a whole. Jennifer Sterling-Folker has argued that this neglect of domestic identity formations has compelled constructivists to fall back on assumed collective interests without fully exploring their bases. There is no a priori reason to assume that state or social identity is created solely at the international level, and there are many instances in which foreign policy can reasonably be argued to have been influenced by domestic culture. Chaim Kaufmann and Robert Pape argue that it was domestic political culture that led to Britain's opposition of the international slave trade in the nineteenth century, for example. Identity would seem likely to emerge first from domestic culture, though it is critical to note that it becomes meaningful only in relationship to the international Other, that an identity informed by a society's conception of itself domestically still exists within the intersubjective web of identities at the international level. Hopf has argued that it would be a mistake to reduce IR theory to a function of strictly domestic state identities, but "social constructivism assumes that a state's identity in international politics cannot be constructed at home alone—it is only in interaction with a particular Other that the meaning of the state is established."[29] Communities and distinctions between them exist both within states and across state borders, and while acknowledging these cleavages vastly complicates the task of explaining international politics, it also enables a theoretical grasp on those historical phenomena that impact IR but seem to defy the model of a sovereign state system as it has often been conjured—political and cultural schisms within states or across borders; the "special relationship" between like-minded states or the labeling of an "enemy within," for example. One strength of the constructivist perspective is its capacity to consider and account for these realities, based on the fact that social constructivism, as Hopf has put it, "assumes no boundary between meanings within and outside the state's official borders. The assumption that meaningful Others exist both at home and abroad differentiates a social constructivist account of the domestic from those that assume either the primacy of the internal or the external or that there are different domains for the two."[30]

Systemic or third-image constructivists focus on the relations between states, arguing that intersubjective identity is generated in the interactions between what can be understood as essentially unitary actors. Second-image analysts tend to emphasize the social and culture structures and dynamics within states, contending that national ideas about Self and Other are derived at least in part from the cultural baggage that states bring to their approach to international politics. First-image analysts emphasize the cognition of individual leaders and the beliefs, values, and psychology of small groups of key decision makers. None of these perspectives is complete and to a great extent they are complementary rather than contradictory; when authors from these different schools disagree it tends to be over what can reasonably be left out in the interest of theoretical parsimony, not whether there is some validity in the claims of analyses emphasizing a different image. What can be lost in these different perspectives, however, is the ways in which the construction of identity at each of these levels feeds, informs, and interacts with what is occurring at the other levels. While culture and ideology at the national level may shape the way that a polity understands itself and by extension its role in the world and appropriate relationships with international others, it is certainly true that the nature of the interactions that state has with other states will also shape its conception of friend and enemy, opportunity and threat. The construction of identity that most directly affects policy occurs within the minds of individual leaders and within small groups of decision makers, but these individuals and groups do not deliberate or act in isolation from their societies or the international system. On the contrary, they are products of their societies; they bring to the process of decision making the cultural assumptions, beliefs, and values that characterize their societies as a whole and will likely choose policies that reflect those values as they understand them, not only because it is politically necessary to do so but also because they tend to share those attitudes. So national identity as an operative force in international politics is not constructed at the international, domestic, or individual level; rather, it is constantly being generated at all three levels in interaction with one another, and consideration of what occurs at each level as well as the nature of the interaction between them is necessary to fully comprehend the role of identity in international politics.

This book will argue that domestic politics and culture are also sites in which social understandings of Self and Other are generated and employed, as are the belief systems and cognition of individual political actors or decision making groups within the government. It will suggest that all of these are locations in which collective social identity is formed and acted upon and that to understand the process by which ideas about international politics come to affect the foreign policies of states, it is necessary to consider each of these levels and the interaction between them.

The set of identities relevant to policy makers is not likely to be limited to self and international other. National identity is critically important for understanding international interactions, but it is not the only form of identity that is significant for policy makers, or indeed for any individual. Identity consists not just of "Self" and "Other" or even "Others," but rather multiple, overlapping layers of selfhood experienced simultaneously. So it is possible for political actors to imagine certain "Others" as their opponents within the sphere of domestic politics, but because of their membership within that community still as members of the primary "We" group, that which is distinct from all international Others. There is not just one operative "We" for national leaders, but many; while the national "We" may be the most significant, leaders may also see themselves and their interests tied to many subnational and transnational groups. A given leader may see ideological kinship creating a bond of solidarity with like-minded groups or leaders in other states, for instance, or may argue that some among his or her own countrymen are, in effect, outsiders even though they are technically citizens. The discourse of anticommunism in the United States in the 1950s, for instance, constructed an enemy that comprised not just international Others but also some Americans, individuals who by virtue of their political attitudes were excluded from the national in-group. In more typical circumstances in democratic states, leaders tend to view their political adversaries as members of the national "We" but not as individuals sharing their political interests, so both partisan and national identity can play a role in determining leaders' policy choices. Thus, for instance, in the era after the 9/11 terrorist attacks, the Bush administration operated from a sense of national identity in making policy, but also presented a perspective on subnational identity that seemed to divide the national entity, which it otherwise depicted as a unified whole. "America" had a clear and specific meaning for the Bush administration, but the administration also represented political opponents within the United States as having a particular identity that tended to parallel those of international Others who opposed the administration's policies but were not overt enemies of the United States. Domestic opponents of the war in Iraq, for example, tended to be represented as naïve, soft, and irresolute, just as some states and international organizations were portrayed not as hostile but as weak willed, irresponsible, and prone to inadvertently helping the enemy due to their unwillingness to act against it.

National identity is commonly thought of as being rooted in one of two distinct bases of allegiance: on the one hand, nations may be formed around bonds of "ethnic or traditional community that shares common linguistic, cultural, racial, or religious characteristics," or on the other, "ideological community composed of a variety of ethnic groups that unite around a set of common beliefs."[31] Japan and Germany might be suggested as examples of the former category and the United States, Switzerland, and Belgium as cases of the latter. This distinction is problematic because ethnicity and ideology are rarely wholly separable in practice; to use Anderson's term, ethnic communities are *imagined* communities just as ideological communities are. They are based on the idea of belonging in the consciousness of their members more fundamentally than they are based on biology. To be Japanese is to be part of an ethnic community, but it is also to be part of a community of shared history and values (it is hard to conceive of the meaning of being Japanese without considering Japanese Buddhism, for example), and in practice it would be both impossible and misleading to prioritize or sever these elements of identity from one another. While the case has often been made that the United States is an unusual society in that its identity is built around a set of ideas rather than the ethnic, religious, or other bonds that tend to characterize other nations, this is an oversimplification. Every nation is built around a set of ideas—often perceptions of ethnic kinship rooted at least as much in belief as in biology, or religious doctrine, but also, critically, of the shared history and values that form national cultures. American identity is comprised in part of an acceptance of common liberal political and economic values, but also revolves around a sense of shared and unique history and culture. Religion is often a critical component of national identity, but not necessarily because it unites people behind an evangelical mission or even universal belief. To be Russian Orthodox is an important part of what it is to be Russian, but many people who consider themselves Russian and Russian Orthodox do not go to church very often, or at all. Thus, religious identity comprises one piece of a larger shared culture rather than a code for operationalizing national identity. While it is true that Shia Islam is a critical element in contemporary Iranian national identity, that element of identity is inseparable from many other factors, including a sense of Persian national history (with very definite recognition of pre-Islamic history) and distinction from the Other—notably from both the West and the Sunni and Arab worlds, and indeed to some extent from Shia Muslims in other states.

It has been suggested that IR theorists "can measure the similarity or dissimilarity of these ideas, and so track relative national identities just as we track relative power" and on this basis predict the likelihood of international conflict and cooperation. Henry Nau contends that "the identities of separate nations may conflict or converge" and that "the United States and the Soviet Union fought the cold war as much because they pursued different national ideas to legitimate the use of force as because they pursued relative national power." While Nau makes a critical point here about the importance of national identity in motivating conflict, he draws a misleading distinction between power and ideology. The cold war superpowers would not have regarded each other as threatening as they did and would likely have pursued much more moderate policies toward one another had they shared similar national identities. Consider by comparison the example of Britain and the United States from 1890 to 1930. Britain, the world's economic hegemon for decades, was rapidly being surpassed in this role by the rise of the United States. Britain was also the world's preeminent naval power and in strictly material terms a much more serious rival to U.S. naval power in the Pacific than Japan. U.S. policy makers throughout this period saw Britain as a strategic and economic competitor, but never an "enemy" in the way that Germany, Japan, and even the far weaker Soviet Union were understood. In this case, as in the cold war, identity is not incidental to definitions of power and interest—it is intrinsic to them.[32]

Nau argues that national identities may also converge, creating the basis for international cooperation and community. Because identity is first and foremost related to the conditions under which force can legitimately be used, converging state identities will tend to create consensus around this question or at least leave states better able to anticipate the use of force by their neighbors. Uses of force by one state in such a community will not be surprising to others in the same community and will tend to be regarded as just. Relations between Russia, Prussia, and Austria during the Concert of Europe tended toward a relatively peaceful balance of power due to shared identities as aristocratic monarchies; the same dynamic is at work today as "the world's great industrial powers share similar democratic national identities and appear to eliminate the balancing of military power from their relationships altogether."[33]

It is clearly not the case that national identity or ideology will define national interests to the exclusion of other factors, only that all factors influencing the definition of national interests are understood through a socio-cognitive process in which national identity and ideology are always intervening variables. As Nau suggests, "Relative national identities can harden or soften the consequences of national power. And identity changes can reduce or increase threats even if there are no power changes. Military capabilities by themselves are not the threat. Who (i.e., the identity of the nation) possesses the capabilities defines the threat. France with hundreds of nuclear weapons is not a military threat to the United States; North Korea with a few nuclear weapons is."[34] Policy makers' judgments regarding the threat posed by another state must necessarily be based on evaluations of both capabilities and intentions. The first of these can be very difficult to know; the second is nearly always impossible to be certain about. Thus, there is virtually always great uncertainty and thus vast room for subjective interpretation surrounding potential threats, and policy makers tend to rely on understandings of identity to fill these gaps in knowledge, just as all human beings tend to rely on heuristic device to make an uncertain and complex world comprehensible. Conceptions of identity will be deployed to answer questions of capability as well as intent. In the absence of incontrovertible intelligence, U.S. leaders are likely to draw conclusions about whether North Korea possesses nuclear weapons from their understanding of whether North Korea is *the kind* of state that would build and conceal such weapons. It is certainly not the case that material capabilities do not matter at all—North Korea cannot actually use nuclear weapons unless it has them, for example, and it can make its threat to do so far more effective by filling the interpretive space in U.S. leaders' perceptions by testing one. But it is true that policy makers' understanding of threats are always filtered through the lens of relative state identity, that this process invariably results in an image of reality that is different from the world as it actually is, and that the result can be an understanding of threats that is sometimes profoundly different from that which neorealists might expect based on objective knowledge of material capabilities alone. Saddam Hussein was judged by U.S. leaders to be a threat to built and use weapons of mass destruction because he had already built and used them in the past, so it is not as if the conclusion that he was likely to do so in the future was without any material basis at all. But the leap from a set of historical facts to apparent certainty about the present and future in Iraq—with virtually no other hard evidence to support such conclusions—shows the profound effect that understandings of relative identity can have on the policy decision process.[35]

Constructivist theory is able to account for these facts by starting from the premise that state interests are not waiting to be discovered by or ontologically prior to the state actors themselves. "Interests" in the constructivist formulation have no intrinsic meaning or value of their own; rather they are functions of identity. According to Hopf, "A state's own domestic identities constitute a social cognitive structure that makes threats and opportunities, enemies and allies, intelligible, thinkable, and possible." "There is no such thing as an unalloyed economic interest," Hopf continues; to determine whether the United States has an interest in investing in Iranian natural gas, for example, one must necessarily consider the intersubjective identity relationship of the two states.[36] Or as Nau has stated, "National identity and national power both define the national interest . . . The national interest begins with what kind of society the nation is, not just what its geopolitical circumstances are."[37]

Clearly, in shaping identity, a significant role is played by perceptions of history; social identity relationships between states are shaped in part by their understandings of how they have interacted in the past. It is important to note that it is perceptions of history that shape identity and thus structure future expectations; history is not so much a set of events as a set of commonly accepted stories about those events, and national history is shaped before and interpreted after through the interpretive lenses of national identity and ideology. There may be a warlike history between states because, on the basis of ideological antipathy, they have seen one another as threats. In this case, their history of conflict will not create but rather reinforce their image of one another as enemy. Similarly, historical facts will be interpreted by different parties in ways consistent with their understanding of their own identity and others'—as the American Civil War is regarded as a war against Southern slavery by some and a war of Northern aggression by others. National ideology both shapes and is shaped by history, constantly creating new stories to comprise the every-changing national mythology, but also giving credence to one or another interpretation of national ideals.

Thus, the idea of a nation is typically constructed around a particular version of history, a set of stories that comprises a national mythology, a "usable past" that structures collective understandings of the meaning of the national "We": where we came from, who we are (and are not), and by extension, how we should act in the world.[38] Michael Kammen argues that the "needs of contemporary culture" require "manipulating the past in order to mold the present."[39] Walter Hixson suggests that "once naturalized and embedded within culture over many generations, national mythology provides a metanarrative—an explanation of the past, present, and future trajectory of a people and a nation."[40] And Robert Jervis argues that leaders' shared understandings of a society's founding will be particularly important in shaping "the concepts and strategies that they later apply to ruling their country and dealing with the world." Stories about the emergence of the nation as an independent entity will tend to be seen as bearing lessons for its future conduct.[41]

Theorists have long argued that the international state of anarchy is moderated by the fact that state interactions occur in an endless series of iterations; states know how their neighbors have behaved toward them yesterday and 100 years ago, and they know they will necessarily have to contend with one another tomorrow. There is thus more pressure for honesty and fidelity to agreements than there would be in a pure, pre-social anarchic state, even if the restraints of law and ethics are more limited in the international domain than they are within domestic societies. Unlike previous paradigms, the constructivist perspective suggests that the social relationships created in these ongoing interactions have a significant impact on the course of international affairs. It is not simply the case that states will tend to view each other as "honest" or "dishonest" on the basis of past behavior, but that they will conceive a tendency toward honesty or dishonesty in their neighbors as one part of a much larger and more detailed identity based not only on past behavior but on a variety of other factors deployed to help place the observed state in a comprehensible relationship with the observer. Past behavior will be one factor that helps the observer to conclude where to place the observed on a continuum of similar or dissimilar, to decide whether They are more or less like Us, and it is from this estimation that the observer will derive conclusions about intentions and likely future behaviors. The more like Us they are, the more likely they are to behave as we do (peacefully and reasonably in the self-estimation of most observers), and the more likely They will be to behave in a friendly way toward Us. Certainly past behavior is part of this process, but like "the national interest," to be meaningful, past behavior requires interpretation, and actions that appear dishonest or aggressive from the perspective of one who already sees the actor as an enemy may appear justifiable or defensive from one's own perspective or that of a "friend."

All communal groups, all "We" groups, are trust based. Social groups function on the basis of such trust—belief that we have the same goals and will cooperate to achieve them, that cars will stop when we cross the street, that the mail will be delivered, that contracts will be honored, and that the rules and norms associated with the group will be abided by. It is this trust that distinguishes society from the state of nature, that allows an individual to leave his or her home without experiencing constant insecurity and fear. "Otherness" is therefore the absence of this trust; the extent to which I understand an individual to be "Other" is the extent to which he or she does not enjoy the trust that I extend to those who I consider "We." So strictly speaking, it is not the international system as such that creates the sense of insecurity associated with "anarchy," but rather the social psychology of the human minds in which anarchy acquires its meaning.

Thomas Risse-Kappen has suggested that actors also infer external behavior from the values and norms governing the domestic political practices that shape the identities of their partners in the international system.[42] In normal, day-to-day social intercourse, identifying areas of commonality between individuals is the primary means by which kinship bonds and feelings of fellowship are constructed. If you and I discover we both love the same music, we unconsciously take this as a hint that we may have more in common. The more sameness we discover, the more we tend to assume is beneath the surface, and the easier we find it to trust one another and thus to behave cooperatively.[43] These kinds of inferences about unknown aspects of an individual's personality on the basis of known aspects are referred to by psychologists as "halo effects."[44] In IR, as William Scott has noted, "favorable characteristics tend to be attributed to liked nations, and unfavorable characteristics to disliked nations."[45] As Jervis puts it, "When one believes that the other state has a general resemblance to one's own, there is a tendency to overestimate the degree of congruence between the structures, norms, and patterns of behavior of the two states."[46]

Nau has argued that identity is intrinsically related to domestic regime type, to "the consensus by which the citizens of a nation agree that only the state can use force legitimately," both internally and externally. The conditions under which most citizens would accept that their government should be able to use force—to compel compliance with its domestic laws or to advance the state's interests and ideals abroad—thus comprise not only a set of legal or political constraints, but also the fundamental premises around which those people define themselves communally. These values are likely to closely parallel each other in their domestic and external applications, Nau argues. "No state is completely schizophrenic," he suggests, with "its behavior abroad consistently deviating from its behavior at home." These behaviors are rooted in a common national value system and bounded by the constraints of political legitimacy within the same framework of national public opinion. These domestic standards have important implications for intersubjective international identity as well, though; if a government represses its own people in ways that run counter to the values of other states, this will tend to construct or reinforce the identity of that state as *both* internally repressive *and* externally aggressive in the eyes of these observers—even if the repressive state has exhibited no aggressive behavior beyond its borders. "When China cracks down on dissidents," Nau contends, the United States tends to assume that "if China treats its own citizens in this manner, it may also use force for similar purposes against outside states."[47]

How is it possible then to explain hostile relationships between states with similar identities or the absence of hostility between states that are not alike? What might be called the "Saudi Arabia Paradox" poses a serious challenge to constructivists, who would emphasize shared ideas, identity, and regime type in explaining international conflict and cooperation. Saudi Arabia and the United States have a close and long-standing diplomatic and security relationship, but government types and social and political values that could hardly be more different. They do share a common material interest, however, in the continued flow of Saudi oil into global markets. If this interest is in itself sufficient to forge a very friendly and enduring interstate relationship, how much can ideas really be said to matter after all? Is it not just material power that distinguishes friend from foe in the end?

This example is a critical one for constructivist theory because it sheds important light on the way that ideas work in the minds of policy makers, of who is being constructed and how, and of which ideas matter and how ideas can work to mitigate and shape one another. Identity and ideology are heuristic devices, means to the end of making the world comprehensible and rational decisions possible, enabling judgments of opportunity and threat. But they are complex and can have multiple nodes and aspects; just as I can define myself as both an environmentalist and a NASCAR fan, it is possible for the United States and Saudi Arabia to hold complex views of one another that can accommodate some tension over different political values within a broader relationship as trading partners with a well-established security relationship. So the United States' desire to buy oil and Saudi Arabia's interest in selling it can be explained within the framework of identity by noting that "vital trading partner" can in fact be an important element of intersubjective identity. What focusing on identity also allows, however, is the differentiation of relationships between states on the basis of the differing aspects of identity that separate or bind them together. Canada is also a significant exporter of oil, and part of the intersubjective identity set between the United States and Canada is also "vital trading partner" as it is between the United States and Saudi Arabia. But beyond that, Canada's identity relationship with the United States is very different; noting this fact helps to explain many of the differences that exist in the U.S.-Canadian relationship relative to the U.S.-Saudi Arabian relationship. If the internal combustion engine became obsolete tomorrow and the United States had no more need for oil, the U.S. relationship with Saudi Arabia would likely change dramatically, quite possibly tending toward greater animosity due to divergent social and political values. In the same scenario, the U.S. relationship with Canada would certainly change as well, but not in the same ways. American and Canadian leaders would likely still construct the relationship between their states as "friendly," despite the absence of oil, due to a continued sense of shared history, culture, and values. Emphasizing relative identity as a unit of analysis does not presume that material assets do not matter in state relationships; these factors can in fact be understood and accounted for within such an identity framework. What this emphasis does as well, however, is to enable the analyst to contextualize material asset relationships and look beyond them to include cultural and ideational factors. Through the perception of a common commitment to the mutually self-serving status quo of the international system and their bilateral trade and security relationship, U.S. and Saudi leaders are in fact members of an imagined community built around shared values. That a particular self-serving relationship can mitigate the effect of divergent cultures and regime types in a given case does not change the fact that diverging identities will tend to generate mutual mistrust and hostility.

Clearly elements of national identity overlap, conflict, and evolve over time. What it means to be African-American, Catholic, a member of a trade union, and U.S. citizen all at the same time is a question being negotiated in countless permutations on a daily basis, sometimes with great conflict—as when the question of whether one could be both "Virginian" and "American" was decided finally only through violence on a scale that few could have imagined at the time. Whether one can be "Walloon," "Belgian," and "European" all at once (or which takes priority) is a question that is still being answered today, without much violence but not without conflict. It does not mean exactly the same thing to be American, French, or Ibo in 2008 that it did in 1868 or 1968, but in all three instances there are important continuities, common threads of belief and value woven through the fabric of identity over that time as well as differences. A Turkish guestworker in Germany may have a very different conception of what it is to be "German" than does a Wehrmacht veteran of World War II; a recent immigrant from Honduras living in South Central L.A. may define "American" somewhat differently than does a fifth generation farmer in Minnesota. But there will be important linkages between their definitions as well, commonalities that can reasonably be thought of as comprising a core national identity among its adherents. Clearly national identity can change over time, typically through gradual evolution and generational adaptation, but sometimes precipitously (postwar Germany is an obvious example, but consider the Soviet Union or Yugoslavia in the 1990s or post-revolutionary Iran). When change occurs, it never eradicates the ideational framework of the past, however; it consists instead of changes in emphases within a very diverse set of beliefs and values and novel adaptations of old ideas to new circumstances.

By definition, all groups are characterized by some type of identity—if they did not have some identifying trait they could not be considered "groups" at all. But "national" identity as a category is somewhat problematic, owing to the fact that while nations exist in many different cultural contexts around the world and in different historical eras, the form, substance, and social and political significance of the "nation" varies greatly with time and place. National identity may be strong or weak relative to other identities—subnational, ethnic, tribal (as in the case of say, Nigeria), or transnational (as perhaps in the European Union)—as sources of state policy. Some states are divided between multiple nationalities or include part of a national group that spans the borders of other states. Certainly one national group in a multinational state sometimes seizes power, in which case the identity ideas of that group will dominate policy. But if this does not happen, the set of values that is shared by the society as a whole will be the only basis for consensus among diverse groups. In a multinational state in which there is strong agreement on societal values between groups, these consensus identity notions can form the basis for effective government and foreign policy (as in Canada, for example). Where there is no strong agreement, governance will not be as effective because it will not draw on the loyalty and consent of as wide a cross-section of society. And there are many cases of variation between these different models with very different outcomes in many societies—notably, Yugoslavia during the cold war had a strong social and communal identity associated with the county as a whole (not merely because it governed effectively or compelled the allegiance of its citizens by force, but also because there was a clear sense of "Yugoslav" identity that existed side by side with ethnic and other identities). Post–cold war Yugoslavia descended into violence largely because this social understanding of a broad national identity collapsed, supplanted by narrower forms of allegiance.

Both states and nations, which tend to be viewed as conceptually and historically stable entities, are in reality both historically and socially contingent.[48] States and nations do not usually converge perfectly with one another, and they do not have the same social meaning everywhere in the world in every historical era. In David Campbell's view, states are "entities which do not possess prediscursive, stable identities . . . states are never finished as entities."[49] Jutta Weldes, Mark Laffey, Hugh Gusterson, and Raymond Duvall argue that "in conventional studies of security, the state is treated as a natural fact, but any particular 'state' is in fact a cultural production." They note that "these imagined national communities are not always well synchronized with state boundaries—as in the case of the contemporary Kurds or Basques, for example. The interests imputed to such nations or ethnic groups are, in fact, often antithetical to those of the state(s) in which they live and in such cases it is the state that is constituted as a danger threatening the identity of the nation."[50] And Charles Tilly has emphasized this misfit between nations and states, arguing that few, if any, states exist on the basis of prior national identity markers such as religion or language, and that the idea of nationality supporting what he refers to as "national states" as opposed to "nation-states" better describes the instrumental role that nationhood plays vis-à-vis the state.[51]

Developing identity within groups is a hardwired function of the human brain, and national identity is one expression of this function on a large scale. But it is neither the first nor likely the last such expression in human history. The nation as it is now understood is an invention of modernity (and late modernity at that; truly modern "nation-states" date only to nineteenth-century Europe, though certainly the development of both the nation and the state as they now exist had been under way for many centuries). Families, tribes, clans, ethnic and linguistic groups, interest groups, localities, regions, civilizations, empires, and the human community as a whole are all alternative human groupings, some of which predated the nation, some of which may supplant it in the future, and all of which can exert a claim on an individual's identity simultaneously without necessarily threatening the viability of that identity as a whole. There is nothing inherently privileged about national or state identity to make these the critical phenomena to be understood in IR for time immemorial. The nation-state system is certainly changing, and there is nothing inevitable about the persistence of this preeminent role for national identity, but at this juncture in history it is the most important site of the identities most critical to the flow of events in international politics. Hall has argued that "actor self-identification is a critical component of a historically changing 'structure of identities and interests' . . . Changes in the prevailing forms of societal self-identification generate changes in this 'structure of identity and interests' and result in epochal change in the international system . . . State interests, institutional forms, and behavior emerge . . . as variable products of the evolution of societal collective identity." State policy and the very notion of states themselves, in other words, are functions of the particular ways in which identity and interests are understood by actors in the international system in any given era. Notions of identity and interest change over time, and the nature of state policies and the state itself change with them.[52]

Thus, if self-perceived national identity can change over time, intersubjective identity relationships at the international level can change as well. Such changes can be precipitous—witness the sudden, dramatic end of the cold war, due not so much to the sudden disappearance of Soviet nuclear weapons as the sudden assertion by Soviet leaders that they no longer regarded the West as an enemy (which in turn made possible dramatic reductions in the weapons stockpiles that had been symptoms of their prior relationship). Here again, the distinction between international and domestic identity seems false and misleading. The West was convinced to abandon its long-held view of the Soviet Union as an enemy both by Soviet actions abroad (notably removing missiles and tank divisions from Europe) and by changes within the Soviet Union itself—political and economic liberalization, which, critically, made the Soviet Union with all its cultural differences and past misdeeds appear to be a society that shared Western political values. After generations of hostility and active war, Germany and Japan became part of a democratic security community in the second half of the twentieth century, a concert of states built around a stunningly new norm of the impossibility of war between the world's leading economic powers. This was able to occur because of changes in the material power structure of the international system—the permanent limitation of German and Japanese military power and the emergence of the cold war. But it also happened because the former adversaries could now imagine international cooperation because they understood each other as sharing common values domestically. These examples suggest that it is not merely unnecessary to segregate notions of identity at the international and domestic levels, it is actually misleading, because the changes that occurred at each level in these instances were intrinsically related, cause and effect of one another.[53]

Authors such as John Gerard Ruggie and John Ikenberry have suggested that international institutions may have an important role to play in this process of state identity formation, going beyond the traditional neoliberal view that institutions can shift the cost-benefit calculus in the foreign policies of their members to conclude that institutions can change the ways in which state interests are understood by fundamentally altering the nature of state identity itself and thus the meaning of anarchy and community in the international system.[54] John Owen argues that state leaders tend to form "transnational ideological groups" with like-minded leaders in other states. These individuals will "tend to derive positive utility from one another's gains vis-à-vis opposing ideological groups . . . [and] perceive losses in their own power from increases in the power of opposing ideological groups in other states."[55] While it is true that the international institutions that comprise the most tightly bonded communities of states are those that include the most politically similar groups of states, it is too simple to say that domestic similarity is the cause and international integration the effect or vice versa. There is instead a frequent tendency for changes in self-perceived state identity and intersubjective international relationships to cascade, reinforcing one another, motivating change at the international institutional level, which in turn tends to foster further change in identity. Historians 100 years hence will likely look at the emergence of postwar liberal democracy in Western Europe and the founding of the E.U. and NATO as simultaneous events, all causes and all effects of one another.

Clearly these forces cannot always be expected to reinforce one another indefinitely, nor always to create stronger communities rather than weakening them. The saga of the League of Nations, for example, stands as a cautionary tale regarding the limited capacity of international organizations to foster communal identity where it does not already exist. Woodrow Wilson expected the League to do just this, to engender a sense of community between its members on the basis of a very broad acceptance of common interests at its inception. We cannot know whether this expectation might have come to pass had history not conspired against it, but the historical record is clear that in the absence of U.S. membership, under the pressure of a world economy collapsing into depression, and with some member states showing no interest in peace or maintenance of the territorial status quo, the League could not create a community of states where one did not exist before. And what was true of the League can still be argued to be true of many international organizations to this day—that they are seen by some states as the creations of larger powers to serve their own interests. This is perhaps the single best explanation for the relative success of regional organizations uniting communities of domestically similar states compared with larger institutions. But this should not be taken to suggest that international organizations cannot be a force shaping state identity and fostering community, only that membership in international organizations is not in and of itself an indication that strong communal bonds already exist.

National identity clearly does not exist in a material sense, nor is it readily quantifiable, in much the same sense that the "international system" is not a tangible entity but an intellectual construct, a shorthand describing a set of relationships without a material reality of its own. Similarly, national identity is a construction, a set of commonly shared conclusions about what defines a people as a people. This notion of identity is complicated by the fact that states are not unitary actors, that they are made of cultures and subcultures as well as idiosyncratic individuals, each of whom has his or her own understanding of what belonging within the community means. And if national identity exists, it is clearly not always reflective of the objective reality of practice within a society; many people in France and around the world think of crepes as French and kebabs and hamburgers as un-French, regardless of the fact that more kebabs and hamburgers than crepes may be eaten every day in France. Americans think of their society as being defined by equality of opportunity, despite the clear fact that equality of opportunity (e.g., between rich and poor in education) is not the reality of the contemporary United States. Identity is not about who we are. It is first and foremost about who we think we are, as operationalized in the context of the world outside ourselves, with its own understandings of who we are.

Thus, for their significance in international politics to be fully understood, the national identities of states must be examined from multiple perspectives. If a society can be assumed to have a more or less coherent sense of its own identity, that self-image is clearly not the only version of identity that matters in international politics—also highly significant are the ways in which other societies perceive that state. The way in which a given society understands itself and the way in which it is understood by another may differ, and the ways in which a given state's identity is understood may differ dramatically between various international Others. The United States tends to see Taiwan as an independent state; China does not. The formal mechanisms of international law and diplomacy might be understood as somewhat weaker versions of the state licensing board—formal recognition and a seat in the United Nations provide a shorthand for the identity of individual states as sovereign entities within international society as a whole, but this does not mean that understandings of the identities of particular states may not vary greatly between other states.

For the purposes of foreign policy analysis, national identity must be recognized as being constructed at the societal and policy-elite level as well as at the level of the international system. There is a political imperative for national leaders to frame their actions within the consensus boundaries of national identity, and they are also products of the cultural environment of those societies themselves, no more free than any other individual to shed the cultural baggage that they have acquired throughout their lives. But they are also in a position to shape the interpretation of national identity and to some degree to shape national identity itself. Social ideas in turn structure the political preferences of members of society, but they are also subject to evolution over time; they do not tend to change quickly, but neither are they entirely rigid or fixed throughout history. Policy elites have some ability to affect this process—for instance, by avoiding or being in contact with external Others, they increase or decrease the exposure of their societies to those Others and encourage change in common understandings of the set of acceptable and appropriate relationships with those Others. H.C. Kelman, for example, argues that "identities are commonly reconstructed, sometimes gradually and sometimes radically, as historical circumstances change, crises emerge, opportunities present themselves, or new elites come to the fore."[56]

Foreign policy analysis does not need to apprehend national identity in a quantifiable way to consider its importance in policy making. The intervening role of policy makers means that national identity does not typically affect policy directly—but the perceptions of national identity by leaders do, and so it is only necessary to comprehend the ways in which national leaders define their nation and the international Others with whom it interacts. This leaves unanswered the question of whether leaders appeal to national identity because they are honestly defining the nation's interests in this way or simply framing for public consumption policies that are actually motivated by material power or security concerns, but it does suggest that a coherent, unimpeachable portrait of national identity is not necessary to illuminate the effects of identity on policy.

Internal government documents concerning national strategy and the practical requirements of policy do not logically need to reference identity; their purpose in the strictest sense is to describe what policy is to look like, what its intended goals are, and what are the technical means by which they will be accomplished. So it is surprising that such documents do frequently include extensive discussion of not only what is to be accomplished and how, but also of who we are. The answers to these questions have embedded within them implications for how policy is to be carried out, but even more importantly suggest *why* it is being done and why it is important that it be successful. Campbell writes, [While one might have expected few if any references to national values or purposes in confidential documents prepared for the inner sanctum of national security policy (after all, don't they know who they are or what they represent?), the texts of foreign policy are replete with statements about the fulfillment of the republic, the fundamental purpose of the nation, God-given rights, moral codes, the principles of European civilization, the fear of cultural and spiritual loss, and the responsibilities and duties thrust upon the gleaming example of America. In this sense, the texts which guided national security policy did more than simply offer strategic analysis of the 'reality' they confronted: they actively concerned themselves with the scripting of a particular American identity.[57]]

This is so because the task of constructing, affirming, and using identity as the intellectual foundation for policy is ongoing at all times among policy makers and the national public alike. Discerning the best choice of ends and means in foreign policy is a complex and never-ending challenge for policy makers; they must decide on a single conception of what they want and how to get it from among an infinite number of possible formulations—and they must choose options that will be politically acceptable within the domestic cultural framework in which they operate as well as effective in accomplishing their goals. In undertaking these choices, national leaders are constantly referring back to their understandings of "who are 'we'" along with "who are 'they'" and "what is the world like in which we interact" because the answers to these questions narrow and focus both the set of goals they might choose and the set of feasible policy means to those ends, limiting their choices and thus simplifying and enabling the decision-making process. This book will argue that the plans for action derived from these identity constructions constitute "ideologies."

Ideology

If, in the simplest sense, identity answers the question, who am I? then on the basis of that answer, ideology answers the question, what do I believe and how should I act on that belief? Like identity, ideologies serve as heuristic devices, cognitive frameworks enabling individuals to manage the complexity of reality by drawing general conclusions from a relatively small set of particular facts. Unlike the broader category of identity, in politics ideology is invariably, explicitly, and consciously normative. Ideologies are systems of belief that translate philosophical principles or values into instructions to act, sets of ideas that are presumed to form a basis for individual behavior rather than simply to be believed. Ideology and identity are mutually interconstitutive; that is, they are constantly informing and informed by one another, just as an individual's sense of who she is in the world both shapes and is shaped by the set of principled beliefs for action she holds. If ideology is one reflection of identity, it is a particularly important one for political analysts in that it is the element that explicitly presumes to dictate political behavior.

"Ideology" has been chosen here as the term that most accurately captures the set of ideas being described in this book, but it should be noted that the definition of the term itself is a subject of debate. Ideology has tended in the past to refer to highly coherent and well-defined systems of belief, such as Christianity or Marxism, but this view has become a matter of scholarly contention as it has been challenged by a more general, inclusive construct. Applied to states, this broader notion of ideology comes to mean something akin to "political culture"; it is a set of general widely and firmly held beliefs that delineate the ways in which people conceive of the multisided relationship between themselves, the polity of which they are members, their government, and the external world. Martin Seliger describes what he refers to as "restrictive" and "inclusive" definitions. The first "comprises the definitions which, like the original Marxian conception of ideology, but on different grounds, confine the term to specific political belief systems. The other category comprises those conceptions which stipulate the applicability of the term 'ideology' to all political belief systems."[58] Walter Carlsnaes (among others) has contested this definition, arguing that this broader conception robs the word of much of its meaning.[59] The distinction between the two notions lies in the level of coherence and narrowness that one demands a belief system must posses to be referred to as an ideology. The restrictive view requires that the given set of ideas provide an explicitly stated, easily definable, and internally coherent system of thought, while the inclusive view sees all political discourse as fundamentally rooted in ideology.[60]

For the purposes of this book, ideology is defined as an internally coherent set of beliefs prescribing an agenda for social or political action. To have political utility and causal significance as a variable in the study of foreign policy, an ideology must be abstract or at least abstractable from particular questions of policy; an ideology is a principled belief system or philosophy. It must also be prescriptive; it cannot be pure theory, but must both answer basic questions about the proper relationship of individuals to state and society and also assert the possibility and desirability of social reform to match these claims.

This notion of ideology is closely related to what Jeffrey Legro has called the "dominant ideas . . . embedded in public discourse and symbols that also represent intersubjective phenomena that attach to group, not individual, orientation." Legro argues that in understanding state behavior it is necessary to consider not only identity and interests, but also these "notions that actors have about how to enact their identity or achieve their interests . . . states become what they do as much as they do what they are, they desire what they do as much as they do what they desire . . . This proposition supports a view of identity that is not a monolithic macrovariable but a collage of different operational ideas that are activated in different contexts and issue areas." "Dominant foreign policy ideas," he adds, "are typically embodied in national debates and speeches, decision-making discussions, symbols, encapsulated lessons of history, and organizational procedures."[61]

In understanding the ways in which dominant ideologies rise and fall, it is vital to note that the role of a particular set of ideas in policy is largely determined by their functional utility for policy makers and society as a whole. As in individual psychology, ideational frames serve the heuristic purpose for whole societies of simplifying the world in order to make it comprehensible and provide a roadmap for action within it. Such intellectual frameworks must be able to predict and explain events in ways that are convincing to a significant proportion of society. Entrenched ideas will tend to remain so only if they are able to serve this role; if events transpire in ways that seem grossly inconsistent with the expectations of the dominant ideational system, space will be created for competing ideas to offer alternative explanations, which, if they are more convincing to enough people in a society than the existing orthodoxy's explanations, can form the basis for a paradigm shift in the intellectual rationale for policy. "Ideas that endure seem to do so because they appear to generate desirable results," Legro argues. "When events generate consequences for societies that deviate from their collective expectations and the consequences are starkly undesirable, change is more likely."[62]

Legro contends that cultural ideas should not be seen as direct catalysts for particular policies but rather as the raw material that is shaped by political processes. "Collective ideational change," he argues, "is inherently political and conflictual." The process of foreign policy change is thus a collective intellectual process involving groups ranging in size from the president and his or her advisers to the entirety of the United States government to the whole of American society, and indeed the whole of world society. Conceptions of self and other and appropriate goals, means, and norms of conduct in international politics are constantly being shaped and reshaped through the mechanisms of politics. Collective ideas are asserted and critiqued by a wide array of competing actors, interpreted and reinterpreted to account for new problems and other changes in society and the broader world. Legro's aim in describing this process is to account for and explain foreign policy change through this lens; I argue here that this framework is also necessary to understanding continuity in the intellectual superstructure of American foreign policy—not merely the policy continuity that comes from the inertia of settled consensus ideas, but also the repetitive patterns of argument and counterargument that have occurred throughout American history. While noting the existence and malleability over time of collective foreign policy ideas adds a valuable insight to the field of IR, to fully understand such ideas it is necessary also to understand where they come from and how they persist over centuries as well as how they rise and fall from year to year or decade to decade. A given set of paradigmatic foreign policy ideas may hold sway for many years but then suddenly be discredited and replaced by an alternative paradigm—as happened with American noninterventionism in the period between the world wars, for example, which eventually came to be replaced by the interventionism of the World War II and cold war eras. But it is also necessary to understand why and how it is that the ideas and rhetoric of noninterventionism and other subsets of American ideology continue to circulate within American culture and reemerge to challenge the new dominant paradigms in later eras. Where do these ideological systems come from, how do they relate to one another, and why is it that these systems of thought continue to recur time and again in American political discourse? This book seeks to build on the work of Legro and others by suggesting answers to these questions.[63]

Consistent with Seliger's restrictive definition, "ideological states" have often been thought of as those that explicitly refer to a well-codified set of beliefs as their guiding principles in policy making, such as Nazi Germany, the Soviet Union, or revolutionary Iran. Distinguishing these states as "ideological," however, risks minimizing the importance of political belief systems that meet the "inclusive" definition in other states. The term "ideology" is used here with the understanding that it refers to the broader definition, and for the purposes of this book an ideology can be thought of as any system of principled beliefs that dictate political action. By this standard, the United States, Turkey, and Japan are also ideological states, because there exists within the political culture of each a set of ideas, rooted in the communal identity of those societies, which forms an ideational framework that both enables and constrains state policy.[64]

Whether nationalism itself can be considered an ideology depends on the what is meant by the term. As a concept, "nationalism" is sometimes characterized as the belief that human beings naturally divide themselves into and show allegiance to national units and that distinct nations have a right to sovereign self-determination. In practice, nationalism is typically not concerned so much with the universal rights of all people as it is with the distinct characteristics and rights of one people. "The nation" is not an ideology if by the nation one means the collection of cultural attributes—typically including understandings of a shared language, ethnicity, history, and art and of the identities of Others—that attract the allegiance of a group of people. Ideologies as defined here are operative ideas in politics; they are not just values but instructions or guidelines for putting those ideas into action. The belief that "we are a distinct nation" is not an ideological belief. The belief that "we are a distinct nation and should therefore respect the rights of other nations," or the belief that "we are a distinct nation and should therefore eliminate all of those among us who are not like us," are ideological beliefs because they translate a value or principle into a plan for political action.

Ideologies affect perceptions of threat. As John Kennedy stated in a letter to Nikita Khruschev, "I am conscious of the difficulties you and I face in establishing full communication between our two minds. This is not a question of translation but a question of the context in which we hear and respond to what each other has to say. You and I have already recognized that neither of us will convince the other about our respective social systems and general philosophies of life. These differences create a great gulf in communications because language cannot mean the same thing on both sides unless it is related to some underlying purpose."[65] Because ideology is rooted in identity, ideological challenges are threats to identity itself. We are what we believe, and if our beliefs are challenged by others, this challenge poses a risk not just to our ideas but to our very notion of self. As Mark Haas explains, "The greater the ideological difference dividing decision makers from different states, the more likely they are to view one another as substantial dangers to both their domestic power and the security of their respective countries . . . ideological variables shape leaders' understandings of the security environment in which they operate, in terms of which states constitute the greatest threats to leaders' key interests and the level of this perceived threat."[66] Ideologically like-minded leaders in different states will also tend to trust one another and to understand their relationship as one based on shared values and interests. Emanuel Adler and Michael Barnett have suggested that like-minded states may form "security communities" in which the use of force is not considered a possibility and cooperative security relations are the dominant norm.[67] Haas finds that ideological antipathy historically exists not just around regime type, but also around economic philosophy and prevailing attitudes about the rights of internal minority groups. States that are less alike on each of these axes are more prone to view one another as hostile and to engage in conflict with one another.[68] Haas's "core claim is that there exists a strong relationship between the ideological distance dividing states' leaders and their understandings of the level of threat they pose to one another's central domestic and international interests."[69]

This approach seems well designed to consider the sources of conflict in the period Haas looks at, 1789–1989, in large part because what we now think of as political ideologies had begun to fully emerge in this period. It is more difficult to explain conflict rooted in ideology before this period because at least in Europe, the international system after the Treaty of Westphalia and before the French Revolution was highly unstable and prone to conflict, despite the fact that its major members shared a similar regime type, being aristocratic monarchies. Conflict within that system was driven not so much by political ideologies as they are now understood as by identity; while Britain and France did not compete because one was democratic and the other not, they did compete in ways that depended on a mutual understanding that they were different from one another, which in turn depended on a set of values, of ideas on both sides of what it meant to be "French" or "English." A focus strictly on ideology, which neglects identity, also has difficulty explaining nationalistic or other conflicts between ostensibly like-minded states with similar governing systems, such as conflicts between authoritarian states like communist Vietnam and China in the 1970s. Ideology is vitally important in determining state policy, but is best understood in the context of its relationship with identity. The fact that Vietnam and China in the 1970s claimed to hold similar ideological beliefs did not erase their sense of historical and cultural difference sufficiently to prevent armed conflict between them. A focus on identity is necessary for understanding the ways in which ideologies emerge.

Michael Hunt has suggested that "ideologies are integrated and coherent systems of symbols, values, and beliefs" arising from "'socially established structures of meaning,'" sets of ideas that are "relatively coherent, emotionally charged, and conceptually interlocking." In the history of the United States, Hunt finds that national ideology has been defined by a vision of national greatness linked to territorial expansion and the exportation of liberal political values, a sense of Anglo-Saxon racial superiority, and a fear of revolution in any form. Hunt asserts that in every era, a small and homogeneous cohort of policy elites have succeeded in making these values define the role of the United States in the world.[70] An approach similar to Hunt's is adopted by Richard Kerry, who considers American ideals historically to have included Democratic Universalism (the notion that the American system of government and society are applicable everywhere), American Exceptionalism (the belief on the part of

Americans that the development of their nation is distinct from the manner in which such evolution has taken place in other parts of the world), and the nineteenth-century Liberal philosophy of Locke, Mill, Jefferson, and others. Kerry views each of these systems of belief as having had an influence on traditional American attitudes toward foreign policy.[71]

Stanley Hoffmann asserts the importance of similar influences on policy, arguing that America's principles are rooted in the Liberalism of the eighteenth and nineteenth centuries. In practice, these ideas constitute "abstract dogmas and moral imperatives, deeply felt and widely shared, setting goals and defining rules of conduct," along with assumptions about how individuals and nations can be expected to act. The nation's historical experience has had a similar and related effect on American attitudes toward foreign policy, creating erroneous assumptions about what is possible in the realm of world politics. "Our past, our principles, and our pragmatism," Hoffmann concludes, "breed not only millennial hopes, but an embattled sense that we are the chosen champions of those hopes—and this buoys and harries us in turn."[72] Hoffmann argues that what he refers to as "America's principles" and "national style" constitute "a truly remarkable tissue of common beliefs and feelings," creating a broad consensus about foreign policy goals within American society.[73]

Citing as an example the historical reluctance of the United States to employ military means to settle civil wars beyond U.S. borders, even in defense of democracy, George Kennan refers to national "principles," as "general rule[s] of conduct by which a given country chooses to abide in the conduct of its relations with other countries." They are unlike policies inasmuch as they are not subject to negotiation. "A country, too, can have a predominant collective sense of itself," Kennan writes, of "what sort of country it conceives itself to be—and what sort of behavior would fit that concept . . . Principle represents, in other words, the ideal . . . of the rules and restraints a country adopts." Principles to Kennan are the necessary cornerstone of successful national leadership on issues of foreign policy.[74]

Though an identifiable set of national identity beliefs has colored American foreign policy throughout its history, emphases on different aspects of this identity and differing interpretations of common aspects have led individuals starting from similar core beliefs to reach very different ideological positions and policy conclusions. On the basis of these diverging interpretations, recurring ideologies have emerged from American identity over time.

Over the course of U.S. history, American identity has been dominated by Judeo-Christian values and traditions and the philosophy of eighteenth- and nineteenth-century liberals, including Locke, Mill, Rousseau, and Jefferson. This thinking has emphasized the preeminent value of the liberty of individuals and states and the efficacy of reason in solving problems, and in doing so, has tended to cloud Americans' understanding of nationalism, leading to either the oversimplification of international issues or fearful aversion to them. Nau has argued that the major poles of American thought historically—isolationism, liberal internationalism, and realism—are all rooted in a common sense of American separatism or exceptionalism. This sense of difference has produced the historical cycle of engagement and disengagement from world affairs, and this aspect of U.S. identity currently mitigates against recognition of global interdependence.[75] In the early United States, a belief in individualism, economic and political freedom, opposition to regulation, and mistrust of government, along with "self-government, distance, and a liberal political ideology" were the "ingredients [that] molded a new identity, even as the political ideology sharpened conflicts and put the new nation on a course to civil war."[76] Seymour Martin Lipset has emphasized a similar set of characteristics in describing American identity: "The United States . . . compared to other Europe-Canadian polities is still more classically liberal (libertarian), distrustful of government, and populist. It gives its citizens more power to influence their governors than other democracies, which rely more heavily on unified governments fulfilling economic and welfare functions. Viewed cross-nationally, Americans are the most antistatist liberal (Whig) population among the democratic nations."[77]

This same liberal philosophy and sense of exceptionalism has also formed the ideological basis for American support for international institution building in periods of historical foreign policy activism, as a sense of the moral superiority of America's founding principles has led U.S. leaders with a strong belief in the utility of American power to advocate for the creation of international institutions based on this model. They have reflected a desire to create a constitutional community—*E Pluribus Unum*—on a global scale and have tended to lead Americans to underestimate the power and potential for violence of traditional nationalism. Woodrow Wilson's argument for a new international order rooted in law and organization after World War I or Franklin Roosevelt's arguments for the creation of the United Nations and Bretton Woods system after World War II were attempts to apply to global politics those liberal principles that were understood to have created a just and stable order in the diverse American polity in the preceding centuries. Thus, as Ruggie has argued, "A multilateral vision of world order is singularly compatible with America's collective self-conception as a nation. Indeed the vision taps into the *very idea* of America."[78]

American identity has also included an understanding of history that has engendered the sometimes contradictory notions of American exceptionalism and the universalizability of the American model of society and politics. American leaders over the course of the past two centuries have consistently held that the United States is a country fundamentally unlike other states in its more just form of government and social organization. They have also consistently claimed that this model of just society is universally applicable; rooted in basic truths about the value of individual sovereignty, its essential structure has been assumed to be appropriate everywhere. Louis Hartz has argued that American "exceptionalism" emerged from the absence of the *ancien regime* of hierarchical aristocratic and religious social order that existed in Europe.[79]

American identity must be understood as rooted most deeply in modernity itself, in the Enlightenment's faith in reason and human agency to create progress. The American founders believed they were carrying the intellectual project of the Enlightenment to its logical conclusion, putting the theories of enlightenment philosophers into practice, creating a new society on the basis of enlightenment principles. That this is the purpose of America and, by extension, of American foreign policy is a belief that remains deeply rooted in American political culture to this day. As Hixson writes, "American history emerged within the broader frame of modernity, which defined itself in contrast with others, perceived as primitive or backward . . . increasingly in the Age of Reason empowered European men sought to direct the forces of history rather than live in the shadow of an omnipotent God . . . Colonialism and imperialism thus flowed from the aggressive expansion of a western European worldview that apotheosized its way of life as ordered, reasoned, and providentially sanctioned."[80]

Americans have tended to believe, in short, that the social and political order established in their country is unique and universally applicable because it recognizes the basic rights of all human beings. But there have been crucial differences over the means—example or activism—that the nation should apply to the promotion of this model abroad, and as a result, this single, basic belief has given rise to very different visions of the nation's proper place in the world. Starting from this core value, it is possible to conclude that the United States should actively export its superior vision of politics and society or that it should protect the uniqueness of this order at home by avoiding engagement with the outside world. This example illustrates the more general complexity of the translation of ideology into policy, because the conclusions leaders have drawn from this belief have depended on a host of ancillary assumptions and values, and the distance separating the policy options that emerge has tended to obscure their common core principles.

Beyond these generalities on which there is broad agreement, profound differences over policy have emerged over more concrete questions of interpretation and emphasis. Contrasting sets of assumptions, each internally coherent and each derived from differing interpretations of national identity ideas, have constituted the foreign policy ideologies at play over the course of American history. The differences between them have tended to be about whether the United States has a material interest in economic stability in more or less of the rest of the world, or the right or duty to champion its own version of political and economic order against other alternatives, or a moral obligation to establish peace abroad. Conclusions about the answers to these questions have tended to be connected with and supported by assumptions about the means of policy—whether the United States has the economic capacity to fund an activist foreign policy or whether its diplomats and military can be effective.[81] Disagreement over the answers to these questions has led individuals to assert very different understandings of what constitutes the national interest and the requirements of national security. The relative importance of American sovereignty and the danger presented to it by participation in foreign politics; the relative importance of promoting justice (meaning a Liberal definition of individual human rights, capitalism, and democracy); the relative importance of foreign trade to U. S. economic prosperity; and the relative value of and danger to the lives of U.S. troops posed by foreign activism—differences over these issues have given rise to the competing ideological systems that have animated each of the pivotal debates that have marked the history of American foreign policy.

Ideology and Identity in the History of U.S. Foreign Policy

The concluding section of this chapter will suggest the ways in which national identity and ideology have shaped the creation of U.S. foreign policy over the course of the past two centuries. It will argue that differences in emphasis and interpretation within this common ideational framework explain the divergent visions of America's world role that have animated the critical foreign policy debates in U.S. history. While national identity comprises the overall socio-cognitive structure within which foreign policy debate occurs, within this broad system particular ideological schools of thought have emerged time and again, such as liberal and conservative isolationism and internationalism. At moments of change in the international system, one of these approaches has gained ascendance over its competitors to define a new foreign policy consensus for the decades that follow. Though the process by which this has occurred is complex, the most important factor determining which approach to the world will triumph has tended to be its ability to convincingly explain the critical events of recent historical memory.

Tony Smith has argued that liberal ideals have consistently shaped U.S. foreign policy, but that the dominant interpretation of these ideas and the subsequent shape of policy have gone through four distinct historic phases. First, in its "pre-classical" phase, American liberal idealism held that the United States was an exceptional society by virtue of its uniquely just political and social values. America was the "ark of liberties of the world" according to Melville, and the "last, best hope of earth" according to Lincoln. Though its democratic values were universal truths, however, in this period the real limits on American power and demands of consolidating the American empire in North America meant that the dominant interpretation of the meaning of this exceptional status for policy was that the United States should lead the world by example, not activism. The liberal reformer John Quincy Adams could counsel against seeking "monsters to destroy" abroad; America's mission was framed by the nation's tradition of seeing itself as a "city on a hill" and by Washington's advice to avoid entangling alliances. The second, "classical phase" of liberal internationalism began with the presidency of Woodrow Wilson, who articulated an expansive global role for the United States on the basis of these same principles. Wilson reinterpreted American ideals to argue for policies that they had not traditionally supported and asserted that the United States now had both the ability and duty to reform the world in its own image. While Wilson's view represented a radical reinterpretation of American philosophy, which would help to mobilize public support for U.S. intervention in the First World War and presaged foreign policy in decades to come, it fell short of permanently altering the U.S. approach to the world in the years immediately following World War I. The United States retreated to its traditional detachment from global political and military affairs after the war, and so Wilson's new thinking left liberal internationalism with the intellectual blueprint for a new foreign policy rather than an actual framework in place. This was to change after World War II, when liberal internationalism entered what Smith refers to as its "hegemonic" phase. Franklin Roosevelt and Harry Truman revived many of Wilson's ideas, which became in many ways the animating assumptions of the post–World War II international system and American foreign policy during the cold war. The idea that world order would be coordinated through a network of international organizations and that promotion of democracy and human rights on a global scale should be the principles driving American foreign policy became the central premises of liberal internationalism from the late 1940s until the end of the cold war. At that point, liberal internationalism entered what Smith refers to as its imperialistic phase, in which its core ideas were reinterpreted once again to support the conclusion that state sovereignty could be compromised in the name of human rights and that the United States should actively promote democracy because democratic values could take root anywhere and would make the world more peaceful.[82]

While it is true that a sense of a liberal, civilizing mission in the world has marked every era of American history as Smith suggests, it is also true that very different interpretations of the appropriate polices to be derived from the nation's core liberal ideals have held sway in different eras, and different views of the answer to this question have been advocated by different individuals in the same era. Divergent foreign policy ideologies—particular policy prescriptions nevertheless rooted in a common sense of national identity—have contested with one another even in periods when there was relatively broad consensus over policy. These distinct ideological interpretations of American identity have tended to follow a number of common themes. Among these are liberal internationalism, which has encouraged the activist promotion of liberal ideals abroad through military force in conjunction with international law and institutions. Liberal internationalist leaders have included Woodrow Wilson, Franklin Roosevelt, and Bill Clinton. Conservative or realist internationalists, such as Richard Nixon in the 1970s or Henry Cabot Lodge in the era of World War I, have also tended to support a large military and activist world role, but have been highly skeptical of international organizations, which they have tended to see as constraining America's freedom of action. Liberal noninterventionists, such as Robert LaFollette in the years before World War II and Henry Wallace in the early cold war era, have argued that the United States should lead by example and focus its resources on social and economic problems at home rather than playing an aggressive international role; these thinkers have often argued that American intervention abroad was imperialistic and immoral. Conservative noninterventionists, such as William Borah in the pre–World War II era or Pat Buchanan in the 1990s, have held that the United States should play a limited world role because its interests are likely to be compromised and its character as a society corrupted by foreign entanglements. These are recurring categories of thought, but individual leaders have frequently combined elements of each to create distinct ideological positions—notably, presidents Theodore Roosevelt, Ronald Reagan, and George W. Bush all took essentially conservative internationalist policy positions regarding the desirability of an assertive, militant world role emphasizing independent freedom of action, but premised their arguments on liberal internationalist notions about aggressively exporting liberal values.

Over the course of the nation's history, American identity has evolved significantly but has retained a consistent core emphasis on exceptionalism and liberal individualism. The term "American" to distinguish the early colonists from the English came into common usage well before the revolutionary period. It was first used by soldiers from the British Isles serving in the American colonies to distinguish themselves from those born in the colonies. It was a term of disparagement, the "American" soldiers being thought by those from Great Britain to be "poor soldiers, Irish papists, and fit only for cutting fascines with the negroes." Campbell argues that "from the 1760s on the English and their culture began to be depicted by many in the colonies . . . [as] morally inferior and even decadent when compared to America . . . Counterposing the degeneracy, licentiousness, and immorality of the Old World with the innocence, decency, and ethics of the New."[83]

Emphasis on differences in both race and culture characterized early American identity.[84] The division of the world into binary categories—the civilized Christian world and the barbaric, heathen Other—had constituted the dominant European worldview since before Columbus, and early American colonial identity depended on an "Indian Other." Campbell argues that the eventual denial of English identity thus posed a tension for Americans because it amounted to a rejection of the identity that had always differentiated Americans from the barbaric Other. In the end, the baseness and corruption of the European Other became in many ways parallel to the non-white, uncivilized, barbarian Other—while Europeans possessed learning and technology, they were depicted as base, vulgar, lacking in the moral advancement that defined true civilization—and thus themselves more like technically proficient barbarians.[85]

A widely shared notion of what it meant to be "American" had certainly emerged well before the political independence of the United States itself. Commonalities of language, custom, religion, economy, and civil society had developed in colonial America, forming the foundation for an inchoate national culture and identity years before the idea of independence had gathered a critical mass of public sentiment behind it. The ideas of the Reformation and the Enlightenment formed the intellectual superstructure that came to support a distinctly American national culture. Through the widespread distribution of newspapers and pamphlets, the printed word formed a vehicle through which colonial Americans, 75 percent of whom were literate, could share ideas and experiences in ways that would come to bind them together as a distinct people.[86]

Even so, the concept of American identity that spurred the Revolutionary War contained within it a residual sense of a kind of transnational English identity. In many cases advocates for revolution framed their appeals with reference to the English Civil War and Glorious Revolution, employing a usable past rooted in English culture even as they sought to sever their community from the English polity. Loyalist sentiment remained strong in the United States throughout the revolution; the notion that Americans were Englishmen did not disappear overnight—and arguably never disappeared entirely at all, to the extent that Americans still retain a sense of cultural kinship and a "special relationship" with Great Britain. But the political project of the Revolution required a conception of self that differentiated the new country from the old, and by the mid-1770s the public discourse of revolution had settled on a distinct set of political ideas that imagined American identity in clearer and more distinct terms than in the past. The popular sovereignty and individual rights ideas of the Enlightenment combined with the Whig tradition of limited government formed the basis for this revolutionary ideology as it was expressed at this time.[87]

The Revolutionary War was a fight by American colonists against the principle of subjugation to rule from afar without democratic representation. But it was also in a sense a war against being ruled at all, a fight for individual as well as national liberation. This idea of the radical freedom of the individual emerged from an American culture that held the idea of self-sufficiency in the wilderness to be a preeminent national virtue. This individualism provided a cultural framework within which the arguments for independence were shaped, but the experience of the Revolutionary War underscored this idea even more deeply in Americans' self-conception, cementing the idea of individual liberty as the highest principle of the American state and engendering a reflexive opposition to "big government" in American political culture. These ideas persisted, and continue to persist, long after the time when solitary frontiersmen conquered the wilderness through their wits and resourcefulness, to the extent that had ever happened at all. Hixson describes the ideological discourse of the American Revolution in these terms: "Natural rights philosophy forged consent behind the idea that governments that governed least, governed best. Faith in virtue, the free market, and opposition to the established church, standing armies, and central government authority . . . The discursive reference to 'We the people' elided hierarchies of race, class, and gender."[88]

The ideology of the Revolution centered on the notion of America as a community guided by the hand of God toward a particular destiny. Even Benjamin Franklin, perhaps the leading rational-humanist among the Founding Fathers, held that "our cause is the cause of all mankind, and we are fighting for their liberty in defending our own. It is a glorious task assigned us by providence." Ten years before the beginning of the Revolutionary War, John Addams said, "I always consider the settlement of America with reverence and wonder, as the opening of a grand scheme and design of Providence for the illumination and emancipation of the slavish part of mankind all over the earth."[89]

Conrad Cherry has argued that the image of America as a nation with a particular destiny ordained by God has been "such a powerful myth for the nation that it has decisively shaped our foreign relations as well as our own internal developments." The conquest of the continent and the victory of their nation in wars "reaffirmed . . . the conviction that America is a nation called to special destiny by God."[90] This sense of being a divinely chosen society contributed to the American belief in the virtue of territorial expansion, the tendency of Americans to believe that their conquest of the continent and, later, other areas of the world was not just good for the United States but good for the conquered as well. "Transcendent religious destiny fueled foreign policy universalism," Hixson argues. "As the Puritans strove to redeem the 'howling wilderness' from the 'atheistical' and 'diabolical' savages . . . Israel's exodus became New England's 'errand into the wilderness,' which became the U.S. mission to the world . . . Religious faith profoundly influenced foreign policy, and especially war, as the United States confronted a procession of 'heathen' enemies, 'godless Communists,' and 'evildoers' in a continuous history of violent conflict."[91]

On the first page of his pamphlet "Common Sense," Thomas Paine wrote that "the cause of America is in great measure the cause of all mankind."[92] Within American culture, victory in the war for independence vindicated the nation's sense of its own exceptionalism and divinely inspired destiny, confirming for many Americans the belief that theirs was indeed a more just and enlightened social order that was destined to guide not just the nation but the world to a better future. As Hixson has put it, "The patriotic narrative emanating from the Revolutionary War vindicated the virtues of divinely sanctioned republicanism and free market capitalism, ushering in a glorious new era not merely for the United States but for all mankind."[93]

As a statement of principles, the Declaration of Independence quickly rose to the status of "American scripture."[94] Jefferson's discourse of a society in which "all men are created equal" and government operates only by the "consent of the governed" coalesced a set of ideas about who Americans were and what their society stood for that captured American identity in a way that had not been done before. It highlights the extent to which nations are imagined communities and national ideas and historical narratives are mythologized, because in practice all Americans did not enjoy equal rights at the time, or in the centuries that would follow. But the Declaration did represent the clearest and most eloquent statement ever made of the principles that Americans believed their society represented. Indeed, one way of conceiving of national identity ideas in general is as the "truths that we hold to be self-evident;" the facts and values that are beyond discussion, which define the parameters of debate rather than residing within them. In the sense that the Declaration reflects a self-conscious effort to codify these ideas, it is an unusual statement of a society's self-conception, an attempt to make explicit what in most societies remains implicit, if still very salient for politics—the dominant shared understanding of who "We" are.

In the decades after the revolution, the meaning of this emerging national identity for foreign policy was less clear; very different visions of national greatness and the appropriate means to achieve it developed among American political leaders even in the first years following independence. One critical moment in the process of coming to a collective understanding of the nation's world role came as George Washington gave his farewell address as he ended his second term as president in 1797. Washington's words of advice to the new nation regarding foreign policy would become in many ways the seminal statement guiding American foreign policy in the century that followed:

> Permanent, inveterate antipathies against particular nations and passionate attachments for others should be excluded . . . Against the insidious wiles of foreign influence . . . the jealousy of a free people

> ought to be constantly awake, since history and experience prove that foreign influence is one of the most baneful foes of republican government . . . The great rule of conduct for us in regard to foreign nations is, in extending our commercial relations to have with them as little political connection as possible. Europe has a set of primary interests which to us have none or a very remote relation. Hence she must be engaged in frequent controversies, the causes of which are essentially foreign to our concerns . . . Our detached and distant situation invites and enables us to pursue a different course . . . we may take such an attitude as will cause the neutrality we may at any time resolve upon to be scrupulously respected . . . Why forego the advantages of so peculiar a situation? Why quit our own to stand upon foreign ground? Why, by interweaving our destiny with that of any part of Europe, entangle our peace and prosperity in the toils of European ambition, rivalship, interest, humor, or caprice?[95]

Washington asked American leaders to redeem the promise of the Revolution by conducting foreign policy in ways that would allow the new nation to pursue its own destiny, free from the ancient rivalries of European power politics. America's physical isolation from Europe and seemingly unlimited natural resources meant that it had no material interest in deep involvement in Europe's affairs, which could only serve to put the new republic's independence and liberal political ideals at risk. The notion that geographical distance, a morally superior social order, and economic self-sufficiency dictated a policy of nonentanglement in European politics acquired the status of unquestioned conventional wisdom in American society. Washington's words in the farewell address became entrenched in national political culture and formed the intellectual foundation of U.S. foreign policy for the next 100 years.

Washington's Secretary of State, Thomas Jefferson, elaborated the logic of these ideas further. Jefferson's philosophy concerning world affairs held that conditions in the Old World caused "the general fate of humanity . . . [to be] . . . most deplorable . . . suffering under physical and moral oppression."[96] America, on the other hand, profited from a wealth of arable land and other resources, and its people were independent farmers, whose lifestyle to Jefferson's mind was healthier and more noble than that of more urban Europeans. The moral superiority of these people over those of the Old World and the superiority of their liberal, egalitarian government created in the United States the potential for a rational utopia. Americans had established the foundations of a society that was in every way more enlightened and just than any that had come before.

Jefferson's vision of a virtuous agrarian society dovetailed with American ideas regarding the nobility of the "common man," who was the repository of a kind of virtue and unvarnished common sense that provided the basis for just and wise democratic governance. Simple, frugal, and hardworking, the economic freedom of a liberal economic system meant that this common man was free to rise as far in society as his own merits and diligence would allow. Perhaps the best statement of this ideal is provided by Benjamin Franklin's Poor Richard's Almanack, which in its aphorisms ("early to bed, early to rise") tended to emphasize the idea that democracy in America meant that anyone could elevate themselves through hard work and virtue.[97] The image of the frontier became an important element in this national philosophy, representing both the wealth of resources that allowed American detachment from the rest of the world, and also the proper vent for American productive energies. Jefferson's notion of America's moral superiority and the need to maintain a kind of quarantine from European affairs in order to protect it was to find an enduring place in the American national psyche.

The tensions that existed within the embryonic American identity—in particular between notions of individual freedom and racial identity, and loyalty to state or region versus to the Union—caused the politics of the new nation to become increasingly unstable in the changing economic and social circumstances of the first-half of the nineteenth century, finally culminating in the Civil War. At its core, the war was about national identity, about which aspects and understandings of it would control the future, since the contradictions in the identity asserted by the Founders could no longer be maintained. In the end, the war would decide this question of identity by force of arms and leave the nation with a new, more deeply entrenched sense of itself. Hixson writes that "only by viewing the nation as the sacred product of providential destiny could such a mammoth bloodletting have been justified on both sides." The carnage, brutality, and terrible waste could only be rationalized by being wedded to some divine purpose in the national mythology; a reckoning for past sins, a purging of corruption that would allow the nation to move beyond its basest habits and finally achieve the destiny that God had intended for it. It was only after the Civil War that the "United States" came to be referred to in the singular rather than the plural in common parlance, to be understood as a single community in the national mind. The war represented a major step in refining and cementing the national identity of the United States as the primary locus of political identification and loyalty in the American polity. Whether the moral obligations of being Virginian were more significant than those of being American was a profoundly significant question in the United States before and during the Civil War. With the end of that war, the question was answered. Though regional, state, and other subnational identities would persist in the decades that followed, from that point onward all of these were legally, politically, and morally subordinate to American identity. With the economic expansion and internal political coherence that this resolution allowed, the nation was poised to play an expanded world role in the decades to come.[98]

By the turn of the twentieth century the United States had become a global economic power. By 1914 it was the world's leading financier and producer of industrial goods, and U.S. businesses were rapidly expanding their overseas activities and ambitions. As the nation's economy changed, the Jeffersonian construction of America's world role was called into question by a generation of imperialist national leaders who sensed the new potential and demands of greater economic power. In the debate that developed over the question of American empire beyond the continental United States in the wake of the Spanish-American War, proponents of expansion often argued that the nation's racial and cultural superiority imposed on it a duty to civilize the less-developed world beyond its borders. If the United States did not play this role, it was argued, the natives it might have protected would be left vulnerable to the amoral brutality of some European power or Japan. Empire would expedite trade, it was claimed, and in any case national honor would not permit territory conquered at the cost of American blood to be simply abandoned. At the time of the Spanish American war, the imperialist senator Albert Beveridge claimed that "God marked the American people as His chosen to finally lead in the regeneration of the world." For Beveridge, the war was part of the "eternal movement of the American people toward the mastery of the world." Admiral Dewey said that the "hand of God" was at work in his victory at Manila Bay. And President McKinley himself said that it was "the providence of God, who works in mysterious ways, that "this great archipelago [the Philippines] was put in our lap." McKinley denied that the United States operated from any willful intent toward imperialism, saying that the responsibility of empire had been "put upon us." "There was nothing else for us to do but to take them all and to educate the Filipinos, and uplift, and civilize and Christianize them," McKinley said (apparently unaware the Christianity had been the predominant religion in the Philippines for centuries). Even Theodore Roosevelt, an ardent advocate of imperialism, claimed that the United Stated had not chosen empire but had "been forced by the exigencies of war to take possession of an alien land," which it would govern with "disinterested zeal for their progress."[99]

American discourse regarding the Philippine occupation was charged with the symbolism of race and gender. "As in Iraq," Hixson has argued, in the Philippines "the United States first liberated the country and then asserted it could not leave because the subject people lacked the capacity to govern themselves." Senator Beveridge said that "in dealing with the Filipinos we deal with children." Ninety percent of U.S. military commanders in the occupation had previous experience in the Indian wars of the American West, and for the country as a whole the counterinsurgency in the Philippines, which killed some 250,000 Filipinos, likely seemed in many ways an extension of the now-mythologized historical experience of "taming" the American frontier.[100]

The arguments of these advocates of empire prevailed, and in the process altered the traditional Jeffersonian interpretation of America's identity to support a new policy consensus. Still accepting Jefferson's premise that American government and society were morally superior to those of the Old World, they departed from the long-standing interpretation of this belief to argue that the United States now had the means and thus a moral obligation to offer the benefits of civilization to the backward peoples of Latin America and the Pacific. But this idea of America as an active moral educator did not yet extend to Europe. The United States had nothing to fear from the childlike, powerless, even inherently inferior people of the uncivilized world in this formulation, but it could still be damaged by too-deep involvement in the fully developed but amoral European political system. Europeans were the intellectual if not moral equals of Americans, and this meant not just that political entanglement with Europe would be dangerous, but also that it was the duty of the United States to protect less developed regions from the corrupt and brutal grasp of European powers. After prolonged debate within American society, U.S. dominion in Latin America, the Philippines, and other parts of the Pacific were widely accepted as coherent with the nation's founding philosophy; American identity had been reinterpreted to support a new set of policies, a new ideological approach to the world.

The anti-imperialists who argued against U.S. occupation of the Philippines had themselves "deeply internalized the Myth of American identity," in Hixson's words. They advocated against the establishment of an American overseas empire not so much because the United States was evil as because it was virtuous. They viewed the occupation as an "un-American foreign policy that eroded crucial distinctions between the virtuous United States and the corrupt Old World of Europe." The Anti-Imperialist League, for example, issued a proclamation rejecting American rule over "foreign territory, without the free consent of the people thereof . . . in violation of constitutional principles, and fraught with moral and physical evils to our people."[101]

With the outbreak of World War I the United States adopted a policy of neutrality ostensibly based on Washington's principle of non-entanglement. In its effects, this policy served the interests of the Allied powers because of Britain's dominance at sea, allowing the allies access to American goods and finances unavailable to Germany. Once the March 1917 revolution in Russia had replaced the Czar with a republican government, the war could be depicted to Americans as a struggle by democracy to defeat imperialism, militarism, and autocracy.[102] And in U.S. popular culture, the image of Germany taking innocent American lives at sea and conspiring against the United States in Mexico came to be seen as a threat to both the physical security and "national honor" of the United States, arousing public anger and destabilizing the cultural tradition of non-entanglement in European affairs.

In this environment, Woodrow Wilson reinterpreted traditional American identity beliefs to support a new policy ideology of intervention completely at odds with the historical practice of American foreign relations. Whereas tradition held that American exceptionalism compelled the United States to stay clear of European politics so that America's uniqueness should be protected from their influence, Wilson argued that American exceptionalsim should instead be a basis for intervention. A more powerful United States had less to fear from the corrupting influence of the European political system, but might now use its unique national institutions as a model to reshape that system in its own image. On the basis of the same identity principles that had formed the intellectual foundation of traditional policy, Wilson radically altered the ideological conclusions derived from them and called for a "war to end war," and to "make the world safe for democracy."

The goals Wilson described for the postwar world amounted to a global application of the American model of political organization: the protection of all states by all others through a system of collective security; universal national self-determination and democracy; equality under international law; and the elimination of national barriers to trade. These ideas represented a distinctly American statement of what was possible and desirable in international affairs. The same philosophy that provided the intellectual framework for America's Constitution led Wilson to the conclusion that the international community could also be united under the banner of shared aspirations and a common acceptance of universal goals. Democracy, individual liberty, and the right to self-determination in political and economic affairs were assumed to be an adequate foundation for a global constitutional community as they had been in American history.

But if American identity was reflected in Wilson's desire to create a constitutional community on a world scale, opponents of intervention in the war also made arguments on the basis of their own interpretations of beliefs which were no less part of the nation's tradition. Ultimately, Wilson succeeded because his interpretation of these ideas seemed better able to explain recent history. It told Americans that theirs was a rational society that desired peace, but also one that valued human rights and democracy and could no longer stand aside as these ideals were threatened abroad. Wilson's arguments seemed to reconcile the contradictory impulses to pursue both peace and justice. He reinterpreted traditional ideas about American identity to allow the kind of civilizing mission that had previously been extended only to the underdeveloped world to be directed at Europe as well. This argument was enabled by the growing perception among Americans that the United States was now economically and militarily powerful enough to accomplish the goals Wilson described without risking cultural or political domination by European powers.

Wilson depicted the conflict as a millennial struggle of good versus evil and unrealistically raised expectations for the postwar world. Many Americans who had supported the war on this basis were disappointed, and in 1920s political opponents of Wilson's globalism were able to tap into this public disillusionment over the war and the Versailles settlement as they argued for a return to a more limited U.S. world role. America had been drawn into World War I against its interests, they claimed, only to discover that its European allies were more interested in empire than an end to war. The lesson taken was that the morally superior American social and political order dictated that the United States should once again stand clear of European power-political struggles as it traditionally had. This ideological prescription came to define the postwar consensus in U.S. foreign policy, serving as the guiding premise of American foreign relations even as Europe once again descended into war in the next decade. Franklin Roosevelt increasingly worked to challenge this isolationist consensus in the late 1930s and early 1940s, arguing in Wilsonian terms for an activist U.S. world role to defend American ideals and the community of peace loving, democratic states. After the close of World War II, those advocating a leading U.S. world role in peacetime argued in traditional identity terms once again that the United States represented a morally superior social and political system, but now claimed that it was the nation's responsibility actively to export these ideals. In light of the widespread perception that the United States had been too passive in the face of international aggression in the 1930s, arguments for the need to actively engage in world affairs and confront Soviet aggression resonated with many Americans both because they drew on the traditional American principles and because they seemed to capture more effectively than other policy arguments the lessons of recent history.

Legro contends that the evolution of foreign policy ideas during and after World War II had important effects for broader conceptions of American identity itself. "Ideas related to foreign policy significantly influenced both domestic attitudes toward government and what might be considered overarching identity. The shift in ideas after World War II meant that the United States no longer saw itself as set apart from the rest of the world . . . As opposed to John Winthrop's 'city on the hill' where America would be a detached model for the amoral monarchies of Europe, the United States after World War II envisioned itself as the 'hill in the city': it embraced international society even as it saw itself as a superior form of political organization, not detached from, but within, that society." Thus, it is not only the case that ideology emerges from identity but also the case that ideology shapes identity. This process suggests at least one way in which national identity can evolve over time, as new interpretations of traditional ideas in new combinations and emphases result from the need to adapt the intellectual basis of policy to the changing material realities of the world. Foreign policy ideas must adapt to changes in technology, relative power, and other shifting demands imposed by the international system; national identity ideas provide the framework within which this adaptation occurs, but are also shaped by it.[103]

Throughout the history of U.S. foreign policy, dominant social constructions of American identity and the identities of other actors in the international system can be seen as critical factors shaping Americans' perceptions of threat and opportunity in world affairs and guiding U.S. leaders' choices about appropriate foreign policy responses. As Irving Janis notes, for example, U.S. military planners failed to anticipate the attacks on Pearl Harbor in 1941 in part because the did not discuss or anticipate

> enemy moves from the standpoint of how the Japanese would view the risks of not attacking the United States, of allowing themselves to be relegated to the status of a third- or fourth-rate power, deprived of all their hard-won territories gained from years of fighting and sacrifice, divested of all national honor. By not examining Japan's alternative from the Japanese military leaders' point of view, the Navy group was able to continue to assume that a Japanese attack against the Pacific Fleet at Pearl Harbor was not just a low-probability event but had practically zero probability.[104]

Among other mistakes, U.S. military planners had concluded that torpedoes launched from airplanes could not be used in Pearl Harbor because the water was too shallow. They assumed that because U.S. torpedoes would not work there, Japanese torpedoes would not either; they imagined an enemy that was no more capable than they were, with no better technology than they had. Janis speculates that it would have violated U.S. planners' "stereotyped view of the enemy as inferior" to have believed otherwise.[105]

A similar process of identity construction can be seen in the comments of Secretary of State Dean Acheson in 1951 regarding the North Korean invasion of South Korea: "The very fact of this aggression," Acheson claimed, "constitute[s] undeniable proof that the forces of international communism possess not only the willingness, but also the intention, of attacking and invading any time they think they can get away with it . . . communism is willing to resort to armed aggression, whenever it believes it can win."[106] Acheson's statement illustrates his view of "communism" as not only an enemy but a unified, rational actor in a way that might easily have had profound consequences for U.S. policy. Since "communism" had undertaken a policy that challenged U.S. interests, it was logically appropriate to respond to communism anywhere, as opposed to responding to the government of North Korea.

The effects of this process of constructing the identity of the communist Other are described by Janis, who argues that "the views of the members of Truman's advisory group concerning Red China's military strength and intentions were based on ideological presuppositions that they shared with all other leading members of the administration and with many other Americans as well."[107]

> One of the dominant stereotypes shared by all members of Truman's advisory group was that Red China was a weak nation, whose main source of potency in world affairs came from its affiliation with the Soviet Union, which meant that China's foreign policy was largely

> dominated by Russia. The members failed to take account of obvious indications that this oversimplified conception might not apply to Red China's possible responses to American troops in Korea. It contributed to their miscalculation of the risk of provoking a full-scale military response if the United States attempted to use its military power to gain control over China's neighbor and ally. Acheson's image of China, quite at variance with the facts . . . was that of a docile puppet of Moscow without a will of its own . . . Even after it became painfully obvious that they had made serious errors in judging what China would do, the group members continued to assume that China was participating in a Russian inspired conspiracy . . . They spoke of China, Russia, and North Korea as a homogenous entity and accepted the notion that "communism" had decided that China should intervene to divert the United states from its anti-Communist role in Europe.[108]

Throughout the cold war, the prevailing understanding of American identity within the United States held that the nation had both a moral and prudential duty to assertively export democracy and lead its allies in the struggle against international communism. Campbell argues that the cold war was constructed in the United States as a contest between civilization and barbarism and that only by understanding this culturally rooted construction can the policy choices of the United States be explained. To see the cold war as a function of objective power realities unmediated by cultural factors is to offer an explanation too simplistic to effectively explain why conflict emerged in the form it did in this case but not in others. Regarding the anti-communist consensus in the United States in the early cold war years, Campbell suggests, "The well-developed antipathy toward communism within the United States stems from the way in which the danger to the private ownership of property it embodies is a code for distinguishing the 'civilized' from the 'barbaric' (or the normal from the pathological) . . . enmity towards communism and the Soviet Union functioned as a code for the inscription of the multiple boundaries between the 'civilized" and the 'barbaric,' the 'normal' and the 'pathological.'"[109] Weldes has claimed that it was the self-identification of the United States as "leader" of the free world against communism during the cold war that prompted U.S. officials to define the presence of Soviet missiles in Cuba as a "crisis," which in turn limited the set of appropriate policy responses.[110] "During the cold war," Weldes writes, "'leadership' anchored the logic of an emphatically masculinist U.S. state identity. The United States was the 'leader' of 'the West' or the 'free world' and the global champion of 'freedom' and 'democracy.'" Weldes notes that this element of U.S. identity as understood by U.S. leaders is apparent in the formative documents of U.S. cold war policy. NSC-68, for example, states that the "absence of order among nations . . . is becoming less and less tolerable," a fact that "imposes on us the responsibility of world leadership," and NSC-7, characterizes the United States as "the only source of power capable of mobilizing successful opposition to the Communist goal of world conquest."[111] According to Schlesinger, Robert Kennedy framed his policy prescription in response to the Cuban missile crisis in terms of traditional American identity. Remembering Pearl Harbor, RFK premised his argument against a military attack on Cuba on the idea that "for 175 years we had not been that kind of country. Sunday morning surprise blows on small nations were not in our tradition . . . a sneak attack would constitute a betrayal of our heritage and our ideals."[112]

U.S. foreign policy during the cold war was underpinned by an intellectual rationale built around the areas of agreement between liberal and conservative (or realist) internationalists. These two groups tended to agree, though for different reasons, that active U.S. engagement in international politics, including robust military spending, a global network of security commitments, and assertive containment of the Soviet empire, including occasional uses of military force, was necessary to defend U.S. interests. This cold war consensus continued to exert a powerful influence in American thinking in the world after the end of the cold war as well. But before 9/11 the United States was a county with little experience of terrorism on its own soil and a well-entrenched sense of its own invulnerability to attack. This was in many ways a vestige of the "splendid isolation" of the eighteenth and nineteenth centuries and certainly inconsistent with the changed nature of the technology available to America's adversaries long before 9/11, but a social fact in the United States nonetheless. The attacks of September 11 thus struck particularly deeply into the American psyche because they called direct attention to the failure of a set of beliefs that were so deeply rooted in American culture. A country with a longer history of terrorism might have reacted differently, but in the United States the effect of 9/11 was nothing less than widespread insecurity approaching psychic crisis. This social reality provided the unique political and cultural environment that enabled the Bush administration to assert the need for a global war against terror involving the unilateral use of force to prevent threats from becoming imminent, and for these ideas to gain significant traction within American society as a whole. It was the delegitimization of old ideas by the events of 9/11 that opened the social and political space to allow the assertion and acceptance of this alternative vision of policy.[113]

If the different strains of ideology competing with one another throughout U.S. history are rooted in a common system of beliefs about American identity, they are also the lenses through which the nation seeks to understand its recent past. Periods of change in U.S. foreign policy have often been characterized by crises in which the ideological claims of some policy makers appear better able to interpret events than others. This capacity to convincingly explain recent history is crucial to the effective assertion of a vision for future policy. Ideological beliefs shape perceptions of historical facts, and one result of this is that individuals often see in events what they expect to see even in the face of overwhelming evidence to the contrary. But historical facts also serve to lend credence to some ideological belief systems over others, enabling those that can most convincingly explain recent events to gain ascendancy and come to dominate future policy. What Americans have believed about the world and the likely future has often depended heavily on how they have come to understand the recent past.

Legro refers to "external shocks" as a common catalyst for change in dominant policy ideas: "Embedded mind-sets endure for relatively long periods of time, but then they change under the pressure of dramatic events, giving way to new ideas that last until the next crisis. While crises are often related to change, exogenous shock remains an indeterminate explanation." But Legro finds this explanation incomplete, noting that "similar shocks seem to have different effects: some lead to change, some do not." To explain these differences, he argues, it is necessary to consider the role of ideas in shaping policy at these moments. "New foreign policy ideas are shaped by preexisting dominant ideas and their relationship to experienced events, sometimes reinforcing the continuity of concepts and infrequently leading to their radical change."[114] When paradigmatic changes have occurred it has been because external events have forced a reconsideration of consensus assumptions about policy. This change remains constrained within a more general, widely and deeply held set of ideas about identity, though at these moments these beliefs may be interpreted very differently than they have been in the past, to support new and sometimes even revolutionary policy choices. This does not occur without dramatic evidence that the established consensus has failed to anticipate or offer effective responses to critical events. Change comes slowly because policy makers and the public are cognitively wedded to established ideas. Thus, over the course of history, major foreign policy adaptation tends to be abrupt and sudden rather than gradual. Crisis and the unmistakable failure of entrenched foreign policy ideas have often been necessary in order for change to occur. The result has been a pattern of "punctuated equilibrium" in the history of American foreign policy.[115] American history has been characterized by long periods of foreign policy consensus, divided by moments of change when a critical mass of society and policy elites come to view a dominant ideology as dysfunctional and seek to replace it.

Ideas mediate power, creating social understandings of the threats and opportunities that face a society, of what it is possible and desirable for that society to do. Shared ideas shape understandings of the meaning of material reality, generating collective knowledge about what can and should be achieved through foreign policy and what cannot or should not be attempted. These shared understandings of a state's power and purpose, which this study has referred to as "ideologies," form the intellectual rationale for particular policies. While the United States clearly had the material capability to expand westward in the nineteenth century, it would not have done so without the social idea of Manifest Destiny. In the interwar period, the United States clearly did possess the potential for the kind of material power necessary to play a major role in global diplomacy, but made a collective choice not to do so because the dominant set of foreign policy ideas of the time suggested that to play such a decisive world role was neither feasible nor desirable. It might be argued that idea sets such as Manifest Destiny or noninterventionism were simply rationales to justify what was understood by their proponents to be in the nation's power interests—that power interests exist prior to the intellectual rationales that justify them, in other words. Political entrepreneurs certainly will seek ideological rationales for what they understand to be in their own or their country's material interest. But to say this only begs the question of how and why these material interests and the possible and appropriate means to pursue them were understood by these individuals to begin with. To ask whether ideas precede power or vice versa is to misleadingly disaggregate these concepts, to make it impossible to see the ways in which they in fact create and instantiate each other in practice. The meaning of power itself is an ideational construct; American power in the nineteenth century required the idea that U.S. economic and military capabilities could be effectively mobilized to expand. Thus, the idea of Manifest Destiny required U.S. power, but so did power require Manifest Destiny. Territorial expansion could not have occurred without the economic and military capacity for conquest of the United States, nor without the idea of Manifest Destiny. If power generates ideas so do ideas frame and define power. To argue that one is simply window dressing for the other misses the truth that while power and ideas may be intellectually separable, in practice they invariably define and constitute one another.

Throughout the course of American history, the political fate of a given ideological position tends to be tied to the fate of the group of individuals espousing it. A group asserting a set of beliefs that seems to better explain recent events than the dominant orthodoxy will find itself rising in status and power as its ideas become more widely accepted. "The broader ideational shift toward internationalism allowed internationalist groups to be more persuasive and hence to gain strength" in the interwar period, Legro argues. Similarly, those espousing a given orthodoxy as it is discredited and overthrown will tend to lose political power as their ideas lose social traction. Isolationists were the dominant political force in Congress throughout the 1930s, but by the mid-1940s their power had evaporated; a few changed their views and were able to survive (Senator Arthur Vandenberg, an early architect of the cold war, had been an isolationist in the interwar period), but often they were voted out of power at least in part because the ideational orthodoxy they represented had ceased to hold sway with the public as a whole.[116]

Legro notes that "some scholars have identified elements of both withdrawal or 'quietism' and 'messianic' activism, of introversion and activism, of pacifism and bellicosity, of intervention and nonintervention in the personality profile of U.S. foreign policy. Different elements, these scholars posit, have dominated in different periods, shifting in a cyclical fashion."[117] This book suggests that these recurring ideological themes have given rise to different policies in different eras based on their ability to explain recent historical events and thus form the basis for broad social consensus around their policy prescriptions, but that they emerge from differing interpretations of a common set of traditional notions of American identity. These bedrock identity constructs are more than just symbols, but the framework within which more specific political ideologies can provide socially viable intellectual bases for particular policies by interpreting, combining, and emphasizing certain elements of identity.

At moments of change in the history of U.S. foreign relations, debates over policy have been driven by competing definitions of national interest derived from a common framework of national identity, a set of general but historically resilient and widely held ideas combining an understanding of the nation's history with traditional liberal assumptions about the just relationship of individuals, government, and society. This broad, interconnected set of core identity concepts provides individual leaders with the intellectual foundation necessary to build support for their policy choices, but also comprises a set of expectations and understandings of acceptable policy among the public. National identity is the socio-cognitive framework within which the contests between foreign policy ideologies occur, limiting debate by implicitly determining which ideas, arguments, and policies are open to discussion and which are not.

Chapter 2

Identity and Ideology in the "War on Terror"

The terrorist attacks of September 11, 2001, revealed to many Americans the fact that their society was vulnerable in ways they had never imagined before. As it was shaped by U.S. political leaders, this sudden, shocking consciousness of insecurity led to a profound change in U.S. political culture, which enabled equally dramatic changes in U.S. foreign policy. The social context created by 9/11 and the Bush administration's framing of the new reality facing the United States are therefore critical variables necessary to an understanding of the course of American foreign relations since then. From the days immediately following the 9/11 attacks, the Bush administration presented a clear, coherent vision of the world in its public pronouncements, constructing an image of reality that defined the identity of America, its enemies, and the rest of the world in ways that served to enable subsequent foreign policy. Realist analyses that focus on material capabilities and interests alone are not sufficient to explain the evolution of U.S. foreign policy in this period because they do not take account of this process. A constructivist perspective that acknowledges the role of ideology and identity in the shaping of policy in this era is necessary for a full understanding of this change.

Foreign policy decision makers are certainly members of the social-cognitive systems of their societies; it would strain credulity to suggest that individuals in positions of power would somehow shed this prior identity, particularly since national leadership roles require individuals to be symbols of their societies and to advocate policies that are at least ostensibly rooted in their societies' values. Though neorealism suggests that societal and leadership identity are subsumed to objective strategic and economic interest calculations, in practice the decision making process is inevitably affected by the individual assumptions and value judgments of policy makers, and these factors are largely functions of the understanding of these leaders of their own society's identity in relation to that of the Other(s) with whom they are interacting. In assessing threats and opportunities and crafting foreign policy, Ted Hopf suggests that a decision maker "reads the other state through her understanding of her own state and that understanding is itself related to the discourses and identities that constitute her."[1] As Jutta Weldes argues, "Officials do not approach international politics with a blank slate onto which meanings are written as a result of interactions among states . . . Their appreciation of the world, of international politics, and of the place of their states within the international system, is necessarily rooted in collective meanings already produced, at least in part, in domestic political and cultural contexts."[2] "The job of constructivists," Hopf adds, "is to find out what is on that slate that decision makers are bringing with them in their interaction with external Others."[3] As Legro puts it,

> States often rely on the guiding influence of dominant ideas in managing their affairs, and it is worthwhile to understand them. This is not a simple task, but it is also not impossible. Such ideas are typically not in a manual or on a website, and deciphering them is aided by cultural expertise. Yet unlike the mental ideas of individuals, which often are difficult to assess, foreign policy ideas are necessarily embedded in public discourse—in symbols, speeches by officials, and even in institutional rules and procedures. These ideas play coordinating and legitimizing functions and are difficult to manipulate for short-term strategic purposes. Collective ideas, therefore, offer clues to the likely behavior patterns of a state . . . what is needed is multisource analysis in rhetoric, past pronouncements, institutional procedures, private discussion, and actual behavior as a check against strategic disinformation.[4]

It is the purpose of this book to pursue this agenda with regard to post-9/11 U.S. foreign policy, to examine the ideational framework through which the Bush administration understood the United States and the world between 2001 and 2007 in order to better explain the administration's policy choices and their outcomes. This will be accomplished by undertaking what Hopf has called the "textual recovery of identity," a methodology designed to "recover the identities and discursive formations that constitute the social cognitive structures" of political society. In employing this approach Hopf suggests that the researcher's role is first and foremost to listen to the subjects, to record and report their own assertions of identity while self-consciously avoiding the imposition of the researcher's own framework for understanding or ordering these ideas. The researcher should not look for particular identities, in other words, but rather allow them to emerge from the texts themselves. This method relies on an interpretivist epistemology that in turn depends, Hopf states, on "phenomenology and induction."

> Phenomenology implies letting the subjects speak, in this case through their texts. Induction involves the recording of these identities as atheoretically as possible . . . The trick is to remain ontologically open for as long as possible before imposing an analytical theoretical order, or closure, on the numerous ambiguities and differences in the text.[5]

The texts to be considered in this case are the statements of officials in the Bush administration, which will be examined with the intent of discerning how in each instance the subject speaking claims to understand the identity of the United States, the identities of America's friends and enemies in the world, and the nature of the international milieu in which they interact. This analysis will begin in this chapter with an examination of the Bush administration's most significant formal statements regarding the "War on Terror" from 2001 to 2007, focusing particularly on the president's State of the Union addresses and other major speeches.[6] In this chapter and those that follow, this study will also examine the statements of U.S. leaders in policy meetings and other venues.

It is important to acknowledge a number of underlying premises of this methodology. Among these are the presumption that "national interests" do not exist a priori but are defined by state foreign policy makers. In this process of interest calculation state leaders will seek to protect and augment national power and security as realists suggest, but leaders' ideology and understandings of the identity of their own society, other societies, and the international environment are critical factors influencing their conclusions about what comprises power and security and how best to pursue them in any given situation. To explain any foreign policy it is therefore necessary to comprehend the ideological and identity lenses through which the architects of that policy perceive the material world.

Political leaders, like all individuals, may make statements that are disingenuous, intended to manipulate the opinions of others to accomplish some political goal. It would be far too simplistic to presume that because a political leader makes a statement that it necessarily reflects his or her true beliefs. This fact represents an important point of caution for interpretivist methodologies: it cannot be assumed that any given statement of any political leader is a window into his or her heart of hearts, or that we can really know what any political actor truly believes.

While interpretivist analyses should be conducted with this point in mind, it does not present an insurmountable hurdle to such methodologies for a number of reasons. First, while it is fair to assume that political speech is intended to shape the opinions of its audience and is thus manipulative by definition, it is also reasonable to assume that political leaders have beliefs and values that play an important role in defining their political goals and that much of political speech is an honest attempt to convince others to share both these goals and the underlying beliefs and values.

Second, while it may not be possible to know what a political actor truly believes, it may be equally or more valuable to policy analysis to know what s/he claims to believe and what s/he understands his or her audience to believe. The substance of national identity is amorphous and highly contestable, but for the purposes of this study it is less vital to understand how the whole of American society understands itself than it is to grasp how U.S. leaders believe it understands itself. When advocating for a particular foreign policy, presidents frequently base their arguments on either implicit or explicit arguments about who "We" are, who our friends and enemies are, and what the world is like in which we live. In making these arguments, a president is likely to reveal what he or she believes about the answers to these questions, but certainly will reveal what he or she believes American society as a whole believes. Both of these variables comprise layers of understanding of national identity, and both are therefore of critical importance in illustrating the ways in which national interests are defined from a constructivist perspective.

Franklin Roosevelt held his own interventionist views in check in his statements about U.S. foreign policy in the late 1930s and early 1940s, mainly because he did not believe that American society as a whole shared his opinions and he did not want to compromise his ability to lead public opinion by staking out a position that diverged from it too radically. It seems likely that this example is to some degree typical of all presidents, who may not state their true policy preferences on every occasion because doing so might compromise their efficacy as political actors. But if not every presidential statement reveals the true beliefs of the speaker, it is nevertheless fair to assume that presidential statements will be consistent with the administration's understanding of the basic beliefs and core values of its audience, which will typically be assumed to be the common values of American society as a whole. Presidents may not always reveal what they think, but they will tend to reveal what they think America as a whole thinks. Statements by the president will tend to be consistent with the dominant system of shared beliefs within the administration. Leaders will seek to avoid outright lying or misrepresentation of important values to their audiences if they can, and will tend to recognize that framing their policy preferences within the context of their own and and society's values will be the most effective strategy for rallying support around those choices.[7]

Thus it is not necessary to comprehend with certainty the true beliefs of U.S. leaders in order to understand the role of identity-ideological factors in policy formation. The public policy statements of leaders will not always fully represent deeper beliefs, but for the purposes of this book it will be assumed that national leaders will seek to avoid making statements that run contrary to their deeply held convictions and understandings of reality. While they may describe the world and their preferred policies in ways designed to garner public support, these descriptions will *tend to be consistent* with their core beliefs and values. More importantly, it is an assumption of this book that leaders will seek to shape policy to approximate their own ideological preferences within the constraints of national political culture as they understand it. In publicly framing foreign policy, in other words, national leaders tend to claim that their own political preferences, determined through their assessment of the nation's interest in the world viewed through their personal cognitive-ideational schemas, are consistent with what they believe to be the public's understanding of national identity. Thus, the arguments of national leaders for particular foreign policies will tend to accurately illustrate both their own individual beliefs, values, and assumptions about threats and opportunities in the world, and their own understanding of the identity and values of their society, since the claim that particular policies are consistent with these societal values tends to be a key assertion of political speech. Such political speech can and should be examined with an eye toward comprehending both what leaders believe and want in the world and what they understand their audience to believe and want.

This approach to understanding the goals and values of the Bush administration is consistent with the image of the rhetorical construction of policy in the administration that emerges from most contemporary accounts. According to many observers, in his speeches George W. Bush was not merely reciting words that speechwriters had written for him. Instead, he provided many of the core ideas within his speeches and expected his speechwriters to craft language around them. In developing his first major address to the nation after 9/11, for example, interviewer Robert Draper quotes Bush as telling his speechwriters that the idea he wanted to convey to the public was that "I am going to be thinking about this every morning when I wake up, for the rest of my presidency." From this thought came the line in the speech, "I will not yield; I will not rest; I will not relent in waging this struggle." In its final form the statement was more stylistically sophisticated, but the essential idea belonged to Bush himself. Bob Woodward's accounts similarly depict Bush as deeply involved in the process of drafting his speeches, proposing and changing specific language, not relying on his speechwriters for major themes but instead expecting them to structure sentences and paragraphs around his ideas and phrases. On the night of 9/11, for example, Woodward describes Bush instructing his advisor Karen Hughes to remove the line "This is not an act of terrorism. This is an act of war" from his address, despite the fact that he himself had said it numerous times that day, because he felt it did not provide the message of reassurance that he sought to convey to the country. He also told his speechwriters to include the sentence "we will make no distinction between those who planned these acts and those who harbor them," specifying that he preferred the word "harbor" over terms like "tolerate" or "encourage" because it was more specific. In both of these accounts, Bush is not a president merely speaking words someone else has crafted for him, but rather the conceptual architect of a message that he relies on speechwriters to capture.[8]

IDENTITY AND IDEOLOGY IN THE FOREIGN POLICY OF GEORGE W. BUSH

Constructivist theory suggests that the ways in which the leaders of states understand themselves and the world around them is a critically important variable in explaining their policy choices. Thus, to evaluate the causes of recent U.S. foreign policy, this chapter will consider the ways in which the Bush administration conceived of the identities of the United States, its friends and enemies, and the environment in which they interacted in the years after September 11, 2001.

This chapter will contend that the following set of core assumptions were the critical ingredients in the Bush administration's construction of the post-9/11 world: that the promotion of democracy and peace were central goals of American identity and foreign policy; that America itself was profoundly vulnerable to extant but invisible threats, both internationally and domestically; that the world was divided into two camps, loosely defined as "civilization" versus "terrorism" or barbarism; that individuals and groups in the "terrorist" camp were irrational and, by virtue of their rejection of civilized norms, not fully human; that opposition to terrorism and undemocratic governments was a continuation of the United States' historic opposition to fascism and other forms of totalitarianism; and that other states which ought to be in the U.S. camp might or might recognize their duty to defend freedom, imposing a moral obligation on the United States to act whether or not international consensus could be reached. The Bush administration's successful assertion of this vision of reality created the political environment that allowed post-9/11 American foreign policy in general, and the war in Iraq in particular, to be carried out.

Foreign policy in the Bush administration has often been referred to as Wilsonian in its moralistic activism and emphasis on democratization.[9] In practice, however, it tended to regard the means of traditional Wilsonianism—internationally coordinated action through multilateral organizations—as marginally useful at most, even while asserting Wilsonian principles as its desired ends. This chapter will evaluate the influence of Wilsonianism on the rhetoric and substance of U.S. foreign policy in the Bush administration. It will argue that the administration's policies were ineffective largely due to its failure to recognize the inherent connection between liberal ends and multilateral means in the logic of traditional Wilsonianism.

Robert Jervis has argued that a central tenet of the Bush Doctrine was that dictatorships tend to pursue aggressive, violent, "evil" foreign policies and were not susceptible to reform or rational deterrence. Overthrowing such governments by force was regarded as legitimate and sometimes necessary for the security of the international system as a whole, which thus required assertive U.S. hegemony to maintain peace. In this respect, Jervis argues that Bush combined aspects of Wilsonian internationalism with a realist conception of the utility of the use of force.[10] Or as Jack Snyder has noted, "Bush promise[d] to fight terror by spreading liberal democracy" and claimed that strict realists had "lost contact with a fundamental reality that 'America is always more secure when freedom is on the march.'"[11]

But while advocating the virtues of democracy, Snyder argues, "the Bush administration [showed] little patience for the complexities of liberal thought—or for liberalism's emphasis on the importance of international institutions."[12] Even as it asserted the importance of liberal principles of law and democracy in contemporary international politics, the administration consistently sought to undermine or dismantle an array of international agreements—notably the Kyoto protocol on climate change, the statute of the International Criminal Court, and the U.S.-Russian Anti-Ballistic Missile Treaty. Most significantly, the Bush administration carried out an invasion and occupation of Iraq without the approval of the United Nations Security Council and despite the opposition of many of its closest allies.

This chapter will begin by comparing the foreign policy discourses of the Wilson and Bush administrations and argue that the Bush administration's stated foreign policy goals were rhetorically consistent with traditional Wilsonianism in their emphasis on American exceptionalism; the utility of force; democratic universalism and the democratic peace; trade liberalization and debt forgiveness; humanitarianism and America's "civilizing" mission; and self-determination. But with regard to the means of foreign policy, the Bush administration departed from the principles of Wilsonian liberalism by disregarding their emphasis on international institutions. This chapter will argue that by ignoring the logical coherence between ends and means in liberal internationalist thinking, this approach undermined its viability as a basis for policy.

Wilsonian Liberalism

Woodrow Wilson was president in an era that saw the most profound political and military crisis in European history up to that time and the emergence of the United States as a global economic and military power. At this pivotal moment, Wilson described a set of principles that provided the ideological orientation for much of U.S. foreign policy in the century that followed and still resonates deeply in American culture today. Though Wilson's name is most clearly identified with twentieth-century liberal internationalist thought, the deeper roots of this philosophy lie in the Enlightenment liberalism of Locke, Mill, Kant, and the American founders. Major themes consistent in this body of thought over time have included the idea that the legal equality of nations should be the central principle of international relations; that international society is improvable and war is not inevitable; that institutions and law are sources of social order; that effective international organizations are both necessary and possible; that democracy and national self-determination are universal rights; that open access to trade and economic opportunity will increase prosperity and reduce the likelihood of armed conflict; that all states are economically interdependent and have an interest in global development; that democracy, economic openness, and peace are inseparable and mutually reinforcing goals; that there is a high degree of commonality between the interests of states; and that human rights are universal. The threads uniting these ideas have been a belief in the common interest of all people in peace and the sanctity of the political freedom and equality under the law for both individuals and nations. Collective security would be a universal system of common defense of all states by all others, applied against any aggressor on behalf of any victim in defense of the principle of national self-determination shared by all societies. Freedom from imperialism, the right to democratic government, and equality under the law have been held to be universal entitlements that transcended cultures. From these principles have flowed a belief in the possibility and necessity of an international constitutional order to serve the common interests of humanity.[13]

Appealing to Congress for a declaration of war on April 2, 1917, Wilson placed intervention in the context of these ideals. The United States would fight, he said,

> for the ultimate peace of the world and for the liberation of its peoples, the German peoples included: the rights of nations great and small and the privilege of men everywhere to choose their way of life and of obedience. The world must be made safe for democracy . . . We have no selfish ends to serve. We desire no conquest, no domination for the sacrifices we shall freely make . . . We are . . . the champions of the rights of mankind . . . Our object is to vindicate the principles of peace and justice in the life of the world as against selfish and autocratic power and to set up amongst the really free and self-governed peoples of the world such a concert of the purpose and of action as will henceforth ensure the observance of those principles.[14]

Wilson argued that U.S. foreign policy should be guided by moral precepts rather than the pursuit of material interests alone. He deplored the traditional realpolitik of European diplomacy, which he viewed as amoral and inclined to produce war.[15] "My dream," he suggested, "is that . . . all shall know that [the United States] puts human rights above all other rights, and that her flag is the flag not only of America, but of humanity."[16] "The government of the United States," he claimed in the second *Lusitania* note, "is contending . . .

for nothing less high and sacred than the rights of humanity." Wilson was the devoutly religious son of a Presbyterian minister, and when he concluded that U.S. intervention in the war was necessary, his religious values informed his understanding of its purposes. "There are times in the history of nations," he argued, "when they must take up the instruments of bloodshed in order to vindicate spiritual conceptions . . . when men take up arms to set other men free, there is something sacred and holy in the warfare."[17]

Wilson held throughout World War I that the United States had no interest in the conflict except in a peaceful and just resolution. He did argue that American policy should serve universal goals for pragmatic as well as ethical reasons though, contending that America could no longer reasonably seek to isolate itself from world politics. The nation's economy was now too large, as well as too dependent on foreign markets and sources of raw materials. In August 1919, Wilson warned Congress that the United States now was part of an interdependent world. "We must face the fact," he said, "[that] in saving Europe, she [the United States] will save herself . . . Europe is our biggest customer. We must keep her going or thousands of our shops and scores of our mines must close. There is no such thing as letting her go to ruin without ourselves sharing in the disaster."[18] Wilson held that while it was naive to think that America could remain detached as before, the country could perhaps exercise a global role "not of exploiting power, but of liberating power, a power to show the world that when America was born it was indeed a finger pointed toward those lands into which men could deploy . . . and live in happy freedom."[19]

In February 1916 Wilson had argued that America "ought to keep out of this war . . . at the sacrifice of everything except this single thing upon which her character and history are founded, her sense of humanity and justice."[20] Intervention could not be justified by anything less than the globalization of American liberal ideals, the creation of a world order based on freedom and equality that would reduce or eliminate the prospect of future wars. In his arguments for intervention, Wilson applied to Europe a concept of an American civilizing crusade that had previously served as a rationale only for American interventions in the developing world, such as the occupations of Cuba, the Philippines, and other U.S. colonial possessions. He expected that this crusade would not merely end the war but mark the beginning of a new era of international peace based on the principles of justice.

Central to this new regime would be cooperative conflict management between democratic powers. The secret and thus undemocratic diplomacy which was seen as one of the causes of World War I would be eliminated. Democracy would supplant autocratic rule and self-determination would replace imperialism. Democracy, international law, and free trade would support one another to form the basis of a more stable, just, and peaceful world order. While the old system of power politics had always been amoral and warlike, Wilson thought that the horrors of modern war now made millennial change so clearly necessary as to be inevitable. From the ashes of World War I would arise a new moral consensus in the world that would form the foundation of a new society of nations.[21]

The spread of democracy would be a critical factor in this new international system, which Wilson claimed would serve the interests of justice as well as peace. He held that democracy was more just and humane than any other form of government because it was premised on the sanctity of individual human rights. The spread of democracy was also necessary for international peace because undemocratic states were prone to external aggression just as they were to repression of their own peoples. "A steadfast concert for peace can never be maintained except by a partnership of democratic nations," Wilson argued. "No autocratic government can be trusted to keep faith within it or observe its covenants."[22]

But Wilson believed that if this new era was to come into being, it would be critically necessary to recognize the intrinsic connection between the *ends* of a more just foreign policy—democracy within states and peace between them—and the *means* of that policy—international cooperation within a system of effective international law and institutions. Recognizing, codifying, and enforcing this new international order would be the task of an international body of states, a league of nations. Wilson had long believed that global interdependence would make such a body necessary, and he first publicly outlined his plan for a world league in late May 1916. In that address, he called for the creation of an organization of states based on self-determination, the equality of nations, and the collective prevention of aggression. American isolation, he stated, was over: "We are participants, whether we would or not, in the life of the world. The interests of all nations are our own also . . . what affects mankind is inevitably our affair as well as the affair of the nations of Europe and Asia."[23]

In seeking to build a new international order, Wilson believed that he was pursuing the ideals of the American Founding Fathers to their logical conclusion. Wilson had been a political scientist and constitutional scholar before he became a politician. He understood

American history as the story of a diverse group of independent polities becoming one through recognition of their common interests and shared values. Respect for the sanctity of individual liberty had united the fractious American colonies into a single society, and this model could be applied to the world as a whole, if only the warring states of Europe could recognize their common interest in living in a world of peace and liberal norms. Democracy, individual liberty, and the right to self-determination could form the foundation of a constitutional community for the world just as they had in America. The United States was a unique society, in Wilson's view, a nation founded on transcendent principles that could form the basis of a new global community of states.

Wilson did not view this globalization of the American model of social and political order as imperialistic, but rather as the opposite: the creation of a system for the defense of national independence and diversity. He believed that one of the most important functions of the U.S. federal government was to protect the rights of states and local communities to govern themselves in ways consistent with their own values, and he imagined the League of Nations playing a similar role in the international system.[24] When international aggression occurred, a collective body would meet it with "common force" to "safeguard right." A permanent organization created for this purpose could provide for all states a "virtual guarantee of territorial integrity and political independence."[25]

Wilson claimed that the League "is going to lead us, and through us the world, out into pastures of quietness and peace such as the world never dreamed of before."[26] He also suggested, more ominously, that a failure to seize the chance for peace on the basis of this new order would have dire consequences for the future. The opportunity to build a more just and peaceful international society would be fleeting; it would disappear

> like a dream in the night, and there issues upon it, in the suitable darkness of the night, the nightmare of dread . . . and there will come sometime, in the vengeful Providence of God, another struggle in which, not a few hundred thousand fine men from America will have to die, but as many millions as are necessary to accomplish the final freedom of the peoples of the world.[27]

Wilson's assertion of universal norms was inextricably linked to a belief in the need for an international community to enforce them; the promotion of democracy and the maintenance of peace were for him intellectually inseparable from a belief in the need for international institutions. He argued that the first priority of U.S. foreign policy for both moral and practical reasons should be the creation of a stable and lasting peace, and this would require recognition that the security of the world was indivisible and required central coercive authority to be guaranteed. A peaceful community of states could be maintained through the common defense of the sovereignty of all its members, Wilson claimed, as long as they all accepted certain basic principles: political democracy, economic openness, international law, and the right of national self-determination. He viewed past wars as nearly always the result of the aggression of one state against another and believed they would become less prevalent in an international system in which democratic nation-states conducted foreign policy fairly and openly. The League would be the center of this international society of democratic states, the first step toward an international community beyond the state of nature. This model could work in world politics as it had in America, Wilson believed, because it was premised on principles of justice and human rights that defied cultures and borders.

Liberal Unilateralism: Ideology in the Administration of George W. Bush

Authors such as Tony Smith have placed George W. Bush's rhetoric squarely in this Wilsonian liberal internationalist tradition. Smith suggests that it was the president's fundamental worldview, rather than insincere political calculation or the opinions of his advisors, that drove his characterization of the world and the American place in it. "His arguments are clearly and coherently liberal," Smith contends. "They place the democratization of foreign states through regime change at the center of the American agenda for world order and thus for national security. This suggests that the president was relying less on his advisors and speechwriters to shape his words than on his own intuitive understanding . . . The president had clearly internalized his argument and would give no quarter in pushing it forward." Smith notes that President Bush was impressed with the book *The Case for Democracy* by Israeli politician Natan Sharansky and had copies distributed among his top foreign policy advisers. In it, Sharansky asserts a version of the democratic peace argument, saying that "while the mechanics of democracy make democracies inherently peaceful, the mechanics of tyranny make nondemocracies inherently belligerent."[28]

In focusing on the spread of democracy as a stated foreign policy goal, Bush was not breaking new ground but in fact echoing a set of ideas that had come to define the intellectual mainstream in both academic and official discourse in the United States in the 1990s. What might be termed a neoliberal internationalist consensus came to dominate the thinking of foreign policy elites of both political parties, and to an extent academic political science, in the post cold war era. Smith suggests that this new liberal orthodoxy was comprised of three major ideas. First was the notion of the "democratic peace," the argument that democracies could be empirically shown not to fight one another and that a world made up of democratic states would therefore be a more peaceful world. Initially asserted by the political theorist Michael Doyle on the basis of his rereading of Immanuel Kant's 1795 "Perpetual Peace," this idea gained currency among political scientists and then political elites of both parties in the 1980s and 1990s. It led many to conclude that an American foreign policy that actively promoted democracy abroad would serve U.S. interests by creating stability and peace, as well as more just and humane living conditions in those societies that became democratic. Second was the notion of the universal applicability of democracy as a system of government, the belief that because the underlying premise of democratic governance was respect for individual rights that were shared by all people, the appropriateness of democracy for a given society was not dependent on the particular historical or cultural conditions of that society. Because everyone in every culture enjoyed the same fundamental human rights, democracy could also be expected to function more effectively and justly than any other governing system everywhere. This idea supported arguments for an activist democracy-promotion agenda in U.S. foreign policy by suggesting that such a policy could eventually succeed anywhere. The third idea was the notion that human rights trumped national sovereignty in at least some cases. Thus, the core principle of the Westphalian state system for the previous four centuries—the sovereign equality of states and legal inviolability of their borders—was directly challenged by U.S. and other Western intellectuals and political leaders of the left in the 1990s. They argued that "ethnic cleansing," genocide, and other gross violations of human rights dictated that the international community had a moral right and even a duty to protect threatened citizens from the actions of their own governments regardless of whether these posed a threat to international peace. The legal and intellectual foundation of the Westphalian principle of unlimited state sovereignty had been unstable at least since the Nuremburg tribunal at the end of World War II, where the very notion of "crimes against humanity" suggested that state governments did not have sole authority to determine what was just and unjust with regard to the treatment of their own citizens within their own borders. The intervening decades had seen few real applications of this principle, but with the collapse of the bipolar international system it gained new currency in the 1990s. An unexpected resurgence of post–cold war nationalism led to staggering violence in Somalia, Bosnia, Rwanda, Haiti, Kosovo, and many other parts of the world, and among liberal internationalists in Washington, D.C. there emerged a consensus that the most extreme horrors perpetrated by governments against their own people should not be tolerated by the international community. While the United Nations was the Clinton administration's preferred vehicle for coordinating the international response to such crises, by the end of its time in office the administration had concluded that it should not condition its willingness to act on U.N. Security Council approval. In Kosovo in 1999, the Clinton administration launched a sustained war against the government of Yugoslavia without the approval of either the Security Council or the U.S. Congress.[29]

Smith suggests that the "template for policy offered by democratic peace theory was used repeatedly (and in theoretical terms, accurately) by official Washington." It aided the administration of George W. Bush in defining usable identities to attach to other states in the world. In many speeches as well as in the *National Security Strategy* document of 2002, the Bush administration asserted that the most important categories dividing kinds of states from one another in its cognitive schema were regime types. Speaking at the National Defense University on March 8, 2005, Bush argued the validity of democratic peace theory and criticized past U.S. policy in the Middle East for failing to recognize the inextricable relationship between internal repression and external aggression. "By now it should be clear that decades of excusing and accommodating tyranny in the pursuit of stability have only led to injustice and instability and tragedy," Bush said. "It should be clear that the advance of democracy leads to peace, because governments that respect the rights of their people also respect the rights of their neighbors . . . When a dictatorship controls the political life of a country, responsible opposition cannot develop, and dissent is driven underground and toward the extreme . . . dictators place blame on other countries and other races and stir the hatred that leads to violence."[30]

In the administration's conceptual framework, democratic states, including Canada, Australia, Japan, South Korea, the states of the European Union, most of Latin America, and others, comprised the "free world." They were members of a community of ideals and interests with the United States; they could be expected to be peaceful and friendly in their relations with America and each other, and it was in the interest of the United States to see them prosper and vice versa. A second category of states were not fully democratic but had friendly relations with the United States and were important to U.S. interests in various ways; these included Russia, China, Turkey, Brazil, and Mexico. A third category were repressive authoritarian states with whom the United States might have important cooperative relationships, such as Uzbekistan or Saudi Arabia; these were problematic because their closed political systems were antithetical to American values and prone to internal instability and radicalism. Some of these closed regimes were already "rogue states" hostile to American interests and values; others were willing to work with the United States, but it was seen as the U.S. role to use its relationship to move these toward democratic reform. A handful of states also comprised "illiberal democracies," a category which allowed that some apparently democratic states were not supportive of U.S. values and goals and explained this apparent contradiction by suggesting they were not in fact as democratic as they appeared—Venezuela under Hugo Chavez and the Palestinian Authority under Hamas were included in this category.[31]

This categorization of states by regime type led to a reframing of the notion of multilateralism by the Bush administration. Since the United States naturally shared interests with democratic societies like itself and naturally found its interests in conflict with nondemocratic regimes, international cooperation and coordinated action would tend to occur within the community of democracies rather than in the venue of the community of states writ large. So when Condoleezza Rice spoke of multilateral ends and means in her confirmation hearing before the Senate Foreign Relations Committee on January 18, 2005, it was a multilateralism of a very particular kind: "First, we will unite the community of democracies in building an international system that is based on our shared values and the rule of law," she said. "Second, we will strengthen the community of democracies to fight the threats to our common security and alleviate the hopelessness that feeds terror. And third, we will spread freedom and democracy throughout the globe."[32]

Neoconservatism

Charles Taylor has written that "it often happens that what start off as theories held by a few people come to infiltrate the social imaginary, first of elites, perhaps, and then of the whole society."[33] In 1968, James C. Thomson blamed the Johnson administration's failures in Vietnam in part on the ideology and military doctrines of just such a small group of intellectuals. Thomson, who had served as Lyndon Johnson's National Security Council Staff from 1964 to 1966, saw the mistakes of that war as in part a result of

> the rise of a new breed of American ideologues who see Vietnam as the ultimate test of their doctrine. I have in mind those men in Washington who have given a new life to the missionary impulse in American foreign relations: who believe that this nation, in this era, has received a threefold endowment that can transform the world. As they see it, that endowment is composed of, first, our unsurpassed military might; second, our clear technological supremacy; and third, our allegedly invincible benevolence (our "altruism," our affluence, our lack of territorial aspirations). Together, it is argued, this threefold endowment provides us with the opportunity and the obligation to ease the nations of the earth toward modernization and stability . . . In a sense, these men are our counterparts to the visionaries of Communism's radical left: they are technocracy's own Maoists."[34]

Much the same argument can be made about the Bush administration, in which many of the unanticipated negative consequences of foreign policy have been directly attributable to the flawed, simplistic premises of the firmly held ideology of a small group of individuals with the capacity to shape public opinion and define policy. The Bush administration was clear about its worldview and clear that its policy choices flowed from this intellectual framework. These ideas are collectively referred to as "neoconservatism."

This section of this chapter will argue that neoconservatism must be understood as an ideology, because it comprised a set of political beliefs that encompassed not only a vision of the world as it is but also a plan of action, an invocation to change the world to make it as it should be. To understand the origins of neoconservatism, it is important to recognize that it was rooted in long-standing conceptions of America as an exceptional society, built on the foundation of individual freedoms that could provide the basis for just government in any culture. In the sense that neoconservatism emerged from these ideas it must be seen as growing out of, rather than departing from, the intellectual history of U.S. foreign policy. But while grounded in these traditional notions of American identity, neoconservatism also represented a radically new set of interpretations of these ideas; it reinterpreted, combined, and emphasized distinct threads in the liberal tradition in ways that had not been done before in history, and in this sense it constituted a revolutionary departure from the past. To understand neoconservativsm as an ideology it is necessary to grasp both its deeper roots in traditional ideas about American identity, the distinct ways in which these ideas were interpreted and employed, and the particular historical circumstances that caused them to become accepted within the Bush administration and broader American society as the appropriate intellectual framework to animate U.S. foreign policy.

Many observers have identified the ideological roots of the Bush administration's approach to world affairs with the Project for a New American Century (PNAC), a Washington think tank founded by conservative commentators William Kristol and Robert Kagan in 1997. Closely identified with other conservative research centers, including the American Enterprise Institute (which housed the PNAC's offices), the PNAC was the intellectual home for a group of foreign policy scholars and practitioners who would become known as neoconservatives, many of whom would come to play central roles in the creation of the Bush administration's foreign policy. The PNAC advocated for the building of U.S. defenses to a point of unassailable primacy to which no other challenger could aspire. Andrew Bacevich has described the neoconservative worldview as being marked by "an extraordinary certainty in the righteousness of American actions married to an extraordinary confidence in the efficacy of American arms."[35] Neoconservatism also focused on the moral necessity of an activist world role, calling for the aggressive promotion of democracy and open markets. It "emphasized changing American foreign policy to become a hegemon and police its international interests as a new kind of benevolent American empire. This would include expanding the military, withdrawing from major treaties, as well as engaging in preemptive strikes against those who would threaten U.S. interests."[36]

Among the leading neoconservative thinkers in the Bush administration, academia, and think tanks in the last decade, probably the most influential were I. Lewis (Scooter) Libby, chief of staff to the vice president; Elliot Abrams, special advisor to the president; Paul Wolfowitz, deputy secretary of defense; John R. Bolton and David Wurmser, State Department officials; Douglas Feith, under secretary of defense; Zalmay Khalilzad, National Security Council official and later ambassador; Richard Perle and Eliott A. Cohen, Defense Policy Board members; Donald Kagan, Yale University professor; Bernard Lewis, Princeton professor; William Kristol, *Weekly Standard* editor; Charles Krauthammer, *Washington Post* columnist; James

Woolsey, former CIA director; Max Boot, Council on Foreign Relations member; and Norman Podhoretz, Hudson Institute fellow. Of the 25 founding members of the PNAC, ten found positions in the new administration of George W. Bush, as did numerous others such as John Bolton and Douglas Feith who were not charter members. While closely associated with the neoconservative movement and certainly sharing many of its ideas, Donald Rumsfeld and Dick Cheney did not have the kind of deep roots in the movement that many of their subordinates did. Notably, Cheney and Rumsfeld seem to have accepted but not been the primary advocates for democracy promotion as a goal of the administration's policy, a central tenet of neoconservative thinking.[37]

On October 1, 2001, just a few weeks after the 9/11 attacks, Kristol and Kagan noted the extent of the neoconservative influence in the Bush White House and enjoined these leaders to be true to the principles they had claimed to stand for when they had signed a letter to President Clinton in 1998 calling for the ouster of Saddam Hussein by force. "The signatories of that 1998 letter are today a Who's Who of senior ranking officials in the administration. Secretary of Defense Rumsfeld, U.S. Trade Representative Robert Zoellick, Deputy Secretary of State Richard Armitage, Deputy Secretary of Defense Paul Wolfowitz, Undersecretary of State John Bolton, Undersecretary of State Paula Dobrinsky, Assistant Secretary of Defense Peter Rodman and National Security Council officials Elliott Abrams and Zalmay Khalilzad. If those Bush administration officials believed it was essential to bring about a change of regime in Iraq three years ago, they must believe it is even more essential today. Last week we lost more than 6,000 Americans to terrorism. How many more could we lose in a world where Saddam Hussein continues to thrive and continues his quest for weapons of mass destruction?"[38]

Among its goals the PNAC listed increased defense spending, confrontation with "regimes hostile to our interests and values," and acceptance of "responsibility for America's unique role in preserving and extending an international order friendly to our security, our prosperity, and our principles." Its statement of principles called for "the resolve to shape a new century favorable to American principles and interests," a "Reaganite policy of military strength and moral clarity . . . to build on the successes of this past century and to ensure our security and our greatness in the next."[39] Beyond this, neoconservative thinking was often associated with the following themes: a Manichean worldview that divided the international sphere into good and evil along ideological lines and a belief that political character is the willingness to choose good over evil; a belief that both military power and the willingness to use it are the fundamental arbiters of interstate relations; a focus on the Middle East as the primary region of concern for U.S. foreign policy and global Islam as the primary ideological challenge for Western liberalism; an understanding of international issues in stark, moralistic terms, leading to a belief that political disagreement is tantamount to a betrayal of the nation; a focus on the Munich analogy over the Vietnam analogy, and an emphasis on the efficacy of American power in influencing world affairs; disregard for traditional diplomacy and its institutional locus, the State Department, along with the perceived amoralism of "realism" and the moral relativism of cultural specialists; a historical orientation toward and nostalgia for the Reagan administration; and hostility toward multilateral institutions and treaties, which were seen as constraining American sovereignty.[40]

For neoconservatives, "stability" and "normalcy" were not necessarily good things, certainly not automatically ends to be sought.[41] "Deterrence," "containment," "realism," "collective security," "confidence building," "dialogue," and "consensus" were dangerous illusions, not appropriate strategies in contemporary international politics.[42] Neoconservative authors tended to refer the Middle East "peace process" in skeptical quotations, regarding it as the misguided or malevolent work of "peacemongers."[43]

A seminal statement of the neoconservative position was the 2000 book *Present Dangers: Crisis and Opportunity in American Foreign and Defense Policy* edited by PNAC founders Robert Kagan and William Kristol. In it, Kagan and Kristol described the risk that "the United States, the world's dominant power on whom the maintenance of international peace and the support of liberal democratic principles depends, will shrink from its responsibilities and—in a fit of absentmindedness, or parsimony, or indifference—allow the international order that it created and sustained to collapse. Our present danger is one of declining military strength, flagging will and confusion about our role in the world."[44] An article by Kristol and Kagan in the summer 1996 issue of *Foreign Affairs* provided another key articulation of the neoconservative worldview. In it, Kristol and Kagan argued that "American hegemony is the only reliable defense against a breakdown of peace and international order. The appropriate goal of American foreign policy, therefore, is to preserve that hegemony as far into the future as possible." They worried that American society was feckless, distractible, naively sentimental, and perhaps weak willed, however, and that Americans might "absentmindedly dismantle the material and spiritual foundations on which their national well-being has been based . . . the main threat the United States faces now and in the future is its own weakness."[45] Kristol and Kagan called for the "benevolent hegemony" of the United States and for the use of preeminent power for the purpose of "actively promoting American principles of governance abroad—democracy, free markets, and respect for liberty." They depicted an America with "the capacity to contain or destroy many of the world's monsters" and a "responsibility for the peace and security of the international order." But the United States was also seen as a society that could be tempted into shirking its responsibilities, into "a policy of sitting atop a hill and leading by example [which] becomes in practice a policy of cowardice and dishonor." The United States therefore needed leaders who could call the country to its moral duty, who could sum up the threats facing the United States in terms reminiscent of NSC-68 at the opening of the cold war. American leaders needed to face the rhetorical task of "preparing and inspiring the nation to embrace the role of global leadership . . . The re-moralization of America at home ultimately requires the re-moralization of American foreign policy."[46]

In the wake of the cold war, Kristol and Kagan argued, America's role in the world "ought to have been obvious. It was to prolong this extraordinary moment and to guard the international system from any threats that might challenge it. This means above all, preserving and reinforcing American's benevolent hegemony." Instead, they claimed, the Clinton administration had failed to rid the world of Saddam Hussein once and for all, had failed to stem the rise of Chinese power and instead had pursued a policy of "appeasement" toward China's "aggressive behavior," and rather than confronting "evil regimes" had "tried to do business with them in pursuit of the illusion of stability."[47]

In light of these failures, Kristol and Kagan advocated "a fundamental change in the way our leaders and the public think about America's role in the world." They called for "a foreign policy based on American hegemony, and the blending of principle with material interest," and an "America capable of projecting force quickly and with devastating effect to important regions of the world." They argued that these capabilities should be used to "set about making trouble for hostile and potentially hostile nations, rather than waiting for them to make trouble for us." They were critical of the narrow, geopolitical conceptions of self-interest advocated by realists and instead called for policies rooted in "honor and greatness in the service of liberal principles."[48]

From its inception in 1997 and throughout the decade that followed, the PNAC and its individual members never ceased arguing for the forceful overthrow of Saddam Hussein's government in Iraq.[49] Regime change in Iraq was a major goal of neoconservatives, but it was also a means to a larger end—fundamentally reshaping the politics of the Middle East as a whole. As Kagan and Kristol wrote in the *Weekly Standard* of January 21, 2002, "A devastating knockout blow against Saddam Hussein, followed by an American-sponsored effort to rebuild Iraq and put it on a path toward democratic governance would have a seismic impact on the Arab world—for the better."[50]

Kristol and Lawrence Kaplan published the definitive neoconservative statement on Iraq, entitled *The War over Iraq: Saddam's Tyranny and America's Mission*, on the eve of the war. In it, they argued that the realist case for containment of Iraq was dangerous because "Saddam has revealed himself to be a pathological risk-taker" who intended "to dominate his region and deter the United States" with weapons of mass destruction. "Today we may attack Iraq with minimal risk because Saddam has yet to acquire a nuclear bomb. Once he does, the equation changes. Then it is we who will be deterred." But overthrowing Saddam was not enough, Kaplan and Kristol asserted. Instead, as with the defeated axis powers of World War II, Iraq should be democratized to serve as an example for the region as a whole. "Iraq's experience of liberal democratic rule . . . could increase pressure already being felt by Teheran's mullahs to open that society. Iraq's model will be eyed warily by Saudi Arabia's theocrats to the south . . . Meanwhile, Iraq could even replace Saudi Arabia as the key American ally and source of oil in the region."[51]

The neoconservative agenda for the Middle East was to shock the region out of its torpor and fundamentally shift the course of history with a single bold stroke. The work of scholars Bernard Lewis and Fouad Ajami was influential among neoconservatives and within the Bush administration, and Lewis and Ajami themselves were frequent participants in meetings with administration officials aimed at strategizing broadly about the Middle East and the war on terror. Their scholarship, typified by Lewis' *What Went Wrong?* and Ajami's *Dream Palace of the Arabs*, tended to construe the Muslim and Arab worlds as tragically resistant to the forces of modernity, resulting in centuries of social and cultural stagnation relative to the rise of the West in the wake of the Enlightenment. In works like "The Roots of Muslim Rage," Lewis argued that it was not the legacy of Western Imperialism that impeded social, economic, and political development in the Muslim world, but rather a cultural refusal to accept the manifest superiority of Western enlightenment ideas. In its refusal to acknowledge modernity, Lewis suggested, Islamic civilization had doomed itself to centuries of slow decline in the face of Western advances. The result was a growing frustration and anger that would eventually provoke a crisis, unless through Western intervention Muslim culture could be radically redirected. The decline of the once-great Muslim civilization was a source of humiliation and rage among contemporary Muslims, as were the corrupt and repressive regimes that governed Arab states, a glaring symptom of the resistance of the Middle East to the waves of democratic reform that had swept much of the rest of the world. American foreign policy in the Middle East had not created this trend, but it had helped to facilitate it in the last century by propping up brutal, nondemocratic regimes because they were pro-American and appeared stable. The net result was a region on the brink of crisis, with the future of the entire world hanging in the balance. Muslim culture was mired in a kind of quicksand that its own history would not allow it to escape. Some outside force was needed to jolt the Muslim world out of its corrupt and reactionary stasis. One democracy in the Arab world would sweep aside generations of inertia and entrenched pessimism by its example. It would demonstrate all that was possible in the Arab world, and what would at first seem a flicker of hope would soon become a conflagration, a burgeoning of democracy that would sweep the region from Tehran to Damascus to Palestine and Riyadh. The festering corruption and stagnation of the Arab Middle East was intolerably and increasingly dangerous for the world as a whole; the only reasonable way to deal with it, challenging and radical though it might be, was through Western intervention to allow Arab and Muslim societies to take the great leap forward they had missed in centuries past, to act as the catalyst that would allow history to begin again.[52]

Support for Israel and the Likud Party in particular was an important aspect of the political ideology of many neoconservatives, in varying degrees. For Douglas Feith, George Packer suggests that "the security of Israel was probably the prime mover." Packer argues that Paul Wolfowitz was motivated more by concern with democracy as a universal principle than with the security of Israel in particular. As a group, neoconservatives placed a very high priority on the defense of Israel because it was the Middle East's only democracy, and because of its security relationship with the U.S. government, if not for moral or ethical reasons.[53]

The neoconservative agenda before 9/11 had not said much about terrorism; it was rooted in an essentially state-based conception of international politics, a view of the world that imagined state governments with radical ideologies and aggressive ambitions as the primary threats to U.S. hegemony. Neoconservatism was an ideology created by cold warriors in an attempt to apply an understanding of cold war history to the post–cold war world; it was not a schema that was especially concerned with the kind of transnational, non-state issues that were a focus of other commentators on the international system of the 1990s. This fact suggests that if the neoconservatives were revolutionaries in some respects, they were also creatures of the world in which they had come of age. Cheney and Rumsfeld, whose offices formed the axis of policy formulation in the Bush administration, were themselves not radical thinkers. In a sense they were the most conservative of conservatives, the ultimate organization men, consummate insiders who brought with them an astonishing history of experience in Washington politics. They had come of age as cold war hawks enraged at the betrayal of the American left in Vietnam, determined to rebuild American strength and prestige in the world. Donald Rumsfeld, George Packer has written, "hadn't formed a new idea since opposing arms control as Gerald Ford's secretary of defense." They were trapped in the modes of thought of the cold war, in particular the idea of a world that was made of states divided by implacably hostile ideologies. This was not the world that existed after the cold war, and these thinkers were singularly unprepared to consider the deep implications of the new threats that didn't fit neatly into this model—failing states; ethno-nationalist conflict; transnational crime and weapons proliferation; environmental degradation; and postmodern, stateless organizations like al Qaeda. When the events of 9/11 forced these thinkers to grapple with the tangible implications of this new world, the usable ideology they found most readily available and seemingly best able to explain what had happened and what should happen next was neoconservatism.[54]

Neconservatives were American nationalists, who viewed the cultivation of American power and the defense of American sovereignty as preeminent values. Yet they were also in a sense cosmopolitans, who saw the American values of democracy and freedom as universally applicable because they were rooted in human rights that did not change from era to era or culture to culture. Their concerns about world affairs tended to focus on the Middle East, because this was the region of the world where threats to American strategic interest intersected most clearly with challenges to American ideals. Neoconservatives tended to be strong supporters of Israel because it was a strategic ally and represented the sole democracy in this region and because, in many cases, leading neoconservatives brought to their worldview a personal and ideological commitment to the idea of a Jewish state.[55] This passionate nationalism distinguished neoconservatives from the rationalistic realism of Republican foreign policy in the tradition of Nixon and President Bush senior. Foreign policy in the Eisenhower administration was conducted more in the pattern of traditional republican realism, but this was likely due to the choices of the president—neoconservatism had clear antecedents in the rhetoric of crusading, moralistic anticommunist activism of figures such as Eisenhower's secretary of state John Foster Dulles. Its division of world politics into two ideological camps competing for world domination echoed the perspective of Paul Nitze and other early conservative cold warriors, most powerfully expressed in NSC-68.

If neoconservatives distinguished themselves from the Republican realist tradition, they disagreed even more ardently with the perspective of liberal internationalists, with whom they shared many conclusions about the globalization of democracy and human rights, in particular. For neoconservative commentators, the liberal internationalism of the Clinton administration was weak, irresolute, vacillating, and dangerously willing to rely on corrupt and ineffective international institutions. The 1990s was a wasted decade from the neoconsertive perspective, a time when U.S. power atrophied and U.S. citizens were allowed to persist in the happy delusion of a world without the appearance of mortal challenges to U.S. interests or values.[56]

But in a deeper sense, neoconservatives inherited important elements of their worldview from the liberal tradition. While rejecting liberal internationalism's emphasis on international law and organization as the means of policy, neoconservatives enthusiastically embraced the idea of global activism and assertive democracy promotion. This ethical commitment to democracy as an end of foreign policy, and the belief that this goal should be pursued aggressively and by military means if necessary, were consistent with the liberal tradition of Woodrow Wilson and other liberal internationalists. Some leading neoconservatives have acknowledged this connection; Robert Kagan, for example, has argued that while neoconservatism may be new, it is not really "conservative" at all. "In foreign policy I am a liberal," Kagan told George Packer. "The conservative tradition in foreign policy is a minimalist, realist tradition." For neoconservatives like Kagan, in Packer's words, "anticommunism was only half a worldview; the other half was democratic idealism, a faith in the transformational power of American values." As the 1990s began, the presidency of

Ronald Reagan and the wholesale collapse of communism around the world seemed to confirm the rectitude of these ideas.[57]

Ultimately, neoconservatism was derived from the traditional American identity concepts stressing democratic liberalism and a moral, civilizing mission. In the particular ways in which neoconservatives interpreted and applied those ideas in the post-9/11 era, they drew on a more specific ideological tradition dating to the early twentieth century at least, in which liberal thinkers of the 1930s and 1940s, and the political philosophy of Leo Strauss regarding the moral duty to defend democracy from tyranny, figure prominently.

By most accounts, Strauss is the towering figure in the intellectual history of neoconservatism. A professor of philosophy at the University of Chicago, many leading neoconservatives of the late twentieth and early twenty-first century were Strauss' students or students of his students. As a young man Strauss had experienced firsthand the dissolution of the Weimar Republic and the beginning of Europe's descent into totalitarianism, events that by most accounts shaped the deeply pessimistic cast of his later work. Stefan Halper and Jonathan Clarke argue that neoconservatives emphasize two aspects of Strauss's philosophy in particular: his identification of the fragility of democracy and belief that democratic societies would struggle to maintain themselves because of the constant challenge that confronting tyranny would pose for them; and his view that the Enlightenment represented a movement away from the religiously rooted conception of virtue that should comprise the foundation of democratic society. Strauss argued that there was a moral duty to oppose tyranny and defend democracy, but he was skeptical of the will or ability of democratic societies to recognize and follow through on this responsibility. Packer argues that "Strauss's intellectual project was to call into question the complacent materialism and secularism of the modern West." His philosophy was an indictment of the bottomless relativism of liberal thought that appealed to many in a generation of students disenchanted with the apparent collapse of social values and shallow narcissism of American culture in the 1960s and 1970s.[58] Strauss wrote that the secularization of political order that accompanied the Enlightenment represented a "movement away from the recognition of a superhuman authority—whether of revelation based on Divine will or a natural order—to a recognition of the exclusively human based authority of the state." He also argued that classical texts contained "hidden writing," meanings that were accessible only to enlightened intellectual elites. The death of Socrates had demonstrated that philosophy was not mere abstraction but a profoundly political act, and the radical and politically challenging meanings of texts were therefore hidden within them for the understanding of a few great minds alone. His 1952 book, *Persecution and the Art of Writing,* held that classical philosophy was written on multiple levels, with the more obvious and uncontroversial ideas being readily available to most readers but deeper, more politically dangerous notions that represented the deepest inquiry into truth being accessible only to a wise and enlightened few.[59] Strauss and Straussians tend to believe that democracy is a superior form of government because it allows the maximum freedom of philosophical inquiry, but that it is also inherently weak due to the tendency of mass politics to be driven by the immediate, the emotional, and the base self-interests of individuals or groups within society. In short, Straussians tend to hold that democracy requires their intervention to save it from itself. This attitude leads to a fundamental tension in Straussian thought, the conclusion that democracy can only be preserved through undemocratic means.[60]

Packer argues that the Bush administration's perspective on intelligence was derived from Straussian assumptions about the nature of political regimes. Straussian philosophy suggests that the type of government in a given society, the nature of its values and traits of its leaders, matter greatly in determining its behavior, both internally and externally. Democracies tend to behave as if their opponents were like them—essentially nonaggressive, behaving more or less rationally and defensively. This presumption is a flaw in democracy, reflecting a refusal to acknowledge the fact that endless competition and deceit are the norm in international politics. There was deep skepticism at the highest levels of the Bush administration, especially in the Pentagon and the vice president's office, about the ability of the CIA to really grasp the dangers that were facing the United States after 9/11, to be able to see threats where they were not apparent as well as where they were expected. The Office of Special Plans in the Pentagon was set up with this purpose in mind, to analyze intelligence with a more skeptical eye, to ask the more frightening questions that the CIA was unable or unwilling to ask.[61]

Strauss argued that an enlightened elite should act behind the scenes of democratic politics, quietly manipulating the masses to mitigate the effects of their base passions or indifference and protecting against the will of aggressive and dangerous totalitarian enemies. The weakness of democratic societies resulting from the fact that their populations were materialistic, easily distracted, and unlikely to recognize or respond to mortally threatening ideological enemies was a recurring theme in Strauss's philosophy. The threat of Islamic fundamentalism represented exactly the kind of implacable ideological challenge that Strauss had cautioned against. Some commentators have argued that the neoconservatives of the early twenty-first century viewed themselves in this context, as an ideological vanguard with unique access to truths hidden to most of their fellow citizens and therefore with a unique responsibility to push politics in the direction required by these truths, regardless of the resistance they encountered. Strauss's philosophy may have suggested to some of his followers that they comprised, as Smith has put it, "something of an intellectual honor society, complete with the conviction that their thinking was necessarily superior to that of the public at large," and justifying their use of "noble lies" to enact policy that was necessary for reasons comprehensible to these elites but not to the general public.[62]

As an intellectual movement, the neoconservatives absorbed from Strauss the notion that ideas matter, that political philosophy is dangerous because it can shape political reality, and that a handful of motivated ideologues in the right places and working in concert could change the political life of the world. They believed that an enlightened few could be the catalyst for much larger change. Packer argues that the neoconservatives of the Bush administration understood themselves to be this intellectual elite, that they believed "they cradle a truth that no one else has the courage or vision to see . . . They conceive of themselves as insurgents, warring against an exhausted liberal establishment that doesn't have the moral clarity to defend itself, let alone the country—that has not principles left to defend. They are the vanguard of democracy."[63]

Beyond this, the influence of Strauss on neoconservative thinking is hard to define fully or with certainty. Certainly some leading neoconservatives were students of Strauss (or students of his students, including Allan Bloom). Paul Wolfowitz, William Kristol, and Abram Shulsky (who would serve on the Pentagon's Office of Special Plans developing intelligence and policy on Iraq) had been Strauss' students, and Lewis "Scooter" Libby had in turn been Wolfowitz's student at Yale. But other thinkers who became known as neoconservatives had little or no exposure to Strauss (including those in earlier generations, such as Irving Kristol, who reached his own conclusions quite independent of Strauss, though he acknowledged the power of Strauss's thought). In short, while Strauss was an important intellectual influence on many neoconservatives, theirs was not a system of thought derived solely from Straussianism; it has intellectual roots that are far more diverse and extend back farther than the influence of Strauss.

Packer argues that neoconservatism's origins were in fact in the radical left of the 1930s and 1940s, that "the original neoconservatives had once been leftists themselves—not ordinary Adlai Stevenson, John F. Kenney liberals but Trotskyites, Lovestoneites, Schachtmanites, and other exotica of the hothouse world of New York intellectuals."[64] Also tracing its pedigree back to the opposition to fascism and communism of the American left in the 1930s and 1940s, Smith argues that neoconservatism throughout its evolution has been defined by the belief that "whatever the shortcomings of liberal democracies, they represent the highest political order we have produced, so that the preservation of this human accomplishment is an imperative moral duty of all citizens. Nevertheless, neoconservatives typically despair that their fellow citizens, especially liberals, are equal to the task."[65] As these liberals became disillusioned with the descent of the Soviet experiment into the tyranny of Stalinism, some of them became equally idealistic and vehement anticommunists. Packer argues that this shift was marked by a continuing "tendency to believe in the power of revolutionary vanguard to change the world . . . without pausing to graze on tasteless facts under the dull sky of moderation," a trait that would continue to define the neoconservatives of later decades.[66]

These militant, liberal anticommunists supported the hard line against first fascism and then communism taken by the Roosevelt and Truman administrations. Their ideas were in tune with the world-encompassing ideological struggle described in NSC-68. They supported the moralistic tenor of John Foster Dulles' anticommunism and proposals to "roll back" communism in the 1950s, but were disappointed with Eisenhower's refusal to put these ideas into practice by more aggressively challenging communism by supporting the French at Dienbienphu and anti-Soviet forces in the Hungarian uprising of 1956. They supported the U.S. confrontation with communism in Vietnam but deplored what they saw as Lyndon Johnson's cautious half measures in fighting the war and his failure to fully engage the American public in the ideological importance of the conflict. They became disenchanted with the excesses of the left in the 1960s and what they perceived as the left's failure of will in Vietnam, which they saw as a result of a naïve refusal to take the threat of global communist expansion seriously. But they were equally critical of what they viewed as the amoral realism of Nixon and Kissinger, their willingness to pursue détente with the Soviet Union in a way that seemed to fly in the face of the moral distinctions between democracy and communist totalitarianism. Vietnam was a turning point in the neoconservative movement, the moment when it became fully identified with the right as the postwar idealism of the left seemed to many neoconservatives to lose its ethical anticommunist moorings and devolve into a dangerous policy of military weakness and moral relativism. This generation of neoconservatives, which included Senator Henry "Scoop" Jackson, Norman Podhoretz, Irving Kristol, and Senator Daniel Patrick Moynihan, instead found common ground with the moralistic anticommunism of Barry Goldwater and later Ronald Reagan. It was also during the late 1960s and 1970s that the next generation of neoconservatives, including future Bush administration officials Paul Wolfowitz, Richard Perle, Elliot Abrams, and Douglas Feith met and worked together in various roles in Washington, in particular the legislative offices of Senators Jackson and Moynihan.[67]

In the 1970's the neoconservatives spoke in the pages of the journal *Commentary* and in the statements of the Committee on the Present Danger of the dangerous and provocative weakness of the United States and perceived Soviet expansion around the world. Jimmy Carter's emphasis on human rights was consistent with neoconservative values, but his unwillingness to rebuild the U.S. military and aggressively challenge communism led to the nadir of postwar U.S. foreign policy from the neoconservative perspective. That the United States should stand by impotently as its diplomats were held hostage in Iran and the Soviet Union invaded Afghanistan in 1979 was, in neoconservative thinking, the result of a collapse of moral will and practical power that had left the United States rudderless and helpless.[68]

In Ronald Reagan, however, the neoconservatives found their true standard-bearer—a president who understood both America's moral purpose and the importance of its military power, who recognized both the absolute malevolence of communism and the real potential of the United States to challenge and destroy it, the practical ability and ethical duty of the United States to reform the world. Now, there was an administration in the White House that would actively confront the evil of communism and free the United States from treaties and international organizations that, in U.N. envoy Jeanne Kirkpatrick's words, only served to "constrain and control American power."[69] But if Reagan's election was a triumph for neoconservatives, there was some tension within his administration between neoconservatives and more traditional conservatives like Kirkpatrick who were willing to support the governments of friendly noncommunist authoritarian states in the interests of stability. Elliot Abrams, Reagan's assistant secretary of state for Latin America and later a defense department official in the administration of George W. Bush, authored a memo in 1981 arguing that the United States should not simply oppose communism but actively and aggressively promote democracy. In 1982, Reagan echoed the same position in a speech at Westminster in which he called for the global expansion of democracy. In it, he said that a "democratic revolution is gathering new strength," around the world. "We must be staunch in our conviction that freedom is not the sole prerogative of a lucky few, but the inalienable and universal right of all human beings."[70]

For the generation of neoconservatives that would populate the Department of Defense and White House in the first decade of the twenty-first century, this speech was a formative moment, a new vision of American foreign policy that would profoundly shape their future thinking.[71] From El Salvador and Nicaragua to Eastern Europe, from Russia to South Africa, from Chile to Tiananmen Square, in the late 1980s and early 1990s the courage of Reagan's convictions seemed to neoconservatives to bear fruit. For the generation of leaders that would populate the highest levels of the George W. Bush administration, the values and example of the Reagan era constituted a defining political experience. Reagan's achievements represented the validation of neoconservative arguments for the generation of thinkers who followed him, but they found the subsequent Bush and Clinton administrations lacking in Reagan's vision and unwilling to consolidate the gains he had made possible. President George H.W. Bush was too cautious, too prudent, too concerned with the niceties of international diplomacy and coalition building, and too much influenced by the tenets of realism to achieve the kind of greatness his predecessor had. The Clinton administration was worse, inclined to let American power stagnate as it flirted with dangerously naïve ideas about multilateralism and threatened to restrain American power in a straitjacket of international law and organization. The consequences of these failures were not immediately obvious in the 1990s, as a relatively peaceful and prosperous world allowed Americans to succumb to the delusion, as they had in the 1920s, that the global struggle between good and evil had ended because no threats were immediately apparent on the horizon. This decade-long dream ended on September 11, 2001, and neoconservatives held that it was fortunate that when it did, America had a president in George W. Bush who would recognize the moral implications of what had happened and take up the responsibility for dealing with them.[72]

On March 8, 1992, the *New York Times* published selections from a leaked Pentagon document that would in retrospect be seen as a formative statement of neoconservative values in defense policy.

Ambiguously titled the "Defense Planning Guidance," it was in fact a sweeping call for the preservation of U.S. hegemony as the defining principle of post–cold war foreign policy. It was authored by Zalmay Khalilzad and Abram Shulsky, who would later become senior officials in the administration of George W. Bush. The report had been commissioned by Dick Cheney and its construction overseen by Paul Wolfowitz. Its primary point was that in the coming decades the "first objective" of U.S. foreign policy should be "to prevent the reemergence of a new rival." High defense spending would enable the United States to maintain and widen its superpower status and discourage any potential competitor from seeking to rival it. The United Nations was not mentioned in the document and as for America's standing alliances, it suggested that in the future "we should expect ... coalitions to be ad hoc assemblies, often not lasting beyond the crisis being confronted."[73]

The administration of George H.W. Bush quickly distanced itself from the document, signaling the isolation of neoconservative thinkers from the mainstream of the administration at that time. But the Defense Planning Guidance would serve as a key statement of neoconservative ideas for the post–cold war world, and its authors and these ideas would soon emerge to form the basis for the PNAC. With the election of George W. Bush, these individuals returned to government, but no longer on the intellectual fringes; now their ideas would take center stage. One indication of this was the adoption, almost verbatim, of the major premise of the 1992 Defense Planning Guidance in the 2002 National Strategy of the United States—that both world security and the security of the United States required U.S. military dominance so far beyond the reach of any potential competitor as to discourage any attempt to catch up. "We must build and maintain our defenses beyond challenge," Bush said at West Point on June 1, 2002. "We will maintain the forces sufficient . . . to dissuade potential adversaries from pursuing a military build-up in hopes of surpassing, or equaling, the power of the United States." Such a policy was beneficial not only to the United States but to the world, it was argued, because U.S. hegemony on such a scale would deter aggressors and prevent expensive and destabilizing arms races.[74]

One difference between the neoconservative philosophy of the post-9/11 era and the principles of the Defense Planning Guidance was their attitude toward the domestic governing regimes of states. The DPG took a realist stance toward regime type, assuming that it was the relative balance of power between states that was America's primary concern; what happened within states was less relevant, and it was certainly not the purpose of American arms to compel foreign governments to reform simply because they engaged in unsavory human rights practices within their own borders. This perspective was not shared by the neoconservatives who advocated for a new foreign policy after 9/11. In their view, the historical lesson of 9/11 was precisely that this approach was shortsighted, that decades of tolerance of repression in the Middle East had come home to roost in lower Manhattan and Northern Virginia. In a world defined by the Manichaean struggle between freedom and repression, authoritarianism anywhere was a threat to democracy everywhere. The United States had both a moral duty and a pragmatic interest in promoting democracy actively and aggressively in every corner of the world.

In part, this change reflects the fact that one of the primary authors of the Defense Policy Guidance, Paul Wolfowitz, now found himself part of an administration in which there was principled support at the highest levels for his moral commitment to democracy promotion, as well as the maintenance of hegemonic power. Regarded by many observers as the leading intellectual architect of the Iraq war, Wolfowitz deserves particular attention as an exponent of the neoconservative ideology within the Bush administration. Wolfowitz came from a liberal background. His father, Jack Wolfowitz, was a Cornell mathematics professor whose family had emigrated to escape anti-Semitism in Poland in 1920. Wolfowitz' upbringing was intellectually rich and politically liberal; admiration for the memory of Franklin Roosevelt and support for the anticommunism of Harry Truman defined the political atmosphere in the Wolfowitz home during his youth.[75] As an undergraduate student at Cornell, Wolfowitz came into the orbit of Professor Allan Bloom, who introduced Wolfowitz to the ideas of Strauss. Wolfowitz would soon leave Ithaca for the first time to enter graduate school for political science at the University of Chicago, where Strauss was teaching. He would go on to serve on the staff of Senator Henry "Scoop" Jackson, as an official in the Arms Control and Disarmament Agency, and as director of policy planning at the State Department under President Ronald Reagan.[76] Wolfowitz also served as the U.S. ambassador to Indonesia, where he became familiar with the liberal reform movement within Islam. David Phillips argues that Wolfowitz saw Iraq through the lens of Indonesia, that he "envisioned Iraq, like Indonesia under President Suharto, as a secular pro-Western anchor for U.S. interests in the Muslim world."[77]

Wolfowitz argued that freedom and democracy were in fact the default state of human politics, that tyranny needed to be actively imposed to compromise freedom. As the natural condition of politics, democracy was therefore possible in any cultural context. When tyranny was overthrown, democracy would tend to reemerge unless some new force acted to subvert it again. Politics in any society would tend toward becoming more democratic unless something acted against this trend, so repressive leaders were constantly struggling to maintain their rule against the natural tendency toward political openness and pluralism. The real political inertia everywhere was toward freedom, so by promoting democracy the United States was not so much creating something that otherwise would not exist as removing the barriers to a process of change that would occur on its own once unconstrained. Because undemocratic regimes were inherently unstable, the presence of one democratic regime in a region would increase pressure for democratic reform among its neighbors as well. Wolfowitz told Jeffrey Goldberg that he felt it was "absurdly unrealistic, demonstrably unrealistic, to ignore how strong the desire for freedom is."[78]

Writing in 2000, Wolfowitz had called for the "universalization of American principles." "Nothing could be less realistic," he argued, "than the version of 'realism' that dismisses human rights as an important tool of foreign policy."[79] In one interview, Wolfowitz objected to the term "export of democracy," saying that it "isn't really a good phrase. We're trying to remove the shackles on democracy."[80] Wolfowitz said in a September 2002 interview with Bill Keller that "you hear people mock [the idea of a democratic Iraq] by saying that Iraq isn't ready for Jeffersonian democracy. Well, Japan isn't [a] Jeffersonian democracy either. I think the more we are committed to influencing the outcome, the more chance there could be that it would be something quite significant for Iraq. And I think if it's significant for Iraq, it's going to cast a very large shadow, starting with Syria and Iran, but across the whole Arab world, I think."[81]

Whatever the neoconservatives may have argued, it is clear that their worldview came to define the policies of the Bush administration only after 9/11. The ideas were there, had been there for decades, but their proponents did not control policy until then. As a body of thought they are critical to understanding the nature of policy change because they provided its guiding principles and specific prescriptions, but these ideas are not the sole cause of the change in U.S. policy in this period. The events of 9/11 reshaped the political environment of the United States in a way that created a vacuum of ideas, a demand for new ideology to better explain a new reality and provide the framework for policy to contend with it. To understand the change in American foreign policy as a story only of events and their consequences, or as a story only of ideas operating independent of events, ignores the critical relationship between the material world and the socio-cognitive milieu in which ideas are contested, rise and fall.

Ideology and Identity in the Bush Doctrine

Arguing that the Bush administration embraced a strategy of American primacy in its foreign policy, Colin Dueck has claimed that the administration "returned to many of the Wilsonian assumptions that characterized the Clinton years." "International structural pressures cannot explain why . . . these changes occurred," Dueck suggests. "The real explanation lies in the influence of distinctive policy ideas, as promoted by leading state officials." Paul Lyons has argued the in his post-9/11 discourse Bush articulated a "right-wing Wilsonianism" rooted in a conception of America as a "City on a Hill," a metaphor fundamental to American identity historically and one with crucial religious as well as political meaning embedded within it. Sandra Silberstein has noted that in referring to the United States as a nation "under God" locked in a struggle against "evildoers," President Bush occupied the role of "national pastor," much as Wilson had done.[82]

Stanley A. Renshon and Peter Suedfeld have pointed to five key elements of Bush's unilateralist Wilsonianism, or what would become known as the "Bush Doctrine": "American preeminence; assertive realism; equivocal alliances; selective multilateralism; democratic transformation."[83] In its first years in office, the Bush administration's single most cogent effort to describe its approach to foreign affairs was its *National Security Strategy of the United States,* issued in September 2002. In its most quoted and controversial clauses this document asserted an American right to "act against . . . emerging threats before they are fully formed" and stated that the United States would "not hesitate to act alone, if necessary, to exercise our right of self-defense by acting preemptively against . . . terrorists."[84]

The *National Security Strategy* described three primary threats to the United States: terrorist groups with global reach; weak states that harbor, assist, and provide havens for such organizations; and rogue states. It asserted that the "greatest danger our Nation faces lies at the crossroads of radicalism and technology. Our enemies have openly declared that they are seeking weapons of mass destruction, and evidence indicates that they are doing so with determination. The United States will not allow those efforts to succeed . . . America will act against such emerging threats before they are fully formed." It claimed that the "leaders of rogue states [are] more willing to take risks, gambling with the lives of their people and the wealth of their nations," than America's adversaries in the cold war who were "generally status quo, [and] risk-averse." Thus, the successful security policy of the cold war, deterrence through mutually assured destruction, would not be appropriate against what Bush in his West Point speech referred to as "unbalanced dictators with weapons of mass destruction." Because rogue state leaders would know they could not win a conventional conflict with the United States, they could be expected, in Bush's words, to "rely on acts of terror and, potentially, the use of weapons of mass destruction—weapons that can be easily concealed, delivered covertly, and used without warning."[85]

But the *National Security Strategy* also framed the interests of the United States in terms that were often overtly Wilsonian. It committed the United States to the defense of "human dignity" and a list of human rights principles echoing the 1948 U.N. Universal Declaration. It spoke of bringing "the hope of democracy, development, free markets, and free trade to every corner of the world." It suggested that "alliances and multilateral institutions can multiply the strength of freedom-loving nations" and described the United States as "committed to lasting institutions like the United Nations, the World Trade Organization, the Organization of American States, and NATO," among others. Downplaying realist concerns about interstate aggression as the most serious threat to global peace, it argued that "America is now threatened less by conquering states than we are by failing ones." It spoke of a "distinctly American internationalism" in which the "United States will constantly strive to enlist the support of the international community." While terrorism was the foremost concern noted in the document, it favored multilateral responses to the problem; "to defeat terrorism in today's globalized world we need support from our allies," it noted, and "wherever possible, we will rely on regional organizations and state powers." It spoke of an "increasingly interconnected world," in which the United States needed to "invest time and resources into building international relationships." It noted that the administration had called for large increases in U.S. support for the African Development Fund and the World Bank's fund for the least developed nations in the world, and expressed support for a new global fund to fight HIV/AIDS organized by the U.N. Secretary General.[86] All of this comprised, in the view of Jackson Diehl of the *Washington Post,* "a Wilsonian promise to 'bring the hope of democracy, development, free markets and free trade to every corner of the world.'"[87]

In December 2005, Secretary of State Condoleezza Rice echoed the sentiments of the *National Security Strategy* in an editorial in the *Washington Post*, arguing that the interdependence of the contemporary world had, in effect, made many of the rules of power politics in the Westphalian system of sovereign states obsolete. Interstate war was no longer the threat it once had been, Rice suggested, but the implosion of social order within states could foster the growth of destructive forces, which could now emerge and move more quickly throughout an increasingly globalized world. "The greatest threats to our security are defined more by the dynamics within weak and failing states than by the borders between strong and aggressive ones," she claimed.

> The phenomenon of weak and failing states is not new, but the danger they now pose is unparalleled. When people, goods and information traverse the globe as fast as they do today, transnational threats such as disease or terrorism can inflict damage comparable to the standing armies of nation-states . . . Weak and failing states serve as global pathways that facilitate the spread of pandemics, the movement of criminals and terrorists, and the proliferation of the world's most dangerous weapons.[88]

Rice asserted, as Bush had done on many occasions, that the moral superiority of democratic governance was not a culturally bounded idea but rather a universal truth. She criticized those who doubted the viability of democracy in non-Western contexts as "dogmatic cynics and cultural determinists," and asserted the "natural right of all people . . . to govern themselves in liberty." And in a profound challenge to one of the core principles of political realism, Rice concluded that the nature of this new international system forced the conclusion that "the fundamental character of regimes matters more today than the international distribution of power"—a claim that G. John Ikenberry felt would make Hans Morgenthau "turn in his grave."[89] As a result, the principled goal of democracy promotion could not reasonably be seen, in her view, as simply an addendum or alternative to the pursuit of national self-interest. "Attempting to draw neat, clean lines between our security interests and our democratic ideals does not reflect the reality of today's world," Rice argued. "Supporting the growth of democratic institutions in all nations is not some moralistic flight of fancy; it is the only realistic response to our present challenges." "If the school of thought called 'realism' is to be truly realistic," she suggested, "it must recognize that stability without democracy will prove to be false."[90]

In January 2002 Bush elaborated on this worldview in his first State of the Union address after the 9/11 attacks. He claimed that Iran, Iraq, and North Korea were "allies" of terrorism and that together they constituted an "axis of evil, arming to threaten the peace of the world." Iraq had demonstrated by its actions that it had "something to hide from the civilized world." Though the particular connections between al Qaeda and these regimes remained murky, it was clear enough that they shared an opposition to "civilized" norms and values.[91]

Though he explicitly praised the "strong leadership" of authoritarian president Pervez Musharraf of Pakistan, Bush claimed that "America will lead by defending liberty and justice because they are right and true and unchanging for all people everywhere."[92] In terms that would have seemed entirely consistent had they been uttered by Wilson, Bush said that

> history has called America and our allies to action, and it is both our responsibility and our privilege to fight freedom's fight . . . we have a great opportunity during this time of war to lead the world toward the values that will bring lasting peace. All fathers and mothers, in all societies, want their children to be educated and live free from poverty and violence. No people on earth yearn to be oppressed or aspire to servitude or eagerly await the midnight knock of the secret police . . . no nation owns these aspirations and no nation is exempt from them. We have no intention of imposing our culture, but America will always stand firm for the non-negotiable demands of human dignity, the rule of law, limits on the power of the state, respect for women, private property, free speech, equal justice and religious tolerance.[93]

Bush returned to these themes in his 2003 State of the Union address, saying that America would accept its responsibility to defend the civilization, peace, and the "hopes of mankind" against a "world of chaos." In this effort the United States would seek to enlist the aid of like-minded countries, but Bush cautioned Americans once again that not every nation would behave honorably, and that U.S. policy could not be hamstrung by the weak willed. "We've called on the United Nations to fulfill its charter and stand by its demand that Iraq disarm," Bush suggested, but "America's purpose is more than to follow a process; it is to achieve a result . . . the course of this nation does not depend on the decisions of others." "We will consult," he said, "but let there be no misunderstanding: If Saddam Hussein does not fully disarm, for the safety of our people and for the peace of the world, we will lead a coalition to disarm him."[94]

Though Bush continued to stress the humanitarian goals of the United States, in his 2004 address particular emphasis was placed on the universal applicability of democracy and its central importance to U.S. foreign policy. Bush chastised critics who doubted the prospects for democracy in the Middle East. "It is mistaken, and condescending," he said, "to assume that whole cultures and great religions are incompatible with liberty and self-government. I believe that God has planted in every human heart the desire to live in freedom."[95] He argued that there were both moral and practical reasons for the United States to promote democracy in the Middle East and around the world. Democratic states would be more stable and friendlier to the United States, Bush claimed; undemocratic societies would breed "despair and anger . . . [and] continue to produce men and movements that threaten the safety of America and our friends." He announced a "forward strategy of freedom in the greater Middle East," in which the United States would "challenge the enemies of reform, confront the allies of terror, and expect a higher standard from our friends." Its goal would be to bolster a set of distinct but related pillars of democratic stability in various states, among which were the "development of free elections and free markets, free press and free labor unions." And he noted the importance of finishing "the work of democracy in Afghanistan and Iraq," which would become exporters of democracy and examples for emulation throughout the region. "Those nations can light the way for others, and help transform a troubled part of the world," Bush said.[96]

Ideology and Foreign Policy in the Bush Administration: A Break with the Past?

Lloyd Ambrosius has argued that both Woodrow Wilson and George W. Bush appealed to traditional American ideals to describe their foreign policy goals:

> During World War I and after September 11, 2001, they both led the nation into war for the avowed purpose of protecting traditional values and institutions at home and of expanding these throughout the world, promising to make freedom and democracy the foundation for peace. . . . Appealing to the old American hope of "freedom just around the corner," both Wilson and Bush proclaimed American ideals to justify their new foreign policies . . . They assigned a redemptive role to the United States, committing it to fight evil and create a new international order.[97]

In a spring 2005 article in the journal *International Security*, Jonathan Monten argued that neoconservatism as expressed in the Bush doctrine "is not unique and its nationalist vision of the United States as a redeeming force in international politics provides an essential point of continuity with preceding generations of grand strategy."[98] William Kristol and Lawrence Kaplan have argued that neoconservative thinking is consistent with the tradition of Teddy Roosevelt, Harry Truman, John Kennedy, and Ronald Reagan. Paul Berman has claimed that it echoes the intellectual tradition of Abraham Lincoln.[99] Anthony Smith disagrees, arguing that "the doctrine conveys a tone of megalomania, a condition that we might argue is out of keeping with many strains of the American tradition, including earlier formulations of liberal internationalism . . . the Bush doctrine was a grand imperial strategy of a sort never seen before in the history of U.S. foreign policy. In its separate parts, such a grandiose design did indeed have its antecedents, but as a formal whole, and in practice, it had no parallel."[100]

Melvyn P. Leffler has argued "that there is more continuity than change in the policies of the Bush administration. Bush's rhetoric and actions have deep roots in the history of American foreign policy." Leffler has placed the liberalism of Bush's freedom agenda in the intellectual tradition of the Open Door, Wilson's Fourteen Points, the Atlantic Charter, and the Truman Doctrine, and argued that even the Bush Doctrine's embrace of American hegemony and preemptive war have precedents in U.S. foreign policy throughout the twentieth century and before.[101] Alternatively, historian Arnold Offner has claimed that Bush's policies represent "an extremely radical and dangerous departure from accepted norms."[102] Adam Quinn has suggested that Bush's foreign policy has intellectual roots in both "Theodore Roosevelt's advocacy of military strength in the service of good and Woodrow Wilson's ideological conviction that American engagement in the world could be made conditional on the pursuit of global reform in line with an idealized conception of American values and practices." As such, Quinn contends, "the Bush worldview should not be seen as a radically new phenomenon, but as a logical outgrowth from the American foreign policy tradition."[103] Halper and Clarke argue that the neoconservatives have made extensive attempts to describe their views as rooted in American tradition, but have very selectively chosen only those elements of history which are supportive of their views and ignored those that are inconsistent. Teddy Roosevelt, Harry Truman, and Ronald Reagan are presidents with whom the neoconservatives associate their views, for example. But while neoconservative authors have emphasized TR's "big stick" imperialism and Truman and Reagan's confrontational approach to the Soviet Union, they have typically ignored TR's diplomatic mediation of the Russo-Japanese War, Truman's building of the United Nations and NATO, and Reagan's willingness to embrace Mikhail Gorbachev and end the cold war.[104]

The Bush administration merged the aspirations of Wilson with the practical approach to policy of Theodore Roosevelt, Henry Cabot Lodge, or Ronald Reagan—national strength and a willingness to apply American power in all its forms internationally, but an absolute refusal to alter U.S. policy to build coalitions within international organizations, or to in any way subject U.S. policies to restraint by the United Nations or other international bodies. But Bush is also distinct from all of these presidents in different ways. That he applied unilateralist means to liberal ends in a way that is inconsistent with Wilsonianism is a central argument of this chapter, but the ideational framework of Bush's policies is also very unlike those of TR and Reagan, two other presidents to whom he is sometimes compared. While TR advocated an activist foreign policy premised on the efficacy of American military power, unlike George W. Bush his vision did not presume that democracy and national self-determination could or should be the ordering principles of politics everywhere in the world—instead, he expected and sought the domination of global politics by Anglo-Saxons and the subjugation of peoples he viewed as incapable of ruling themselves by those more able to do so. Similarly, while Bush shared with Reagan a sense of moral purpose in foreign policy, he did not share Reagan's willingness to accept authoritarian stability as an outcome consistent with U.S. interests, nor Reagan's aversion to directly involving the U.S. military in sustained foreign wars, nor Reagan's ultimate ability to engage in serious and transformative diplomacy with ideological adversaries.

As Ambrosius has noted, comparisons of Bush and Wilson focusing on their ideological kinship have tended to neglect the

> disparity between ends and means in the foreign policies of these two presidents...Historians who have placed Bush in the mainstream of the American diplomatic tradition, moreover, have exaggerated historical continuity by ignoring his willingness to use unprecedented means of preemptive war to achieve traditional Wilsonian goals . . . Bush affirmed only Wilson's goals, not his methods. He and the neoconservatives who guided his conduct of U.S. foreign relations had espoused the Wilsonian vision of global democracy, but they sought to achieve it through unilateral means. In so doing, they unwisely and dangerously resorted to the folly of empire.[105]

While critical of Bush's foreign policy, however, Ambrosius does not explore the ways in which this inconsistency between ends and means led to specific policy consequences. This study seeks to make this connection by arguing that the administration's failure to quickly establish stable democracy in Iraq after the fall of Saddam Hussein's government was a direct result of its pursuit of liberal ends through illiberal means.

Bush's foreign policy represents a historically unprecedented attempt to pursue liberal ends through hegemonic, unilateral diplomacy and military force. But the irreconcilable tension in the intellectual framework of the Bush administration's policies rendered them ineffective in promoting democracy and stable peace in Iraq and elsewhere in the world. Chris J. Dolan has argued that the Bush administration undertook a policy of systematically "chipping away at a host of treaties and conventions they believed constrained U.S. power." The administration's policies "deprived international institutions the necessary powers to respond to nontraditional security issues such as conflicts over natural resources, public health and infectious diseases, international crime, and environmental degradation," in Dolan's view, leaving "little or no room for consideration of proposals for new forms of global governance to address nonsecurity issues and nontraditional, yet very real, threats."[106] The Bush administration pursued policies that ignored or were overtly hostile to the structure of laws, norms, and institutions that defined the post–World War II liberal international system, even as they were rhetorically premised on the defense of the core principles of that system. As Ikenberry suggests, the administration embraced "a liberal argument about security and world order and used it in a way that [was] subversive of the postwar liberal international order." While the administration consistently professed its belief in the Wilsonian goal of universal democracy, it just as consistently failed to appreciate the importance of operating within the international legal and institutional framework that accompanied the expansion of global democracy—the "norms, expectations, relations, modes of affiliation—that democracies create," and which are part and parcel of the democratic peace.[107] The major flaw in the Bush administration's approach to foreign policy, and the source of many if not all of its failures in international affairs, was a refusal to recognize and act upon the intimate and mutually supportive connection between democratic institutions *within* states and legal and institutional structures *between* them. As Ikenberry argues, the leaders of the Bush administration "learned that the spread of democracy may have a 'peace effect.' But they [were] still completely blind to the more general security advantages and opportunities of liberal international order."[108] As a consequence of this disconnect between ends and means, history is likely to remember the Bush administration primarily for its foreign policy failures.

CHAPTER 3

"WITH US OR AGAINST US"

CONSTRUCTING AMERICA, ITS ENEMIES AND THE WORLD

This chapter will illustrate the ways in which the Bush administration constructed identities for the United States and other actors in the international system, and conceived of the environment within which they interacted in the years after 9/11. It is important to note that in this process the Bush administration was both constrained and empowered by both preexisting U.S. political culture and the material reality of events. The administration had an opportunity to interpret the meaning of 9/11 and argue for an appropriate response, but in doing so it was limited, as always, by the nation's common understanding of itself, its traditional conception of national identity. The administration was similarly faced with a political culture which it had some power to shape but which was ultimately beyond its absolute control. While the Bush administration may have done much in the months after 9/11 to condone or even cultivate an environment of insecurity in the United States, it did not create this environment—the material facts of the events of 9/11 would have had powerful effects on American culture in any case. Thus, the constructions of identity of Self and Other that the Bush administration asserted in the months and years that followed must be understood as attempts to shape but also to act within the confines of what Stuart Croft has called a "social process of crisis." This process involved complex interactions between events, the preferences of policy makers, and popular culture writ large. Croft agues that the interpretation of 9/11 within American culture both reflected and reinforced preexisting American images of the United States and global Others to enable the foreign policy initiatives of the Bush administration. Susan Willis identifies this culture of post-9/11 America as one in which a climate of paranoia prevailed, exemplified by phenomena such as the Washington, D.C. snipers and anthrax scares, and in which "the intellectual atmosphere . . . was such that opinion deviating from the officially sanctioned narrative of good vs. evil was actively discouraged, the majority of the media toeing President Bush's warmongering line."[1]

The events of 9/11 were immediately constructed within the Bush administration and in its public statements as acts of war, requiring a military response. Five minutes after American Airlines flight 777 crashed into the Pentagon, Bush spoke with Vice President Cheney on the phone. "We're at war," he said, immediately placing the events in a specific context that would drive future discussion and ultimately U.S. policy. A little less than an hour later, Bush spoke with Cheney again. "We're going to find out who did this," the president said. "And we're going to kick their asses." Later that day, as Bush spoke with Donald Rumsfeld from Air Force One, he again represented the events of the day in very particular terms. "It's a day of national tragedy" he said, and "we'll clean up the mess and then the ball will be in your court and [JCS chairman] Dick Myers's court."[2] On the same day, Bush was also already publicly asserting a clear vision of the identity and motives of the attackers and of the United States in relationship to them. "America was targeted for attack because we're the brightest beacon for freedom and opportunity in the world," he said in a nationally televised address on the night of September 11. "And no one will keep that light from shining . . . America and our friends and allies join with all those who want peace and security in the world."[3]

Meeting with congressional leaders shortly after 9/11, Bush said that the enemy was not just a particular group but "a frame of mind" built on hatred. "They hate Christianity," Bush said. "They hate Judaism. They hate everything that is not them."[4] Returning from meetings with his top military and foreign policy advisors at Camp David in the days after the attacks, Bush spoke to the press on the White House lawn. He referred to the 9/11 attackers as "evil" or "evildoers" seven times. He described the attacks as "barbarism" and the attackers as "burrowing into our society and then emerging . . . [to] fly U.S. aircraft into buildings full of innocent people and show no remorse." The U.S. response would be a "crusade," he said.[5] Meeting with his senior foreign policy advisors in the days following 9/11, Bush would refer to the terrorist threat as "a cancer."[6]

Stephen Walt has argued that references to alternate ideological systems as "contagions" or "infections" to be contained are a virtual constant in the rhetoric of state leaders confronting regimes founded on different principles.[7] They suggest an underlying assumption, or sometimes an explicitly stated understanding, that internal politics will affect foreign policy, that regimes espousing different ideologies also tend to be externally aggressive, seeking to export their beliefs. The notion that bad ideas can spread like a communicable disease was part and parcel of the domino theory that rationalized the U.S. response to communism during the cold war, just as the idea that global Islam was "sick," infected with the disease of radicalism and requiring drastic intervention, was a common theme in neoconservative rhetoric about the war on terror.[8]

In the months that followed, Bush and other administration officials would often refer to the terrorist enemy as "barbaric" and suggest that the United States fought for "civilization." Mark Salter notes that these constructions harken back to earlier imperial discourses that used the separation of the civilized Self from the barbaric Other as a rationale for conquest and war without restraint. He suggests that "within the European imperial context, 'barbaric' societies were viewed as lacking the conditions of European civilization. 'Barbarians' were both feared and patronized. The presence of 'barbarians' legitimized the rhetoric of the 'civilizing mission.'"[9] In R.B.J. Walker's words, "The possession of 'civilization' justifies the conquest of 'barbarism.'"[10] The refusal of barbarians to accept the limits of civilized rules of warfare meant that those constraints also did not apply to the armies of civilized states when they fought barbaric adversaries. The barbarians would not restrain themselves, so the forces of civilization could not be expected to do so either. As Jürgen Osterhammel has put it, "Colonial wars were viewed as wars to spread 'civilization' to adversaries who were said to lack civilized rules of conduct . . . Methods of warfare that in Europe were morally and legally barred were considered legitimate in the face of an enemy who did not seem to subscribe to the same cultural code."[11] After September 11, Salter argues, "in rhetorically distancing these terrorists and 'barbarians,' the administration hopes that all manner of extra-legal international violence will be tolerated by the society of nations."[12]

Gerrit Gong has argued that the differentiation of the "civilized" from the "barbaric" in European history symbolized the expression of a single European identity, the assertion of the idea that compared with the rest of the world, European societies were fundamentally similar to one another in their shared cultural advancement. "Civilization" became understood as both the dominant rationale for European hegemony over the "uncivilized" world and the underlying principle of the system of international law built by Europeans to apply to the world as a whole. Gong argues that for many centuries, this notion of civilization was applied to the practice of foreign policy as a means of distinguishing those who were worthy of self-rule from those who could and should legitimately be the subjects of European empires. In World Wars I and II these same tropes of civilization and barbarism were applied within Europe as a means to distinguish "Us" from "Them" on the basis of values and practices, enabling the treatment of the Other in ways that would not be appropriate for members of the civilized in-group.[13] Robert Ivie has argued in similar terms that "the language of savagery is indigenous to US political culture as the trope that legitimises war and empire." "Throughout U.S. history, from America's 18th century revolution to the post–World War II American century and from Cold War to the present open-ended war on terror," U.S. foreign policy has been, in Ivie's view, "a continuing quest for empire under the sign of civilisation and democracy."[14] Ikechi Mgbeoji has referred as well to "the enduring notion of the civilised self and the barbaric other . . . [which] has continued to animate international policy" throughout much of human history.[15]

In an address to both houses of Congress two weeks after the 9/11 attacks, Bush elaborated further on the administration's understanding of the identities of the terrorists, the United States, and the rest of the world. He described the attackers as believers in a simplistic ideology, with unlimited political goals and an unquenchable hatred for the United States rooted in an irreconcilable conflict between value systems. The 9/11 terrorists were "enemies of freedom," practicing a "fringe form of Islamic extremism." "The terrorists' directive commands them to kill Christians and Jews," he said, "to kill all Americans and make no distinctions among military and civilians, including women and children." This particular antagonism to the United States emerged from perceptions of the American social and political system and the American "way of life" rather than the U.S. world role. "They hate what they see right here in this chamber, a democratically elected government," Bush argued. "They hate our freedoms, our freedom of religion, our freedom of speech, our freedom to vote and assemble and disagree with each other."[16] Conflating al Qaeda and the Taliban, Bush held that

> in Afghanistan we see Al Qaeda's vision for the world. Afghanistan's people have been brutalized. Many are starving and many have fled. Women are not allowed to attend school. You can be jailed for owning a television. Religion can be practiced only as their leaders dictate. A man can be jailed in Afghanistan if his beard is not long enough.[17]

But the terrorists' ambitions were not limited to Afghanistan or the Middle East, Bush suggested. "Al Qaeda is to terror what the Mafia is to crime," he said, "but its goal is not making money; its goal is remaking the world and imposing its radical beliefs on people everywhere."[18]

The world itself had changed on 9/11, Bush asserted. "Night fell on a different world," he claimed, a world in which "freedom and fear are at war." "This is civilization's fight," Bush held, "the fight of all who believe in progress and pluralism, tolerance and freedom." "The civilized world," he said, "is rallying to America's side." But in any case, this new environment would not admit neutrality or indecision. "Every nation in every region now has a decision to make. Either you are with us or you are with the terrorists . . . From this day forward, any nation that continues to harbor or support terrorism will be regarded by the United States as a hostile regime." Bush suggested that in this new world there could be only two identities, with implacable hostility their only possible relationship. "Freedom and fear, justice and cruelty, have always been at war," he said, "and we know that God is not neutral between them."[19]

The United States, for its part, was "a country awakened to danger and called to defend freedom." Bush likened 9/11 to previous eras in American history both in its impact on the nation's psyche and the ethical responsibilities it implied for foreign policy. September 11 had been the only attack on American soil in 136 years, he said, except for "one Sunday in 1941." About al Qaeda he added that "we have seen their kind before. They are the heirs of all the murderous ideologies of the 20th century . . . they follow in the path of fascism, Nazism and totalitarianism." They were enemies to be challenged, but also to be feared. "They are . . . sent to hide in countries around the world to plot evil and destruction," he claimed, and enjoined Americans to "live your lives and hug your children . . . even in the face of a continuing threat."[20]

This theme of invisible, looming danger emerged more noticeably in Bush's State of the Union address four months later, where he noted that the war in Afghanistan had revealed

> the depth of our enemies' hatred in videos where they laugh about the loss of innocent life. And the depth of their hatred is equaled by the madness of the destruction they design. We have found diagrams of American nuclear power plants and public water facilities, detailed instructions for making chemical weapons, surveillance maps of American cities and thorough descriptions of landmarks in America and throughout the world . . . Thousands of dangerous killers, schooled in the methods of murder, often supported by outlaw regimes, are now spread throughout the world like ticking time bombs, set to go off without warning . . . tens of thousands of trained terrorists are still at large.[21]

Now the terrorists, who had previously been described as evil and aggressively violent, seemed "mad," maniacal—as irrational, indiscriminate, and unavoidable as an unseen, ticking bomb. Bush called on all nations to "eliminate the terrorist parasites." They were no long simply evil; they had become *inhuman*.[22]

And while the 9/11 attacks had been framed immediately afterward primarily as the actions of wicked men, now they were contextualized within the international system of states more familiar to U.S. foreign policy. While al Qaeda had earlier been depicted as the inheritor of previous evil ideologies against which the United States had contended, now it was linked with despotic regimes in contemporary states. Among these were North Korea, which Bush said was "arming with missiles and weapons of mass destruction, while starving its citizens;" Iran, which was also "aggressively pursu[ing] these weapons and export[ing] terror, while an unelected few repress the Iranian people's hope for freedom;" and Iraq, which was continuing "to flaunt its hostility toward America and to support terror." "States like these, and their terrorist allies," Bush claimed, "constitute an axis of evil, arming to threaten the peace of the world. By seeking weapons of mass destruction, these regimes pose a grave and growing danger. They could provide these arms to terrorists, giving them the means to match their hatred."[23]

But why would it be assumed, in the absence of any clear evidence of strong ideological or political kinship between any of these states and al Qaeda, that any of them would be tempted to provide WMD to that group, given the enormous potential cost to them of doing so? Bush hinted at an answer to this question when he suggested that by its actions, Iraq had demonstrated that it had "something to hide from the civilized world." Though the particular connections that might exist between al Qaeda and these regimes remained murky, it was clear enough that they shared an opposition to "civilized" norms and values. The "axis of evil" provided not just a framework for understanding the U.S. relationship to Iraq, Iran, and North Korea through the comparative historical lens of World War II, but also a mechanism for making al Qaeda and the 9/11 attacks comprehensible within the Westphalian system of sovereign states. If the terrorists were "allies" of states, it should be expected they would share tactics and technology—since this is what allies do. And if the enemy was not an amorphous terrorist organization but an alliance of states, it would be easier to imagine attacking and defeating it within an intellectual and bureaucratic framework that had developed primarily to coerce and deter sovereign states.[24]

If the truly evil regimes in the world were relatively few in number in the administration's construction, so were the "civilized" states who would recognize and respect their responsibility to band together. Like the townspeople in *High Noon*, who abandon the Sheriff as outlaws approach because they are unwilling to commit themselves to a common defense against evil, many states in the world might refuse to accept their duty. "Some governments will be timid in the face of terror," Bush said, but added "make no mistake about it: If they do not act, America will."[25] In the months before the war in Iraq, that administration suggested that the leaders of France and Germany, for example, were driven more by narrow self interest than by concern for the threat to world security posed by Saddam Hussein. Bob Woodward contends that Bush believed that diplomacy was stalled not over legitimate concerns about force or the presence of WMD but because of "the ascendancy of power in Europe." Saddam had picked up these signals from French President Jacques Chirac and German Chancellor Gerhard Schroeder, Bush thought, and they had emboldened him to think he might still be able to manipulate the world community, to wriggle away once again. Bush's opinion of Tony Blair, the administration's staunchest supporter among European leaders, was quite different though; Bush told Blair's communications director Alistair Campbell at one point that "your man has cojones."[26]

A number of authors have commented on the prevalence of analogies of the old west in the Bush administration's rhetoric surrounding al Qaeda and the "War on Terror," as well as on the presence of metaphors of both war and crime. Michael Sherry has suggested that the Bush administration's framing of the world after 9/11 contained elements of both paradigms, noting that Bush described his approach to the hunt for Osama bin Laden by saying "there's an old poster out west, as I recall, that said, 'Wanted: Dead or Alive'" and "announced a 'Most Wanted Terrorist list' as part of his effort to 'round up'—both cowboy and cop words—'the evildoers.'"[27] As in the old west, in the war on terror the struggle to enforce law in a lawless society led Bush to depict U.S. policy as both war and a fight against crime. Wyn Rees and Richard Aldrich have argued that U.S. responses to 9/11 tended to be framed in the language of war as the result of a "historically determined strategic culture" defined by a "'national security' approach towards this threat [that] has emphasized unilateralism." In contrast, "Europe, based on its own past experience of terrorism, has adopted a regulatory approach pursued through multilateralism."[28]

If others could not be counted upon to act in the name of justice in a state of anarchy, the United States had already risen to the challenge in early 2002, Bush argued. America had "saved a people from starvation and freed a country from brutal oppression, he claimed. "The mothers and daughters of Afghanistan were captives in their own homes, forbidden from working or going to school. Today women are free, and are part of Afghanistan's new government" "The Islamic 'street' greeted the fall of tyranny with song and celebration" in Afghanistan, Bush said.[29]

Within Bush's circle of top advisors, Afghanistan was understood to comprise both the Taliban and al Qaeda—organizations that were often conflated into one and that were depicted as the enemy to be destroyed—and the Afghan people, who were imagined to be the innocent victims of the oppression and brutality of these groups, and were therefore to be saved.[30] As the administration planned its attack on Afghanistan, Bush nevertheless wanted Afghans to see the United States as a force for good, a society that would help them even as it was bombing and invading their country. He wanted a large-scale humanitarian aid mission to begin along with the military war, and asked his advisors "Can the first bombs we drop be food?" "I was sensitive to this [accusation] that this was a religious war, and that somehow the United States would be the conqueror," Bush said. "And I wanted to be the liberator." This was not merely a political or public relations concern for Bush, though, as he told Bob Woodward—it was a moral and religious duty. "We've got to deal with suffering," he said; "there is a human condition that we must worry about in times of war. There is a value system that cannot be compromised—God-given values. These aren't United States-created values. There are values of freedom and the human condition and mothers loving their children... We're all God's children."[31]

The Taliban itself was seen within the administration as comprised of only a relatively small core of true believers surrounded by a much larger contingent of less-committed hangers-on. Administration discussions of the Taliban often made a distinction between "moderate" and "hard-line" elements within the organization. When presented with a CIA report suggesting that a massive bombing campaign might demoralize and cause many Taliban to desert, Bush told CIA director George Tenet, "I want more of this."[32]

With the war in Afghanistan under way, in his 2002 State of the Union Address Bush claimed that "America will lead by defending liberty and justice because they are right and true and unchanging for all people everywhere."[33] In terms that would have seemed entirely consistent had they been uttered by Woodrow Wilson, Bush said that

> history has called America and our allies to action, and it is both our responsibility and our privilege to fight freedom's fight . . . we have a great opportunity during this time of war to lead the world toward the values that will bring lasting peace. All fathers and mothers, in all societies, want their children to be educated and live free from poverty and violence. No people on earth yearn to be oppressed or aspire to servitude or eagerly await the midnight knock of the secret police . . . no nation owns these aspirations and no nation is exempt from them. We have no intention of imposing our culture, but America will always stand firm for the non-negotiable demands of human dignity, the rule of law, limits on the power of the state, respect for women, private property, free speech, equal justice and religious tolerance.[34]

Bush revisited many of these same themes in his State of the Union address the next year. He said that his administration did not want war, and was driven by just and humanitarian concerns: "We seek peace . . . If war is forced upon us, we will fight in a just cause . . . we will bring to the Iraqi people food, and medicines, and supplies and freedom." He reminded his audience that the threat of terrorism was constant and closer than many might imagine. "There are days when our fellow citizens do not hear news about the war on terror," he said, but "there is never a day when I do not learn of another threat, or receive reports of operations in progress, or give an order in this global war against a scattered network of killers." He reminded Americans that "outlaw regimes that seek and possess nuclear, chemical, and biological weapons . . . could also give or sell those weapons to terrorist allies, who would use them without the least hesitation."[35] And he placed the threat once again within a clear historical context:

> America's duty is familiar. Throughout the 20th century, small groups of men seized control of great nations, built armies and arsenals, and set out to dominate the weak and intimidate the world. In each case, their ambitions of cruelty and murder had no limit. In each case, the ambitions of Hitlerism, militarism and communism were defeated by the will of free peoples, by the strength of great alliances and by the might of the United States of America . . . Now, in this century, the ideology of power and domination has appeared again, and seeks to gain the ultimate weapons of terror. Once again this nation and all our friends are all that stand between a world at peace and a world of chaos and constant alarm. Once again we are called to defend the safety of our people and the hopes of all mankind. And we accept this responsibility.[36]

American foreign policy would shoulder the responsibility to defend civilization, peace, and the "hopes of mankind" against a "world of chaos." In this effort the United States would seek to enlist the aid of like-minded countries, but Bush cautioned Americans once again that not every nation would behave honorably and U.S. policy could not be hamstrung by the weak-willed. "We've called on the United Nations to fulfill its charter and stand by its demand that Iraq disarm," Bush suggested, but "America's purpose is more than to follow a process; it is to achieve a result . . . the course of this nation does not depend on the decisions of others." "We will consult," he said, "but let there be no misunderstanding: If Saddam Hussein does not fully disarm, for the safety of our people and for the peace of the world, we will lead a coalition to disarm him."[37]

Bush continued to argue that certain regimes—North Korea, Iran, and Iraq in particular—shared a place with al Qaeda on the other side of a morally bifurcated world.[38] On one side were the forces of peace, democracy, and "civilization;" on the other, the forces of aggression, totalitarianism, and barbarism—two camps that Reinhold Niebuhr in an earlier era might have called the "children of light and the children of darkness." Much of Bush's analysis of Iraq focused on the personality of Saddam Hussein, who Bush characterized as "a brutal dictator, with a history of reckless aggression, with ties to terrorism, with great potential wealth" and an intent "to dominate a vital region and threaten the United States." Bush described Hussein as a man who had made agreements for his own purposes and then cynically violated them. "To spare himself, he agreed to disarm of all weapons of mass destruction. For the next 12 years, he systematically violated that agreement." He had continued to pursue weapons of mass destruction, Bush charged, despite the horrific cost of this policy to his country, resulting from his self-imposed "isolation from the civilized world." Bush noted Hussein's disrespect for the United Nations in particular as evidence of his distance from the norms of international society "He has shown instead utter contempt for the United Nations," Bush said, "and for the opinion of the world."[39]

In short, Bush argued that past behavior demonstrated the Saddam Hussein was irrational or perhaps mentally deranged. "Trusting in the sanity and restraint of Saddam Hussein . . . is not an option," Bush claimed. Bush also presented a clear description of Hussein's future intentions that was fully consistent with the image of Hussein as a megalomaniacal sociopath. "With nuclear arms or a full arsenal of chemical and biological weapons,"[40] Bush suggested,

> Saddam Hussein could resume his ambitions of conquest in the Middle East, and create deadly havoc in that region. And . . . evidence from intelligence sources, secret communications, and statements by people now in custody, reveal that Saddam Hussein aids and protects terrorists, including members of Al Qaeda. Secretly, and without fingerprints, he could provide one of his hidden weapons to terrorists, or help them develop their own. Imagine those 19 hijackers with other weapons, and other plans -- this time armed by Saddam Hussein. It would take one vial, one canister, one crate slipped into this country to bring a day of horror like none we have ever known.[41]

A year later, in January, 2004, Bush continued to characterize the United States and its friends and enemies in the world in similar terms. "The terrorists," who he described as "killers who hide in caves," continued "to plot against America and the civilized world." As a group, they were depicted as immoral, violent, even animalistic (Bush noted that Saddam Hussein was also "found in a hole"). And in Iraq they had fought without honor, outside of the norms of civilized conduct: they were "thugs and assassins" who "ran away from our troops in battle [but] are now dispersed and attack from the shadows." Those resisting the U.S. occupation of Iraq, Bush said, were "enemies of freedom [who] will do all in their power to spread violence and fear."[42]

Michael V. Bhatia has examined the process of labeling violent non-state actors, the cognitive and political implications of naming, and "the contested relationship between the actual nature of a movement and the name applied, particularly in terms of the attempt to identify the essence or true nature of a movement and how this relates to other dissenting or surrounding factors." "Once assigned," Bhatia suggests, "the power of a name is such that the process by which the name was selected generally disappears and a series of normative associations, motives and characteristics are attached to the named subject." To label an individual or group "terrorist" (or "soldier" or "civilized") is to create an identity for that actor which serves to structure expectations about its motives and likely behavior—and thus constrains the set of relationships which might exist between the observer and actor being named. "Soldiers" are motivated by limited political goals and are likely to behave honorably within a clearly defined code of conduct, but this is not true of "terrorists." "Civilized" actors are capable of rational negotiation; "barbarians" are not. Naming is a cognitive and heuristic process but also a political one, consciously intended by political actors to shape social understandings of the world to suit their preferences, and thus to be examined with a high degree of skepticism. While the Bush administration might not have been doing anything fundamentally new in identifying its enemies as "terrorists," as Bhatia suggests, "the long historical relationship between the naming of opponents, empire and colonialism, as well as the manner in which the global media frame armed conflict, only provide further reason to doubt the truthfulness of the names assigned, and their ability to address the micro-realities involved in these conflicts and movements."[43]

If America's enemies were terrorists, thugs, and assassins, Bush argued the United States itself had sought and was operating in Iraq with the support of a broad international coalition of states. But he added that there was "a difference . . . between leading a coalition of many nations, and submitting to the objections of a few," noting that "America will never seek a permission slip to defend the security of our people."[44]

Bush defined not only American goals in his State of the Union address in 2004, but America itself. And he did it in terms, once again, that sounded unmistakably Wilsonian. "America is a nation with a mission," he said,

> and that mission comes from our most basic beliefs. We have no desire to dominate, no ambitions of empire. Our aim is a democratic peace—a peace founded upon the dignity and rights of every man and woman. America acts in this cause with friends and allies at our side, yet we understand our special calling: This great republic will lead the cause of freedom . . . The cause we serve is right, because it is the cause

> of all mankind. The momentum of freedom in our world is unmistakable—and it is not carried forward by our power alone. We can trust in that greater power who guides the unfolding of the years. And in all that is to come, we can know that his purposes are just and true.[45]

In his 2005 State of the Union address, Bush expanded on the process by which democracy would spread, it's practical as well as ethical importance to the United States, and the identities and motives of those who opposed it. "The victory of freedom in Iraq will strengthen a new ally in the war on terror," he argued, "inspire democratic reformers from Damascus to Tehran, bring more hope and progress to a troubled region." The "advance of freedom," he said, "will lead to peace." But if whole regions of the world were allowed to remain "in despair and grow in hatred, they will be the recruiting grounds for terror, and that terror will stalk America and other free nations . . . Our men and women in uniform are fighting terrorists in Iraq, so we do not have to face them here at home."[46]

Once again, Bush described a world of two warring camps, one representing "tyranny and terror," "hatred," and "ideologies of murder;" the other "hope" and "the force of human freedom." The terrorists, Bush said, were "violently opposed" to what they saw as the "evil principle" of democracy. They sought "to impose and expand an empire of oppression, in which a tiny group of brutal, self-appointed rulers control every aspect of every life."[47]

Bush claimed that the United States, on the other hand, had the "ultimate goal of ending tyranny in our world." He suggested that the United States sought to "build and preserve a community of free and independent nations, with governments that answer to their citizens, and reflect their own cultures." Bush argued that the aggressive, imperialistic nature of the terrorists' ideology constituted "one of the main differences between us and our enemies," in that "the United States has no right, no desire, and no intention to impose our form of government on anyone else"—despite the fact that the U.S. military was occupying Iraq and Afghanistan and had installed governments much like the U.S. government in both states.[48]

Bush once again sought to place contemporary events in an historical context, arguing that Americans had an obligation not only to their own interests in the present but to the future. "Our generational commitment to the advance of freedom . . . is now being tested and honored in Iraq," he said. "The victory of freedom in Iraq will . . . lift a terrible threat from the lives of our children and grandchildren." And he again evoked the memory of Franklin Roosevelt, quoting him as saying, "'Each age is a dream that is dying, or one that is coming to birth.' The liberation of Europe from fascism was only a dream, until it was achieved. The fall of imperial communism was only a dream, until one day it was accomplished." Bush noted that the tide of history was on the side of democracy, which had a "great momentum in our time, shown by women voting in Afghanistan, and Palestinians choosing a new direction, and the people of Ukraine asserting their democratic rights and electing a president."[49]

In his 2006 address, Bush returned to the theme of historical trends and responsibilities, but now employed this argument as part of a broader appeal to resist isolationism. Arguing that "the advance of freedom is the great story of our time," Bush noted that

> in 1945, there were about two dozen lonely democracies in the world. Today, there are 122 . . . it is a privilege to serve the values that gave us birth. American leaders from Roosevelt to Truman to Kennedy to Reagan rejected isolation and retreat, because they knew that America is always more secure when freedom is on the march . . . America rejects the false comfort of isolationism. We are the nation that saved liberty in Europe and liberated death camps and helped raise up democracies and faced down an evil empire. Once again, we accept the call of history to deliver the oppressed and move this world toward peace . . . Our own generation is in a long war against a determined enemy.[50]

He suggested that at stake in the nation's choices were not just its interests but its "honor" and "character," which would be compromised if the temptation to "retreat from our duties in the hope of an easier life" was not resisted. Having previously argued in Wilsonian terms that democracy, international law, and peace were mutually supportive, in his 2006 State of the Union address Bush included another element in this formulation that would have been familiar to Wilson: free trade. "We will choose to build our prosperity by leading the world economy," he said "or shut ourselves off from trade and opportunity."[51]

The theme of global interdependence and the need to reject isolationism resonated throughout Bush's 2006 address, even as he returned to constructions of the United States and its enemies that had echoed since 9/11. "Every step toward freedom in the world makes our country safer," he argued. "We seek the end of tyranny in our world," he said, because "on September 11, 2001, we found that problems originating in a failed and oppressive state 7,000 miles away could bring murder and destruction to our country." "We cannot find security by abandoning our commitments and retreating within our borders," Bush said,

> if we were to leave these vicious attackers alone, they would not leave us alone. They would simply move the battlefield to our own shores. There is no peace in retreat. And there is no honor in retreat. By allowing radical Islam to work its will, by leaving an assaulted world to fend for itself, we would signal to all that we no longer believe in our own ideals or even in our own courage. But our enemies and our friends can be certain the United States will not retreat from the world, and we will never surrender to evil.[52]

As for the motives and intentions of the terrorists and undemocratic leaders, Bush's conception was clear, simple, and unwavering. "Dictatorships shelter terrorists and feed resentment and radicalism and seek weapons of mass destruction," he claimed, and "terrorists like bin Laden . . . seek to impose a heartless system of totalitarian control throughout the Middle East and arm themselves with weapons of mass murder." "Their aim is to seize power in Iraq and use it as a safe haven to launch attacks against America and the world." As it had been with Nazi Germany and the Soviet Union, the ultimate goal of America's enemies in the War on Terror was nothing short of global domination. Their hope, Bush said, was to "break our will, allowing the violent to inherit the earth."[53]

The leaders of the Bush administration consistently argued that the United States' ideals transcended cultures and borders, that they were not simply national values but principles that applied to all people everywhere. In a speech at Princeton University on September 30, 2005, Condoleezza Rice said, "We must be serious about the universal appeal of certain basic rights. When given a truly free choice, human beings will choose liberty over oppression . . . And human beings will choose to be ruled by the consent of the governed, not by the coercion of the state . . . These principles should be the source of justice in every society and the basis of peace between all states."[54] In an address at West Point on June 2, 2002, President Bush said that "when it comes to the common rights and needs of men and women, there is no clash of civilizations. The requirements of freedom apply fully to Africa and Latin American and the entire Islamic world. The peoples of the Islamic nations want and deserve the same freedoms and opportunities as people in every nation."[55] And on February 26, 2003, at the American Enterprise Institute, Bush said that "human cultures can be vastly different. Yet the human heart desires the same good things, everywhere on Earth. In our desire to be safe from brutal and bullying oppression, human beings are the same . . . For these fundamental reasons, freedom and democracy will always and everywhere have greater appeal than the slogans of hatred and the tactics of terror."[56]

In his Second Inaugural address Bush said that "there is only one force of history that can break the reign of hatred and resentment, and expose the pretensions of tyrants, and reward the hopes of the decent and tolerant, and that is the force of human freedom . . . So it is the policy of the United States to seek and support the growth of democratic movements and institutions in every nation and culture, with the ultimate goal of ending tyranny in our world."[57] In the same speech, Bush connected what he argued were the universal values forming the basis of the American identity with the nation's contemporary mission in the world: "From the day of our founding, we have proclaimed that every man and woman on this earth has rights, and dignity, and matchless value, because they bear the image of the Maker of heaven and earth. Across the generations we have proclaimed the imperative of self-government because no one is fit to be a master and no one deserves to be a slave. Advancing these ideals is the mission that created our nation . . . Now it is the urgent requirement of out nation's security and the calling of our time."[58]

Bush suggested that the promotion of freedom in the world was a moral, even holy responsibility. It was not America's will that people be free, but God's will. American foreign policy was simply the mechanism for accomplishing this sacred end—by whatever means necessary. "Freedom is not America's gift to the world," Bush told Bob Woodward in an interview. "Freedom is God's gift to everybody in the world . . . I believe we have a duty to free people. I would hope we wouldn't have to do it militarily, but we have a duty."[59] The United States was, in Bush's formulation, an exceptional nation, with a destiny to rise above narrow parochial interests to bring freedom to the world. This moral mission made the United States unlike any other country in history; as Condoleezza Rice wrote in 2000, "We may be the only great power in history that prefers greatness to power and justice to glory."[60]

With regard to the international community, in both its internal and public discourse, the administration argued that its policy of pushing toward war in Iraq with or without U.N. approval was in fact a defense of the international order and the U.N. itself. On February 5, 2003, as Bush and Rice met with 20 key members of Congress in the White House, Rice argued that "Iraq is critical to reestablishing the bona fides of the Security Council . . . We tried sanctions, we tried limited military operations, we tried resolutions. At some point war is the only option." Further weapons inspections would not work because of the nature of the adversary, Rice argued. "The Iraqis love this game, they're comfortable with it, they know how to defeat it . . . He's hiding a lot. I'm quite certain we'll find a lot of it."[61]

The administration's clearest public statement of its understanding of the United Nations as an institution came with President Bush's speech to the U.N. General Assembly on September 12, 2002. "All the world now faces a test, and the United Nations a difficult and defining moment," Bush said. "Are Security Council resolutions to be honored and enforced, or cast aside without consequence? Will the United Nations serve the purpose of its founding, or will it be irrelevant?" Bush referred to the history of the League of Nations and its failure to act in the face of a surging tide of aggression and tyranny, reflecting the administration's broader intellectual framing of the post-9/11 era in the mold of World War II. This was a rhetorical strategy, but also a function of the cognitive framework that dominated within the administration.[62]

Bush deplored what he saw as the U.N.'s emphasis on process, on talking over action, on endless deliberation as threats mounted.[63] As he and his advisors had planned it, the intent of his U.N. speech was to shame the world community, to question its honor, to call it out for its cowardice. Bush had no taste for the sterile, inoffensive diplomatic tone that he identified with typical discussions at the U.N. As Draper puts it, "He *wanted* them to be offended! Calling them on their complicity—they *needed* to feel their honor stung . . . Bush thought he was doing the UN a favor by shaming it. It didn't occur to him, as he hammered away at the delegates consciences, that this might not feel at all like a favor—a mighty, fabulously privileged country telling lowly nations how and when they must act."

Bush said of his speech at the United Nations that it was also addressed to Saddam Hussein, that it was an attempt to let him know that Bush was serious. "When the president of the United States walks in and gives a pretty powerful speech in front of a world body, the message to Saddam Hussein should've been, 'This guy's serious . . . And I don't believe he took me seriously," Bush said. "I don't. I think it's more of the same, in his mind. And I tried hard to make him understand that one way or the other, we were going to deal with the threat."[64]

Constructing Iraq

From the perspective of strategic realpolitik, the choice of the United States to go to war with Iraq in the spring of 2003 is in many ways a puzzling one. It may be that President Bush and his advisors believed there would be some geostrategic advantage to the United States served by occupying Iraq, but if they did, this motive was inextricably wrapped up with other ideas about the identities of the United States and other international actors. Though Iraq possesses vast deposits of oil, access to that oil would have been more easily gained by removing U.N. sanctions restricting its sale than by using military force to seize it. The first Gulf War had demonstrated that Saddam Hussein's regime might attempt to destroy oil resources rather than let them fall into enemy hands, and in the event, the violence and political instability that followed in the wake of the U.S. invasion in 2003 seriously restricted the amount of oil flowing from the country in the years that followed. Iraq had possessed weapons of mass destruction and the Bush administration claimed to believe that it still did, but even the existence of such weapons would pose at most an indirect threat to the United States itself, and Iraq was only one of many states in the world with WMDs in their military arsenals. By going to war with Iraq the United States risked alienating popular opinion in many strategically important Muslim states, as well as diverting resources and public attention away from the ongoing war in Afghanistan. Why then would the Bush administration have chosen war with Iraq? This section of this chapter will argue that the answer to this question can be found in the Bush administration's socio-cognitive construction of Saddam Hussein's Iraq, the United States, other friends and enemies of America in the world, and the international system in which they interacted.

In the months leading up to the invasion of Iraq in the spring of 2003, the Bush administration based its case for the necessity of war on a coherent narrative describing the past, present, and future of Iraq's relations with the United States, its regional neighbors, and the wider world. In this narrative Saddam Hussein was a megalomaniacal despot, prone to violence and brutality beyond the norms of civilized society. He was a deranged, evil man, leading a regime with the technological capacity to produce chemical, biological, and nuclear weapons in enormous quantities and use them against targets throughout the region and around the world. In this story Saddam was perhaps psychotic, but not irrational. He was careful, meticulous, calculating, concealing complex weapons programs for years and doggedly rebuilding them after they were destroyed. He was motivated by his own ego ambition for political and military dominance in the Middle East, and by extension by hatred for the United States, the most important obstacle standing in the way of that ambition. Thus, he could be expected to form strategic alliances with terrorist groups and provide them with weapons of mass destruction which they would then deliver to the United States, bringing harm to his enemy without the risk of accountability for his regime.

Speechwriter David Frum described Bush's thinking about Iraq, saying the president felt that if the United States could overthrow the Ba'athist regime, "it could create a reliable American ally in the potential superpower of the Arab world. With American troops so close, the Iranian people would be emboldened to rise against the mullahs. And as Iran and Iraq built moderate, representative, pro-Western regimes, the pressure on the Saudi Arabia and other Arab states to liberalize and modernize would intensify. It was quite a gamble—but also quite a prize."[65]

In a meeting with members of the House of Representatives on September 26, 2002, Bush described Saddam Hussein as "a terrible guy who is teaming up with al Qaeda. He tortures his own people and hates Israel." "It is clear he has weapons of mass destruction—anthrax, VX; he still needs plutonium and he has not been shy about trying to find it," Bush said. He added that the "time frame would be six months" to Iraq having a nuclear bomb if it could acquire the fissile material.[66] In early April 2002, Bush told ITV reporter Trevor McDonald that "the worst thing that could happen would be to allow a nation like Iraq, run by Saddam Hussein, to develop weapons of mass destruction, and then team up with terrorist organizations so they can blackmail the world." The issue in Iraq was not weapons inspections, Bush said. "This is an issue of [Saddam] upholding his word."[67]

In a speech in Minnesota on November 3, 2002, Bush described Saddam as "the kind of guy that would love nothing more than to train terrorists and provide arms to terrorists so they could attack his worst enemy and leave no fingerprints. Later in Sioux Falls he told a crowd that Saddam "can't stand America. He can't stand some of our closest friends. And not only that: He is—would like nothing better than to hook up with one of these shadowy terrorist networks like Al Qaeda, provide some weapons and training to them, let them come and do his dirty work, and we wouldn't be able to see his fingerprints on his action." In Dallas Bush said, "this is a man who told the world he wouldn't have weapons of mass destruction, promised he wouldn't have them. He's got them."[68]

In a press conference on March 6, 2003, Bush argued that [Saddam is a threat. And we're not going to wait until he does attack . . . Saddam Hussein and his weapons are a direct threat to this country . . . If the world fails to confront the threat posed by the Iraqi regime . . . free nations would assume immense and unacceptable risks. The attacks of September the 11th, 2001, show what enemies of America did with four airplanes. We will not wait to see what . . . terrorist states could do with weapons of mass destruction . . . September the 11th changed the—the strategic thinking, at least as far as I was concerned, for how to protect our country . . . Used to be that we could think that you could contain a person like Saddam Hussein, that oceans would protect us form his type of terror. September the 11th should say to the American people that we're now a battlefield, that weapons of mass destruction in the hands of a terrorist organization could be deployed here at home.[69]]

The case that Saddam Hussein was "undeterrable," that he could not be prevented from acquiring or using weapons of mass destruction through the threat of reprisal, rested on four basic assumptions: that Hussein was malicious and would act out of evil motives; that he was "unbalanced," a "madman"; that he had already used weapons of mass destruction, against Iraqi Kurds and Iranian troops during the Iran-Iraq war; and that he had a tendency to act recklessly on the basis of serious miscalculations. There was evidence in Hussein's past behavior that tended to cast doubt on these claims—that he had not used WMDs against coalition forces in the first Gulf War, for example, and that in that case the United States had contributed to his belief that it would not intervene when U.S. ambassador April Glaspie told him that the United States had no position on border disputes such as that between Iraq and Kuwait. Perhaps the best reason to believe that Hussein could be deterred from using weapons of mass destruction was the fact that he had, in fact, been deterred from using them during the 1991 Gulf War. Faced with certain military defeat by an overwhelmingly superior opposing force, Hussein did not try to counterbalance this force by using unconventional weapons—which was exactly what the Bush administration argued he would try to do by giving WMDs to terrorists. In the decade of incursions into Iraqi airspace and more sustained attacks on the country that had followed the 1991 war, Hussein had not provoked the United States by shooting down a U.S. aircraft or otherwise instigating a war, but this evidence tended to be explained away or simply ignored by the Bush administration.[70]

The administration's most important single statement of its case for the necessity of war in Iraq came on October 7, 2002 in Cincinnati, Ohio. With a congressional vote authorizing the president to use force looming, Bush described the administration's rationale for war by detailing a vision of the identity of the United States, its friends and enemies in the world, and the nature of the international system in which they interacted. He began the speech with a sweeping indictment of Iraq's regime which focused not only on its past behavior but on what it would do in the future, in both cases making assumptions about the answers to these questions which were derived from the administration's general worldview and particular cognitive construction of the Iraqi government. "The Iraqi regime . . . possesses and produces chemical and biological weapons," Bush said. "It is seeking nuclear weapons. It has given shelter and support to terrorism, and practices terror against its own people. The entire world has witnessed Iraq's 11-year history of defiance, deception, and bad faith." The president then immediately framed this description of Saddam Hussein's Iraq in the context of an understanding of 9/11: "On September the 11th, 2001, America felt its vulnerability . . . We resolved then . . . to confront every threat, from any source, that could bring sudden terror and suffering to America."[71]

Bush described Saddam Hussein as "a homicidal dictator who is addicted to weapons of mass destruction," "a murderous tyrant who has already used chemical weapons to kill thousands of people . . . has tried to dominate the Middle East, has invaded and brutally occupied a small neighbor, has struck other nations without warning, and holds an unrelenting hostility toward the United States." While there were many unsavory and undemocratic regimes in the world, Bush argued, "by its past and present actions, by its technological capabilities, by the merciless nature of its regime, Iraq is unique."[72]

Saddam Hussein's regime had also flouted the norms of international society by building its weapons in secret and in violation of international agreements. Part of Bush's case against Saddam was built on the argument that in addition to being murderous, he was a liar, that besides behaving brutally he had behaved dishonorably. This fact as much as any other seems to have formed the basis for the administration's conclusion that the Iraqi regime could not be considered part of the "civilized" world, and indeed had consciously cut itself off from that world. "Every chemical and biological weapon that Iraq has or makes is a direct violation of the truce that ended the Persian Gulf War in 1991," Bush argued. "Saddam Hussein has chosen to build and keep these weapons despite international sanctions, U.N. demands, and isolation from the civilized world." In a private meeting on December 18, 2002, Bush told Spanish president José María Aznar that Saddam was "a liar and he has no intention of disarming . . . Saddam is using his money to train and equip al Qaeda with chemicals, he has harboring terrorists."[73]

In Cincinnati, Bush argued that Iraq had the capability—and implicitly, the intent—to strike at U.S. interests in the Persian Gulf and to kill Americans both in the Middle East and the United States itself. [Iraq possesses ballistic missiles with a likely range of hundreds of miles—far enough to strike Saudi Arabia, Israel, Turkey, and other nations—in a region where more than 135,000 American civilians and service members live and work. We've also discovered through intelligence that Iraq has a growing fleet of manned and unmanned aerial vehicles that could be used to disperse chemical or biological weapons across broad areas. We're concerned that Iraq is exploring ways of using these UAVs for missions targeting the United States. And, of course, sophisticated delivery systems aren't required for a chemical or biological attack; all that might be required are a small container and one terrorist or Iraqi intelligence operative to deliver it.]

In the same speech, Bush claimed that Saddam Hussein had proven "links to international terrorist groups." He had "provided safe haven to terrorists . . . finance[s] terror and gives assistance to groups that use terrorism to undermine Middle East peace." "We know that Iraq and al Qaeda have had high-level contacts that go back a decade," Bush asserted.[74]

> Iraq has trained al Qaeda members in bomb-making and poisons and deadly gases. And we know that after September the 11th, Saddam Hussein's regime gleefully celebrated the terrorist attacks on America. Iraq could decide on any given day to provide a biological or chemical weapon to a terrorist group or individual terrorists. Alliance with terrorists could allow the Iraqi regime to attack America without leaving any fingerprints . . . Saddam Hussein is harboring terrorists and the instruments of terror, the instruments of mass death and destruction. And he cannot be trusted. The risk is simply too great that he will use them, or provide them to a terror network.[75]

Bush stated in September 2002 that "you can't distinguish between al Qaeda and Saddam when you talk about the war on terrorism. They're both equally as bad, and equally as evil, and equally as destructive . . . the danger is that al Qaeda becomes an extension of Saddam's madness and his hatred and his capacity to extend weapons of mass destruction around the world."[76] In fact, Saddam Hussein and Osama bin Laden never seem to have had much in common but antipathy for the United States. Al Qaeda was a transnational movement with one overarching, transnational goal—the creation of a single, politically indivisible Muslim community. Al Qaeda's ideology was thus fundamentally hostile to the secular Arab nationalism represented by Iraq's Ba'ath party and regarded the leaders of such states as infidels. Hussein, for his part, took as his political model not

Mohammed but Josef Stalin. Throughout the First Gulf War and the decade of confrontation with the United States that followed, he appears to have very carefully calculated the degree of force he allowed to be used in order to avoid a full-scale U.S. attack. The idea that such a leader would provide weapons of mass destruction, acquired at great expense and risk, to terrorist organizations with no loyalty to and indeed deep enmity toward his regime, to be used where, when, and against whom they saw fit, simply defies all past history and common sense. Robert Harvey has argued that to lump Saddam and al Qaeda together as the administration did "is on par with equating Nazism and Soviet communism during the interwar period as examples of European extremism, and represents the kind of quasiracist dismissal by Washington of difference between Arab countries and political movements that most irks people in the region."[77]

After the war in Iraq had begun, two high-ranking al Qaeda leaders, Abu Zubaydah and Khalid Sheikh Mohammed, told U.S. interrogators in separate interviews that there were no ties between al Qaeda and Iraq. They said that while al Qaeda leadership had discussed the idea of trying to work with the Ba'athist regime in Iraq, Osama bin Laden had rejected it because he did not want to owe Saddam Hussein anything or be dependent upon him.[78]

While Bush's claim that Hussein's regime could give weapons of mass destruction to a terrorist organization at any moment it chose would have been true had it actually possessed any of these materials, the same could be said of any of the many countries possessing weapons of mass destruction, including U.S. allies and the United States itself. The salient aspect in Bush's argument in this regard was therefore not his stated point that Saddam *could* do this so much as his implicit point that Saddam *would* do this. In part, this presumption was based on past behavior—Saddam was indeed unusual among contemporary world leaders in that he had ordered chemical weapons used in acts of interstate warfare and domestic repression. But neither he nor any state leader had ever given weapons of mass destruction to a terrorist organization. The presumption that Saddam Hussein was likely to do so was thus built not on a pattern of past practice but rather on a construction of the identity of the Iraqi leader and his government by the Bush administration, in turn built in part on perceptions of that regime's prior behavior. It was this identity construction that led the administration to conclude that this was not only an enemy, but the kind of enemy that might go to such extremes even though it had not done so in the past.

Bush continually linked Saddam Hussein's Iraq to September 11. Though the president never explicitly claimed that Hussein was somehow responsible for 9/11, he repeatedly argued that the actors and forces responsible for 9/11 were phenomenologically related, and moved between his framing of 9/11 and impending war in Iraq in such a way that the rhetorical proximity of the issues suggested a relationship between them even where none had been explicitly stated. As he had from the days immediately after 9/11, Bush drew no distinction in the lead up to the war in Iraq between transnational terrorist groups and enemy states; they were both part and parcel of the axis of evil, the single anti-civilizational movement that threatened America. "Terror cells and outlaw regimes building weapons of mass destruction are different faces of the same evil," Bush said. "We have seen that those who hate America are willing to crash airplanes into buildings full of innocent people. Our enemies would be no less willing, in fact, they would be eager, to use biological or chemical, or a nuclear weapon."[79]

The Bush administration derived from its construction of the Iraqi regime a clear picture of not only Iraq's existing military capabilities, but the future trajectory of its ambitions and intentions. Despite what now appears to have been exceedingly scant hard evidence of existing Iraqi WMD programs, to say nothing of evidence of future intent to use such weapons or give them to terrorists, Bush declared in October 2002 that "Saddam Hussein still has chemical and biological weapons and is increasing his capabilities to make more." "He is moving ever closer to developing a nuclear weapon," Bush stated, and "has held numerous meetings with Iraqi nuclear scientists, a group he calls his 'nuclear mujahideen'" Globalization compounded the implications of such actions for the United States, the ease of movement of people and materials that defined the contemporary world order meaning that the existence of even a small amount of dangerous material in the hands of even a few individuals could profoundly threaten vital U.S. security interests. "If the Iraqi regime is able to produce, buy, or steal an amount of highly enriched uranium a little larger than a single softball," Bush claimed, "it could have a nuclear weapon in less than a year. And if we allow that to happen, a terrible line would be crossed. Saddam Hussein would be in a position to blackmail anyone who opposes his aggression. He would be in a position to dominate the Middle East. He would be in a position to threaten America. And Saddam Hussein would be in a position to pass nuclear technology to terrorists."[80]

Beneath these statements lay a complex, well-developed web of assumptions and understandings of the identity of the Iraqi regime which allowed the Bush administration to fill in the gaps in technical knowledge about Iraq's weapons programs that had emerged since the departure of the U.N. weapons inspectors in the late 1990s—substantive questions about what Iraq had and what it could do. But derived from these same identity understandings were even more important conclusions about Iraq's intentions and ultimate goals—questions about what Iraq would do with materials at its disposal. The existence of weapons stockpiles or WMD programs in different parts of the world would not in itself constitute a threat to the United States in the eyes of the Bush administration or any presidential administration. It was the answer to the second set of questions, the conclusion that Saddam Hussein's regime was likely to use or provide such weapons to terrorists if it had them, that formed the basis for the administration's judgment regarding the extreme seriousness of the threat.

For its part, the United States in Bush's narrative was a society which valued peace but felt an obligation to act against injustice and in defense of international law. In accepting the necessity of using force against Iraq America was acting on behalf of the common interests of the international community, Bush claimed, and would be supported by a broad coalition of allies. "Many nations are joining us in insisting that Saddam Hussein's regime be held accountable," he argued. "America is challenging all nations to take the resolutions of the U.N. Security Council seriously . . . to make the demands of the civilized world mean something."[81]

Bush's narrative included a construction of the United States which emphasized a particular set of values and understandings of the nation's historical experience. The administration interpreted the lessons of the 9/11, World War II, and the cold war to mean that the international environment was a fundamentally insecure and dangerous one from which the United States could not insulate itself, and that weakness or appeasement in the face of aggression would only whet the appetite of the aggressor. "The dictator of Iraq is a student of Stalin," Bush said, and "the longer we wait, the stronger and bolder Saddam Hussein will become."

> As Americans, we want peace—we work and sacrifice for peace. But there can be no peace if our security depends on the will and whims of a ruthless and aggressive dictator . . . Failure to act would embolden other tyrants, allow terrorists access to new weapons and new resources, and make blackmail a permanent feature of world events. The United Nations would betray the purpose of its founding, and prove irrelevant to the problems of our time. And through its inaction, the United States would resign itself to a future of fear. That is not the America I know . . . We refuse to live in fear. This nation, in world

> war and in cold war, has never permitted the brutal and lawless to set history's course. Now, as before, we will secure our nation, protect our freedom, and help others to find freedom of their own . . . The attacks of September the 11th showed our country that vast oceans no longer protect us from danger. Before that tragic date, we had only hints of al Qaeda's plans and designs. Today in Iraq, we see a threat whose outlines are far more clearly defined, and whose consequences could be far more deadly. Saddam Hussein's actions have put us on notice, and there is no refuge from our responsibilities. Like other generations of Americans, we will meet the responsibility of defending human liberty against violence and aggression.[82]

Bush also framed the prospective war in terms that emphasized the United States' moral responsibility to defend traditional liberal human rights. "On Saddam Hussein's orders," he argued, "opponents have been decapitated, wives and mothers of political opponents have been systematically raped as a method of intimidation, and political prisoners have been forced to watch their own children being tortured." The United States had a moral duty as well as a prudential responsibility to challenge such practices, Bush claimed, based on the premises of its own national philosophy and founding: "America believes that all people are entitled to hope and human rights, to the nonnegotiable demands of human dignity. People everywhere prefer freedom to slavery; prosperity to squalor; self-government to the rule of terror and torture. America is a friend to the people of Iraq." Bush argued that if war were necessary to enshrine these values in Iraq it would be an acceptable sacrifice in defense of the humanitarian interests of the Iraqi people. With the end of the Iraqi regime, even as a result of war with the United States, "the first and greatest benefit will come to Iraqi men, women, and children," Bush said. "The oppression of Kurds, Assyrians, Turkomans, Shia, Sunnis, and others will be lifted. The long captivity of Iraq will end, and an era of new hope will begin."[83]

Throughout the prewar period, the Iraqi people were depicted by the Bush administration as innocent, helpless victims of Saddam's brutality. During the American occupation of Iraq, this characterization continued, with terrorist insurgents now in the role of oppressor but the Iraqi people still in need of American aid. Throughout the occupation, references to Iraq as a child and the Iraqi people as children were common in discussions between the administration's top officials. Deputy National Security Advisor Stephen Hadley frequently referred to Iraq as an "abused child," emotionally scarred and with a continuing need for the parental care of the United States. Rumsfeld argued for a sterner style of parenting, repeating that the United States needed to let Iraq stand or fall on its own; he frequently used the comparison to a parent needing to let go of the back of a bicycle as their child learned to ride. Rice took an approach between the other two, at one point saying, "Let's let them try to pedal on their own, but we better be there to catch them . . . if you take your hand off the bicycle and it goes over a ravine that's not a very good thing either . . . How do you judge that they're capable enough?"[84] In the 2000 campaign Bush had similarly referred to Saddam Hussein in terms that sounded like he was disciplining a misbehaving child: "If we catch him developing weapons of mass destruction in any way, shape, or form, I'll deal with him in a way that he won't like," Bush told PBS commentator Jim Lehrer. "He just needs to know that he'll be dealt with in a firm way."[85] Iraqis were often depicted in the internal discourse of the administration as childlike in the sense that they were too violent or unsophisticated to govern themselves without U.S. tutelage. David Berreby has argued that this is a typical rhetorical and cognitive strategy for rationalizing the domination of one group by another, to "suggest lesser-human status." "Despised kinds can be depicted as childish and flighty," Berreby contends, "be they Greek slaves of Roman masters, black slaves of American masters, homosexuals in mid-twentieth-century America, or women in many male-dominated societies."[86]

Optimism for Iraq's future after the war was an element of the Bush administration's worldview that was informed by historical memory of World War II and the cold war, along with a broader sense of the efficacy of military force in accomplishing political and social goals. In World War II the American military victory had been completely decisive, and the occupations of Germany and Japan were peaceful and quickly produced very stable and prosperous democratic states. At the end of the cold war the sudden demise of the Soviet-supported governments throughout Eastern Europe demonstrated that even apparently stable and entrenched autocracies could be deeply unpopular among their own populations by virtue of their repressiveness, and if visibly weakened were prone to sudden collapse. In most cases the fall of those long-standing governments was followed by the rise of more democratic regimes with minimal bloodshed. This had been the case throughout Eastern Europe (Romania being one notable exception), as well as in the Soviet Union itself, and had occurred on the watch of the administration of George W. Bush's father, which included many of the younger Bush's closest advisors in key positions. In any event the president argued in 2002 that the negative consequences of war for Iraq's people would be slight compared to the severity of the oppression they suffered under Saddam; a worse outcome than the status quo was simply unimaginable, Bush held: "The situation could hardly get worse . . . for the people of Iraq. The lives of Iraqi citizens would improve dramatically if Saddam Hussein were no longer in power . . . Freed from the weight of oppression, Iraq's people will be able to share in the progress and prosperity of our time."[87]

Beneath this optimistic view of Iraq's future after the fall of the Ba'athist regime was also a critical assumption about the world-changing power of America—its military, its economy, its culture and ideas. A key element in the Bush administration's worldview as expressed in its public statements regarding Iraq was a belief in the almost limitless capacity of the United States to create social and political change, literally to reshape the world through its material power and transcendent values. "The United States and our allies will help the Iraqi people rebuild their economy and create the institutions of liberty in a unified Iraq at peace with its neighbors," Bush argued. "By our resolve, we will give strength to others. By our courage, we will give hope to others. And by our actions, we will secure the peace, and lead the world to a better day."[88]

The dominant ideas in the Bush administration served not merely to guide or enable policy, but effectively determined it by leaving no alternative to war with Iraq. If the administration's consensus assumptions were correct, they led inevitably to the conclusion that not only was war justified, but that not going to war would be dangerously irresponsible. As Andrew Flibbert has put it, the administration "launched the war because these ideas framed the status quo in Iraq as a serious foreign policy problem, with forcible 'regime change' as the only viable solution . . . Its belief in the unity of American enemies left it with little alternative to war, given the danger such a reality would pose."[89]

Historical Analogies

In seeking to understand the world after September 11 and to shape and publicly advocate for its foreign policies to meet the challenges of that world, the Bush administration relied on two primary historical analogies—World War II and the cold war. In addition, shared understandings of the 1991 Iraq war and 2001 war in Afghanistan played an important part in shaping the expectations of both political and military leaders of the kind of war they would face in Iraq in 2003 and the most effective means by which to fight it. Of these analogies, however, certainly the mythologized memory of World War II was the most significant in defining the Bush administration's worldview, providing a social meaning for the 9/11 attacks and forming the ideational basis for the policies chosen to respond to them in the years that followed. Comparisons of the era after 9/11 to World War II are abundant in the public statements and speeches of Bush and his chief advisors. Condoleezza Rice wrote in the *Washington Post*, for example, that "much as a new democratic Germany became a linchpin of a new Europe, so a transformed Iraq can become a key element of a very different Middle East in which the ideologies of hate will not flourish." And in a November 2002 interview, Paul Wolfowitz said he expected that Chalabi's Iraqi National Congress "would return to Baghdad and assume the reins of power, just as General Charles DeGaulle and the Free French returned triumphantly to postwar France." In addition to this kind of public statement, however, the administration's leaders often referenced the symbolism of World War II in private as well; the president himself wrote in his diary on September 11, for example, that "the Pearl Harbor of the 21st century took place today."[90]

For the Bush administration, the interpretive emphasis on World War II was intimately connected with notions of democratic universalism. The United States had democratized Germany and Japan after the war, proving wrong many skeptics who doubted the cultural fitness of these societies to adapt to democratic governance. "There was a time when many said that the cultures of Japan and Germany were incapable of sustaining democratic values," Bush said in his March 6, 2003 speech at the American Enterprise Institute. "Well, they were wrong. Some say the same of Iraq today. They are mistaken. The nation of Iraq, with its proud heritage, abundant resources and skilled and educated people is fully capable of moving toward democracy and living in freedom."[91] This analogy ignores a number of critical differences between the cultural and historical circumstances of these occupations, attention to which might have prepared the Bush administration for a longer, harder military endeavor in Iraq than it anticipated.

As part of the larger construction of the war on terror and war in Iraq as analogous with World War II that was dominant within the administration, American officials tended to associate the Ba'ath Party with the Nazi Party of Hitler's Germany. According to Jeffrey Record, for the Bush administration "Hitler easily translate[ed] into Saddam Hussein," and on this basis Bush and his advisors came to assume "that all Iraqis but Saddam and a few of his henchman would welcome a U.S. invasion and this would be like Eisenhower's liberation of France." This belief in turn served to enable the administration's "expectations of an early regime implosion, which among other things would spare U.S. forces the prospect of protracted urban warfare in Baghdad." These comparisons were oversimplified in a number of ways which had important social and political consequences within Iraq. Among the most apparent of these is the fact that while in the 1930s and 1940s the Nazi Party did not have a history or identity that was really separable from the ideology and leadership of Adoph Hitler, the Ba'ath party was in fact a transnational political movement that had existed before Saddam Hussein's rise to power in Iraq and was therefore distinct from Saddam in the minds of Iraqis and comprehensible without reference to his rule. In short, while Saddam Hussein had used the Ba'ath party to control Iraq, it was possible for Iraqis to believe in the party without supporting him the same could not be said for Hitler and the Nazi party, which was not a meaningful entity when dissociated from the Fuhrer. As Ali Allawi has put it, in Iraq "People believed that Saddam had usurped the Ba'ath and had distorted its otherwise 'credible' record to suit his own purposes. After all, were not Ba'athists also victims of his terror? The argument began to be made that there were both 'good' and 'bad' Ba'athists; that most members joined the Party to secure, keep or procure advancement in a job; that the Ba'ath Party had played a useful role in 'modernising' society, and so on."[92]

The main reason the Bush administration viewed the prospective occupation of Iraq as analogous to the post–World War II occupations of Japan and Germany may have been that it served the purposes of cognitive consistency. Because the war against terrorism was conceived as being analogous to the previous ideological struggles in which the United States engaged, and because the occupations of Japan and Germany were widely understood to represent the kind of successful democratization exercises that the administration hoped to accomplish in Iraq, the examples of Japan and Germany fit well with the other pieces of the ideational framework the administration had constructed to describe the identity of Iraq and the meaning of war there. A better analogy might have been the U.S. occupation of Vietnam, where the United States dispatched its military to support a feeble and unpopular government of its own creation and found itself mired in a civil war in which its enemies were amply armed and supported by ideological allies from outside the country. Unlike Germany, Iraq had no tradition of democratic government. Unlike both Germany and Japan, Iraq did not have an advanced, diversified industrial economy but had long depended on oil as its primary source of revenue. While there were important social schisms in Japan and Germany (notably along economic class lines), the aristocratic tradition in each society had been thoroughly undermined by war; the kinds of ethnic and religious divisions that would become violent fault lines in Iraq simply did not exist in either Japan or Germany. In both Japan and Germany, liberal reform elements were co-opted by the fact that the U.S. occupier had replaced totalitarian regimes of the far right, and nationalist conservatives were pressured to cooperate with the occupiers because American-style democratic capitalism represented an alternative to socialism and the United States was at least a formidable ally against the rising tide of global communism. For both Germany and Japan, Russia was a traditional enemy of much longer standing than the United States, and actively opposing the U.S. occupation was understood to imply the risk of a much more dangerous vulnerability to Soviet domination. Throughout the period of the cold war, the bipolar international system and prospect of communist subversion created pressure for Germany and Japan to democratize and align tightly with the United States in foreign policy, but no such ideological pressure was present in Iraq.[93]

The United States also sent much larger occupying forces to Japan and Germany than to Iraq; the occupation of Japan involved 23 divisions comprising some 500,000 troops, well over three times as many as were sent to Iraq. In the case of Iraq, U.S. leaders' need for cognitive consistency between a belief in the efficacy of U.S. military force in creating democracy, and a belief in the doctrine of "military transformation" calling for small, nimble, technologically advanced forces, led to the conclusion that Iraq could be like Germany and Japan without anything like the troop strength used in those occupations. And perhaps most significantly, both Germany and Japan had been utterly devastated and exhausted by nearly five years of war before U.S. occupation forces arrived. Their military forces had been demolished, their civilian populations decimated, their industry and infrastructure reduced to ruins. The defeat of Japan and Germany was complete, comprising not just strategic military victory by the United States but the thorough demoralization of the defeated societies and the utter delegitimization of their previous governments. As former secretary of the navy James Webb has written, "Our occupation forces never set foot inside Japan until the emperor had formally surrendered and prepared Japanese citizens for our arrival. Nor did MacArthur destroy the Japanese government when he took over as proconsul after World War II. Instead, he was careful to work his changes through it, and took pains to preserve the integrity of the imperial family."[94] Nationalists who advocated military struggle against the occupier had little credence among the civilians of postwar Japan and Germany, and this fact set these occupations far apart from both Vietnam and Iraq, where the arguments of such nationalists could be heard by civilians with an intact sense of national pride and will to resist, whatever their opinions might be of the political ideologies and actors around whom resistance was organized.[95]

If World War II provided an important analogy for the post 9/11 era, then the cold war served a similar, if less prominent role as well. In particular, in many accounts George W. Bush sought to model his presidency on those cold war leaders such as Truman and Reagan who he regarded as distinguished by the courage of their convictions, their moral certainty and bluntness, and their steadfast willingness to confront the reality of evil in the world. In the months after 9/11 Bush read Dean Acheson's memoir of the early cold war, *Present at the Creation*. Both Bush and Rice professed to admire Truman's resolve, the way in which he recognized U.S. power and political capital in the post World War II era and sought to actively use it to reshape the international system to serve U.S. interests.[96]

Though Bush often imagined himself as a bold, plain spoken architect of a new world order akin to Harry Truman, Truman himself had denounced the idea of preemptive or preventative war. "We do not believe in aggression or preventative war," Truman said in a radio address in 1950. "Such war is the weapon of dictators, not free democratic countries like the United States." Certainly the Soviet Union in 1950 was an existential threat to the United States in a way that went far beyond any threat posed by Iraq, and the Soviet Union had demonstrated that it possessed atomic weapons. Some in Truman's military wanted to eradicate this threat before it fully matured—the commandant of the air force's Air War College asked Truman for the order to conduct a nuclear first strike against the fledgling Soviet nuclear weapons facilities, explaining that "with it [the atomic bomb] used in time, we can immobilize a foe [and] reduce his crime before it happened." Truman fired the commandant.[97]

The end of the cold war also provided a recurring analogy within the Bush administration. One official has described Paul Wolfowitz as often speaking about postwar Iraq in meetings as being "like Eastern Europe with Arabs," briefly turbulent but ultimately stable and ready to be directed onto the path of democracy.[98] The collapse of the Soviet client regimes in Eastern Europe in 1989—events that as officials of the previous Bush administration, Wolfowitz, Rice, Cheney and others had experienced firsthand—were understood in George W. Bush's administration as a story of one after another apparently stable authoritarian government collapsing as soon as it became apparent to its people that they could openly challenge it. As such, the end of the cold war in Europe was interpreted to support the conclusion that the Ba'athist regime in Iraq, if it were destabilized, would quickly collapse but leave intact most of the social and governmental structures necessary to maintain order in the country. As in East Germany or Czechoslovakia, the ruling party and its leaders would go but after a brief period of turmoil, social order would return. Like Saddam's government, these Eastern European regimes had also been states that ruled through repression and fear, but the appearance of control had belied their underlying weakness. There were very significant differences—not least the fact that no foreign power had invaded Czechoslovakia or East Germany to encourage their citizens to rise up, and in fact their motivation to do so was laden with a nationalistic sense of hostility to governments which were seen as puppets of a foreign empire, the Soviet Union. These distinctions do not seem to have merited much attention in the Bush administration, in which many of the officials who had served in the Reagan and H.W. Bush White Houses as the cold war came to an end instead simply interpreted the common "brittleness" of the Soviet satellites and Iraq as providing a clear picture of the likely response to a U.S. attack.[99]

Finally, especially with regard to military strategy, the wars in Iraq in 1991 and Afghanistan in 2001 served as analogies which tended to be understood within the administration to suggest that the 2003 war in Iraq would be fought between conventional military forces and would be over quickly. The war in Afghanistan was also understood within the administration as having demonstrated the effectiveness of the doctrine of 'transformation"—heavy reliance on technology and a light footprint on the ground to overthrow a hostile regime with minimal expense and risk of casualties. David Phillips suggests that General Jay Garner's Office of Reconstruction and Humanitarian Assistance (ORHA) the first agency of the U.S. government to attempt to govern postwar Iraq, assumed it would be contending with the aftermath of the 1991 war, "focus[ing] its planning on a humanitarian emergency involving the displacement of more than a million Iraqis, including the possible use of WMD." "ORHA also anticipated oil-well fires and Iraq's neighbors sending in troops," Phillips suggests, but "None of these contingencies came to pass." Michael Gordon and Bernard Trainor have argued that similar comparisons were made within the military command structure, with commanding general Tommy Franks and the Defense Department's Central

Command (CENTCOM) basing their planning for the war largely on the memory of 1991. "During the Desert Storm campaign Saddam Hussein's Republican Guard was the best equipped and most loyal force," Gordon and Trainor argue. "Franks and his generals continued to regard the Republican Guard as their principal adversary . . . But it would be the paramilitary Fedayeen that represented the principal challenge in Nasiriyah, Samawah, Najaf, Kifl, and Diwaniyah, and that fought ferociously in Baghdad as well." Gordon and Trainor suggest that this analogy also prevailed within the U.S. intelligence services, and in particular drove the CIA's assumption that Iraqi troops would surrender en masse, as had occurred in the 1991 war.[100]

Thomson suggests that a similar process of institutional "abuse and distortion of history" occurred within the Johnson administration at the time of the Vietnam War. "Vietnamese, Southeast Asian, and Far Eastern history has been rewritten by our policy makers . . . to conform with the alleged necessity of our presence in Vietnam," Thomson claimed. "Highly dubious analogies from our experience elsewhere—the 'Munich' sellout and 'containment' from Europe . . . have been imported in order to justify our actions." If historical analogies are significant, however, their importance derives not so much from whether they represent "correct" or "incorrect" interpretations of history, as from the ways in which they were socially understood and used by groups of policy makers and whole societies. Some analogies become significant rallying points for particular policy prescriptions not only because they suggest what is likely to happen and what should be done about it in the future, but especially because they seem to offer some insight on what has occurred in the recent past. So many Americans and the Bush administration itself saw the post-9/11 era as analogous to World War II not primarily because Saddam Hussein was like Hitler—this comparison was often made, but it was a product rather than an underlying assumption of this World War II analogy. The social background which enabled this analogy and gave it its broad public appeal was generated by 9/11 itself—the attacks were like Pearl Harbor; they demonstrated the nation's vulnerability in a world more dangerous than Americans had realized before; they suggested a stark ideological conflict ahead, a world divided between good and evil. Jack Snyder wrote about the significance of the World War II and cold war analogies for the Bush administration and the United States as a whole after 9/11: "The Rumsfeld generation grew to political maturity inculcated with the Munich analogy and the domino theory," Snyder suggested. "It is true that an opposite metaphor, the quagmire, [was] readily available for skeptics to invoke as a result of the Vietnam experience. But after the September 11 attacks and the easy victory over the Taliban, the American political audience [was] primed for Munich analogies and preventative war, not for quagmire theories."[101]

American Political Culture after 9/11

How was the Bush administration able to shape a broad, bipartisan coalition in support of the war on the basis of the ideological arguments and identity constructions outlined above? Certainly, not all of those Americans who supported the administration's choice for war were partisan Republicans or believers in neoconservative ideology; the war enjoyed widespread public support extending well beyond these groups, including among many liberal internationalists and Democrats who otherwise opposed the administration's policy agenda. Andrew Flibbert has argued that the dominant assumptions within the Bush administration "diffused throughout the country to help generate a pro-war ideational community that included a majority of Americans, acquiring enough discursive hegemony to sustain the American march to war from 2001 to 2003."[102] The war was widely supported because the Bush administration appealed for it in terms which referenced deeply held American values and identity precepts, and interpreted traditional American beliefs to support an explanation of recent history that resonated with many Americans in the post 9/11 social environment.

The Bush administration was able to shape a coherent public understanding of the meaning of the September 11 attacks that would be used to publicly rationalize its subsequent foreign policy choices. But the impact of the administration's ideas about foreign policy cannot be separated from the social context that was created by the attacks themselves. The Bush administration helped to frame this context and used it, but did not create it from scratch. To understand the significance of the administration's ideology as a cause of foreign policy, it is necessary to recognize that the social understanding of the need to implement that ideology, within the administration and throughout American society as a whole, would not have existed without the material fact of the 9/11 attacks. The administration used this social environment to build support for its policies, but even before it could begin to interpret the events of 9/11 for public consumption, public opinion was very supportive of the use of force in general and against Iraq in particular. In a Gallup/CNN/*USA Today* survey taken three days after the 9/11 attacks, for example, 88 percent of those polled said they thought the United States should take military action in retaliation for the attacks. A CBS News/*New York Times* poll taken on September 20, 2001, found that 92 percent of those surveyed favored "military action against whoever is responsible." The same CBS/*New York Times* survey found that 68 percent of those polled favored military action against those responsible even if it meant that "many thousands of innocent civilians may be killed."[103]

Despite the lack of evidence of any Iraqi connection to the 9/11 attacks, a Harris poll taken two days after they occurred found that 78 percent of those polled believed it was "very likely" or "somewhat likely" that "Saddam Hussein was personally involved" in the attacks. A Gallup/CNN/*USA Today* poll taken on September 21–22, 2001, found that 90 percent of those surveyed felt that "Removing Saddam Hussein from power" should be a "very important" (68 percent) or "somewhat important" goal of military action after the terrorist attacks. 79 percent felt that "preventing Iran, Iraq, and North Korea from developing weapons of mass destruction" should be a "very important" goal of military action, despite the fact that none of these states had any demonstrated connection to the attacks. A PSRA/*Newsweek* poll taken on October 11–12, 2001, found that 81 percent of those surveyed supported using military force against Saddam Hussein and his military in Iraq. A November 27, 2001, ABC News/*Washington Post* poll found that 78 percent of respondents supported the forcible removal of Saddam from power. As it began in the spring of 2003, the war in Iraq was supported by more than 70 percent of the U.S. public, with Gallup/CNN/*USA Today* polls showing between 76 and 71 percent support between March 20 and March 24–25. An ABC News/*Washington Post* poll taken in April 2003, found that 77percent of those questioned said they thought the war with Iraq was part of the war against terrorism.[104]

Polls in the same period found that Americans in the aggregate also tended to share the Bush administration's understanding of the United States as a benevolent force in the world, and a country committed to the defense and promotion of democracy in its foreign policy. A Zogby poll taken between September 5–9, 2003, found that a combined 93 percent of Americans polled felt that it was either "very accurate" or "somewhat accurate" to describe the United States as "a good friend and ally of people who desire freedom" (with 65 percent responding "very accurate"). 87 percent said they believed it was "very" or "somewhat" accurate to describe the United States as "a force to promote the values of freedom and democracy." A Gallup/CNN/*USA Today* poll taken between November 14–16,

2003 found that 56 percent of those polled felt that the United States had "a responsibility to help other countries rid themselves of dictators and become democracies."[105]

The tone of commentary in the American media in the days immediately after 9/11 was bellicose, and to a large extent this would have been true regardless of the statements of the Bush administration. Senator John McCain said that the attacks were an "act of war" that demanded military retaliation. Former secretary of state Lawrence Eagleburger told CNN's Judy Woodruff that "we know who these people are" and it was time to "kill some of them" by any means necessary, including nuclear weapons.[106] Douglas Kellner argues that "The U.S. corporate media continued to fan the war fever and there was an orgy of patriotism such as the country had not seen since World War II. Media frames shifted from 'America under Attack' to 'America Arising,' 'America Strikes Back,' and 'America's New War'—even before any military action was undertaken." Flags appeared everywhere in the United States—first outside private homes and then on television, on billboards, as decals on cars, on web sites and in countless other locations. Television shows including *The West Wing* and *Law and Order* used computer animation to place American flags into scenes in their programs."[107]

9/11 left Americans with a new and profound sense of vulnerability, but vulnerability by itself was not a guide to specific action. This new sense of being in the world was malleable—it might have been interpreted as cause to reatreat into isolationism, to strengthen international alliances or bolster the United Nations, or to advocate unilateral militarism. Though the choices of the Bush administration were clear, it is important to note that there was nothing inherent in the events of 9/11 themselves to make those particular choices inevitable. These events did not have a fully developed social meaning until one was ascribed to them by political leaders and public discourse in American society as a whole. It is not events themselves that matter in international politics but rather the commonly accepted meanings which are attached to them, and these meanings are to a large extent what political leaders make them to be. Garnering popular support for policy depends on political leaders' ability to convince society as a whole that the meaning they assert for particular events is in fact the appropriate one, that their explanation of recent history is more accurate than competing understandings. Kathleen Hall Jamieson and Paul Waldman have argued that presidential power is largely derived from that ability to "develop and disseminate frames or interpretations that are accepted by the press and the pubic and as a result become the lenses of which they are unaware but nonetheless shape how we think about political affairs."[108] In the weeks and months after 9/11, the Bush administration demonstrated this power, developing from its neoconservative ideology and advocating to American society a cognitive framework through which the events of 9/11 could be explained and a future course of action charted.

While the neoconservative movement is often, and rightly, seen as the intellectual incubator of the war in Iraq, it is important to note that the choice for war was supported by a broad cross-section of the American public, and by many intellectuals and policy makers of the liberal internationalist cast as well. Tony Smith has argued that academics and public intellectuals of the left provided critical support for the process of moving the United States toward war. In many cases, liberal internationalists failed to really challenge Bush's choice for war in Iraq largely because they did not disagree with its ends but only its means. Smith argues that many Democrats whose foreign policy preferences were shaped by Kantian and Wilsonian thinking formed a critical basis of support for war in Iraq. He notes that the Progressive Policy Institute of the Democractic Party's National Leadership Council and the Project for the New American Century "were effectively mirror images of one another" when it came to the war on terror. The PPI issued a document entitled "With All our Might: A Progressive Strategy for Defeating Jihadism and Defending Libety." Its authors were "liberal hawks;" neo-Kantians and Wilsonians who argued for an assertive and militaristic democracy promotion and ant-terrorism agenda. Peter Beinart, an editor of the *New Republic*, wrote a book entitled *The Good Fight: Why Liberals—and only Liberals—Can Win the War on Terror and Make America Great Again* which echoed these same sentiments.[109]

Thomas Friedman provided another example when he wrote in the *New York Times* on March 3, 2006 that "A majority of Americans, in a gut way, always understood the value of trying to produce a democratizing government in the heart of the Arab-Muslim world." On January 8, 2004, Friedman wrote that the "global war on terror . . . amounts to World War III—the third great totalitarian challenge to open societies in the last 100 years . . . What we can do is to partner with the forces of moderation within these societies to help them fight the war of ideas. Because ultimately, this a struggle with the Arab-Muslim world, and we have to help out allies there, just as we did in World Wars I and II." In addition to having a significant influence on public opinion himself, Friedman was expressing the views of many liberal internationalists, often Democrats, who had supported the military interventions of the Clinton administration in the 1990s, and were willing in the wake of the 9/11 attacks to accept the Bush administration's rejection of multilateralism to serve ostensibly liberal goals.[110]

When liberal internationalists found common cause with the Bush administration and its plans for war in Iraq, they broke with their own traditional ideological principles not because they supported an aggressive democracy-promotion agenda abroad or because they believed that the force of American arms could fundamentally alter the international system. They broke with the liberal internationalist tradition by accepting the severing of multilateral means and liberal ends implied by the Bush administration's argument that if the U.N. Security Council would not act then the U.S. should act alone, in not conditioning their support on the sanction of the world community.

The liberal internationalists of the post 9/11 era were the inheritors of a specific, well-defined tradition of foreign policy thought. But as always, that body of ideology was mediated and understood through the lens of recent history, and the examples that dominated recent history in this instance were the frame of 9/11—which was interpreted to mean that the United States was vulnerable and could not delay action while waiting for international approval—and of Bosnia and Kosovo, liberal internationalist wars in which international approval and coordination had proven cumbersome and had hindered an effective response. In Bosnia, the United States failed to use military force to affect an end to the war during its first four years because policy became mired in negotiations with allies about how to act. The presence of U.N. peacekeepers on the ground was eventually seen by many as a hindrance to the actions that might have ended the war. In Kosovo, when it became clear that the U.N. Security Council would not endorse a U.S.-European war to stop Serb forces from brutalizing Kosovar Albanians due to parochial Russian interests, the United States and NATO simply ignored the U.N. and went to war anyway. The result was a complete rout of the Serb forces and the eventual collapse of Slobodan Milosevic's government, a clear victory in a just cause in the eyes of some liberal internationalists. In this case, the lesson taken by many observers was that even the coordination of the war through NATO had involved an excessively complex and ponderous decision-making process that had hindered the conduct of the war. The liberal internationalist construction of the United States was summed up by Madeleine Albright, who on February 18, 1998 said that "If we have to use force, it is because we are America. We are the indispensable nation. We stand tall, and we see further into the future."[111] The liberal wars of the 1990s had cemented in the minds of many liberal internationalists the idea that force could be effective in the defense of human rights, but that international approval for such force was perhaps desirable but not absolutely necessary and would complicate the prospects for success in any case. Thus, in Smith's words, when in 2003 "it became apparent that Washington would not work through the United Nations, indeed that it would spur its NATO allies and mock the pretensions of the European Union . . . [Many liberal internationalists] joined the war party, having been convinced by the logic of the neoconservative position that once American leadership had proved its worth, unilateralism would show itself to be the high road to multilateralism, for others would quickly support Washington's mission, realizing it was for the common good."[112] Operation Iraqi Freedom thus had its origins "not just from the neoconservatives, however culpable they might be in their own way, but also from the neoliberal establishment, which had done so much to make the democratization process seem so relatively easy to envision in Iraq."[113]

Ultimately the social-ideational constructions which formed the basis for the war in Iraq were to a large extent created by the effects of the 9/11 attacks on American society, as well as on the small cohort of national leaders surrounding and including president Bush. As Moises Naim has written, "The ultimate enabler—or the factor that made the other enablers possible—was September 11, 2001. Americans felt the attacks like a blow to the head: numbing and disorienting. September 11 was so painful, surprising, and threatening that confusion and suspension of disbelief became natural reactions." The effect of 9/11 on U.S. popular culture was not simply to create fear, but to cause fundamental understandings of the world to be cast into doubt. If the world was really so much more threatening than it had previously appeared, then what other facts should be suspect, and indeed could facts and evidence provide a secure basis for critical judgment in international politics at all? The Bush administration's argument that Iraq should be attacked not because it had WMD's, but because it could *not* be known *not* to have them, made more sense to many Americans than it otherwise would have in the social context of insecurity, uncertainty, and doubt that held sway in the years after September 11, 2001.[114]

Chapter 4

Identity and Ideology in the Policy Process

Individual and Social Psychology in the Bush Administration

Michael Gordon and Bernard Trainor have argued that with regard to the war in Iraq

> President Bush and his team committed five grievous errors. They underestimated their opponent and failed to understand the welter of ethnic groups and tribes that is Iraq. They did not bring the right tools to the fight and put too much confidence in technology. They failed to adapt to developments on the ground and remained wedded to their prewar analysis even after Iraqis showed their penchant for guerrilla tactics in the first days of the war. They presided over a system in which differing military and political perspectives were discouraged. Finally, they turned their back on the nation-building lessons from the Balkans and other crisis zones and fashioned a plan that unrealistically sought to shift much of the burden onto a defeated and ethnically diverse population and allied nations that were enormously ambivalent about the invasion. Instead of making plans to fight a counterinsurgency, the president and his team drew up plans to bring the troops home and all but declared the war won.[1]

The Bush administration's policies in Iraq were premised on a host of flawed assumptions which led to unrealistic expectations and non-existent or unworkable plans. This chapter will seek to explain how this happened by examining the dominant ideological and identity constructions that held sway within the administration and the social-psychological environment in which the president and his advisors discussed policy and made key decisions.

To make this case it is necessary to consider the ways in which constructivism as a body of theory connects with social psychological theories of decision making. Constructivism holds that dominant ideas are critical variables in the interactions of states, but ideas by themselves obviously cannot affect policy. Ideas reside in the minds of individuals and can be shared in groups, and it is these individuals and groups—whether of ten or ten million—that put ideas into practice. So to understand the ways in which ideas shape policy, it is necessary to understand the social-psychological process of decision making and implementation; it is necessary, in other words, not merely to identify a set of ideas that animated policy but also to understand the particular ways in which those ideas were acted upon by policy makers, since process will inevitably shape outcome. Both individual and social psychology matter in the process of generating and operationalizing identity, and cannot be understood as distinct from one another without obscuring this process as a whole. Individual leaders have idiosyncratic attitudes and preferences, but policy choices are shaped in social environments ranging from small groups to whole societies to the global community. To see individual leaders creating policy on the basis of individual preferences or personality alone is to disaggregate the individual from the social in a way that can only be destructive of a real understanding of the ways in which humans acquire and apply knowledge.

In the past, constructivist and psychological theories of decision making have not tended to speak as directly to one another as often or intentionally as might be expected, with the result that there have not been as many bridges built between these bodies of theory as might be hoped. The psychological approaches of scholars such as Irving Janis (*Groupthink*) and Robert Jervis (*Perception and Misperception in International Politics*) are essentially rationalist in the sense that they presume a reality exists that leaders should see, but that leaders sometimes fail to see this reality correctly because of an identifiable set of psychological tendencies related to individual cognition (in Jervis's formulation) and group dynamics (in Janis's). Failure to see correctly is correlated with policy ineffectiveness; Janis focuses on "fiascoes" because the fact that policy has gone badly wrong, has failed to achieve its goals and resulted in unintended negative consequences indicates that pathological decision making has occurred. Both Janis and Jervis seek to explain leaders' choices for policies that are costly or do not achieve their desired ends and they find the explanations in errors of individual cognition and dysfunctional policy processes.

These approaches to foreign policy analysis complement constructivist theory by illustrating the ways in which particular constructions of Self and Other come to be shared by policy makers and shape their choices and the ways in which particular constructions will lead to destructive and unintended outcomes. In turn, constructivist theory provides a broader context within which the significance of these social and psychological factors can be understood by emphasizing that shared ideas comprise the socio-cognitive environment of international politics. But constructivists also tend to argue that for policy makers there is not a single correct reality but rather an infinite number of discreet facts, which even if perceived accurately, depending on how they are interpreted and the emphasis placed on each, lend themselves to a wide array of conclusions about threat and opportunity, of what the national interest is and how to pursue it. Policy makers do not perceive "reality" so much as one among many potential "realities," and the choice of which depends on the identity and ideological frames that individuals, decision-making groups, and whole societies bring to the process of understanding the world.

As Legro puts it, while "the psychology literature in international relations has illuminated the dynamics of change in the ideas that individuals hold . . . given its focus on the human mind, psychology has been less helpful in explaining how individual ideas come together to affect national ideas." Individuals and groups are neither entirely rational free agents nor prisoners of social structures with no autonomy of their own. They do exercise real choice, but their behavior is nevertheless informed and constrained by the beliefs and values shared within the group and those of their society as a whole. Group dynamics are "embedded . . . in broader organizational, political, and cultural constellations," as Paul 't Hart, Erik Stern, and Bengt Sundelius argue, and "social and political psychologists cannot afford to ignore the broader institutional forces that govern the perceptions, calculations, and behavior of real-world policy makers." Human psychology is certainly relevant to an understanding of the policy choices of individuals and groups, in Legro's view—"After all, there is no group or national 'mind' that can think the way the human mind can. At a basic level, idea change must involve individual psychology . . . [but] change in collective ideas is as much a social process as a psychological one." To focus strictly on individual psychology as the root of policy decisions is to ignore the social basis of many of the ideas held by individuals. "The formulation of national beliefs involves both some set of individual ideas and some conception of how individual ideas connect or aggregate to form the collective ideas that orient the group (states)." And, as Vertzberger notes, "A group is more likely to reflect cultural values than individual decision-making" because cultural ideas are likely to comprise a basis of common values shared within the group.[2]

Social-Psychological Factors and the Construction of Iraq after 9/11

As a starting point for considering the internal social psychology of the Bush administration as it affected foreign policy in the years after 2001, it is important first to acknowledge the likelihood that the very personal experience of the 9/11 attacks had a profound effect on the ways in which these policy makers conceived of the world around them in the months and years that followed. Just as someone who has a had a traumatic experience like being in a car accident will tend to be more anxious riding in cars for some time afterward, terrorism became a focus of concern for many Americans after 9/11 to an extent that was probably far out of proportion with the actual likelihood of further terrorist attacks directly affecting them. As Robert Jervis has put it, "If people do not learn enough from what happens to others, they learn too much from what happens to themselves." While the trauma of those events had a powerful impact on American society as a whole, this is likely even more true for the leaders of the Bush administration, who experienced the events of 9/11 in very personal ways which most Americans did not. The president and his closest advisors knew that the White House had very likely been a target of the 9/11 attackers; certainly Donald Rumsfeld and his staff knew very well that they might easily have been victims of the attack on the Pentagon. These individuals walked through the rubble, met the grieving families, saw and felt the consequences of the events of 9/11 firsthand. While there was a generalized fear among Americans of a "second wave" of attacks in the weeks that followed, that fear must have been experienced very differently by those who understood that they were probable targets, that they had a duty to keep those attacks from happening, and that they bore some responsibility for having failed to prevent the first attacks. The days, weeks, and months after 9/11 were a time of fear and rumor in American society at large, but how much more intense and uncertain must that time have been for policy makers who were being deluged with information unavailable to almost anyone else—frightening, disconnected bits of data that seemed to portend further violence without revealing, where, when, or how it might occur, or what could be done to prevent it? President and Mrs. Bush were awakened suddenly on the night of September 11 itself and told that a plane was heading down the Potomac River, possibly intending an attack on the White House. It is impossible to know the effect of that experience, and the less-intense but always present fear that another night, it might not be a false alarm, on the worldview of the president in the months and years that followed, but it seems safe to assume that the psychological impact would have been very real. In the weeks after the attacks Bush had been told that if an airliner taking off from Washington, D.C.'s National Airport was taken over by terrorists it could be crashed into the White House in just 40 seconds. "I'm in the Lord's hands," he had told American Red Cross director Bernadine Healy.[3]

Many of the critical assumptions that would drive U.S. foreign policy after 9/11 were already established in the hours immediately after the attacks, as the senior members of the Bush administration worked to craft the president's first substantial public response in a nationally televised address that evening. Fundamental conclusions about the nature of the attacks—that they were acts of war rather than crimes—and the identities of America's enemies who had carried them out—"terrorism" broadly, including states who harbored terrorists, rather than al Qaeda narrowly—were reached within hours after the attacks and would remain fixed in the administration's public rhetoric and shared internal understanding from that point forward. That America represented the forces of good in a Manichaean world, and that the United States possessed power, especially military power, sufficient to coerce or destroy any enemy and enact its will in that world, were also assumptions that were already in evidence in the administration's first reactions to the attacks and would not shift thereafter. When Bush told his senior advisors in a meeting on the night of September 11 that "we have to force countries to choose," his unstated assumption was that United States was an actor with the power to compel such a choice, and that the rest of the world was made up of countries that could be compelled. That the attacks were acts of war that required a forceful response was an unquestioned assumption within the Bush administration from the moment they occurred, and one that arose at least in part from personal emotion and experience as well as rational calculation. Bush liked to open every cabinet meeting with a prayer, and when on September 14, 2001, he asked Donald Rumsfeld to lead it, among other things the defense secretary prayed for "patience to measure our lust for action."[4]

On September 13, 2001, Bush told a reporter how he saw the United States after 9/11 and understood the events of the previous days. "Make no mistake about it, this nation is sad," he said. "But we're also tough and resolute. And now is an opportunity to do generations a favor, by coming together and whipping terrorism; hunting it down, finding them, and holding them accountable. The nation must understand, this is now the focus of my administration . . . now that war has been declared on us, we will lead the world to victory." When Bush met with King Abdullah of Jordan on September 28, 2001, he described the feelings of Americans as he saw them at that point, but perhaps also his own: "Our nation is still somewhat sad," he said. "But we're angry. There's a certain level of blood lust, but we won't let it drive our reaction . . . We're steady, clear-eyed, and patient . . . but pretty soon we'll have to start displaying scalps." As Colin Powell reported (in the words of Bob Woodward) in the days after the attacks "Bush was tired of rhetoric. The president wanted to kill somebody."[5]

On September 11 itself, the first thoughts of many senior members of the Bush administration were about Iraq. Just minutes after being evacuated from his Pentagon office Paul Wolfowitz told aides that he suspected Iraqi involvement in the attacks. At 2:40 p.m. on that day, Donald Rumsfeld met with his staff in the building's operation center with the dust and smoke from the attacks still apparent in the room. One of Rumsfeld's aides noted that in this meeting the secretary raised the prospect of war with Iraq in response to the attacks. "Hit S.H. [Saddam Hussein] @ same time—not only UBL [Usama bin Laden]," the aide recorded Rumsfeld suggesting. Rumsfeld asked a Pentagon lawyer to discuss with Paul Wolfowitz Iraq's "connection with UBL." Meeting with Bush's war cabinet the following day, Rumsfeld asked whether the attacks did not present an "opportunity" to go to war in Iraq.[6] The next day, Bush himself ordered his counterterrorism chief Richard Clarke to "see if Saddam did this. See if he's linked in any way." When Clarke responded, "But Mr. President, al Qaeda did this," Bush said "I know, I know, but . . . see if Saddam was involved. Just look. I want to know any shred." Six days after the attacks Bush told his national security team "I believe Iraq was involved."[7]

In conflating Iraq and al Qaeda, U.S. leaders were drawn to false conclusions about not only the nature of the threats confronting them, but also the appropriate responses. U.S. military thinking was bounded by the entrenched culture of preparedness for interstate war. Having a hammer, every threat facing the administration looked like a nail. Thus it was that Donald Rumsfeld argued for war against Iraq after 9/11 in part because Afghanistan lacked a large number of "good targets" amenable to being destroyed by the kinds of weapons in the U.S. arsenal. Bush told Bob Woodward that in the days following September 11,

Rumsfeld was actively advocating for a war of global scope and seeking places other than Afghanistan to demonstrate U.S. military power, not least to convey the impression of global war to the American people. "Don, wisely—and I agreed with this—was looking for other places where we could show the war on terror was global," Bush said. "He was the man who was insistent upon boots on the ground to change the psychology of how Americans viewed war."[8] Rumsfeld's perspective on the military response to 9/11 seems to have been animated by a desire to choose an enemy to match the military's capabilities, rather than bringing the most appropriate means of statecraft to bear against the enemy who had actually carried out the attacks. When after raising the idea of attacking Iraq Rumsfeld was told that there was no evidence pointing to an Iraqi role in the terrorist attacks and that the likely perpetrators were in Afghanistan, Rumsfeld's response was "I don't want to put a million-dollar missile on a five-dollar tent."[9]

Despite immediate differences about whether Iraq should be a first target in the war on terror, the members of Bush's National Security Council (NSC) did share an array of core assumptions about Iraq. At the NSC meeting shortly after 9/11 in which Rumsfeld raised the possibility of attacking Iraq, Powell disagreed, saying the focus should be on al Qaeda. However, as Bob Woodward describes the meeting, there was nevertheless a broad consensus over goals and means; the key difference was over timing. "Everyone at the table," Woodward writes, "believed Iraqi President Saddam Hussein was a menace, a leader bent on acquiring and perhaps using weapons of mass destruction. Any serious, full-scale war against terrorism would have to make Iraq a target—eventually."[10]

Thus, in the days immediately after 9/11, a number of powerful and essentially unquestioned consensus assumptions had already become entrenched among the president and his advisers. That the use of military force should form the primary U.S. response was first among these; questions about where, when, and how force should be used were more intensely debated, but that the United States was going to war does not seem to have been a point of protracted discussion among the president and his advisers. Whether Iraq should be among the first targets in the war was discussed at length, but the fact that this was considered at all, and that even among those who opposed going to war with Iraq the issue was not if, but when, suggest assumptions worthy of some interrogation, given that there was no evidence that Iraq was involved in the attacks.

At least part of the reason for this immediate focus on Iraq can be explained by Robert Jervis' observation that "Perceptions are influenced by immediate concerns ('evoked sets') as well as by more deeply rooted expectations. A person will perceive and interpret what is at the front of his mind." Many international issues came and went over the course of the 1990s, but Iraq remained in the foreground of American foreign policy throughout the entire decade. In the years since the end of the 1991 Gulf War, U.S. and allied pilots patrolling the two large no-fly zones over Iraq had entered Iraqi airspace some 150,000 times. They had been targeted by Iraqi radar on hundreds of occasions and had dropped hundreds of munitions on Iraqi targets. Weapons inspections, discussions in the United Nations Security Council, "Oil for Food," threats of force and uses of force—year after year, Iraq never left the American agenda. It was a glaring, unsolved issue in a region of vital concern, and Saddam Hussein was the most obvious and most defiant enemy of the United States in the world. Iraq was America's "evoked set" on the morning of September 11, 2001, so perhaps it should not be surprising that officials of the Bush administration—and the American public more generally—immediately thought of Iraq as they sought to understand the causes of the terrorist attacks. Nor should it be surprising, for the same reason, that a group of officials and an entire society for whom the evoked set after 9/11 had become "terrorism" should see terrorists everywhere, including in Iraq. It is worth noting that neoconservatives in the Bush administration who had focused much of their energy in recent years on the threat posed by Iraq were not alone in finding confirmation for their fears in 9/11 and an explanation for 9/11 in their prior concerns. Opponents of corporate globalization quickly identified the terrorist attacks as examples of the costs of globalization and the backlash against it. Jerry Falwell, who had argued for many years against America's social liberalism and gay rights in particular, saw in 9/11 divine retribution for these sins. Anti-Semites claimed that the attacks were the result of a Jewish conspiracy. As Jervis suggests, "People perceive incoming information in terms of the problems they are dealing with and what is on their minds when the information is received."[11]

Jervis argues further that "the process of drawing inferences in light of logic and past experience that produces rational cognitive consistency also causes people to fit incoming information into preexisting beliefs and to perceive what they expect to be there." Ole Holsti has demonstrated, for example, that John Foster Dulles accepted without much skepticism information about the economic failings of the Soviet Union that corresponded to his established views, but required contrary evidence to be overwhelming before he would take it seriously.[12]

Jervis argues that "this means not only that when a statesman has developed a certain image of another country he will maintain that view in the face of large amounts of discrepant information, but also that the general expectations and rules entertained by the statesman about the links between other states' situations and characteristics on the one hand and their foreign policy intentions on the other hand influence the images of others that he will come to hold." Thus the leaders of democratic states will be quicker to see hostile intentions in the actions of dictators than in those of the leaders of other democracies.[13]

Jervis could easily have been writing about the Bush administration's claims of Iraqi connections with al Qaeda in 2002, or its claims that the country was heading toward stability in late 2003, or its argument that Iraq was not in the throes of a sectarian civil war in 2005, when he referred to cases in which "evidence is being ignored, misremembered, or twisted to preserve old ideas. Instead of the correct perception of facts that are clear in retrospect, we find strained interpretations and tortuous arguments." But in addition to making immediate judgments on the basis of unquestioned assumptions and worldviews, in the Bush administration this tendency was eventually institutionalized in a process of intelligence gathering and analysis that seemed intentionally designed to find information supportive of an existing ideology. "Ignoring discrepant information or assimilating it to preexisting beliefs will perpetuate inaccurate images and maintain unsatisfactory policies," Jervis has written. But since policy makers operate in a world of complex, incomplete, and often contradictory information, established worldviews are necessary and indeed desirable to the extent that they allow national leaders to make sense of this complexity and guide policy with vision along a coherent path. Real problems arise, Jervis suggests, "only when the assimilation of incoming information involves violations of generally agreed-upon rules for treating evidence." This seems to have been the case in the Bush administration, when institutional processes for intelligence analysis were systematically short-circuited by a small group of individuals who shared a set of beliefs and oriented the entire national security bureaucracy to prove they were correct and create policy around them.[14]

Planning for War in Iraq: Individual Values and Group Identity

Similarly, Jervis might have been writing about the Bush administration's assumption that Iraq possessed weapons of mass destruction when he wrote that "If a decision-maker thinks that an event yields self-evident and unambiguous inferences when in fact these inferences are drawn because of his pre-existing views, he will grow too confident of his views and will prematurely exclude alternatives because he will conclude that the event provides independent support for his beliefs. People frequently fail to realize that evidence that is consistent with their hypothesis may also be consistent with other views." Bush and his advisors simply failed to seriously examine the other motivations that might have driven Saddam Hussein to refuse to reveal the absence of WMDs in Iraq, because the assumption that they were there was so deeply entrenched in the internal decision-making culture of the administration that it was not open to serious question.[15]

Jeffrey Record argues that while Bush was not personally dedicated to the ideological agenda of the neoconservatives before 9/11, the terrorist attacks caused him to embrace these ideas with a passion, and that it was this conversion more than any other single cause that led to the choice of war in Iraq. As an account in the *National Journal* put it, after 9/11 Bush "borrow[ed] wholesale from neoconservative arguments about how the United States should reposition itself in the world and use its unprecedented power." Robert Jervis has argued that seizing upon these ideas was akin to a religious conversion for Bush, that "Bush's transformation after September 11 may parallel his earlier religious conversion: just as coming to Christ gave meaning to his previously dissolute personal life, so the war on terrorism has become the defining characteristic of his foreign policy and his sacred mission." Many of the leading officials in the Bush administration were dedicated believers in neoconservative principles before 9/11, but it is not clear that the president was, or that he had any well-developed worldview regarding foreign affairs at all. The 9/11 attacks created a sudden and urgent need for a coherent intellectual framework to describe the world and prescribe the appropriate ends and means for action within it. The administration needed such a framework both because it required a coherent rationale upon which to base its public arguments for policy, but more fundamentally because as individuals and as a group, the president and his advisors needed an intellectually coherent plan for action in order to be able to act at all. Though the president may not have been a neoconservative true believer before the 9/11 attacks, neoconservatism as an ideology was close at hand, consistent with his existing opinions and attitudes, and actively being advocated by a significant number of his advisors. Whether the president or the public would have accepted the neoconservative foreign policy agenda as they did without the 9/11 attacks is an open question. On the basis of what did occur, however, it can fairly be said that ideas mattered in creating policy in this case, but that their particular effects were determined both by the content of the ideas themselves, and also by the historical moment in which social and political conditions allowed them to come to define policy. It cannot be said that neoconservative ideas by themselves controlled history at this moment, but rather that the convergence of these ideas with a particular set of historical circumstances brought them to the fore and caused them to become the intellectual framework for policy in the years that followed.[16]

Bush loathed the very idea of doubt in the face of adversity. "I know it is hard for you to believe," he told Bob Woodward, "but I have not doubted what we're doing . . . There is no doubt in my mind we're doing the right thing. Not one doubt." When Rice told Bush in the early weeks of the Afghan war that there was some "hand-wringing" among his advisors about the failure of the Taliban regime to collapse, Woodward reports that Bush "jerked forward . . . He hated, absolutely hated the very idea, especially in tough times." "A president has got to be the calcium in the backbone," Bush told Woodward. "If I weaken, the whole team weakens. If I'm doubtful, I can assure you there will be a lot of doubt. If my confidence level in our ability declines, it will send ripples throughout the whole organization. I mean, it's essential that we be confident and determined and united . . . I don't need people around me who are not steady . . . And if there's kind of a hand-wringing attitude going on when times are tough, I don't like it."[17]

In an interview on August 2, 2002, Bush told Woodward that his attitudes toward the world were deeply connected to a sense of moral mission, that they were not strictly rational or calculated but personal and emotional. "I loath Kim Jong Il," Bush shouted at Woodward. "I've got a visceral reaction to this guy, because he is starving his people. And I have seen intelligence of these prison camps—they're huge—that he uses to break up families, and to torture people . . . it appalls me . . . It is visceral. Maybe it's my religion, maybe it's my—but I feel passionate about this . . . And I feel that way about the people of Iraq, by the way . . . there is a human condition we must worry about." The United States, he said, was in a "unique position right now. We are the leader . . . we're never going to get people all in agreement about force and use of force . . . But action—confident action that will yield positive results provides kind of a slipstream into which reluctant nations and leaders can get behind and show themselves that there has been—you know, something positive has happened toward peace." Woodward concluded that Bush's "vision clearly include[d] an ambitious reordering of the world through preemptive and, if necessary, unilateral action to reduce suffering and bring peace."[18]

At least according to accounts published thus far, Bush's moral certainty about his course of action never seems to have wavered throughout the march to war from 2001–2003. Powell, Bob Woodward notes, thought it was clear that "the president was convinced it was both 100 percent correct and moral" to go to war in Iraq. Bush himself seems to have had few doubts, or at least not to have expressed them. He did note that one "meaningful moment" for him came in a meeting with Rice and Elie Wiesel in late February, 2003, when Wiesel said to him "It's a moral issue. In the name of morality, how can you not intervene?" Bush claimed that he saw this as a "confirming moment. I said to myself, Gosh, if Elie Wiesel feels this way, who knows the pain and suffering and agony of tyranny, then others feel that way too. And so I am not alone."[19]

Bush deplored the concept of "nuance," even the word itself. On one occasion when he heard Rice use the term with a visiting diplomat, Bush added with an air of disdain that "nuance is a word that we use in foreign policy." Powell's deputy Richard Armitage, having seen Bush's distaste at the word, learned to substitute "hurdle" or "problem" or any other term instead. When he saw lines in his draft speeches in which diplomatic language seemed to be trying to obscure or soften a point, Bush would aggressively challenge his speechwriters about why it was not more clearly, strongly stated. "What the hell does that mean," he would ask. "Who wants to own up to it?" Robert Draper has argued that the inclusion of the statement "We will make no distinction between the terrorists who committed these acts and those who harbor them" in Bush's address to Congress in the week after 9/11 reflected his personal desire to find moral clarity at the expense of subtlety or nuance. This attitude permeated deeply into the culture of Bush's inner circle of foreign policy advisors. Equivocation, moderation, or uncertainty were equated with weakness, suggesting a lack of moral fiber. As Rice put it to a group of reporters, the administration's attitude was that "nuance isn't always good when you're talking about terror and bad regimes—nuance is not a good thing."[20]

Related to this drive to find moral certainty and banish subtle distinctions, Draper argues that optimism and a belief in his own personal power to overcome hardship were fundamental elements of Bush's personality. He had overcome business failures, dependence on alcohol, political defeats, and the monumental challenge of the

9/11 crisis. He saw questioning as wavering, doubting as weakness, indicative of a lack of moral clarity. He believed that he and those around him should make decisions and then stick with them—which meant no "hand-wringing," no skepticism, especially in public. Public departures from the administration's message were a betrayal of loyalty, and loyalty was an expression of that same moral certitude that Bush valued above all other virtues. As the war dragged on and became increasingly unpopular, however, Draper suggests that in the eyes of advisors "Bush's optimism grew less reflexive and more self-consciously determined. Aides heard it from him, time and again: 'It takes an optimistic person to lead.' 'Who's going to follow a leader who says, "Follow me, things are going to get worse"?' 'I'm the calcium in the backbone.'"[21]

Bush said about his days at Yale, at the height of the cold war and Vietnam War, that "I used to always wonder about people who always worried about nuclear war, trying to imagine what it would be like to walk around thinking, 'A bomb's gonna hit.' I always try to enjoy myself. I never try to be so heavy that I can't see the bright side. I'm an optimist . . . Only later, the more I heard about how the Vietnam War was conducted, the more disillusioned I got. It was more of the fact that the soldiers weren't allowed to fight. We put people in harm's way, and it was a political war."[22]

Drawing on this understanding of history, Bush's personality inclined him toward an approach to the management of the Iraq war that stressed both the autonomy of the military, unwavering support for policy decisions that had been made, and loyalty and dedication to the mission of the group among the advisors who surrounded him. Bush did not seek to micromanage military policy in Iraq, but he also did not manage the process of oversight of the war among his advisors in a way that encouraged, or indeed tolerated, open and honest assessment and critical introspection. In interviews with Draper, Cheney, Bremer, Card, Rice, and Hadley all noted that U.S. military commanders in their regular video conferences never said that they needed more troops. This was taken within the administration to mean that despite media reports to the contrary, the war was not going badly, that things were OK. In fact what it may have indicated is that the ironclad refusal to reconsider decisions or brook internal dissent at the top levels of the administration permeated well down into the military bureaucracy. The administration's approach to internal criticism was not to address the problem being identified but to obscure it by eliminating or questioning the loyalty of the critic, and this tendency toward an enforced orthodoxy around established ideas and policies seems to have become even more rigid as the problems in Iraq mounted and external criticism increased. White House Chief of Staff Josh Bolten, Rice, and her deputy, Robert Blackwill, all commented to Draper that they found the regular military briefings repetitive and seemingly intended to reaffirm the president's sense of the military's loyalty to the mission. "Mr. President, let me just say that the men and women of your armed forces have the greatest confidence in this mission," they would begin, leading Blackwill to mutter to Rice that it was "the same briefing—it's like *Groundhog Day*."[23]

On the rare occasions when outside critics had access to the Bush administration and expressed their dissent, it tended to be summarily dismissed. On January 5, 2006, 13 former secretaries of state and defense were invited to meet with the president and be briefed on the war in Iraq in a one hour meeting. After the briefing, about 15 minutes were left for discussion, much of which was occupied with complimentary comments by Melvin Laird and George Schultz. When Madeleine Albright finally suggested that the Iraq was damaging U.S. alliances and distracting the administration from other concerns such as China and Iran, Bush said "I can't let this comment stand." His administration could walk and chew gum at the same time, he said, and shortly thereafter the former secretaries were shepherded out for a photo opportunity, from which the president quickly departed. A number of the participants were left to "marvel at the encounter's thorough lack of substance."[24]

The failure of the Bush administration to critically review and reassess policy in Iraq in the first years of the war was a result of the ideology and identity constructs that held sway within the administration, expressed and operationalized through a policy process in which questioning established policies or consensus assumptions was equated with disloyalty. This kind of dysfunctional decision making process was not unique to the Bush administration; as Irving Janis and other authors have noted, it is a risk for all groups in which shared belief systems and investment in a set of policies create strong pressure for group cohesion around those ideas. In a sense, for Bush and his advisors, a particular set of shared beliefs and policy choices were the identity of the group; they defined its history and purpose, and comprised the set of interests that its members had in common, so any challenge to those values and choices risked being seen as an attack on the group's identity itself. Janis notes that this is typical of group decision making, and has argued that these factors can give rise to what he famously termed "Groupthink"—"a mode of thinking that people engage in when they are deeply involved in a cohesive in-group, when the members' strivings for unanimity override their motivation to realistically appraise alternative courses of action." A dominant characteristic of Groupthink, according to Janis, is the tendency of group members to remain "loyal to the group by sticking with the decisions to which the group has committed itself, even when the policy is working badly and has unintended consequences that disturb the conscience of the members. In a sense, members consider loyalty to the group the highest form of morality."[25]

't Hart, Stern, and Sundelius have argued that a small group can become an emotional refuge for leaders, a place where they know they are surrounded by like-minded colleagues who share their values and are working for the same goals. Their political destinies are connected, and they each have a firsthand understanding of the predicaments they face, which is not shared by the outside world. The group can become a site of emotional support, but of course this role may render the group unable to also be a place where alternative views are invited and thoroughly vetted, where self-critical questioning of assumptions can occur. "One important function of high-level bodies of government . . . is to articulate and embody the core values and norms advocated by the chief executive, the organization as a whole, or the prevailing policy paradigm . . . The need to project and maintain dominant beliefs and values also plays out in the group setting itself . . . The group effectively becomes a kind of 'psychic prison' for its members."[26]

Janis argues that "the more amiability and esprit de corps among the members of a policy-making in-group, the greater is the danger that independent critical thinking will be replaced by groupthink, which is likely to result in irrational and dehumanizing actions directed against out-groups." The group of senior officials and advisors who surrounded Bush in the first years of his administration was not marked by particularly amiable relations among all of its members—the bureaucratic tension and bad blood between Powell and Armitage on the one hand and Rumsfeld and Cheney on the other now seems clear. But once Powell and his supporters had been marginalized, what was left was a core of advisors who shared a deeper ideological kinship, and a political allegiance to one another of longer standing, than any group of U.S. leaders in recent memory, perhaps any in history. In particular, Rumsfeld and Cheney had a close and mutually supportive political relationship that spanned decades, and surrounded themselves with subordinates in Wolfowitz, Feith, Libby, and others who held a uniform, cohesive and fully articulated view of the world that brooked little dissent. Condoleezza Rice seems to have viewed her role as confidante to the president rather than advocate for an alternative foreign policy vision to counter the neoconservatives; she accepted their policy conclusions in any case. In Bush, Cheney and Rumsfeld found a president who seems to have had broad instincts tending toward a nationalistic, moralistic foreign policy in the image of Ronald Reagan, but lacked a fully integrated and refined world-view. In the aftermath of September 11, Cheney, Rumsfeld, and their cohort offered a coherent ideology to fill this void, and their vision of American foreign policy came to dominate administration thinking so thoroughly as to admit no dispute or criticism at all. In this respect Janis' suggestion that the tighter the group the more extreme the effects of Groupthink seems confirmed in this case.[27]

Bush reported being told by a European leader that the best way to hold together the international coalition in the Afghan war was to be open to the views of other states, to listen and be responsive. Bush reported he had dismissed this view, saying "my belief is the best way that we hold this coalition together is to be clear on our objectives and to be clear that we are determined to achieve them. You hold a coalition together by strong leadership and that's what we intend to provide." In Bush's view, leadership was a product of moral certainty and forceful, resolute actions, not endless diplomatic dithering. Others would be drawn in not by America's willingness to listen but by its sense of purpose, its conviction that it was right and its determination to act, alone if necessary. According to Woodward, Bush believed that he was "an agent for change," that it should be his role to "state a new strategic direction for policy with bold, clear moves. And because it would be the policy of the United States, the only superpower, the rest of the world would have to move over, would adjust over time." He modeled himself on Lincoln, he said, recognizing that "The job of the president is to unite a nation to achieve big objectives." "The job of the President," Bush told Robert Draper in an interview, "is to think strategically so that you can accomplish big objectives. As opposed to playing mini-ball. You can't play mini-ball with the influence we have and expect there to be peace. You've got to think, think BIG."[28]

Rice also said she believed that Bush saw himself as a reformer, a president who would change the world and let history judge his actions, but who would not accept being seen as reactive or a mere caretaker of the status quo. She saw him in the mold of Harry Truman, recognizing the dangers facing the United States and using American power to confront them and reshape the international system in the bargain. "I will seize the opportunity to achieve big goals" Bush said, and "there is nothing bigger than to achieve world peace." In February 2007,

Bush told Robert Draper "I truly believe we're in the process of shaping history for the good. I know, I firmly believe, that the decisions I have made were necessary to secure the country . . . I made the decision to lead. And therefore there'll be times when you make those decisions—one, it makes you unpopular; two, it makes people accuse you of unilateral arrogance. And that may be true." As one Bush adviser told journalist Ron Susskind, the administration's attitude was that the skeptics and critics beyond the White House walls lived "in what we call the reality-based community" in which people "believe that solutions emerge from your judicious study of discernible reality . . . [but] we're an empire now, and when we act, we create our own reality. And while you're studying that reality—judiciously, as you will—we'll act again, creating other new realities, which you can study too, and that's how things will sort out. We're history's actors, and you, all of you, will be left to just study what we do."[29]

Janis suggests that among the symptoms of groupthink are "an illusion of invulnerability . . . which creates excessive optimism and encourages taking extreme risks," "an unquestioned belief in the group's inherent morality," which leads "the members to ignore the ethical or moral consequences of their decisions," and "stereotyped views of enemy leaders as too evil to warrant genuine attempts to negotiate, or as too weak and stupid to counter whatever risky attempts are made to defeat their purposes." The consequences of these tendencies are "incomplete survey of alternatives . . . incomplete survey of objectives . . . failure to examine risks of preferred choice . . . selective bias in processing information at hand [and] . . . failure to work out contingency plans." As Vertzberger puts it, "Decision-making groups that . . . believe in the superior capabilities of their members due to their past achievements ('the best and the brightest'), or have faith that they are being guided by some divine power, will develop a sense of invulnerability and be more prone than other decision-making groups to take risky decisions." Janis notes that such a sense of 'unlimited confidence' was pervasive among the "New Frontiersmen" of the Kennedy administration. According to a confidant of Robert Kennedy at the Justice Department, decision making about the Bay of Pigs invasion was marked by a feeling among the president's advisors that "with John Kennedy leading us and with all the talent he had assembled, nothing could stop us. We believed that if we faced up to the nation's problems and applied bold, new ideas with common sense and hard work we would overcome whatever challenged us."[30]

On March 19, 2003, after giving the command for war, Bush went for a long, solitary walk around the White House grounds. "I prayed as I walked around the circle," he said later. "Going into this period, I was praying for the strength to do God's will . . . I pray that I be as good a messenger of His will as possible." When asked whether he spoke to his father about matters of policy, Bush said that "he is the wrong father to appeal to . . . there is a higher father that I appeal to." Bush was a devout Christian, who said many times that his foreign policy principles were intended to serve the will of God, that God had placed him in the presidency for a purpose, that the United States in its war on terror was fighting evil with God on its side. From this perspective, it follows that whatever hardships might be faced along the way, a foreign policy blessed by divine support must ultimately be destined to succeed. Given this aspect of Bush's personality, it seems possible that the kind of undue confidence Janis refers to may have been underpinned by a spiritual belief system in Bush's case. Walter Hixson has argued that Bush "sincerely believed it was the nation's mission, under God, to 'rid the world of evil' by invading the Middle East and bolstering the biblical land of Israel. Bush, like Woodrow Wilson, backed by substantial public consent, believed in these words; he thus internalized the discourse that drove the nation's militant interventionism."[31]

It is possible that Bush and his advisors understood themselves to be on the side of history, invulnerable due to the superiority of their ideas or the favor of divine providence. Janis writes that "An important symptom of groupthink is the illusion of being invulnerable to the main dangers that might arise from a risky action in which the group is strongly tempted to engage. Essentially, the notion is that 'If our leader and everyone else in our group decides that it is okay, the plan is bound to succeed. Even if it is quite risky, luck will be on our side.'"[32]

Jervis writes that individuals will also tend to "spread apart" alternatives after a decision has been reached, coming to see the rejected options as really much worse than they had understood at the time of the initial decision, and to view the selected alternative as really much better than was known at the time. And as the costs of a policy rise, the increasing investment may come to be seen as itself justifying continuation along the same path. This seems particularly likely to be true in cases of war, when the costs of policy are far greater than in other circumstances because they are measured not just in dollars but in human lives. "Their sacrifice must not have been in vain" is not in fact a reasonable justification for continuing a wrongheaded policy, but it is often represented as if it were one. "The costs of war," Jervis asserts, "can lead to an increased evaluation of winning and/or an overestimation of the probability of success." Thus there develops a fallacy that what is regarded as necessary is therefore also possible, and that past sacrifices raise the stakes of current decisions and thus justify future sacrifices. This kind of thinking is apparent in the Bush administration's arguments about Iraq. In an interview with Robert Draper, for example, Bush said "I'm driven a lot by—in my mind exists many of the conversations I've had with families. It's replayed quite often. About making sure that their child is not, their memory is not—that the sacrifice is *worth* something, that it's *worth* something going in, that it's *worth* it to promote democracy, that it's *worth* it to see it through. And I feel the same way."[33]

Janis suggests that a sense of invulnerability often goes hand in hand with a decisionmaking group's construction of the identity of itself and the international Others it has identified as enemies or rivals. "We are a strong group of good guys who will win in the end," the in-group self-construction dictates, and conversely, "our opponents are stupid, weak, bad guys." "One of the symptoms of groupthink is the members' persistence in conveying to each other the cliché and oversimplified images of political enemies embodied in long-standing ideological stereotypes." Janis notes that the dominant view of Fidel Castro within the Kennedy administration at the time of the Bay of Pigs invasion was as a "weak, 'hysteric' leader whose army was ready to defect; he was considered so stupid that 'although warned by air strikes, he would do nothing to neutralize the Cuban underground.'"[34]

The same psychological dynamic seems to have been at work within the Bush administration, where the capabilities of the Iraqi military and the effectiveness of any likely resistance to the U.S. occupation were consistently and repeatedly dismissed. Saddam's regime was assumed to be "brittle," unpopular within Iraq and therefore inherently unstable once the mechanisms of brutality and fear through which it maintained its authority were undermined. In discussions with Franks on January 9, 2002, Rumsfeld asked a question that seemed almost to answer itself: "If dozens of key targets could be destroyed simultaneously, would that put pressure on the regime, cause it to crumble and preclude the need for a long war requiring a large force?" Within the administration the dominant image of the Ba'athist regime in Iraq was that of an empty shell, outwardly solid but so corrupt within that it would quickly collapse under pressure, perhaps minimal pressure. This understanding implied an image of the Iraqi people as well, which suggested that they were so deeply hostile to Saddam's government that they would view an attack by a foreign power as an opportunity to overthrow him rather than rallying behind him, that they would view the United State as an ally against a common enemy—the government of Iraq—rather than as a foreign threat to Iraq's independence.[35]

Franks further clarified the military's assumptions about the war and image of Iraq as a country when he briefed Rumsfeld on ongoing war planning on January 17, 2002. His briefing focused on Iraq's conventional military assets, which Franks noted had been diluted by years of sanctions to the point of severely limiting their offensive capabilities. The Republican Guard was 15 percent smaller than it had been in 1991, the regular army 35 percent smaller. The Iraqi air force had 60 percent fewer aircraft than it had in the first Gulf War. The Iraqi navy had gone from being "a joke" to being essentially nonexistent. Franks' discussion did not focus on the prospect of irregular or guerilla war; he suggested that the U.S. military expected to fight a conventional war of maneuver much as it had done in 1991, and that under this scenario its military advantages were immense.[36]

Franks also discussed the expected response of the Iraqi people to a U.S. invasion, saying that the Iraqi population was likely to support the U.S. invasion once it became clear that the United States was sincerely committed to the goal of overthrowing Saddam. "The more the U.S. became involved, the less the people of Iraq would support the regime," Franks said. Bob Woodward claims, however, that this conclusion "was based less on solid intelligence from inside Iraq than assumptions about how people *should* feel toward a ruthless dictator. The paucity of U.S. human intelligence sources inside Iraq meant evidence about Iraqi popular opinion or likely reaction to an American invading force was thin." U.S. planning assumed that the Iraqi military would surrender en masse, that whole units of significant size—battalions or even brigades—would put down their weapons and give up, at which point they would be placed in military POW camps. At an NSC meeting on March 12, Feith had told the president that the postwar plan was to "not immediately demobilize all the people and put them on the street, but use them as a reconstruction force." Three to five regular army residual divisions would form the core of a new army, depoliticized and subject to civilian control. The assumptions underlying these plans seem to have been derived from the experience of the first Gulf War, in which large numbers of Iraqi troops did surrender to U.S. and allied forces, and from CIA estimates that whole units might do the same this time.[37]

But in the first Gulf War, even when Iraqi forces had in fact surrendered in significant numbers, there was not a single instance of a whole brigade or division surrendering en masse. The expectation, shared by the CIA and U.S. military, that this would occur in this instance seems to have been based largely on wishful thinking and unquestioned assumptions about American identity as understood by Iraqis. As Gordon and Trainor put it, "At CENTCOM, the plan was to use members of the Iraqi Regular Army who had capitulated to control the country's borders and take on other tasks that the overstretched allied troops would be faced with . . . Rarely has a military plan depended on such a bold assumption. The Bush administration was not only confident that it would quickly defeat the Iraqi military but also counted on Iraqi forces to work under American supervision and even to help police the occupation."[38] Rice said that "the concept was that we would defeat the army, but the institutions would hold, everything from ministries to police forces . . . You would be able to bring new leadership but we were going to keep the body in place." When Iraqi forces simply went home rather than surrendering, the large pool of manpower that American planners had expected to be waiting in prison camps to be used for reconstruction did not materialize.[39]

While the administration did focus much of its attention on the possibility of the Iraqi military using chemical or biological weapons, it did not anticipate the possibility of a sustained guerilla insurgency. Bush said that "The idea of Zarqawi fomenting sectarian violence—he was successful in doing that, which is something we didn't spend a lot of time planning for. We planned for what happens if Saddam and his people dug into Baghdad." This conclusion was derived from a number of core assumptions about American and Iraqi identity that drove the administration's operative ideology. Bush and his advisors appear to have accepted the argument that sectarian divisions in Iraq had been largely created by Saddam Hussein's regime for its own purposes, in Bush's words, "to create a sense of need for a strong central state and to keep people off balance." Most critically, they also believed that the United States would be seen by Iraqis as it saw itself—as a force for liberation and democracy, rather than an imperial occupier.[40]

In this case, cognitive dissonance seems to have worked hand in hand with the administration's sense of American power and the enemy's weakness, and the political premium placed on "steadfastness," the need to avoid being seen to "flip-flop" on issues. Jervis describes cognitive dissonance as the state that exists when two seemingly contradictory pieces of information appear to an individual to be true at the same time: "two elements are in a dissonant relation if, considering the two alone, the obverse of one element would follow from the other." Without necessarily consciously acknowledging they are doing so, human beings will shape their mental systems of belief and knowledge to avoid such contradictions. Two hypotheses describe this process: "1. The existence of dissonance, being psychologically uncomfortable, will motivate the person to try to reduce dissonance and achieve consonance. 2. When dissonance is present, in addition to trying to reduce it, the person will actively avoid situations and information which would likely increase the dissonance."[41]

Political leaders understand that they are expected to show the courage of their convictions, to make tough decisions and then stick with them. This social and political dynamic reinforces and is reinforced by the tendency of all individuals to try to maintain cognitive consistency, to believe that their understanding of the world is correct and seek information with bolsters this view and discard that which does not. This process of doubting and deemphasizing discrepant information and seeking consonant information is known as "selective exposure." The emergence of cognitive dissonance due to exposure to dissonant information may actually come to make the individual hold his or her views even more strongly. Rather than learning from new information and altering his or her conclusions, the actor may become even more convinced of the correctness of the original position.[42]

Through this process, Jervis contends, "many crucial errors occur not because decision-makers arrive at the wrong answers, but because they ask the wrong questions. This often involves taking too many things for granted and failing to scrutinize basic assumptions." Whether because of the psychological discomfort of cognitive dissonance or other factors, this process clearly seems to have been at work within the Bush administration. Once the decision for war with Iraq was reached, both the premises of that decision and questions about the consequences flowing from it were simply closed to serious scrutiny or discussion within the president's group of top advisors. Even as it became clear that occupied Iraq was descending into chaos and open revolt, evidence of these facts was dismissed within the administration as distortions of reality by the liberal media. Within the president's circle of advisors, the premium placed on moral certainty and loyalty to the group and its decisions became, in effect, a resolute determination to refuse to acknowledge the realities of the eroding situation on the ground in Iraq. As George Packer has described it, the president and those closest to him "maintained an almost mystical confidence in American military power and an utter incuriosity about the details of its human consequences . . . The president had . . . been told what he wanted to hear—by his vice president and national security adviser, by his secretary of defense and his secretary's deputies, by Kanan Makiya and other exiles, by his ardent supporters in think tanks and the press, by his own faith in the universal human desire for freedom." The policy choices of Bush and his advisors were rooted in a firmly held and strongly shared ideology and set of identity constructions, and their response to the fact that these policies were failing was to simply write off, deny, and ignore the evidence that this was so.[43]

This was, Packer suggests, not simply because of the difficulty of changing a policy, but because for the president and those around him the war became a measure of themselves as well as their ideas and management skills. "Bush's war," Packer argues, "was run with his own absence of curiosity and self-criticism, his projection of absolute confidence, the fierce loyalty he bestowed and demanded. He always conveyed the impression that Iraq and the war on terror were personal tests. Every time a suicide bomber detonated himself, he was trying to shake George W. Bush's will. If Bush remained steadfast, how could America fail?"[44]

Jervis writes that "a person is less apt to reorganize evidence into a new theory or image if he is deeply committed to the established view. Commitment here means not only the degree to which the person's power and prestige are involved but also—and more importantly—the degree to which this way of seeing the world has proved satisfactory and has become internalized." In late 2003, as the occupation dragged on and violence seemed to gain momentum in Iraq, Powell thought that the administration had become increasingly isolated from outside criticism, unhealthily wedded to the path that had been chosen and the decisions that had been made. There was no one, Powell felt, who could push for a critical review of policy without having their own loyalty cast into doubt. As Bob Woodward put it, Powell thought that "now that Bush and the administration had to live with the consequences of their Iraq decisions, they were becoming dangerously protective of those decisions . . . There was no one in the White House would could break through to insist on a realistic reassessment . . . who could go to Bush and say, Pay attention, you're in trouble."[45]

James Thomson, who served on the National Security Council staff at the height of the Vietnam War, wrote in 1968 that the policies of the Johnson administration in Vietnam had been marked by what he termed the effect of "human ego investment." "Men who have participated in a decision develop a stake in that decision. As they participate in further, related decisions, their stake increases," Thomson noted. "To put it bluntly: at the heart of the Vietnam calamity is a group of able, dedicated men who have been regularly and repeatedly wrong—and whose standing with their contemporaries, and more important, with history, depends, as they see it, on being proven right. These are not men who can be asked to extricate themselves from error."[46]

Thomson's arguments about the social psychology of decision making and the dynamics of bureaucratic politics as explanations of the U.S. debacle in Vietnam were trenchant in their time, and unsettlingly accurate in describing the Bush administration's approach to Iraq. He wrote of "the banishment of real expertise" from decision making about Vietnam, the "replacement of experts, who were generally and increasingly pessimistic, by men described as 'can do guys.'" It is easy to see a parallel with the way in which the State Department's "Arabists," with training and experience in regional politics, culture, and language—and generally more skeptical about the Bush administration's plan for war in Iraq—were systematically excluded from planning for and participation in the occupation, at least initially. Thomson refers to the "domestication of dissenters" within the policy process, the practice by which dissident voices are allowed to occasionally express objections to the group's consensus but are then ignored and marginalized, leaving the sense that a diverse range of opinions have been entertained when they really have not. In this regard Thomson refers to George Ball, in-house critic of Lyndon Johnson's war in Vietnam, but could just as easily be describing Colin Powell and Richard Armitage, Bush's domesticated critics up until the point where their dissident views could no longer be tolerated. Even more damningly, Thomson describes the enabling effect of what he terms "Bureaucratic detachment" and "Crypto-racism" on Vietnam policy, noting that physical distance and racial identity constructions were necessary, if subconscious, factors operating within the minds of policy makers, without which they could not have contemplated violence of the kind and scale they carried out.[47] "In quiet, air conditioned, thick-carpeted rooms," Thomson writes,

> such terms as "systematic pressure," "armed reconnaissance," "targets of opportunity," and even "body count" seem to breed a sort of game theory detachment . . . which may have been compounded by a traditional Western sense that there are so many Asians, after all; that Asians have a fatalism about life and a disregard for its loss; that they are cruel and barbaric to their own people; and that they are very different from us (and all look alike?) . . . the upshot of such subliminal views is a subliminal question whether Asians, and particularly Asian peasants, and most particularly Asian communists, are really people—like you

> and me. To put the matter another way: would we have pursued quite such policies—and quite such military tactics—if the Vietnamese were white?[48]

There is no doubt that President Bush and his advisers recognized at an intellectual level that Iraqi civilians and even insurgents were human beings. But the administration's leaders were nevertheless able to implement the policies they did in part because they shared a constructed identity of the enemy as "terrorists" who were barbaric, brutal, duplicitous, and disdainful of human life, and they never had to confront firsthand the consequences of their choices for the enemy or Iraqi civilians because of the great physical distance at which these occurred. The effects of the war for Iraqis were for the most part abstractions to those orchestrating it in Washington, D.C., and this made possible an emotional separation from the human costs of the war, which in turn enabled it to be carried out.

Among Bush's circle of advisors, how the United States was seen by its enemies abroad, and in particular how they as its leaders were seen, was a recurring source of concern. That they would not be taken seriously, or would be dismissed as unwilling to carry through on their threats, was regarded as a potentially grave problem. A consistent theme in the administration's discourse about America's world role was the belief that the United States was seen by its enemies as soft, weak, irresolute. Bush and his advisers would often refer derisively to the Clinton administration's bombing of al Qaeda targets from the air as "pounding sand," a practice that President Bush suggested to an interviewer had led America's enemies to view the United States as weak willed. "Launching a cruise missile into some guy's, you know, tent, really is a joke . . . people viewed that as the impotent America . . . a flaccid, you know, kind of technologically competent but not very tough country . . . I do believe there is the image of America out there that we are so materialistic, that we're almost hedonistic, that we don't have values, and then when struck, we wouldn't fight back. It was clear that bin Laden felt emboldened and didn't feel threatened by the United States." Bush would often repeat in private conversations and one-on-one interviews that he was concerned about the ways in which his words and actions would be seen at home and abroad; that he felt it was important not only to be firm and resolute but to appear this way to Americans and the world. He believed he had "a responsibility to show resolve," he told Bob Woodward. "I had to show the American people the resolve of a commander in chief that was going to do whatever to win.

No yielding, no equivocation. No, you know, lawyering this thing to death, that we're after 'em. And that was not only for domestic, for the people at home to see. It was also vitally important for the rest of the world to watch." Other world leaders were "watching my every move," he said, and "it's very important for them to come in this Oval Office . . . and me look them in the eye and say, 'You're either with us or against us." Bush believed that leadership that was strong and certain would create a "slipstream," drawing followers into its wake.[49]

Similarly, Cheney argued in a principals meeting on October 9, 2001 that U.S. policy needed to be driven by a recognition that the United States was, and must be seen around the world, as the preeminent global power. He argued that the administration should encourage its allies in the Northern Alliance to seize the Afghan capital of Kabul rather than wait and risk the appearance of a quagmire. "We as a superpower should not be stalemated," he said. Cheney believed, in Bob Woodward's words, "that other governments would not be willing to step up until they were convinced that the United States meant business. He agreed with Rumsfeld that they had to look people in the eye and say, This is going to happen." This view dovetailed with the long-standing neoconservative argument that the U.S. withdrawal from the Vietnam War, and subsequently from smaller conflicts in the Muslim world such as Lebanon and Somalia, had created a dangerous impression in the minds of America's enemies that while rich and technologically advanced, the United States did not have the stomach for a sustained fight and if bloodied, could be expected to retreat quickly. Thus, staying the course in Iraq became not simply a strategy toward final victory but in fact an end in itself; the United States needed to demonstrate that it was not a paper tiger, that it would not run when the costs of staying started to rise. But in its dedication to the principle of maintaining and demonstrating its commitment and will above all else, the Bush administration fell prey to the fallacy that steadfastness was all or nearly all that was required for victory, and that resolve should not be challenged by self-doubt or introspection. Thomson suggests that the same misconception was at work in the Johnson administration, where he argues policy failure arose in part from the belief that "Vietnam posed a fundamental test of America's national will . . . [that] all we needed was the will, and we would then prevail . . . [and that] those who doubted our role in Vietnam were said to shrink from the burdens of power, the obligations of power, the uses of power, the responsibility of power.[50]

Structural Assumptions about Iraqi Identity

On December 21, 2002, George Tenet and other CIA officials briefed the President, along with Rice and Cheney, on the case for weapons of mass destruction in Iraq. This was a much anticipated meeting, the occasion for the airing of the intelligence community's best estimate of Iraq's capabilities. The case presented was built almost entirely on circumstantial evidence and assumptions, with little really conclusive data. Bush was told that some 3,200 tons of precursor chemicals usable for making chemical weapons were unaccounted for, along with components for biological weapons and 6,000 shells dating to the 1980s. Photos were shown of what "appeared" to be an effort to clean up a spill at a documented chemical weapons site. Iraq was known to have unmanned aerial drones capable of flying within a 500-kilometer range, possibly capable of delivering chemical or biological weapons. The transcript of a radio message in which Republican Guard officers referred to "nerve agents" was presented. Bush was told that Saddam convened his top nuclear scientists frequently and had conversations with them that "implied" that work on a nuclear weapon might begin again soon. At the end of the presentation, Tenet declared that "it's a slam dunk case."[51]

Shared consensus assumptions about what Iraq was and who its leaders were led to conclusions about what they were likely to do, including the belief that the Iraqi government was continuing to develop weapons of mass destruction. These assumptions became so deeply entrenched within the Bush administration that they came to dominate policymaking without ever being methodically interrogated. Individuals often use identity constructions to reach conclusions about the motivations of others, but when they do, their judgments are frequently subject to what the social psychologist Lee D. Ross has referred to as the "fundamental attribution error," in which they attach motivations to fixed identity traits rather than particular circumstances more often than they would in understanding their own actions. Thus, if I arrive at work late I am liable to explain this to myself as a result of the fact that I overslept because I was especially tired or because my alarm clock did not go off. If my colleague arrives late I am more likely to attribute this to his cultural background or personality—his people have different attitudes toward punctuality, he's lazy or flighty—even though I would never use such factors to explain my own behavior. In the case of the Bush administration's decision making about Iraq, this kind of attribution error seems to have played an important role in shaping conclusions about what kind of war Iraqis would fight.[52]

The president and his advisors drew conclusions about the likely Iraqi response to a U.S. invasion based on their shared understanding of the national identity of Iraq as a society and the kind of regime that ruled it, including their sense of Saddam Hussein as an individual. They assumed that Iraq was a centralized state that would engage in the kind of war that states typically fought, but that the same kind of duplicity and immorality that had characterized Saddam's peacetime efforts to develop weapons of mass destruction would lead him to use these weapons in wartime. And they assumed that the Iraqi regime was so corrupt and repressive that it must be deeply unpopular with the Iraqi people, who would recognize the United States as what it understood itself to be—a force for liberation—and abandon the Iraqi government to support the American invasion force. These assumptions were apparent when, in Crawford, Texas on Friday, December 28, 2001, President Bush and his top foreign policy advisors were presented with a detailed plan for war in Iraq. Franks briefed the president and his advisors on the military's assumptions about the war, among which were the belief that "Iraq possessed WMD capacity, so the U.S. would have to plan to fight against it in a potentially contaminated battlefield." Vice president Cheney noted that "we're going to have to really look hard at how we protect ourselves against the use of weapons of mass destruction, both in the field as well as in the rear." At a meeting on January 9 to follow up on the Crawford meeting, Rumsfeld's first question for Franks was "what would be done if Iraq used weapons of mass destruction?" From the very start, planning for war with Iraq within the Bush administration proceeded from the premises that the primary goal of the war would be to remove Saddam Hussein from power—and therefore that Saddam's fall would constitute victory, by definition—and that the Iraqi government possessed WMDs and was likely to use them in combat. Rumsfeld told the Senate Armed Services Committee on September 19, 2002, that "Very likely all they need to complete a [nuclear] weapon is fissile material—and they are, at this moment, seeking that material—both from foreign sources and the capability to produce it indigenously." Cheney said on *Meet the Press* on March 16, 2003 that "We know [Saddam Hussein] has been absolutely devoted to trying to acquire nuclear weapons... And we believe he has, in fact, reconstituted nuclear weapons."[53]

The belief that Iraq possessed weapons of mass destruction and might give them to al Qaeda became a firmly held conviction within the Bush administration, despite the fact that there was, in retrospect, no solid evidence for this conclusion whatsoever. Numerous observers have reported that the depth of this certainty among some of Bush's advisors, and the way in which it moved among them and gained the status of unquestionable fact, seemed somehow pathological, like a virus that spread among hosts and took control of them. Robert Draper suggests that "the conviction that Saddam Hussein was an imminent threat to America and therefore necessitated removal by force began as a kind of communicable agent" within the Bush administration. Draper contends that Cheney, Libby, Wolfowitz, and Feith believed this well before September 11, but that after the attacks "the contagion swept through the Beltway and insinuated itself into the minds of many—including the White House national security adviser and the president of the United States." David Frum recalled that Dick Cheney had made a point of emphasizing concerns over the connections between states with weapons of mass destruction and terrorism in internal campaign discussions in the summer of 2000, soon after Cheney had joined the ticket. Cheney was worried about weapons of mass destruction even in Afghanistan, asking in a meeting on Tuesday, September 25, 2001 "can we do a good enough job of identifying targets in Afghanistan that relate to BW/CW," and arguing that "it should be a top priority." Colin Powell told Bob Woodward that he felt Cheney had "the fever," an "unhealthy fixation" with Iraq, and that with Cheney, "nearly every conversation or reference came back to al Qaeda and trying to nail the connection with Iraq . . . Powell thought that Cheney took intelligence and converted uncertainty and ambiguity into fact." When asked later about Cheney's role in the process of going to war, Bush said that "he's not feverish. Fever to me is this kind of delirious—He's in control. So, no. I felt a conviction." Karl Rove agreed with Powell though, telling Bob Woodward in an interview that Powell's characterization was right, that Cheney's focus on al Qaeda and Iraq was "a real fever."[54]

Even Powell, in the first term the administration's in-house dissenter, was convinced that Saddam did possess WMDs or at least the intent to develop them. He agreed with Cheney when the vice president argued "why in the world would he subject himself for all those years to U.N. sanctions and forgo an estimated $100 billion in oil revenue? It makes no sense!" In his February 5, 2003 address to the United Nations Security Council, Powell argued that "we know that Saddam Hussein is determined to keep his weapons of mass destruction; he's determined to make more." As for Iraq's links with terrorism, Powell claimed "ambition and hatred are enough to bring Iraq and al Qaeda together."[55]

Jervis's suggestion that individuals tend to "see the behavior of others as more centralized, planned, and coordinated than it is" perhaps offers some insight into the process by which the Bush administration came to conclude that Saddam Hussein's regime had links to al Qaeda. To see all unity in the hostile forces arrayed against the United States, to draw connections where no evidence of such connections exist, may be in part a function of the human mind's "drive to squeeze complex and unrelated events into a coherent pattern." If it is politically useful to do this, as it certainly was for the Bush administration, this does not necessarily mean that it was entirely cynical or insincere. Indeed, it seems likely that it was politically useful for the Bush administration precisely because it was cognitively useful for many Americans in exactly the same way it was for those making policy within the administration—it simplified a complex and threatening world in a way that attracted support because it was cognitively satisfying. It made sense, at a visceral if not an intellectual level; it was a coherent description of the world, it left no troubling loose ends demanding further explanation.[56]

"Coherence and consistency are further imposed on the world by the propensity of actors to see others as trying to maximize the same set of values in different situations and in different periods of time," Jervis argues. "This can be misleading when the other's decisions are the outcome of shifting interactions among conflicting forces and interests." U.S. leaders assumed that because Saddam Hussein had been developing and concealing weapons of mass destruction before, he must still be doing so, for the same reasons he had done it before. The belief that someone understood to be an enemy is implacably hostile is particularly difficult to dislodge. As Jervis suggests, "Some beliefs are especially resistant to change . . . the most important type of political image of this kind is the 'inherent bad faith model,' which can provide an explanation for almost any possible behavior the other may engage in. Hostility needs no special explanation, and conciliatory actions can be seen as an attempt to lull the perceiver into lowering his guard."[57] For Saddam Hussein, external pressure had changed the balance of incentives, compelling him now to conceal the fact that he did not have WMDs. This was difficult to perceive from without in the absence of any change in behavior, and in fact it seems likely that obscuring the absence of WMDs was an intent of Iraqi policy, that it was a positive goal of Saddam to leave his enemies as he understood them—Iran, the United States, and Iraqi civilians who might rise up against his rule—with the false impression that he had WMDs that he might use if attacked.[58]

Saddam Hussein's policy of refusing to offer proof that Iraq had no weapons of mass destruction seems to have been intended largely to hold Iraq's traditional adversary Iran in check, rather than being a policy whose primary audience was the United States and United Nations, as tended to be assumed by U.S. policy makers. Lieutenant General Raad Majid Hamdani, commander of the II Republican Guard Corps, claimed that Saddam deliberately hid the fact that Iraq had no weapons of mass destruction in order to maintain a policy of "deterrence by doubt" toward Iran. "His political strategy was to keep Tehran in check by maintaining some measure of ambiguity over Iraq's WMD," Gordon and Trainor have written. Chemical weapons had proven highly effective in balancing Iran's advantage in numbers in the Iran-Iraq war, blunting the "human wave" attacks of tens of thousands of Iranian soldiers. Saddam also appears to have believed that fear of WMD attacks were what kept the U.S. military from marching on Baghdad in 1991, and that the perception that his regime possessed such weapons was a deterrent to popular uprisings. The international outcry against Iraq's failure to comply with weapons inspections was a minor problem compared to a full-scale revolt against his government or an Iranian attack, and in any case, as Gordon and Trainor suggest, "According to his associates, [Saddam] did not consider the United States a natural adversary. He saw no reason why the Americans would want to invade Iraq. And he believed the Americans had no stomach for a bloody war." When an Iraqi warplane had accidentally attacked a U.S. Navy ship in the Persian Gulf during the Iran-Iraq war, Saddam was surprised that the United States protested diplomatically rather than striking Iraq, Iraqi officials told their U.S. interrogators. The United States had retreated after suffering small numbers of casualties in both Lebanon and Somalia, and the first Bush administration's 1991 decision not to advance on Baghdad was motivated by the same desire to avoid casualties, Saddam believed. These were the analogies that underpinned his understanding of the United States and its leaders, and on the basis of these examples he felt that a protracted war in which the United States would risk large numbers of casualties was not likely. As one senior official in Saddam's government put it, the feeling in his inner circle was "No one is as good at absorbing U.S. precision munitions as Iraq. So if that's all the Americans have got, it's not a threat to our national survival."[59]

According to Iraqi officials captured by coalition forces, as it became more apparent that the United States might launch a full scale invasion of Iraq, in December 2002 Saddam Hussein met with his Revolutionary Command Council, military commanders, and senior Ba'ath Party officials to deliver the surprise announcement that Iraq did not, in fact posses any weapons of mass destruction. He gave instructions to make sure that all traces of anything associated with WMD at every level of the state security and military infrastructure should be expunged, as he was hoping to make an unimpeachable statement to the United Nations that Iraq was in full compliance with its agreement to eliminate WMD, which would deny the Bush administration its rationale for war. These announcements, according to Saddam's deputy prime minister Tariq Aziz, had a devastating effect on morale among Iraqi leaders. It seems likely that the efforts of the Republican Guard and other agencies to make sure that no trace of WMD remained anywhere in their arsenal were what was seen by U.S. satellites and overheard by U.S. intelligence in the photos and radio transcripts cited by Colin Powell in his pivotal address to the U.N. Security Council. Powell (and U.S. intelligence officials and the Bush administration generally) interpreted this evidence to mean that Iraq was indeed seeking to hide WMD, because this interpretation fit well with established understanding of the nature of the Iraqi regime and its policies.[60]

U.S. leaders failed to recognize that Iraqi military planners, according to Gordon and Trainor, worked from the premise that the threats facing them came from three distinct levels—international, regional, and domestic.[61] The Bush administration tended to assume that Iraq's policies were directed at the United States, when in fact they were concerned with the Iraqi regime's perceived enemies domestically and regionally as well as with the United States. For Iraq's government to risk war with the United States by not cooperating fully with weapons inspections did not make sense to U.S. planners *unless* the regime was hiding something. But doing so, even at the risk of the war with the United States, did serve the Iraqi government's other goal of deterring an Iranian attack or domestic uprising by threatening to use chemical weapons against either. The U.S. administration did not see these as possible Iraqi motives because it was too wedded to its own perspective and unable to conceptualize the security environment faced by the Iraqi regime from its point of view.

Planning for the American invasion, Iraqi military leaders devised a defense based on the Russian winter campaign against Napoleon's army. In this plan, the Iraqi military would avoid direct, large-scale confrontations with coalition forces and instead allow them to advance. Small Iraqi units and irregular tribal forces would "chew" on the American invasion force as it drew further inland, gradually wearing it down until the territory it was forced to occupy, the losses it was constantly suffering, and the supply lines it was forced to maintain eventually became unbearable and forced a withdrawal. The Iraqi desert would be like the Russian snow, crippling and degrading the American force in concert with the Iraqi military. But Ali Allawi claims that "Saddam was greatly concerned that the American strategy was not so much about invading the country; rather, through intensive bombings and undercover sabotage, to create the conditions for a Shia uprising. The fear of a serious domestic challenge to its power was what governed the military strategy of the former regime." Saddam reportedly rejected his generals' defense plan in large part because it relied on arming Iraqi tribes, and Saddam was at least as concerned, if not more, about a domestic uprising against his rule than about a foreign invasion. Instead, the defense plan adopted by Saddam involved concentric circles of forces around Baghdad, each a defensive redoubt behind which Republican Guard units would be concentrated. Only Special Republican Guard forces would be allowed inside the city itself, as a precaution against a coup. When this plan was leaked to German intelligence and subsequently passed along to American officials, U.S. leaders dubbed the innermost defensive circle around the city as the "Red Line," which they interpreted to be the trigger point at which chemical weapons would be used as a last defense against the advancing U.S. military.[62]

The assumption that the enemy was and would continue to act as a conventional, centralized state marked the Bush administration's thinking about Iraq as it had earlier deliberations about Afghanistan and al Quaeda. At a principals meeting on October 9, 2001, Cheney and the other members of the group grappled with the difficulty of dealing with an enemy in al Qaeda that might possess weapons of mass destruction. Rumsfeld and Cheney in particular framed their points in the language and assumptions of the cold war, the first Gulf War, and the state-centered international system more generally. Could Osama bin Laden be deterred from using WMDs as the Soviet Union and Iraq had been, they asked. Cheney feared that bin Laden could not, but Bush wondered whether "sponsoring nations of UBL, those that support him, might have some influence with him," and asked, "should we send some message, public or private?" The strategy is reminiscent of the attempts by the Nixon administration to use its relationships with the Soviet Union and China to influence the policies of the government of North Vietnam, but this approach in this instance raises a serious question about to what extent if at all the dynamics of state interest and traditional realpolitik diplomacy could reasonably be applied to U.S. relations with an ideologically driven non-state actor such as al Qaeda. Bush himself seems to have equated victory over the Taliban and al Qaeda with the eradication of a small group of key individuals. He reportedly kept in his desk a "scorecard," provided by the FBI, with the names and photos of 22 leaders of the Tailban and al Qaeda, which he checked off as each was killed or captured.[63]

In an October 15, 2002 memo, Donald Rumsfeld compiled a list of the things that might go wrong in the coming war with Iraq. On the list were the prospect of another state taking advantage of the U.S. focus on Iraq by challenging U.S. interests elsewhere; that "Iraqi intelligence services, who have a global presence including inside the U.S., could strike the U.S., our allies, or other deployed forces in unconventional ways;" that "Fortress Baghdad could prove to be long and unpleasant for all;" and that "Iraq could experience ethnic strife among the Sunnis, Shiites and Kurds as had happened before." Notably, Iraq was seen as a state willing and able to launch terrorist attacks against the United States, but Rumsfeld does not appear to have focused on the prospect of unconventional war in Iraq itself. Iraq was seen through the lens of the global war on terror, as a state likely to use terrorism beyond its borders as a tactic, but at the same time also as a conventional military power that would fight essentially the same kind of war it had fought against the United States in 1991—the kind of war the United States was prepared to fight and expected easily to win. Rumsfeld's thinking about the "what ifs" seems to have been constrained both by the administration's worldview and by the Pentagon's doctrinal culture.[64]

Bureaucratic Politics and Intelligence

Paul Bremer suggests that the view that the Iraq war would involve a quick military victory followed by a very short occupation and handover of power to a new Iraqi government was widely held in the top echelons of the Bush administration. "In part, this optimism was based on the relative ease of a military campaign that had been described as a 'cakewalk,'" Bremer argues, "and it appeared to be encouraged by the predictions of some Iraqi exiles." Bremer suggests that the notion of an "early transfer" of power was administration shorthand for this idea, and that it was "animated in part by their aversion to 'nation-building.'"[65]

The exiles Bremer refers to were part of an organization known as the Iraqi National Congress (INC), which was led by an Iraqi-born former banker, Ahmad Chalabi. Much of the administration's understanding of what was likely to occur in Iraq after the war commenced seems to have been garnered from intelligence and opinions provided by this group. Leading neoconservatives in the Pentagon viewed Chalabi as the appropriate leader of the liberated Iraq, but a serious bureaucratic dispute over this issue developed between the Office of the Secretary of Defense and the Vice President's office, on one hand, and the CIA and State Department on the other.

Chalabi had been an acquaintance and political ally of key neoconservatives for decades. He had met Albert Wohlstetter, whom Wolfowitz described as one of his most influential teachers, while at the University of Chicago, and had introduced Wohlstetter to Richard Perle in 1985. Gordon and Trainor have written that "the CIA considered him a scoundrel who, it charged, bilked the Petra Bank in Jordan out of millions and was little more than a poseur as a London-based guerrilla fighter. The State Department thought he was a master manipulator with little constituency inside Iraq. But Perle, Wolfowitz, and aides in Cheney's office saw him as a talented and dedicated organizer . . . [with a] single-minded focus on stirring a rebellion in Iraq."[66] Whatever else he might have been, Chalabi was an avid student of U.S. domestic politics and history. In one interview he suggested that he "followed very closely how Roosevelt, who abhorred the Nazis, at a time when isolationist sentiment was paramount in the United States, managed adroitly to persuade the American people to go to war. I studied it with a great deal of respect; we learned a lot from it."[67]

The question of interest for this study is not who Chalabi was or how or why he made the claims that he did about Iraq, but rather why he was apparently widely believed by senior Bush administration officials. History will render its judgment on Ahmad Chalabi; at best he is likely to be seen in the end as a cunning and self-serving political manipulator, at worst as a polished con man and charlatan. But for the purposes of foreign policy analysis the critical question about Chalabi should be why did skilled and experienced political leaders with access to the evidence that should have led them to know better, instead put their faith in the assurances of such a man? David Phillips's answer to this question is that "Smart U.S. officials allowed Chalabi to spin them because they badly wanted to believe what he said. Suspending their disbelief, some envisioned Chalabi . . . mobilizing vast legions to take over and reshape Iraq. Chalabi systematically provided the rationale for going to war and promised that coalition forces would be greeted as liberators. The information Chalabi provided also affected Pentagon plans for postwar Iraq. Rumsfeld's decision to send too few troops was influenced by Chalabi's claim that he controlled a vast underground security network whose members would stand up as soon as they saw the Americans."[68]

In some respects the goals and perspective of Chalabi and the INC were quite different from those of the Bush administration. The neoconservatives, for their part, were moralistic nationalists. They were interested in the purposes of American power not just for Iraq, but for the world. Iraq was a means to an end. For the Iraqi dissidents, Iraq was the end. They were not interested in ideology so much as the fall of Saddam Hussein, and saw American power as perhaps the only tool capable of accomplishing that purpose. For one group that goal was proximate, for the other it was the end in itself—but on the necessity of that goal they did agree.[69]

In the years leading up to the war, Chalabi and the INC initially participated in a State Department initiative known as the "Future or Iraq" project. Beginning in April 2002 and involving some seventeen federal agencies, the Future of Iraq Project brought together some 240 expatriate Iraqis, including members of every major ethnic group and political sect. It produced reports totaling some 2000 pages on topics including education, health, sanitation, agriculture, the economy, infrastructure, energy, government finances, security, and law. Though by most accounts these reports did not constitute a complete occupation plan, they certainly represented the most extensive effort of the U.S. government to imagine in detail the ways in which Iraqi government and society might function after Saddam Hussein and the pitfalls and challenges that might accompany his regime's fall. But the INC suspended its participation in the project when disputes arose between the INC leadership and other Iraqi exiles, and subsequent DoD planning for the occupation appears to have studiously ignored the voluminous reports the project produced.[70]

Upon arriving in Baghdad, U.S. officials realized that Ahmad Chalabi did not in fact enjoy a wide base of public support among Iraqis. One State Department official noted that "the biggest surprise was that divisions between exiles and other Iraqis were much deeper than between Iraq's ethnic or religious groups." A senior U.S. official recalled that at his first press conference, Chalabi was "jeered more than cheered" by the Iraqi audience. "It was embarrassing," the official said. "We had to help bail him out." Public opinion polls at the time revealed that Chalabi's approval ratings among the Iraqi populace were lower than Saddam Hussein's. U.S. occupation authorities would later cut their ties with Chalabi after it was discovered that he was providing intelligence to Iran.[71]

Before the war however, Chalabi and the INC regularly supplied elements of the administration with intelligence about Iraq's weapons programs and other matters. At a meeting of the Defense Policy Board on September 19, 2001, for example, Chalabi told the assembled advisors to the Pentagon's leaders that Iraq's military was large but internally weak, ill equipped, and badly demoralized. Saddam's government could be overthrown by Iraqi insurgents supported by U.S. airpower, he claimed. The Iraqi military would help to stabilize the situation after Saddam's fall, and Iraq would emerge as a modern, stable, U.S. ally in the Middle East. The intelligence gathering efforts of the INC were funded by the State Department until the end of 2002 and the Defense Intelligence Agency thereafter. "Major recipients" of the information gathered by the INC were the Office of Special Plans in the Pentagon and John Hannah, a special assistant for national security in the Office of the Vice President.[72] The information supplied by the INC was evidently very influential in shaping the administration's view of Iraq, and Ahmad Chalabi came to be favored by many administration neoconservatives as the choice to lead the country after Saddam's fall. "When it came to nation-building," Phillips writes, [the Bush administration did not have a detailed program. All it had was one person—Ahmad Chalabi—whom neo-conservatives wanted to anoint as Iraq's future leader. Chalabi provided bogus intelligence on Iraq's weapons of mass destruction (WMD). He convinced the Pentagon that Iraqis would welcome coalition forces 'with flowers.' When concerns were raised about chaos after Saddam's removal, Chalabi claimed to control an underground security structure with tens of thousands of Iraqis, which he would activate as soon as coalition forces entered Baghdad . . . Though the INC's information came with an overt agenda, administration hawks did not question its reliability, nor did they listen to concerns raised by the CIA and the State Department's Bureau of Intelligence and Research.[73]]

Another leading member of the INC with close ties to the Bush Administration was Kanan Makiya, a scholar and author whose book *Republic of Fear* was a scathing catalog of the extremes of Saddam Hussein's brutality. Makiya was an acquaintance of Richard Perle and Paul Wolfowitz who would become a confidant of Dick Cheney's as well in the months leading up to the war in Iraq.[74] In late 2002 Makiya frequently traveled to Washington, D.C. to meet with civilian officials at the Pentagon and then with Cheney, Rice, and Bush at the White House. For Bush, one particularly influential meeting occurred on January 10, 2003, when he met in the Oval Office with three leading Iraqi exiles: Makiya, Hatem Mukhlis, and Rend Franke. "I believe in freedom and peace," Bush told them. "I believe Saddam

Hussein is a threat to America and to the neighborhood. He should disarm but he won't, therefore we will remove him from power. We can't make him change his heart. His heart is made of stone." Makiya told the president, "You're going to break the mold . . . You will change the image of the United States in the region. Democracy is truly doable in Iraq. Force for destruction can be turned to force for construction. Iraqis are a technically able people." American troops would be greeted with "flowers and sweets" one of the Iraqis told Bush. Bush asked questions about basic living conditions in Iraq—was their starvation, what would people need for the future, what were the Iraqi political elites like.[75] When Bush asked these exiles if ethnic and religious differences in Iraq would "turn into hatred, leading to civil conflict and more disasters," all three told him they would not. These divisions were a product of Saddam's rule, they said, manipulated by his regime to entrench its own control. With democracy and responsible leadership, they were unlikely to spawn conflict. When Makiya criticized the CIA and State Department for failing to support Chalabi and the INC as Iraq's government-in-waiting, Bush asked Rice "is this true?" apparently unaware of the intense bureaucratic conflict that was raging between the executive agencies over this question. Rice did not deny it, Khalilzad said it was true, and Cheney said only that there were "differences" between the agencies. Rice, Card, and Fleischer all said after the fact that they felt this meeting had a significant impact on Bush.[76]

The Bush administration's confidence in Chalabi, Makiya, and the INC was part of a larger web of assumptions and ideological premises that worked together to support the expectation of a quick military victory and very brief occupation of Iraq. It was not through some oversight that serious planning for postwar Iraq did not take place, but because it was considered unnecessary. The Bush administration constructed an image of Iraq and the events that would define the war and its aftermath in such a way that a large U.S. force was simply not required, and such U.S. forces as were necessary would not need to stay long. As one defense department official put it, "Rummy and Wolfowitz and Feith did not believe the U.S. would need to run postconflict Iraq . . . Their plan was to turn it over to these exiles very quickly and let them deal with the messes that came up." This image of Iraq fit very coherently with the administration's principled commitment to the ideas of military transformation and opposition to peacekeeping and "nation building." Despite all evidence to the contrary as Iraq descended into violent chaos in the summer and fall of 2003, the supporters of this vision persisted in believing that it had been basically correct. Dick Cheney approached Colin Powell in the fall of that year and stuck a finger in Powell's chest, saying "If you hadn't opposed the INC and Chalabi, we wouldn't be in this mess."[77]

Support for Chalabi and the INC would be the most significant issue in what emerged as a serious bureaucratic battle within the Bush administration during the months leading up to the invasion of Iraq. Around the first of January, 2003, Douglas Feith conferred with Stephen Hadley about developing an office in the Pentagon for post war planning in Iraq. The result was the creation, by presidential order on January 20, of the Office of Reconstruction and Humanitarian Assistance (ORHA). The office would be led by former General Jay Garner, but who would serve beneath Garner on its staff soon became a point of intense debate between the State Department and Pentagon. Two State Department staffers, Tom Warrick (who had coordinated the "Future or Iraq" project), and Meghan O'Sullivan (a top sanctions specialist), were ordered to leave ORHA by Rumsfeld. When Powell intervened, Rumsfeld told him that ORHA should not be run by people who were not supportive of the administration's agenda, which Powell interpreted to mean not supportive of Ahmad Chalabi and the INC, favorites of the Pentagon. Though O'Sullivan was later quietly reinstated to ORHA, the dispute presaged an intense bureaucratic struggle over Iraq policy that was to come. Vice President Cheney seems to have been closely allied with Rumsfeld and the civilian leadership at the Pentagon in this process, arguing that the State Department, including Powell, were not sufficiently committed to the goal of democracy in Iraq. "We've got an obligation to go stand up a democracy," Cheney argued in one meeting. "We've got to fundamentally change the place. And we've got to give the Iraqi people a chance at those fundamental values we believe in."[78]

The circle of neoconservative advisors around the president concluded that those individuals and agencies who did not share their views should be isolated from the processes of both making and implementing policy. This meant that the State Department, seen by the neoconservatives as an ideological adversary, should be supplanted in dealing with Iraq by the neoconservative-dominated Defense Department. This shift in the institutional balance within government would have profound implications for postwar Iraq. James Dobbins, who was deeply involved in postwar reconstruction efforts in Haiti, Somalia, Bosnia, and Kosovo, has argued that the placement of postwar responsibility for Iraq in the Pentagon meant that "rather than use the structures that had done our nation building for the past decade, we created a completely new structure. We transferred responsibilities from State and the Agency for International Development to the Department of Defense for things the Department of Defense had never been responsible for."[79]

At the highest levels of the Bush administration there was also deep skepticism about the will or ability of U.S. intelligence and the CIA in particular to see the real depth of the threats facing the United States. Dick Cheney was especially dubious about the Agency's capabilities, recalling how badly it had underestimated Saddam's WMD development program before the first Gulf War—when, as was revealed after the fact, Iraq had been perhaps only a year or two away from having a functional nuclear bomb, unbeknownst to U.S. intelligence. In June 2002 the CIA delivered a report to the administration entitled "Iraq and al-Qaeda: Interpreting a Murky Relationship," which emphasized the wariness with which Saddam and al Qaeda viewed each other but did not exclude the prospect of "limited offers of cooperation" between them. A number of leading administration officials did not think the report went far enough, and for neoconservatives it became a symbol of the CIA's naivete (within the CIA, the report was a source of controversy because many analysts felt it was influenced by political considerations and went farther than the known facts would support). Within the Pentagon, Feith assigned two officers to the task of looking at the intelligence to see if the CIA had underestimated the threat. They concluded that the Agency had discounted a possible Iraq-al Qaeda connection too readily; they argued that a purported meeting between 9/11 plotter Mohammed Atta and Iraqi intelligence agents in Prague had actually occurred, through it had been roundly discounted by the CIA.[80]

As a result of this skepticism and bureaucratic antipathy toward the CIA, Rumsfeld ordered created within the Office of the Secretary of Defense an "Office of Special Plans" (OSP). Under the leadership of Douglas Feith, the OSP was charged with reviewing intelligence on Iraq to find in it what the CIA could not or would not. In Feith's words, its ambiguous title was a gentler acronym for what was really an "office of Iraq policy;" in the view of some observers it was in fact a rogue intelligence operation. In practice, the OSP functioned to seek out evidence of Iraqi weapons of mass destructions and connections between the Ba'athist regime and al Qaeda. In this role, it served to reinforce the dysfunctional social-psychological effects of the neoconservative ideological orthodoxy within the Bush administration. It was a bureaucratic reflection of the administration's tendency to adhere doggedly to its ideological worldview and process information in ways that supported that view, rather than altering its understanding of the world to match new information. It provided an institutional mechanism to shape intelligence to support the conclusions the administration had reached about Iraq.[81]

With regard to the bureaucratic infighting between the State and Defense Departments, Draper argues that "the battles that counted were the ones in the White House, where [Rumsfeld] had a powerful ally in Dick Cheney and a talent for winning over Bush." Draper claims that Rumsfeld was able to appeal, in a way that Powell was not, to Bush's sense of himself as a maverick. Rumsfeld told his staff that the way to win White House approval for an idea was to represent it as the "Big New Thing." Bush saw himself as a reformer with a historical mission; Rumsfeld's contrarian, abrasive attacks on the bureaucratic establishment within his own department and elsewhere dovetailed with Bush's own sense of his administration's purpose. Powell, on the other hand, was the consummate Washington, D.C. insider—focused on careful, measured, diplomacy, on subtlety and process rather than radical change. Of Rice, Draper suggests that she "valued her access to the president and endeavored to maintain it at all costs. As national security adviser, she saw her role as that of facilitator rather than opinion leader . . . Condoleezza Rice would be Bush's information broker and sounding board, rather than the person who incessantly ruffled his feathers with opinions that he did not share." Rice argued that the administration's worldview was an expression of Bush's fundamental beliefs and values. Draper reports that she told a close friend that far from exercising influence over Bush, "I'm internalizing his world."[82]

At the end of Bush's first term in office, as the Iraq war escalated and Powell prepared to leave the State Department, Powell met with Bush to tell him that the national security decision-making process was broken, that decisions were not undergoing the skeptical and self-conscious vetting and review that they should. But this may have been by design as much as by accident; in nearly every account, Bush is consistently depicted as a president who made decisions intuitively and did not like to revisit or cast doubt onto what had been decided, and who entrenched these values in the inner circle of advisors who surrounded him. Citing "former state department officials," Gordon and Trainor contend that "Bush had picked Cheney and Rumsfeld for a number of reasons and their tough-minded approach to the exercise of power was one of them. It was a troika. The president would preside, the vice president would guide, and the defense secretary would implement."[83]

The neoconservatives "questioned Powell's commitment to democracy in the Middle East . . . Cheney and Rumsfeld distrusted those who were close to Powell. The neocons wanted to marginalize anyone who questioned their plans to reinvent Iraq and push radical reform across the Middle East."[84] As Saddam's regime was collapsing, on April 9, 2003 Cheney held a small dinner party with a few of his closest political allies—Ken Adelman, Scooter Libby, and Paul Wolfowitz. The conversation turned to Powell and his role in the lead up to war. "Colin always had major reservations about what we were trying to do," Cheney said.[85] Looking back on his time as secretary of state, Bush said that "Powell is a diplomat . . . And you've got to have a diplomat. I kind of picture myself as a pretty good diplomat, but nobody else does. You know, particularly, I wouldn't call me a diplomat. But, nevertheless, he is a diplomatic person who has got war experience."[86]

The administration persisted in defending its expectations of an easy victory and the need for only a small occupation force in Iraq in the face of significant, persistent objections from many of its own political allies (to say nothing of its opponents) and in some cases from within the White House and Pentagon. For example, in 2002 Major Jeff Kojac of the NSC staff produced a report entitled "Force Security in Seven Recent Stability Operations." It made the point that if the United States were to maintain in Iraq the same ratio of troops to civilian population that had existed in Kosovo, a total of 480,000 troops would be required. If the ratio that existed in Bosnia were used, 364,000 troops would be needed in Iraq. If Afghanistan were the measure, only 13,900 troops would be needed, but Kojac pointed out that more urbanized populations generally required more forces—and Iraq was more urbanized than either Kosovo or Bosnia, with roughly 75 percent of the Iraqi population living in cities as compared to about 50 percent in Bosnia and Kosovo. In Afghanistan, just 18 percent of the population lived in cities. Kojac briefed Rice, Hadley, and Eric Edelman (Libby's deputy and Feith's eventual replacement at the Pentagon), but the report seems to have spurred little second guessing of Rumsfeld's plan within the White House. The dominant interpretation of the report seems to have been that it only showed that Kosovo and Bosnia, Clinton administration exercises in nation-building, had involved too many troops; Afghanistan was a better template for Iraq because it represented the Bush administration's new approach to intervention without nation-building.[87] Bremer states that as he prepared to depart for Iraq, he gave to Rumsfeld a Rand Corporation report suggesting that the U.S occupation force should be some 500,000 troops (the report based this figure on post war U.S. occupations including Germany,

Japan, Somalia, the Balkans, and Afghanistan, applying the ratio of 20 troops per thousand residents to Iraq's population of 25 million). "I think you should consider this" Bremer told Rumsfeld. But, he adds, "I never heard back from him about the report."[88]

Similarly, On February 28, 2003, Robert Perito, an expert on peacekeeping operations with extensive experience in the Balkans, was invited to the Pentagon to speak to the Defense Policy Board about postwar operations in Iraq. The Iraqi police and army would not be ready or able to provide security in the wake of military defeat and governmental collapse, Perito said. The United States also would not be able to rely on allies or international organizations to fill this role as it had in previous cases, and the regular U.S. military was not well suited to peacekeeping because it was focused on its war-fighting role. "Given the political and practical realities," Perito's briefing notes said, "It's doubtful the U.S. will be able to turn to the EU, NATO and OSCE, which provided police and legal experts in Bosnia and Kosovo." Therefore, Perito recommended the swift creation of a "stability force" of some 2500 police and legal experts. "Experience in the Balkans, East Timor, and Afghanistan shows that a coalition force will have to deal with high levels of violence for the first two years of the mission," Perito said. "Like the U.N. Police in Haiti, Kosovo, and East Timor, these police officers should be armed and have 'executive authority' to make arrests, conduct investigations and use deadly force." He was thanked for his briefing but did not hear back from anyone at the Defense Department again.[89]

Meeting privately with House Republican Majority Leader Dick Armey in the fall of 2002, Cheney laid out the administration's case for war. He described the serious underestimations of Iraq's WMD capabilities by U.S. intelligence before the first Gulf War, the advances in technology since that that allowed such weapons to fit into a suitcase, the likelihood that Saddam Hussein's government would give such weapons to groups like al Qaeda, and the impossibility of finding WMD's in Iraq short of war. "You'll never find the stuff until you get in there and clean out everything else," Cheney said. When Armey responded "you're going to get mired down there," Cheney shook his head. "We have great information," he said. "They're going to welcome us. It'll be like the American army going through the streets of Paris. They're sitting there ready to form a new government. The people will be so happy with their freedoms that we'll probably back ourselves out of there within a month or two."[90]

The administration's conclusions about how the Iraqi people would greet coalition forces invading their country were clear and often repeated. Wolfowitz said in a March 11, 2003 speech to the Veterans of Foreign Wars, "The Iraqi people understand what this crisis is about. Like the people of France in the 1940s, they view us as their hoped-for liberator." Meeting with Congressional leaders on March 17, 2003, Cheney told Senator Joseph Biden that "I think we'll be greeted as liberators . . . but there are scores to be settled. It's a tough neighborhood. We'll provide security." Cheney said on *Meet the Press* in March, 2003 that "I think things have gotten so bad inside Iraq, from the standpoint of the American people, my belief is we will, in fact, be greeted as liberators." "I don't think it would be a tough fight," Cheney said in September 2002. Similarly, Richard Perle argued that "Saddam's army will defeat Saddam . . . there may be pockets of resistance, but very few Iraqis are going to fight to defend Saddam." Even months before 9/11 occurred, Perle had claimed that Saddam would be deposed within a year. Three days before the United States launched its first attacks in Iraq, Cheney said that he thought the Iraqi regular army might not fight and that "significant elements of the Republican Guard . . . are likely to step aside." In early March 2003, Rumsfeld met with a number of top aides and asked for their best guesses about the duration of the war. Notably, the premise of his question was that the war ended when Saddam fell: "how long to achieve regime change?" The estimates ranged from seven days to one month, with Wolfowitz expecting the shortest war.[91]

These views dominated within the Bush administration, but they were, in the words of National Defense University Professor and former head CIA analyst on Iraq Judith Yaphe, "fantasy." "They had a strategic vision that we would face no opposition, that everyone would surrender, that Iraqis would throw rose petals and rice, and people would welcome us as conquering liberators," Yaphe suggests. When this belief proved false, the administration had difficulty adapting to this reality in large part because of the cognitive shift required in abandoning a firmly held belief. As Wolfowitz said later, "It was difficult to imagine before the war that the criminal gang of sadists and gangsters who have run Iraq for 35 years would continue fighting."[92]

Of all the errors that might be ascribed to the social psychology of the administration, the unquestioned assumption that the United States would be seen as it saw itself—as a benevolent force for liberation and democracy, rather than an imperialist foreign occupier—was perhaps the most tragically significant for policy. The Bush administration was certainly not the first to be guilty of this kind of mistake—Janis notes that the Kennedy administration's sense of itself was similarly assumed to be shared by the rest of the world. When it became clear that U.S. involvement in the Bay of Pigs invasion would not remain a secret from the world press, Kennedy and his advisors concluded that noncommunist countries would most likely support the policy in any case because, "'After all, we are the good guys.'" Jervis argues that "the inability to recognize that one's own actions can be seen as menacing and the concomitant belief that the other's hostility can only be explained by its aggressiveness help explain how conflicts can easily expand beyond that which an analysis of the objective situation would indicate is necessary." This inability can lead to self-fulfilling prophecies, as perceived adversaries become real adversaries due to defensive overreactions. In the case of the United States, this tendency is compounded by the fact, as George Kennan has put it, that "It has never occurred to most Americans that the political principles by which they themselves lived might have been historically conditioned and might not enjoy universal validity"[93]

The Bush administration succumbed to the same error. It failed to perceive the way in which its actions would be understood elsewhere in the world because it fell victim to the fallacy that the way in which it understood itself and its motives was the only way of understanding them, or at least the way in which they would to be understood by outside observers who were not cynically self-interested or ideologically anti-American. In stating that other countries were either "with us or against us" after 9/11, the Bush administration appears to have legitimately believed that it was acting out of moral certainty and conveying to the rest of the world a sense of resolve. But what was meant to suggest firmness was in fact taken in many places as indicating a reckless militancy and lack of judgment. As Francis Fukuyama wrote one year after the 9/11 attacks, "Americans are largely innocent of the fact that much of the rest of the world believes that it is American power, and not terrorists with weapons of mass destruction, that is destabilizing the world."[94] The Bush administration acted consistently from this kind of ignorance, as if because its intentions were clear and its cause just from its own point of view, anyone who opposed it must be either naïve or hostile. Jeffrey Record has argued that this entrenched insensitivity to the perspectives of others was rooted in the neoconservative ideology itself:

> At the root of the problem is the failure of the neoconservatives who have provided the intellectual and doctrinal foundation for the Bush administration's foreign policy to grasp the fact that others do not see

us as we see ourselves—that is, as a benign and historically exceptional force whose moral and political values are universally appealing . . . The neoconservative view is that America is not just virtuous but self-evidently virtuous, and that its power therefore should not be feared but welcomed. This . . . led, among many other things, to confident prewar predictions that the war against Iraq would be a "cakewalk," that all Iraqis other than Saddam and his henchmen were dying to be liberated and occupied by an invading American army (the analogy was made to France's liberation in 1944), and that Saddam's regime would collapse like a house of cards at the first knock of American military power. The neoconservatives inside the Bush administration know they are right; they have no self-doubt; and they believe the United States can mold the world in its own values and interests.[95]

Chapter 5

Policy Consequences of Identity and Ideology

The Bush Administration and the War in Iraq

The Bush administration's policies in Iraq were driven by discursive constructions of the identities of the United States, Iraq, and other actors in the international system that became dominant among the handful of leaders at highest levels of the U.S. military bureaucracy and within the White House. These constructions were revealed in the statements of the president and his top advisors that form the intellectual basis for the administration's public case for war, but these public positions were highly consistent with the statements of these same officials in private or during closed-door meetings in the same period. These identity formulations guided policy toward war and shaped the administration's expectations of what would occur afterward, and within these constructions are embedded the assumptions that gave rise to the two most notable failures of the Iraq war: the belief that Iraq possessed weapons of mass destruction and posed a threat to U.S. national security requiring the use of preemptive force; and the belief that postwar Iraq would move quickly to stable democracy with minimal need for support by a long-term U.S. military presence. This chapter will describe the specific policy consequences in Iraq of these identity constructions and the ideological precepts that defined the parameters of foreign policy discourse within the Bush administration.

Andrew Flibbert has identified four sets of mutually reinforcing ideas that formed the ideational basis for the administration's choice for war in Iraq: "Belief in the necessity and benevolence of American hegemony, a Manichaean conception of politics, a conviction that regime type is the principal determinant of foreign policy, and great confidence in the efficacy of military force." Together, Flibbert has argued, "these ideas had a constitutive effect on the administration's understanding of U.S. interests and policy options. More specifically, they defined the social purpose of American power, framed threats to the United States, and determined appropriate solutions to core problems."[1] Similarly, David Hastings Dunn has argued that "an understanding of the Bush administration's decision to go to war in Iraq "is impossible without an appreciation of the centrality of the role of ideas in contemporary US foreign policy. Some of these ideas are as old as the republic (such as American exceptionalism and moral certainty), some developed during the Cold War, and others still derive from the Bush administration's self-identification of itself as 'neo-Reaganite' in both domestic and foreign policy—promoting the values and playing the role that Reagan did in the early 1980s." Among the ideational "drivers" of Bush's Iraq policy, according to Dunn, were a realist opposition to appeasement, a belief in U.S. providence and American exceptionalism, a commitment to assertive unilateralism, including a willingness to use military force, and a tendency toward threat inflation and conflation.[2]

In explaining the administration's belief that Iraq possessed weapons of mass destruction and was likely to use them or give them to terrorists, and the belief that the U.S. war in Iraq would lead quickly to democracy and stability that would allow a withdrawal of most U.S. troops after a very short occupation, a few central assumptions and values are key. Among these were a Manichaean view of world politics that suggested that the conflict in Iraq was part of a broader global war on terror in which the forces of freedom and civilization were pitted against the unified forces of barbarism and evil; a faith in the efficacy of American military power to create political change and reshape the international order; a belief in the universal viability and moral superiority of the American model of democratic governance; and the presumption that the United States was a benevolent power fighting for transcendent values and would be seen as such by Iraqis. These ideas combined to support the conclusion that American forces would be greeted as liberators by grateful Iraqis and that while Iraqi society would require the paternalistic support of the United States to be educated in the norms of democracy, the universal appeal of liberal values would lead to the quick emergence of stable prosperity in Iraq. From before the war's beginning and throughout its prosecution these ideas dominated official thinking about Iraq at the highest levels of the Bush administration, leading to a generalized failure among top policy makers to understand the conflict from their adversaries' cultural and cognitive perspective. These ideas proved highly durable, crippling the administration's capacity to adapt its policies in the face of growing evidence of the flaws in its previous assumptions.

A Manichaean sense of international politics led the administration to the conclusion that despite their ideological antipathy toward one another, al Qaeda and Saddam Hussein's Ba'ath Party were natural allies since they were both hostile to the United States. The view of Iraq as a state that posed a direct threat to the United States and would use terrorism to accomplish its goals was in evidence within the Bush administration as early as September 12, 2001, when the president asked his counterterrorism coordinator to seek out connections between Iraq and the terrorist attacks. Bush is reported to have said at National Security Council (NSC) meetings in the days that followed, "Many believe Saddam is involved . . . He probably was behind this in the end . . .. I believe Iraq was involved, but I'm not going to strike them now. I don't have the evidence at this point."[3]

Robert Jervis has noted the cognitive-psychological tendency to see unity among enemies,[4] and it would seem possible for this tendency to influence the social construction of reality that occurs within groups, including groups of policy makers or whole societies. It is worth noting that President Bush's private suspicion that Iraq was involved in the 9/11 attacks also appears to have been shared by large segments of the American public immediately afterward with little evidence to support this conclusion.

Vice President Cheney argued in August of 2002 that the streets in Basra and Baghdad were "sure to erupt in joy in the same way the throngs in Kabul greeted the Americans."[5] Appearing on *Meet the Press* on March 16, 2003, Cheney said that he believed that "we will, in fact, be greeted as liberators."[6] Paul Wolfowitz stated a similar conclusion in a prewar interview in the *Detroit News*: "Our principal target is the psychological one, to convince the Iraqi people that they no longer have to be afraid of Saddam . . . and once that happens I think . . . you're going to find Iraqis out cheering American troops . . . I think ethnic differences are there in Iraq but they're exaggerated."[7] The assumption that Iraqis would greet American troops as liberators was a common claim by Bush administration officials, and was premised on a number of the central assumptions of the administration's worldview noted above. The Manichaean view that Saddam Hussein was an evil despot whose demise would be celebrated by

Iraqis tended to obscure the sectarian and other cleavages in Iraqi politics, divisions that predated Saddam but which were certainly critical to understanding his regime's grip on power. Despite the clear contempt of many Iraqis for Saddam and his Ba'ath Party, attitudes among Iraq's Sunnis were distinctly more mixed than among the Shia and Kurds among whom Saddam was more uniformly loathed.

The expectation of a grateful Iraqi reception for American forces was also rooted in a benign self-construction of U.S identity within the administration, and a tacit assumption that Iraqis would also see the United States as Americans did. This view reflected a serious oversimplification of the attitudes of many in Iraq toward the United States. As Major Michael Eisenstatdt, a U.S. Army intelligence officer and expert on Middle East security issues has suggested, Iraqi perceptions of and responses to the 2003 U.S. invasion cannot be understood "without understanding the end of the '91 war, especially the distrust of Americans" it engendered among Iraqi Shia.[8] At the end of the first Gulf War the first Bush administration had exhorted the Shia population of Southern Iraq and the Kurdish population in the North to revolt. When they did, the Iraqi military counterattacked and brutally put down the uprisings, killing untold thousands. The U.S. military stood by, offering no help or support to the uprisings, and even initially allowing the Iraq military to use its helicopters to facilitate these attacks. Though the United States would spend much of the next decade building what amounted to a stable, autonomous Kurdish state-within-a-state in Northern Iraq, Shia in the country's South would continue to endure both Saddam's repression and the crushing economic effects of Western-sponsored sanctions throughout this period. This experience certainly colored the mindset of many of the Iraqi Shia who witnessed the American occupation of 2003, whose reactions tended more toward reticence and mistrust than grateful support.

The Bush administration's identity construction of the Iraqi regime also formed the basis for its prewar conclusions about Iraq's weapons of mass destruction programs. In seeking to understand and predict the behavior of the Iraqi regime in the absence of hard evidence about its capabilities, the administration drew inferences about Iraq's intentions consistent with its understanding of the regime's identity, failing to perceive motives that did not fit within this construction. David Kay, who headed the postwar U.S. search for Iraq's purported weapons of mass destruction, said that his extensive interviews with those involved in Iraq's weapons programs led him to the conclusion that Saddam Hussein had not believed that the United States would actually invade and was more fearful of his own population, of Iraqi Shia and Kurds, than he was of the United States. His motives were defined primarily by his domestic political context, a reality for most political leaders but one that the dominant cognitive framework of the Bush administration did not account for and could not accommodate. "Totalitarian regimes generally end up fearing their own people more than they fear external threats," Kay said. "We missed that."[9] Thomas Ricks quotes one senior military specialist in Middle East intelligence as believing that Saddam Hussein's concerns about his domestic power base were also reflected in his limited challenges to Western enforcement of the U.N. no-fly zones over Iraq throughout the 1990s. "He was doing enough to show his people he was confronting the mighty United States, but no more than that . . . it was calibrated to show defiance, but not to provoke us."[10] Saddam's policies regarding WMD programs may well have been motivated by the same concerns, his refusal to cooperate with weapons inspectors driven by a domestic political interest in defying the West and intimidating his own population as well as regional neighbors. On the basis of its construction of the identity of Saddam Hussein and his regime, the Bush administration came to believe that Iraq was building WMDs, and that this could only be for the purposes of aggression and terrorism. In reality, the Iraqi government's policies seem to have been undertaken in a calculated attempt to hide the fact that Iraq could not effectively reconstitute its WMD programs, at least after 1998. The Bush administration's inability to consider this possibility even in the absence of hard evidence of Iraq's advanced WMD development, resulted from its identity construction of Iraq's regime and a failure to comprehend the perspective of the international Other.

The Bush administration asserted a moral and legal entitlement, even a duty, to use force unilaterally to overthrow the government of any state that posed a potential threat to the United States by seeking weapons of mass destruction. Though the administration did seek to enlist a coalition of states in the effort to implement this policy in Iraq, its case for war did not make strengthening international organizations and multilateral cooperation for arms control in the future a high priority. Indeed, as Christopher Dolan has suggested, "the American case for war was made in the context of a strategic doctrine that placed a priority on maintaining U.S. global supremacy, the power to utilize preemptive and preventive force, a firm rejection of deterrence and containment, and a strong dismissal of traditional approaches to non-proliferation."[11]

In Iraq, the Bush administration carried out a war without the approval of the United Nations Security Council and with few allies willing to provide a sustained presence of combat troops. As a result, the U.S. effort was immediately viewed as an illegitimate and self-serving American enterprise by people and governments around the world, and crucially, by many in Iraq, who came to oppose the U.S. occupation either actively or passively. Reluctance to engage in long-term "nation building" and peacekeeping operations had been a major theme of Bush's 2000 campaign for the presidency, a principle he had echoed in a major speech at the Citadel military academy just before taking office. Bush's defense secretary Donald Rumsfeld was also deeply skeptical about such operations, outlining his opposition to them in a speech entitled "Beyond Nation Building" just a month before the war in Iraq began. Administration planning for the war assumed a very short stay for most U.S. troops, who would be replaced by a multinational force that would include British and Polish-led divisions and a Muslim force made up primarily of troops from the Gulf states. Foreign constabularies from countries including Denmark, Italy, Portugal, South Korea, and Singapore would also participate in the occupation under the U.S. plan, which was outlined in a document entitled "Iraq Phase IV: Gaining Coalition Commitment" prepared by the joint staff of the Pentagon in the first months of 2003. Bush himself told reporters on Sunday, March 16, 2003, that "in the post-Saddam Iraq, the U.N. will definitely need to have a role. And that way it can begin to get its legs back, legs of responsibility back."[12] As Michael Gordon and General Bernard Trainor have described the administration's plan, "Few of the potential contributors had been wholehearted supporters of the war, but the administration assumed they would be willing to help keep the peace in a relatively benign Iraq." They further argue that "In making the case for its preemptive war . . . the Bush administration made it clear that it was prepared, if need be, to act unilaterally. But the consolidation of the United States' gains assumed that Washington would eventually elicit the cooperation of others: the Iraqis and allied nations that in the main were all too happy to keep their distance from postwar Iraq."[13]

Had the war in Iraq been conducted by a large and committed multinational coalition of forces operating under the authority of the United Nations, it very likely would have been perceived differently both within Iraq and by the world community as a whole. The U.S. military was capable of overthrowing Saddam Hussein's government but was unable to provide security and basic humanitarian needs such as power and clean water for much of the Iraqi population for many months after the regime's fall. Additional combat forces, police, and technical specialists from other U.N. member states might have provided the means to ensure security and a reasonable quality of life in Iraq after Saddam's departure. Forces from other Muslim and Arab states might have allowed for the coalition to avoid the image of Western occupiers that many Iraqis came to associate with the U.S. military. In other recent occupations, including Bosnia, Kosovo, and Afghanistan, multinational efforts coordinated and supported by the United Nations, NATO, and the European Union were crucial to postwar peace operations providing stability and security. This model might have been effectively applied in Iraq as well. But this was not possible because the Bush administration had severed the connection between multilateral means and liberal ends in traditional Wilsonian liberalism. The administration's unwillingness to build real international support for the war through the United Nations left much of the international community thoroughly alienated from U.S. policy in Iraq and uninterested in cooperation in the postwar stabilization effort. Once violence began to surge in Iraq in the summer of 2003 and beyond, there was little incentive for foreign governments, NGO's, or the United Nations to make a substantial effort to help end a conflict that had been started without their consultation or consent.

At the highest levels of the Bush White House and throughout the military bureaucracy it was assumed that Saddam Hussein's military, if it fought at all, would fight a conventional war in which it would be quickly defeated. Fears that this might not occur tended to stress the use of nonconventional weapons, such as chemical or biological weapons, but not nonconventional tactics. In fact, there was some evidence to suggest that elements of the Iraqi military were being prepared for a protracted guerilla war. Prewar intelligence indicated that Saddam Hussein had distributed copies of the film *Black Hawk Down* among his senior commanders, for example, that caches of explosives, small arms and other weapons were being distributed throughout Iraq, and that tens of thousands of Iraqi prisoners had been released before the war, perhaps to provide manpower for loosely organized bands of guerilla fighters. The Ba'ath Party itself had been from its earliest days a guerilla organization that still retained the localized cell structure characteristic of guerilla groups. Taken together, and along with the clear disparity of conventional capabilities that would argue strongly against a strategy of confrontation with the U.S. military on its own terms from the Iraqi perspective, these factors suggest a generalized failure to understand an international conflict from an adversary's point of view throughout the U.S. political and military structure. The assumptions of the Bush administration were defined and bounded by a worldview that did not take account of the perspective of the Iraqi regime, and thus failed to adequately predict the ways in which that regime would act in the face of an American attack.[14]

Why, then, did senior military and civilian leaders within the Bush administration assume that the war they were likely to fight in Iraq would be a conventional conflict much like the 1990 Gulf War instead of a guerilla war? Jervis argues that "people who favor a policy usually believe that it is supported by many logically independent reasons."[15] For Donald Rumsfeld and others in the Bush administration, planning for war in Iraq was marked by a tendency to see military doctrine and neoconservative ideological assumptions confirming and supporting one another. Administration officials subscribed to independent and separable assumptions about the prospects for democratic stability in Iraq and military restructuring; the need for cognitive consistency between these premises pushed these leaders to the conclusion that victory in Iraq could be achieved with a small force.

By many accounts Donald Rumsfeld felt that the primary mission that would distinguish his tenure as secretary of defense was reform of the military to emphasize war fighting by faster, lighter and more technologically advanced forces. Rumsfeld and other senior Bush administration officials were adherents of what had become known as the "Revolution in Military Affairs," or RMA. This idea, which had gained currency in U.S. military culture in the 1990s, held that new technology now enabled a small, technologically sophisticated force to defeat a much larger one by clearing away the "fog of war," using technical means to see the enemy clearly and quickly devastate its central nervous system—its command, control, and communications infrastructure. Military planners who subscribed to this concept advocated for a small, agile, force equipped with the most advanced technology to perceive the battlefield more accurately in real time, enabling it to destroy an enemy's ability to coordinate its actions, effectively decapitating it. Rumsfeld believed that the leadership of the U.S. Army in particular was out of step with the times, too wedded to twentieth-century military doctrines involving capturing and holding ground with tank divisions and infantry, too invested in the heavy military equipment these doctrines depended on—the so-called legacy systems of the cold war. Notably, early in his tenure as secretary, Rumsfeld fought and won a bureaucratic battle with army leadership over the Crusader artillery system, one such piece of military hardware. Infantry divisions were expensive to maintain, slow to move, and lent themselves to the kind of quagmire occupation that the Vietnam War had become. The United States did not need the large conventional force that had won World War II, Rumsfeld believed. Instead, it needed smaller numbers of nimbler, more advanced ground forces capable of overthrowing an enemy regime and then departing (leaving the process of postwar rebuilding to others), complemented by advanced airpower, satellite systems, and missile defense. Under Rumsfeld, this agenda "acquired the aura of an official ideology" within the Pentagon.[16]

In the Bush administration's planning for war in Iraq, there was a cognitive consistency between the belief that this approach to warfare was the future of the U.S. military and the belief that U.S. forces would be greeted as liberators and quickly turn over power to a stable Iraqi government. For Rumsfeld and others in the administration, the assumption that the United States was essentially a benevolent force and would be understood as such by the Iraqi population, went hand in hand with the belief that Iraqi society would quickly return to stability because the promise of democracy would alleviate the prospects for political violence, and the conviction that the war could be won and the occupation carried out with a fraction of the force employed in the first Gulf War. Over the months leading up to the war, Rumsfeld and his staff would be locked in an ongoing, occasionally public argument with the Pentagon's senior uniformed military officers over the size of the U.S. invasion force, with Rumsfeld pushing for a small force consistent with the doctrine of military transformation. At one point Rumsfeld suggested the possibility of an invasion force comprised of just 10,000 troops, though this was very likely a bargaining position in the bureaucratic struggle over this issue within the Pentagon rather than a serious proposal. The force that finally invaded Iraq in March of 2003 would be roughly 145,000 troops including both British and U.S. forces. Planning for the war assumed a goal of removing all but 35,000 U.S. troops from Iraq by the end of the summer of 2003, just six months after the initial invasion.[17]

In late 2001, Rumsfeld summoned senior military leaders to discuss planning for war in Iraq. Central Command's existing plan, labeled OPLAN 1003–98, called for the deployment of some 500,000 troops to Iraq. Rumsfeld felt this number was too large and this plan would require too much time to execute. When asked by General Myers how many troops he thought would be sufficient, Rumsfeld responded that he did not see why more than 125,000 would be needed and even that might be too many.[18] He believed that the war in Afghanistan had demonstrated the effectiveness of small numbers of technologically sophisticated forces as a substitute for mass.[19] Rumsfeld also told Franks that of those troops who would be deployed, a significant number would be en route as the war in Iraq began. If the war ended quickly, some of those troops who had not yet arrived would not be deployed at all, but simply sent home. Thus, Rumsfeld's planning for the postwar occupation of Iraq assumed a number of U.S. forces potentially even smaller than the total number allotted for the war. Once the war was over—the end of the war in this plan being associated with the fall of the Ba'ath regime—the reason for sending more troops would already have been achieved, so there would be no purpose in landing any who had not arrived already.[20]

Rumsfeld approached the task of approving force deployments with the eye of corporate accountant seeking constantly to control costs and increase efficiency. He "regularly told Pentagon officials that the United States had sent more forces and supplies than were needed, that the Iraqi military was weaker than it had been in 1991." As one former senior general who watched the development of the war plan put it, "The secretary of defense cut off the flow of divisions, saying the thing would be over in two days."[21] In April 2003, as Saddam Hussein's regime teetered and then collapsed, Rumsfeld pushed the issue of the number of troops needed with Franks. Both the army's First Calvary and First Armored Divisions were in the process of being deployed; initially Franks insisted that both were needed, but eventually he relented under pressure from Rumsfeld, who officially cancelled the deployment of the First Cavalry Division on April 21. Tom White, the civilian army secretary, said that "Rumsfeld just ground Franks down" on the issue.[22]

White also suggested that the Army's "working budgetary assumption was that ninety days after completion of the operation, we would withdraw the first fifty thousand and then every thirty days we'd take out another fifty thousand until everybody was back. The view was that whatever was left in Iraq would be de minimis."[23] Pentagon plans had assumed a relatively stable and secure environment in Iraq that would allow for most U.S. troops to be withdrawn by the fall of 2003, leaving a force of no more than 70,000 and possibly as few as 30,000 by that point.[24]

A belief in the capacity of American power to transform the world was clearly in evidence in the Bush administration's thinking about the prospect of war in Iraq. Bush claimed before that war that he intended to "seize the opportunity to achieve big goals. There is nothing bigger than to achieve world peace . . . There is a human condition that we must worry about . . . As we think about Iraq . . . it will be for the objective of making the world more peaceful.[25] This belief went hand in hand with what Andrew Flibbert has called "an abiding faith in the efficacy of military force as an instrument of U.S. foreign policy." "With the ongoing revolution in military affairs," Flibbert has suggested, observers in and out of the administration expected American military prowess to be unrivalled in the early twenty-first century, delivering greater firepower and costing fewer U.S. casualties than at any prior moment in history . . . Such confidence in the efficacy of force was linked to a view of Middle East politics as exceptionally brutal and therefore resistant to subtler means of external influence."[26] As PNAC fellow Reuel Marc Gerecht put it in December 2001, "We have no choice but to re-install in our foes and friends the fear and respect that attaches to any great power . . .Only a war against Saddam Hussein will decisively restore the awe that protects American interests abroad and citizens at home."[27]

In the Bush administration's worldview "the United States, unlike any other great power in human history, was deemed capable of playing a dominant but entirely benevolent role in world politics, since U.S. intentions were believed to be irreproachable. The purported absence of American imperial ambition—'America has no empire to extend or utopia to establish'—derived from a sense of American exceptionalism . . . a hegemonic America served as keeper of the global order and was entitled to defend its primacy from both latent threats and open acts of defiance."[28] Thus, the use of preemptive force, which would have been intolerable by another state, was justified in the case of the United States by virtue of America's unique benevolence and the fact that as the guarantor of global stability, America was a unique target for the forces of radicalism and violence in the world.

Many authors have noted the importance of American "exceptionalism" in the intellectual history of U.S. foreign policy, the belief that the United States is a unique society, a "city on the hill" unlike other nations. In fact there is nothing particularly "exceptional" about the fact that Americans have viewed their country as distinct and special; it is certainly possible to find in the foreign policy rhetoric of many societies over time expressions of pride in unique aspects of national culture. What has distinguished American exceptionalism from the cultural pride of other societies is the idea that, at least in politics, what has made America exceptional is not in fact culturally bounded but universally applicable. The enlightenment principles of the American founding, the belief that individual liberty and popular sovereignty could create a better and more just society, have been asserted as ideas that could be applied anywhere, and could knit together the most fractious and diverse polities under a banner of common respect for human dignity and freedom. Japanese and German nationalists of the early twentieth century certainly held that their national cultures were unique and destined for greatness, but tended to equate these ideas to one degree or another with race. They assumed that their racial-cultural superiority entitled them to dominion over others who were inferior in these ways, so they would not have held that what made their cultures exceptional were principles universalizable to all human beings. American political philosophy and the orthodox myths of the American historical experience describe a set of beliefs that are consciously blind to race and culture. It is because of this distinction that Americans have been able to engage in the practices of imperialism while simultaneously arguing that that they have no empires to build, and have often viewed policies that would be loathsome if intended by others to achieve the dominance of one culture over another as moral obligations when carried out to confer the blessings of liberty and universal human rights on people living under tyranny.

The importance of the Bush administration's belief in the transformative power of Western democracy is demonstrated by the great stock the administration placed in the prospect of Iraqi elections in early 2005. Consistent with its presumption of the pacifying effects of democratic rule, the administration hoped that these elections would undercut the growing insurgency and put Iraq on a path toward stability and an eventual end to the U.S. occupation. Iraqi prime minister Ayad Allawi, the U.N.'s Lakhdar Brahimi and others warned the administration that Sunnis would boycott the elections and thus be disenfranchised in the government that would emerge. The CIA also warned that the elections would leave Sunnis disenfranchised and thus might further escalate violence. After one CIA briefing in which these points were raised Bush looked at the briefer and asked derisively "is this Baghdad Bob?" "I'm not hearing that from anyone else but the CIA," Bush said. "I'm depending on the prospect of the elections and an elected government to get the insurgency down and get the security improved."[29]

In retrospect the elections seem to have been seen by many Iraqi Shia as an opportunity to assert Shia power in the country, and had that effect. The government which emerged was supported by little sense of common civic interest between political parties primarily formed around ethnic, religious, or clan loyalties. It was a government with little power over militias and other armed groups throughout the country, and indeed was more controlled by these groups than in control of them. An understanding of the history and culture of Iraq might have led administration officials to the conclusion that the elections of 2005 would have produced these effects. But the dominant ideational orthodoxy within the Bush administration entailed a firm conviction that democracy could quickly take root in any cultural setting because the principles of democratic governance were rooted in universal human rights.

"We're sticking with the elections," Bush repeated to his advisors. Privately he expressed anger at the failure of Iraqi leadership, at the fact that national leaders of the caliber needed were not stepping forward to assert control and lead the country. "Why don't they take charge of their own destiny?" Bush asked in a January 10, 2005 NSC meeting. As the administration's attempts to build a stable Iraqi government proceeded slowly in the spring of 2006, White House Chief of Staff Andy Card recalled Bush's rising frustration. "Where's the leader?" he repeated. "Where's George Washington? Where's Thomas Jefferson? Where's John Adams, for crying out loud? He didn't even have much of a personality." Bush's sentiments suggested the depth of his administration's belief that the American model of democratic government was universally applicable, and would bring peace to Iraq if only it could be implemented there.[30]

It was a dominant assumption within the Bush administration that democracy would lead to peace and stability in Iraq, and that a democratic constitutional structure would lead to open, pluralistic politics—rather than the dominance of one group within society over others, or the use of democratic processes to seize power by groups with no long-term interest in democracy. That Islamic religious principles and identity would play a formal role in Iraq's postwar governing structures seems not to have been considered by the Bush administration, for whom an understanding of democracy was simply presumed to imply an American style separation of church and state. Similarly, the idea that political parties would tend to coalesce around ideological and policy differences as in the United States rather than sectarian and other forms of identity, seems to have been an unquestioned premise lying beneath the administration's understanding of "democracy" as it would apply in Iraq. The administration's expectations about politics in postwar Iraq simply did not take account of either the unique aspects of Iraqi culture or those elements of U.S. and Western culture that formed the hidden foundations of democracy as it was understood by the administration.

Constructing the Insurgency

On August 19, 2003, a truck bomb destroyed the United Nations compound in Baghdad, killing 22 people including the U.N. envoy Sergio Vieira de Mello. The next day, Bush met with his National Security Council. His characterization of these events in this private meeting was much akin to his public rhetoric. "An ugly day for freedom," he told his advisors. "Terrorists want us to retreat and we cannot. We need to redouble our efforts against terror . . . Groups that respond by pulling out of Iraq are simply giving in to the killers and rewarding them." The discussion that followed revealed much about the way in which Bush understood the identity of the United States and its enemies in Iraq. Bush said that in its public response, the administration's "theme should be that the Iraqis should not allow foreign fighters to come into Iraq . . . we need to play on a sense of nationalism that will motivate Iraqis to cooperate with us to exclude the foreigners."[31]

This assertion seemed to overlook the fact that by far the largest group of foreign fighters in the country was Americans, and the increasingly apparent reality that much of the insurgency was motivated by the very nationalism that Bush sought to inspire—directed against occupation by a foreign power, the United States. Speaking to reporters two days later Bush revealed more about the way in which he understood America and its enemies in the ongoing war, saying that Iraq represented "a continuing battle in the war on terror . . . we found resistance from former Ba'athist officials. These people decided that, well, they'd rather fight than work for peaceful reconstruction of Iraq because they weren't going to be in power anymore. I also believe there is a foreign element that is moving into Iraq and these will be al Qaeda-type fighters. They want to fight us there because they can't stand the thought of a free society in the Middle East. They hate freedom. They hate the thought of a democracy emerging. And therefore, they want to violently prevent that from happening." He elaborated further in his radio address of August 23, saying that progress in Iraq "makes the remaining terrorists even more desperate and willing to lash out against symbols of order and hope, like coalition forces and the U.N. personnel. The world will not be intimidated. A violent few will not determine the future of Iraq, and there will be no return to the days of Saddam Hussein's torture chambers and mass graves."[32]

In the months that followed, Bush would claim that "The violence we have seen is a power grab by these extreme and ruthless elements. It's not a civil war. It's not a popular uprising. Most of Iraq is relatively stable. Most Iraqis, by far, reject violence."[33] In April 2004, U.S. administrator Paul Bremer said that he thought rising violence in Iraq was motivated by the fact that Iraqis "feel somewhat guilty that they were not able to liberate themselves. So there is a lot of perverse resentment."[34] In his memoir of his time in Iraq, Bremer consistently refers to the insurgency as being made up of Ba'athist and al Qaeda elements, but he does not acknowledge that to some extent it was a nationalist movement.

In fact, some Iraqi forces had been fighting a guerilla war against the United States from the very beginning. In some of its first combat engagements of the war the U.S. military would face the kinds of guerilla forces and tactics that would be seen again and again in the years to come. In Nasiriyah, the U.S. Marines encountered house to house urban fighting involving one after another ambush attack by Iraqi forces dressed in civilian clothes. The repeat of the Gulf War that the administration and U.S. military had planned for was not to be; the fall of Saddam Hussein's government would not signal the end of the war, but merely another stage in what was to a certain extent a guerilla conflict from the outset.[35]

Though the capabilities of Iraq's regular military had degraded as it sat idly through the 1990s, deprived of resources by virtue of the international sanctions in place on the country, the Ba'athist regime built up its paramilitary and special forces for internal security. Volunteer militias known as al Quds had existed throughout the country, but it was decided that these would not be sufficient, and in 1994 a special force known as the Fedayeen was founded under the leadership of Uday Hussein. These units were trained in small arms tactics and tasked with the protection of Ba'ath Party headquarters and other important sites that the regular army had failed to defend effectively in the uprisings of 1991. The Fedayeen's mission was largely domestic control; in the case of an uprising, it was to work with local militias loyal to the government to contain the rebellion for long enough for Republican Guard forces to move in and crush it. Caches of automatic weapons, mortars, and rocket-propelled grenades were secreted throughout the country for the use of the Fedayeen in such an emergency. Heavy artillery was requested as well, but Saddam Hussein reportedly denied this request for fear that such weapons might fall into the hands of opponents of the regime. The Fedayeen was not explicitly intended to serve as a guerilla force if the regime fell ("There were some things you just didn't talk about, because of morale," one former Iraqi general said), but in the event they were well equipped and positioned to play this role. U.S. intelligence, suffering from a lack of human sources on the ground in Iraq in the 1990s, appears to have failed to fully comprehend these developments, which of course could not be detected by the spy satellites on which U.S. observers relied.[36]

Over the months that followed the Ba'athist regime's fall, these irregular forces formed one significant source of support for the development of a wide array of militant resistance groups. Rumsfeld argued in the spring of 2004 that growing violence was the work of "thugs, gangs, and terrorists . . . we're facing a test of wills . . . we will meet the test."[37] Rumsfeld did not acknowledge any distinction between the disparate elements of the growing insurgency. Rhetorically he lumped former-regime loyalists together with religious jihadists, and conflated the wars in Iraq and Afghanistan under the broader rubric of the "War on Terror." "Coalition forces will continue to root out, capture, and kill remnants of the former regime until they no longer pose a threat to the Iraqi people," he said. "Two terrorist regimes have been removed, but we still have terrorist enemies in Afghanistan and Iraq and across the globe who are seeking to harm our people."[38]

In fact, the insurgency that developed in the early years of the Iraq war was highly diverse and decentralized, making it a difficult enemy for the U.S. military, with its conventional, state-oriented war-fighting culture to find and fight. The collection of predominantly Sunni insurgent groups that emerged initially can be loosely categorized into two broad camps: the first, affiliated or ideologically aligned with al Qaeda in Iraq, included groups such as Jaysh Ahl-ul-Sunna (the Army of the People of the Sunna) and Jaysh al-Taifa al Mansoura (the Army of the Victorious Party), which would eventually become more formally organized under the mantle of the Majlis Shoura al-Mujahidden, or Mujahideen Advisory Council. These groups tended to include both Iraqis and foreign fighters and were organized around the appointment of undisputed local leaders know as Amirs. The second broad grouping of insurgent organizations, more secular and overwhelmingly made up of Iraqis, included at least ten distinct groups and numerous subdivisions, notably Jaysh al-Islami al-Iraqi (the Islamic Army of Iraq), Jaysh 'Umar (the Army of Omar), Jaysh Muhammad (the Army of Muhammad), and Kataib Thawrat al-'Ishrin (the Battalions of the 1920 Uprising). These groups often included elements of the former Iraqi military; the French Journalist Georges Malbrunot concluded that the Islamic Army of Iraq (which captured and held him hostage for some four months), led by former intelligence officers, was comprised of at least 15,000 members and was well organized and funded. According to Allawi, these insurgent groups tended to be held together by family or tribal loyalty and devotion to radical forms of Islam, and often some combination of these factors. This ideological motivation, along with an organizational structure based on cells generated ad hoc for specific tasks and the implicit support for them that existed among the broader Sunni population, made these groups difficult for U.S. intelligence to uncover or penetrate. After some major confrontations with U.S. forces in Fallujah and elsewhere early in the war, the tactics of these groups shifted toward avoiding direct, large scale contact with the U.S. military and toward taking advantage of the security vacuum in much of the country by moving into territory undefended by coalition forces and withdrawing again when confronted with major coalition attacks.[39]

It was the most religiously-oriented of these Sunni groups that were mainly responsible for the waves of bombing attacks against Shia and other civilians in the years that followed. The Bush administration and the U.S. media typically referred to these as "suicide bombers," but this term mischaracterizes the intent of the individual being labeled, whose primary goal is not in fact to commit suicide (though of course this is a consequence of his or her actions), but to destroy something or someone else. To call someone a suicide bomber is to suggest that they are first and foremost suicidal, and by extension unstable and irrational, when in fact the main intent of their actions is an act of political violence that may be quite rational within the framework of assumptions and values they hold. It fit with the Bush administration's worldview to describe such attackers as psychotic, evil, and isolated actors, but this is very likely not how they saw themselves, and the implications for American policy of failing to understand this difference were significant. A "suicide bomber" who acts to achieve a specific military and political goal as part of a larger, ideologically motivated organization such as al Qaeda is engaging in a very different activity than a delusional person who takes their own life or another person's because they are driven by their mental illness to do so. To conflate the two served the purpose of ideational clarity and cognitive consistency in the Bush administration, but it also played a significant role in undermining the effectiveness of U.S. foreign policy in Iraq.[40]

One member of Jaysh Muhammad, one of the largest insurgent groups, was quoted in *Newsweek* in August 2003 as saying that he fought because "The Americans have occupied our land under a false pretext, and without any international authorization. They kill our women and children and old men. They want to bring the Jews to our holy land in order to control Iraq, to achieve the Jewish dream."

Newsweek's correspondent concluded that the insurgents of Jaysh Muhammad were driven by a combination of Sunni Islam, nationalism, and anti-Semitism. An insurgent in the Ramadi area interviewed by the *Guardian* in October 2003 claimed that he fought because "We do not want to see our country occupied by forces clearly pursuing their own interests, rather than being poised to return Iraq to the Iraqis."[41]

As for the Shia insurgent movements, the largest and most influential was comprised of militias loyal to the cleric Muqtada al Sadr. Sadr was described by Bremer as "a rabble-rousing Shiite cleric" and a "young firebrand."[42] Throughout his memoir, Bremer consistently refers to Muqtada al-Sadr by his first name, as if speaking about a child. He suggests that his view was that Sadr was a radical revolutionary—"I'd received increasingly disturbing reports about Muqtada from our able regional coordinator from the Center South, Mike Gfoeller," Bremer writes. "He described Muqtada as a 'Bolshevik Islamist' who understood only one thing, raw power, and who would stop at nothing to get it."[43]

The view of Moqtada al-Sadr and his followers held by U.S. officials was quite different from that held by many Iraqi Shia. As violence and insecurity rose in the weeks and months after Saddam's fall, Sadr's forces stepped in to fill the vacuum. "Sadr's followers did everything from protecting the mosques to acting as traffic police and picking up the garbage. Despite his youth and inexperience, Sadr gained support from seminary students and the masses of impoverished Shia."[44] And though Sadr's was clearly a Shia movment, the Sadrists consistently maintained a public stance of unity with Sunni Islamists which emphasized the rhetoric of nationalist resistance to foreign occupation. Allawi writes that "The Sadrists always claimed that they were Iraqi nationalists, and therefore publicly eschewed sectarian differences between the Shia and the Sunni."[45]

Allawi argues that the failure of the Bush administration to recognize the possibility of this kind of nationalist resistance to the U.S. occupation was rooted in its reliance on the view of the Iraq suggested by scholars such as Bernard Lewis, who tended to argue that Shia Muslims, as the Middle East's perpetual outsiders and victims of the domination by the Sunni majority, would be natural allies in the American agenda to reform the Middle East because of this status. What this belief ignores, Allawi suggests, is the fact that the Shia do not necessarily see themselves first as a minority sect within Islam but as Muslims. They tend to believe that their faith is Islam in its true and legitimate form, and thus the idea that they would embrace the presence of Western armies on Muslim land or rapprochement with Israel simply because of their religious identity was fundamentally misguided.[46]

Many insurgent groups appropriated "the symbols and rhetoric of national resistance to the foreign occupier." They sought to appeal to "Iraqi patriotism, a revulsion at the invasion of the country by foreign armies, and a feeling that Iraq's integrity as a country had been violated." In particular, "the Sadrists' public posture was based on a patriotic rejection of the occupation . . . Whatever individuals might have felt about the direction in which Saddam and the Ba'ath Party were taking Iraq, it could not warrant acceptance of such a dramatic upending of the political order. It was this sense of loss and disempowerment that fed the main wellsprings of the 'nationalist' resistance."[47]

Allawi argues that the administration's particular "categorization of the insurgents translated into ineffective military actions against the insurgency."[48] He claims that these misguided and counterproductive policies were rooted in fundamental misunderstanding of Iraqi society and Sunni identity in particular:

> The Bush administration shared with others a gross misconception related to the response of the Sunni Arabs to their loss of power and prestige. This was probably most disturbing to observers, not least to those Iraqis who thought that after a sullen period of resentment the Sunni Arabs would adjust to the changed circumstances and seek to find a place in the new constellation of forces in the country. The insurgency was almost an exclusively Sunni Arab affair, notwithstanding the two half-rebellions of Moqtada al-Sadr in 2004. The sense of loss and defeat was made even more poignant by the fact that it was a totally unexpected force that achieved the impossible—the dethronement of the community from centuries of power in favour of, as they saw it, a rabble led by Persianate clerics . . . [The insurgency was a] form of existential struggle, where the Sunni Arabs' entire history and identity were at stake.[49]

An October, 2003 National Intelligence Estimate produced by the CIA concluded that the insurgency had its roots in essentially local factors, deep social grievances and hostility toward the presence of foreign troops on Iraqi soil. But the NIE was essentially ignored within the administration. National Intelligence Council Chairman Robert Hutchings concluded that "Frankly, senior officials simply weren't ready to pay attention to analysis that didn't conform to their optimistic scenarios."[50] The Bush administration's construction of the identity of both Iraq and the United States precluded the possibility of a nationalist resistance to U.S. occupation, which was understood by the Bush administration to be a means to the liberation of the diverse array of groups held together by the authoritarian rule of Saddam Hussein. While the administration appears to have believed that these groups could remain united under the more benevolent rubric of Western democracy, at the highest levels it utterly failed to anticipate the power of subnational sectarian loyalties or the strength of Iraqi nationalism and the hostility that this sentiment would quickly engender toward Western soldiers on Iraqi soil. As Gareth Stansfield has written, American policy in Iraq was premised on the "implicit belief that most people in the world are post-ethnic individualists, like Americans believe themselves to be." As a consequence of this assumption, Stansfield contends, "the continuing hold of ethnic and sectarian allegiances was underestimated. The violence and the centrifugal forces we are witnessing in today's Iraq are the reckoning for the 30 years of war that the Sunni-dominated regime waged against the Shias and the Kurds."[51]

Iraqi Culture and the Occupation

The Bush administration not only failed to recognize that Iraqi nationalism would be a factor challenging and complicating the U.S. occupation, but particularly failed to note that resistance to Western imperialism was in fact one of the defining facets of this Iraq national identity. Prior to the Mongol destruction of Baghdad in the thirteenth century, Iraq was a center of world civilization; after that experience its global importance was much diminished, and under Ottoman rule in later centuries Iraq would be administratively divided into three regions, centered around Mosul, Baghdad, and Basra. The reunification of Iraq under British control in the early twentieth century amounted to the re-creation of an Iraqi political community paralleling the Iraqi cultural identity that had never entirely vanished, and the earliest defining experience of this political community was one of armed revolt against European colonial rule. Resistance to the British occupation of the early twentieth century, a historical precedent with eerie parallels to the current U.S. occupation, played a critical role in establishing the ways in which modern Iraqis would understand what it meant to be Iraqi.[52] Feisal Amin Rasoul Al-Istrabadi has argued that Iraq's "national history has fostered a true sense of national Iraqi identity that cannot be lightly dismissed. Indeed, as UN officials continually assert, it has been clear for some time that a significant segment—it is difficult to quantify the percentage precisely—of the current insurgency is now composed of Iraqi nationalists fighting against what they perceive as a potential break-up of the country by outside forces."[53]

A basic understanding of Iraqi history and culture should have belied the belief that most Iraqis would readily embrace a Western occupying force or an American-backed puppet government. As Allawi puts it, "Iraq is one of the most invaded and violated territories in the history of the world, and over a long period of time the people who lived in the country had developed survival and accommodation skills that would confound the most determined of occupiers." "None of this should have come as a surprise" to U.S. leaders, Allawi asserts. "There were enough pointers in Iraq's recent past to show the likely response of Iraqis to the massive jolt of a physical occupation by foreign powers, and the effects that a violent upending of apparently stable relationships would have on the varied components of society." Allawi argues that it was not Iraq's ancient history but the era of the Arab conquest of the region, the rise of Islam, and the centuries of Ottoman-Persian contention over it that followed that gave contemporary Iraq a usable past to the extent that it had one at all. "It is to this period . . . that the modern predicaments of Iraq can be traced," he writes. "the conflict that arose from it remained essentially unreconciled and unresolved, even with the passing of centuries . . . For over two millennia, Iraq had either been the centre of a world empire or, more often, part of another country's empire. It was only in modern times that the geopolitical unity of Iraq became established—neither as a contrived state, as many would later claim, nor as a nation in the full sense of the word."[54]

Given this history, the rhetoric of freedom and democracy that U.S. leaders assumed to be universally meaningful did not in fact translate into the language and culture of Iraq with anything like the same significance it conveyed in the United States. Because the principles of liberal philosophy did not have the same relationship to the shared social identity of Iraqis that they did for Americans, couching the war and occupation in these terms did not resonate with Iraqis in the ways that the administration anticipated it would. U.S. leaders had failed to realize that the social power of these words and ideas was not inherent in them as abstract concepts, but in fact was rooted in the political culture and dominant historical narrative of the Western tradition. U.S. leaders believed they were making a case on the basis of universal ideals, and failed to grasp that the meanings of the words associated with those ideals were to a large extent culturally dependent.

The Bush administration's belief in the transcendent appeal of Western-style democracy obscured its understanding of the distinctive aspects of Iraqi history and culture that would have argued against its predictions of a quick war ending with a stable and democratic Iraq. While U.S. leaders identified Saddam Hussein as the primary source of political violence in Iraq, Nimrod Raphaeli has argued that violent political change has been the historical norm in Iraqi politics; the belief that the promise of democracy in Saddam Hussein's absence would lead to a rapid and peaceful power transition was premised on embedded American cultural assumptions rather than a clear understanding of Iraqi history. "Modern Iraqi culture is also marked by tribalism and violence," Raphaeli argues:

> On October 29, 1936, Iraqi general Bakr Sidqi led the first military coup in the Middle East. He was assassinated less than a year later. While military coups became frequent in Middle Eastern states, Iraq set another first when, on July 14, 1958, it became the scene of the first Middle Eastern coup to culminate in the execution of the head of state. Another coup led to the execution of General 'Abd al-Karim Qasim, the 1958 coup leader. Several other leaders subsequently died under suspicious circumstances. After a short-lived 1963 attempt to seize power, the Baath party tried again and consolidated control after a 1968 coup. In 1979, vice president Saddam Hussein deposed the president, General Ahmad Hassan al-Bakr, who subsequently died from apparent poisoning. Very few Iraqi leaders die of natural causes.[55]

Iraqi historian and sociologist Ali al-Wardi argues that the Bedouin tradition continues to form the basis of modern Iraqi identity. The three elements central to Bedouin culture according to Wardi are tribalism, raiding, and chivalry, each of which is in turn rooted in the concept of *taghalub*, or predominance. "The Bedouin individual seeks to persuade by the force of his tribe, his personal strength, and his sense of superiority. Because of a lack of rules to adjudicate conflict, Bedouins use force to avenge transgressions. This, Wardi argues, explains why there is near permanent war in Bedouin society. 'War in the desert is the reality; peace is a fleeting phenomenon.'"[56]

Widely regarded as among the most insightful analysts of Iraq society, al-Wardi wrote extensively about the effects of nomadism and the way in which multiple social cleavages—sect, tribe, and region, among others—overlapped against the backdrop of Iraq's history of subjection and resistance to empire. Al-Wardi described, in the words of Ali Allawi, "a fragmented social order interacting within the framework of a tumultuous historical legacy. It emphasised the disjointed nature of Iraqi society, held together by geographic imperatives of coexistence in the same space rather than a common sense of shared history or purpose." Allawi notes the fact that the insights of leading scholars such as al-Wardi "might have provided a counterbalance to the range of ill-considered and ahistorical assessments of Iraq that governed the planning for the war and its aftermath" within the Bush administration. It is not possible to say that al-Wardi's rendering of Iraqi society is the "correct" view, that it is more accurate than the neoconservative view that tended to downplay social cleavages and believe them manageable under the aegis of democratic universalism. But at a minimum it can be understood as a credible alternative to the neoconservative construction, and one with enormous implications for U.S. policy in Iraq. It is not necessary to accept one perspective over the other to nevertheless conclude that American policy might have been better prepared for the range of possible Iraqi reactions to a U.S. occupation had it been informed by an understanding of the work of scholars such as al-Wardi.[57]

The organization created within the U.S. Department of Defense to govern postwar Iraq was the Office of Reconstruction and Humanitarian Assistance, under the leadership of former Army General Jay Garner. Garner himself acknowledged that ORHA had been "an ad hoc operation, glued together over about four or five weeks' time. [We] didn't really have enough time to plan."[58] Garner's ORHA staff had almost no Arabists on it at first, and despite his desperate need for expertise, Garner was "instructed by Secretary of Defense Rumsfeld to ignore the Future of Iraq Project."[59] Cheney, Rumsfeld, and the neoconservatives as a group opposed the participation of the State Department in general and its Arabist Middle East experts in particular in the planning for and implementation of postwar governance in Iraq. The primary reasons seem to have been a belief among the neoconservatives that the State Department Arabists did not share their belief that Iraq could become a Western-style democracy, that they had been responsible for the failed policies of the past in which undemocratic governments had been propped up in the interest of stability, and that they did not support Ahmad Chalabi and the Iraqi National Congress as the future rulers of Iraq.[60]

Phillips has written that "ORHA's planning for the 'day after' was based on a set of assumptions that all proved to be wrong," largely based on memories of the aftermath of the 1991 Gulf War. "The United States anticipated oil-field fires, a massive humanitarian crisis, widespread revenge attacks against former leaders of Saddam's government, and threats from Iraq's neighbors. None of these events came to pass."[61] When Garner and his ORHA staff arrived in Baghdad they were few in number and utterly overwhelmed by the scale of the devastation wrought by the war and subsequent looting.

Looting in the days following Saddam's fall was widespread and astonishingly destructive, constituting nothing less than a disaster for Iraq, as well as for the image of the United States in the minds of many Iraqis. "They stole everything," Garner said of the looters. "They stripped the wiring out of the walls, took the plumbing, and they torched the buildings." Looting destroyed Baghdad's electrical grid, leaving the city with little or no electricity for months, shutting down refrigeration and impairing access to water. Mobs plundered hospitals, universities, and every government ministry, often leaving nothing behind and frequently destroying the buildings and everything in them. Virtually every item in the National Library and National Museum was stolen or destroyed, including irreplaceable historical records and artifacts dating from the very dawn of human civilization. Looters stole tons of high explosive and yellowcake uranium from nuclear facilities. While the looting was worst in Baghdad, it occurred in many places throughout the country, as more than 150,000 U.S. and coalition troops stood by all the while. U.S. inaction in the face of such wanton destruction suggested to many Iraqis that U.S. forces must be either unable or unwilling to stop it, and that as an occupier the United States was therefore either callously self-interested or impotent. British envoy John Sawers wrote in an internal memorandum to British leaders dated May 11, 2003 that the soldiers of the U.S. Third Infantry Division "are sticking to their heavy vehicles and combat gear, and are not inclined to learn new techniques. Our Paras company at the Embassy witnessed a U.S. tank respond to (harmless) Kalashnikov fire into the air from a block of residential flats by firing three tank rounds into the building. Stories are numerous of U.S. troops sitting on their tanks parked in front of public buildings while looters go about their business behind them. Every civilian who approaches a U.S. checkpoint is treated as a potential suicide bomber."[62] In the months that followed, there was scant access to clean water, sanitation, and electricity in many places in Iraq. Unemployment in postwar Iraq was 65 percent, and in many neighborhoods crime and violence became rampant.[63]

In late June 2003, Thomas Friedman wrote,

> The Bush Pentagon went into this war assuming that it could decapitate the Iraq army, bureaucracy and police force, remove the Saddam loyalists and then basically run Iraq through the rump army,

> bureaucracy, and police force . . . What happened instead was that they all collapsed, leaving a security and administrative vacuum, which the U.S. military was utterly unprepared to fill. The U.S. forces arrived in Iraq with far too few military police and civilian affairs officers to run the country. As a result, the only way U.S. troops could stop the massive looting was by doing the only thing they knew how: shooting people. Since they didn't want to do that . . . Iraqi government infrastructure, oil equipment and even nuclear research sites were stripped bare. As a result, we are not starting at zero in Iraq. We are starting below zero."[64]

Paul Bremer replaced Garner as the U.S. civilian authority in Iraq in May, 2003, and with him ORHA was supplanted by the Coalition Provisional Authority (CPA). As Bremer describes them, his first concerns in Iraq were with the image of the United States held by Iraqis, and his first impulse was to change that image by using military power, to demonstrate that the United States had the ability, the will, and the sovereign authority to use lethal force where and when it saw fit. In his first meeting with Garner and a group of about 30 senior staff members after landing in Iraq, Bremer stated that "Establishing law and order will be our first priority . . . the media coverage of the unchecked looting makes us look powerless . . . When the American led forces occupied Haiti in 1994, our troops shot sixteen looters breaking curfew and the looting stopped."[65]

The first orders Paul Bremer gave as administrator of the CPA implemented a program of de-Ba'athification and dissolution of the Iraqi military. In retrospect these orders were perhaps the most catastrophic decisions made by the United States in postwar Iraq. They were handed down by Bremer in the very first days after he arrived in the country, and carried out over the strong objections of the outgoing head of ORHA Jay Garner and the CIA chief of station. They undercut the efforts at reconstruction that Garner had begun, which had depended on the large-scale use of the Iraqi military for rebuilding efforts, and destroyed ongoing negotiations between U.S. officials and Iraqi military officers that sought to begin payments to former soldiers with the ultimate goal of pacifying and gaining their support for the U.S. occupation effort. As a practical matter, they deprived Iraqi society of bureaucrats and technicians at every level of government, from those running the ministries to teachers and low-level government functionaries, ending the careers and pushing to the embittered margins of society many thousands of people whose skills were desperately needed to reestablish a functioning government and economy. They deprived vast numbers of individuals of their incomes, creating hardship for many times that number who were their dependents and removing these workers from the already devastated national economic base. They also deprived Iraq of hundreds of thousands of security forces at a time when postwar Iraqi society was marked by widespread criminal violence bordering on chaos. Hundreds of thousands of men were left without jobs, humiliated, and often with access to weapons. The Iraqi army, one of the few symbols of national identity, was eradicated with the stroke of a pen. Faleh Jabar, a scholar of the Ba'ath Party and senior fellow at the U.S. institute of Peace, has argued that "abruptly terminating the livelihoods of these men created a vast pool of humiliated, antagonized, and politicized men." Colonel John Agoglia, deputy chief of plans for the U.S. military's Central Command in 2003–2004, argued that Bremer's orders marked "the day that we snatched defeat from the jaws of victory and created an insurgency." Lieutenant Colonel Alan King, a civil affairs officer in the Third Infantry Division, claimed that "when Bremer did that, the insurgency went crazy. May was the turning point . . . when they disbanded the military, and announced we were occupiers—that was it. Every moderate, every person that had leaned toward us, was furious."[66]

Bremer suggests that his de-Ba'athification order was "the single most important step I had taken as administrator," because "it clearly demonstrated that we intended not just to throw out the brutal tyranny of Saddam, but also to establish in its place a new political order."[67]

De-Ba'athification had the effect of decimating the managerial ranks of many of Iraq's social, political, and public works bureaucracies, precisely at the moment when skilled managers and technicians were most needed to repair these institutions and return them to some semblance of their prewar functions. Among many Iraqi Sunnis in particular, de-Ba'athification was seen as an indication of America's imperial ambitions in Iraq because of the Party's nationalist and anticolonial ideology. While some members of the Ba'ath Party had joined for ideological reasons, others joined out of fear, or out of professional ambition or necessity, or because they felt they had no choice. Membership in the Party was a prerequisite for civil service employment, so nearly all professors, doctors, and engineers were members. The Party's ideology was deeply entrenched in the formal practices of Iraq's education system and elsewhere in the national culture. And it was intimately associated with a sense of nationalism and independence from Western domination. As Phillips writes, "Ba'athist values were taught in schools and emphasized in the workplace. Building on the anticolonial movement of the 1950s and 1960s, Ba'athism and Iraq's national identity became synonymous. Both were fundamentally about asserting independence from Great Britain and establishing equality with the West. Iraqi nationalism was strongest among the beneficiaries of Ba'athist rule." For many Iraqis and particularly for many Sunnis, the Ba'ath party was at least in part a symbol of national self-determination and anticolonialism. So the dismantling of the party was not necessarily seen by these individuals as the eradication of a mechanism of tyranny and oppression as U.S. officials intended, but rather as the destruction of a symbol of national identity and resistance to foreign control, playing directly to the fears of nationalistic Iraqis that the United States was yet another European power seeking to subject Iraq to its rule and exploit the country's resources. De-Ba'athification was intended to establish an image of the United States as liberator in the minds of Iraqis, but due to a failure on the part of U.S. policy makers to understand the meanings of their actions in the context of Iraqi culture, the actual effect for some Iraqis was likely just the opposite—to confirm that that United States was indeed an oppressive colonial power.[68]

Bremer's dissolution of the Iraqi army made no distinction between the roughly 9000 officers who were members of the Ba'ath party and the rest of the 400,000-man force. It effectively left all of them without jobs, compensation, or prospects. Thousands of Iraqi soldiers appeared daily outside the gates of the U.S. embassy after Bremer's order, protesting and displaying signs with messages such as "Dissolving the Iraqi army is a humiliation to the dignity of the nation." Major Mohammed Faour, a former member of Iraq's Special Forces, has suggested that many military officers were prepared to work with the Americans, but "You can't put half a million people with families and weapons and a monthly salary on the dole. . . They'll turn against you." The social and economic effects of the elimination of the Iraqi army certainly extended far beyond the individual soldiers as well; since the average Iraqi family had six members, the number of lives affected directly or indirectly was likely closer to 2.4 million.[69]

The social implications of the dissolution of the Iraqi army almost certainly surpassed Bremer's expectations or intentions. Bremer said he believed that the army was regarded with deep suspicion by the Kurds and other minority groups due to its history of brutal repression, and that it was seen by the Shia as both an instrument of their subjugation and an institution that enshrined discrimination against them in its structures of authority. Many neoconservatives seem to have viewed the Iraqi military as one among many vestiges of Saddam's brutal rule, an organization that was tainted by its history of complicity in Saddam's crimes and therefore not much to be missed. From the point of view of many Iraqis, however, the nation's armed forces were understood quite differently. The army was in many ways the only truly national institution in Iraq, and the county's military history was a source of much of the unifying national mythology that gave Iraqis a sense of identity broader than tribe or sect. As Allawi describes it,

> The Iraqi army had played an almost mystical role in the narrative of modern Iraqi history. The Iraqi public was never told of the army's excesses in its various campaigns against tribes, Kurds, Assyrians, and other rebellious groups. It was seen as a preserver of the nation's core values, and heroic myths were built around its supposed victories and triumphs . . . Its battles in the 1948 war in Palestine and in the 1973 October war were given an epic dimension, and schoolboys were drilled in the virtues of the armed forces as upholders of martial values and pan-Arabism . . . [In the Iran-Iraq war] the army, in the Ba'athist regime's propaganda, was given the additional role of 'guardians' over the eastern gateway of the entire Arab world . . . The security services were detested, and very few could muster any arguments for keeping them. The armed forces, on the other hand, generated considerable sympathy and respect throughout Iraq . . . the decades of indoctrination about the Iraqi armed forces had left a deep impression on the public at large, who reckoned that the army was an integral part of the identity of the state of Iraq.[70]

Driven by a Manichaean conception of politics that viewed all vestiges of the old regime as intolerable, de-Ba'athification and the dissolution of the Iraqi army did incalculable damage to Iraq's economy and the ability of its state structures to govern. Tareq and Jacqueline Ismael have argued that these policies "resulted in the complete collapse of Iraqi state infrastructure . . . [and] created a political and social vacuum, and pre-Ba'ath party social institutions (the tribal, religious and communal formations already emergent under sanctions) were the only agencies left to fill the security vacuum precipitated by the loss of administrative control."[71]

With regard to its physical presence in the country, Bremer's Coalition Provisional Authority acted as an imperial enclave largely detached from the society around it. Larry Diamond has summed up the causes and consequences of the disconnect between the Iraqi view of the Coalition Provisional Authority and the CPA's view of itself as follows:

> The coalition lacked the linguistic and area expertise necessary to understand Iraqi politics and society, and the few long-time experts present were excluded from the inner circle of decision-making in the CPA. Thus the coalition never grasped, for example, the fact that although most Iraqis were grateful for having been liberated from a brutal tyranny, their gratitude was mixed with deep suspicion of the United States' real motives (not to mention those of the United Kingdom, a former colonial ruler of Iraq); humiliation that the Iraqis themselves have proved unable to overthrow Saddam; and unrealistic expectations of the postwar administration, which Iraqis expected to quickly deliver them from their problems. Too many Iraqis viewed the invasion not as an international effort but as an occupation by Western, Christian, essentially Anglo-American powers, and this evoked powerful memories of previous subjugation and of nationalist struggles against Iraq's former overlords.[72]

Packer writes that "Almost all of Bremer's confidants were Americans. The Arabic-speaking ambassadors with years of experience in the Middle East had less access to the administrator and less work to do than his small coterie of trusted aides from Washington. An Iraqi who was close to the CPA told me that, in general, the less one knew about Iraq, the more influence one had." A contractor in the Green Zone commented that life there was "like Plato's Republic . . . all of these well-meaning, smart people who want to do the right thing . . . But they never leave here and they have no idea what's happening in the country they're supposed to be building. It's totally absurd." Allawi describes the Green Zone as "a world of its own, ever more distant and alien from the rest of the country . . . an enclave where the culture of small-town America combined with the trappings of vice-regal administration. This created a curious 'bubble' environment divorced from the travails and life-threatening risks in the rest of the country, with ever more dense concentrations of Iraqi central government offices and officials, parliamentarians and politicians."[73]

Phillips argues that Bremer's "iron will made him seem more like a viceroy than a partner to the Iraqi people."

> By the end of his tenure . . . Iraqis were complaining to me about his imperious and authoritarian ways. Arab Sunnis were angered by Bremer's decrees dismantling institutions they had dominated for decades. Arab Shia blamed Bremer for failing to build bridges to

> prominent clerics such as Grand Ayatollah Ali al-Sistani. The Kurds were upset by Bremer's efforts to strong-arm them into power-sharing concessions with other Iraqis . . . Influenced by Ahmad Chalabi and his neo-con backers, Bremer made the decision to purge Iraq of the Ba'ath Party . . . [which to Sunnis] appeared like an effort to marginalize Arab Sunnis, who dominated the Ba'ath Party.[74]

Bremer has written that he believed that what he referred to as the "shock absorbers" of democratic society—democratic elections and institutions, civil liberties and other mechanisms through which social tension could be expressed and alleviated before it exploded into violence—would be sufficient to address Iraq's sectarian divisions if only they could be put into place quickly enough. For many Sunnis, however, the fall of Saddam Hussein's government represented not so much an opportunity for democratic free expression as the loss of a privileged power position and the realization of longstanding fears about what the country's Shia majority might do if it gained real power. For many Shia, it was not so much an opportunity for power sharing as a chance for the political realization of their demographic dominance, and perhaps for some a chance to exchange the role of oppressed for that of oppressor.

Since the dominant thinking within the Bush administration held that what Iraq needed was the creation of the institutions of democracy on top of what were essentially intact social structures and government bureaucracies, the administration's first post-military wave of occupation officials was largely comprised of policy experts. Some were Iraqi exiles with an interest in control of one or another government agency. Others were young Washington political apparatchiks, often with little or no knowledge of the country or the region, but with ample ambition and an ideological commitment to the administration's goal of transplanting democratic institutions onto the Iraqi body politic.[75]

Bremer's policies came to be seen by many Iraqis as designed to provide only the appearance of real democracy. He resisted quick nationwide direct elections as impracticable and potentially dangerous, saying that "elections that are held too early can be destructive . . . if you start holding elections, the people who are rejectionists tend to win." Bremer delayed and then cancelled plans for a national conference on governance that had been announced by Garner in April, 2003. His opposition to speedy, direct nationwide elections put him at odds with the influential Ayatollah al-Sistani, making it appear that despite its rhetoric the United States was not actually interested in implementing democracy in Iraq.[76]

Bremer named an Iraqi Governing Council that was broadly representative of the ethnic and sectarian diversity of the country, but which had little real authority. It was empowered to name interim ministers, propose a budget, and authorize the drafting of a new constitution, but was subject to the control of the CPA and was in reality far closer to an advisory committee or symbolic figurehead than a sovereign government. Ultimately, Phillips suggests that "The Governing Council had little standing with Iraqis, who saw it as an extension of the U.S. government and a rubber stamp of the CPA . . . With its headquarters in the heavily-fortified Green Zone, the Governing Council was distant and incomprehensible to most Iraqis." In a Friday sermon at the Imam Ali Mosque, al-Sistani said the Governing Council was unelected and illegal.[77]

Former CENTCOM Commander General Anthony Zinni has argued that the U.S. military's "biggest flaw is that we never take time to understand the culture. Some things we do that make perfect sense to us do not make perfect sense in another culture. As a result, look at the mistakes we've made in Iraq day by day."[78]

One example of the consequences of this failure of cultural sensitivity is suggested by a key element of the doctrine applied by the U.S. military in Iraq, the concept of "presence." A carryover from prior missions in Bosnia and Kosovo, the principle behind this approach was that much of the military's role was to reassure the civilian population by being very visible, patrolling frequently and on foot, and interacting at a personal level with the population. While this strategy was crucial to reinforcing the public sense that U.S. forces were capable of and intent on keeping the peace in Bosnia and Kosovo, however, the public's attitudes were quite different in Iraq and the "presence" mission had a very different effect. As Army civil affairs officer Lt. Christopher Holshek put it, among a civilian population that viewed the United States as an occupying force "the presence of troops . . . becomes counterproductive." In Thomas Ricks' view, in its application to Iraq the presence doctrine failed "to understand the centrality of Iraqi pride, and the humiliation Iraqi men felt to be occupied by a Western army."[79]

As Holshek put it, "Two o'clock in the morning, your door bursts open. A bunch of infantry guys burst into the private space of the house—in a society where family honor is the most important thing—and you lay the man down, and put the plastic cuffs on? And then we say, 'Oops, wrong home?' In this society, the guy has no other choice but to seek restitution. He will do that by placing a roadside bomb for one hundred dollars, because his family honor has been compromised."[80] Allawi agrees that [The measures that were used to confront the insurgents were . . . deeply offensive to the cultural and religious mores of what was still a tribal society. It is not so much that the US forces deliberately trampled over these sensibilities, rather that they were generally ignorant of them. The searching of homes without the presence of a male head of household, body searches of women, the use of sniffer dogs, degrading treatment of prisoners, public humiliation of the elderly and notables, all contributed to the view that the Americans had only disdain and contempt for Iraq's traditions. These stories of American insensitivity to local customs grew in the telling and became in the hands of the insurgents and their sympathisers a deliberate programme on the part of the USA to undermine the religious and cultural roots of the country.[81]]

For many Iraqis the image of the United States as occupier was shaped by the behavior of American troops more than by any other factor. Images and stories of violence by American forces resulting in the death or injury of Iraqi civilians became commonplace in occupied Iraq, as U.S. troops engaged in combat against a shadowy enemy came into contact with a vulnerable civilian population. The practices of American forces varied greatly from time to time, place to place, and unit to unit, but stereotypical images quickly emerged of U.S. troops massacring civilians when their cars failed to stop at checkpoints, U.S. bombs destroying civilian houses, the doors of private homes kicked in at all hours of the day and night, the humiliation of Iraqi prisoners held by the Americans, and the even more indiscriminate and unaccountable practices of U.S. contractors. A great number of these occurrences multiplied into an even greater number of rumors and retellings, firmly establishing the notion of the Americans as a brutal and wanton occupation force among many Iraqis. As George Packer describes the situation in late 2003, "As time went on and suicide bombings increased, checkpoints became the scenes of great danger, Far too many Iraqis, sometimes families with children, went down in a hail of gunfire when they failed to understand the bewildering array of signs and hand signals and orders shouted in English." Packer suggests the "daily screaming of obscenities and the spectacle of men thrown to the ground and zip-cuffed played a crucial part in fixing Iraqis' early impressions of the occupation. It was often their first direct encounter with any of the thousands of Americans in their country."[82]

Packer argues that many Iraqis' experience of the American occupiers involved a bewildering contrast between nurturing support and brutality. "Niceness and nastiness seemed to be two conjoined sides of their personality: Love me or I'll kill you." Packer describes the story, carried by the *New York Times*, of a 51-year old Iraqi shopkeeper who was beaten and urinated on by U.S. soldiers, then sent to a U.S. hospital where his injuries were tended with the same care as those of the U.S. soldier in the next bed. "At the base they beat and tortured me," he told a nurse. "Here they treat me like a human being . . . I'm really confused."[83]

The attitudes of U.S. officials toward Iraqis were often imperious, dismissive, or overtly paternalistic as well. On September 16, 2003 Bremer told a group of new Iraqi ministers that "like it or not—and it's not pleasant being occupied, or being the occupier, I might add—the Coalition is still the sovereign power here." He told Wolfowitz about the Iraqis that "these people couldn't organize a parade, let alone run a country." On September 8 he had published an editorial in the *Washington Post* under the title "Iraq's Path to Sovereignty," in which he referred to the U.S. presence in Iraq once again as an "occupation"—which when translated into Arabic was the word *ihtilal*, an offensive term implying the humiliation of foreign domination and invoking comparisons to the Israeli occupation of Arab territory.[84]

In his memoir of his tenure in Iraq, Bremer often depicts himself in a fatherly role in his relationship with the Iraqi people. In some cases he is the compassionate father caring for a sick, defenseless child; in other cases he is the stern father, regretfully but unflinchingly applying force to chastise Iraqi militias when they will not submit to the rules made for them. Bremer writes that in his first days in Iraq, while touring an Iraqi hospital he saw a critically ill Iraqi girl, tiny for her age, lying helpless in a hospital crib. "Seeing this suffering baby, it hit me like a thunderclap: I was responsible for her, and for thousands like her. Having authority as an administrator meant nothing if I couldn't bring some improvement in the lives of ordinary Iraqis."[85] Bremer describes Iraq as a "badly wounded society." He reports describing the Iraqi people to President Bush as "psychologically shattered," and telling the president that "Most Iraqis have had no experience with free thought. They vaguely understand the concept of freedom, but still want us to tell them what to do."[86]

As one example of this attitude, Bremer writes that in the early morning hours of April 6, 2004, he was awakened by the sounds of AC-130 gunships firing their cannons into the neighborhoods of Sadr city. Bremer describes the "weird chainsaw buzz" as the AC-130's cannons, 20 millimeter Gatling guns capable of firing 6,000 rounds per minute, fired into densely populated urban neighborhoods in the predawn darkness. "Small bands of Muqtada's militiamen were holed up in government buildings they had seized, refusing to surrender. The gunship was blasting them out." Bremer's reflection on the event is marked by the chiding tone of a stern parent, resigned to the necessity of punishing a wayward child but unsympathetic and detached in the knowledge that the punishment is necessary. "I'm glad I'm not on the receiving end of that," Bremer recalls thinking, "But we hadn't started this fight. Muqtada had."[87]

In an August 15, 2003 nationally televised address to the Iraqi people, Bremer went further still, equating himself with a benevolent God as he told Iraqis of his plans for them. With a scriptural cadence and air of divine authority, he began his address saying [I am Paul Bremer, administrator of the Coalition Provisional Authority. The Prophet Jeremiah told us: 'For surely I know the plans I have for you, says the Lord, plans for your welfare and not for harm, to give you a future of hope.' The present difficulties of the Iraqi people are manifest. The problems are there for all to see. But things will not remain as they are. There is, before all Iraqis, a future of hope. You will live in dignity. You will live in peace. You will live in prosperity. You will live in the quiet enjoyment of family, of friends, and of a decent income honestly earned. You will live in an Iraq governed by and for the people of Iraq. These things will come to pass.[88]]

The Bush administration's political ideology and constructions of identity formed the basis for its policies in Iraq, but it is also important to note the effects of the particular organizational and bureaucratic contexts in which these ideas shaped policy. The small group of policy makers around President Bush seems to have been marked by unusual intellectual coherence and unusual isolation from alternative perspectives. A clear ideational consensus about the role of the United States in the world became firmly entrenched at the highest levels of the Bush administration in the years after 9/11, imposing a rigid orthodoxy within this small group. Policy debates were constrained within this ideological framework, becoming arguments over tactics rather than critical considerations of strategy or the underlying premises of policy, even when unfolding events were clearly casting these into doubt. It is striking to note that among the president's top foreign policy advisers—Rice, Cheney, Rumsfeld, Tenet, and Powell—only Powell seems to have expressed any serious reservations about the administration's rationale for war with Iraq and assumptions about its likely outcome to the president. Given what appear in retrospect to be glaring flaws in the administration's logic about these issues, this level of agreement seems astonishing. Had any other member of this group counseled strongly against the war, and certainly if one or more had publicly advocated against it, it is possible if not likely that the administration would have been forced to choose another course.

George W. Bush seems to have sought to model his presidency on that of Ronald Reagan, emphasizing once again the moral purposes of American power over what was seen as the pragmatism lacking in passion that characterized Bush's father's administration. But the trait that allowed Reagan's administration to cement its place in history was not simply the strength of its moral and ideological convictions. It was Reagan's ability to look beyond his and his administration's dominant assumptions, to understand that under Mikhail Gorbachev something legitimately new was happening in the Soviet Union and embrace and encourage that change rather than persisting in the hidebound hostility of the cold war. Bush and his advisors reflected Reagan's millennialism, his emphasis on the moral duty of America to change the world. But they demonstrated none of the Reagan administration's capacity to reconsider its own assumptions and adapt.

One indicator of Bush's unwillingness or inability to question the ideological orthodoxy of his administration in the face of contradictory evidence came during an interview he gave on *Meet the Press* on February 8, 2004, nearly two years after the initial invasion of Iraq: "First of all, I expected to find weapons," Bush said. "There's theories as to where the weapons went. They could have been destroyed during the war. Saddam and his henchmen could have destroyed them as we entered into Iraq. They could be hidden. They could have been transported to another country, and we'll find that out . . . Saddam Hussein was dangerous with weapons. Saddam Hussein was dangerous with the ability to make weapons."[89] Within the administration, the belief that Iraq's WMDs would eventually be found seems to have persisted long after the collapse of Saddam Hussein's government. Chief U.S. weapons inspector David Kay reported frequently getting bits and pieces of intelligence directed to him from the vice president's office—snippets of information that he was asked if he had seen, indicating in one case that Iraqi WMDs might have been smuggled to Syria, in another that they were hidden in Lebanon's Bekaa valley. At one point Cheney asked Kay to interview an Iranian informant who Kay knew the CIA had already labeled a "talented fabricator." "Cheney had a stock of interpretations and facts that he thought proved a case and he wanted to be sure that you examined them," Kay said. Cheney seems to have been aggressively asserting his own understanding of the answer to the Iraqi WMD puzzle, seeking pieces of information that fit within the administration's shared cognitive framework and relaying those to Kay in an apparent attempt to spur Kay's team to a wider discovery that would confirm the administration's view.[90]

Another example of the depth of the intellectual intransigence within the Bush administration was its steady refusal to acknowledge that the Iraqi insurgency was growing and that the country was descending into civil war. Classified reports in November 2003 showed that there had been about 1000 enemy-initiated attacks in Iraq in the previous month. When Bush met with the National Security Council on November 11, CIA Near East Division head Rob Richer stated that "we are seeing the establishment of an insurgency." "I may have to disagree with you," Rumsfeld responded. "I need more data," Bush said, "I don't think we are there yet." Deputy Secretary of State Richard Armitage said later that sitting in this meeting he concluded that Bush was in denial about the realities of Iraq.[91] Both Powell and Armitage suggested that the tone of absolute certainty, the complete absence of doubt expressed in the president and vice-president's public statements were repeated in private as well. "They cannot have any doubts about the correctness of the policy because it opens too many questions in their minds, Armitage thought."[92] He came to believe that in the Bush White House, any reconsideration of a decision, any questioning of accepted assumptions, any reservations or critical thinking, were regarded as indications of disloyalty, evidence that the doubter was not "on the team." Powell generally met with Bush for roughly 20 minutes per week, but vice-president Cheney was often there and Powell became convinced that Cheney would later suggest to Bush that Powell's doubts indicated that he was not a team player. Powell and Armitage came to believe that that dominant mindset at the highest levels of the Bush administration was one in which diplomacy was seen as indicative of weakness and equated with appeasement.[93]

Bush himself identified an unwavering, undoubting commitment to principles and policy choices as the defining element of his presidency and something he expected of those around him. He said about his circle of advisors that "it's essential that we be confident and determined and united . . . I don't need people around me who are not steady . . . And if there's kind of a hand-wringing attitude going on when times are tough, I don't like it."[94]

Jay Garner, the first head of the U.S. civilian occupation and reconstruction effort in Iraq, returned to the United States in the late spring of 2003. On June 8, 2003, he met first individually with Rumsfeld, and then with Rumsfeld together with Bush, Cheney, and Rice. In his one-on-one meeting with Rumsfeld he said that he felt the CPA had made three profound mistakes—the extent of de-Ba'athification, disbanding the military, and marginalizing the Iraqi leadership group. But there was "still time to rectify this" Garner told Rumsfeld." "They're all reversible." Rumsfeld's response was a flat rejection of Garner's concerns: "I don't think there is anything we can do," he said, "because of where we are . . . we're not going to go back." In his meeting with Bush, Cheney, and Rice, Garner told stories of Iraqi clerics who appealed to him to make Iraq the 51st U.S. state, of the many people who told him "God bless Mr. George Bush," of the progress and the triumphs of newfound freedom he had seen in Iraq. He did not mention the deep concerns he had expressed to Rumsfeld. "Once again," Bob Woodward has written in his description of this encounter, "The aura of the presidency had shut out the most important news—the bad news . . . It was only one example of a visitor to the Oval Office not telling the president the whole story or the truth. Likewise, in these moments where Bush had someone from the field there in the chair beside him, he did not press, did not try to open the door himself and ask what the visitor had seen and thought." For his part, Garner argued afterward that there would have been no point in his expressing his deeper concerns about the direction of the occupation, simply because it would not have made a dent in the cognitive orthodoxy around the president. "The door's closed," Garner said about this meeting. "And I think if I had said that to the president in front of Cheney and Condoleezza Rice and Rumsfeld in there, the president would have looked at them and they would have rolled their eyes back and he would have thought, 'Boy, I wonder why we didn't get rid of this guy sooner?'" "They didn't see it coming," Garner said. "As the troops said, they drank the Kool-Aid."[95]

Conclusion

Identity and Ideology in the Making of U.S. Foreign Policy

American identity comprises a set of general but widely held and historically resilient ideas encompassing the traditional Liberal values of individual rights, limited government, and popular sovereignty, accompanied by a sense of American exceptionalism rooted in the belief that because its government and social order are founded on these universal principles, grounded in fundamental human rights and therefore a basis for just government anywhere, the United States has a unique place in the world and historical destiny. This broad, interconnected set of ideas forms the socio-cognitive environment within which debates over U.S. foreign policy occur, with varying ideological understandings of the appropriate U.S. world role emerging from differences in emphasis and interpretation within this common identity framework.

Within this superstructure of national identity, particular ideological themes, such as liberal and conservative noninterventionism and internationalism, have emerged time and again over the course of U.S. history. During moments of change in the international system, one of these sets of ideas has typically gained ascendance over its competitors to define a new foreign policy consensus for the decades that follow. The most significant factor determining which foreign policy ideology will come to dominate in any given era has tended to be its ability to convincingly explain the critical events of recent history. Thus, the American policy of neutrality and detachment from world affairs pursued throughout the 1920s and 1930s emerged from an ideology of noninterventionism, rooted in a particular interpretation of American identity, which became widely accepted after World War I due largely to widespread public disillusionment and belief that involvement in the war had been a mistake. This noninterventionist consensus was overturned when many Americans became convinced in the wake of the Japanese attack on Pearl Harbor that it no longer represented the appropriate set of guiding principles for foreign policy. It was supplanted by the ideology of global activism and intervention, again drawn from core American identity principles but deriving very different policy conclusions from those ideas, which formed the intellectual basis for U.S. foreign relations throughout the cold war.

In the years after September 11, 2001, the Bush administration described an ideological agenda specifying a clear set of policy prescriptions, which once again was derived from a particular interpretation of traditional ideas regarding American identity. In the wake of the 9/11 attacks this ideological framework met with widespread acceptance among the U.S. public because it effectively framed the events of the recent past within a comprehensible reading of American identity. The administration articulated a set of policies on this basis, grounded in a meta-narrative that connected familiar ideas about what the United States represented in the world with an argument about the nature of the threats facing American society at that time. The core assumptions that were the key elements in the administration's construction of the post-9/11 world were that the assertive promotion of democracy should be the central goal of American foreign policy; that America itself was profoundly vulnerable to real but invisible threats, both abroad and at home; that the world was divided between the forces of "civilization" and "terrorism" or "barbarism"; that individuals and groups in the "terrorist" camp were irrational and, by virtue of their rejection of the norms of civilization, not fully human; that the contemporary war against terrorism was a continuation of the United States' historic struggles against fascism and other forms of totalitarianism; and that other democracies might not recognize their duty to defend freedom, imposing a moral duty on the United States to act alone if necessary.

In his speeches, Bush often alluded to the threat of terrorism on American soil, frequently referring to unspecified numbers ("thousands" or "tens of thousands") of terrorists, invisible but at large somewhere in the world. Having rejected the norms of civilization, they "hid in shadows and caves"—but also, unseen, in cities around the world. They were depicted as "irrational," "mad," driven by "ideologies of murder" to kill without compunction or restraint. They were "evil men," "parasites," who aggressively sought to destroy freedom in every part of the world. Their sanity could not be trusted, and bent on global domination, they could not be negotiated with or deterred. Along with the states of the "axis of evil," these groups represented the preeminent threat to America and its allies in a new bipolar international system—the forces of tyranny and barbarism allied against the forces of "freedom." In Bush's view, the September 11 attacks represented the latest battle in a war between "freedom and fear" that had been fought throughout history. And in this war, he argued, "God is not neutral."

If this was the enemy, the United States was, in Bush's view, an altruistic state that had no material interests of its own to serve, no desire for empire or gain, but that did acknowledge a moral obligation to defend human freedom when it was threatened. Bush frequently framed his description of American identity in historical terms—the United States was the nation that had defeated fascism and communism and had been a beacon of democracy for generations. Today's Americans, he often reminded his audiences, were the caretakers of that legacy, secured by the sacrifices of their parents and grandparents, just as al Qaeda and the "axis of evil" were the inheritors of the legacy of twentieth-century totalitarianism.

If the lines of division in this bipolar world were clear to the Bush administration, it was acknowledged that others who had a similar responsibility to defend freedom might not be willing to do so. Thus the administration found itself making the paradoxical argument that in order to defend international law and norms, it might be necessary to disregard the role of international institutions like the United Nations in policy making. This was not, Bush suggested, because the United States was contemptuous of the international community, but exactly the opposite—the United States honored the obligations of the U.N. Charter and international law so highly that it was willing to act alone if necessary to defend them, when other, more narrowly self-interested states chose to hinder the cause of multilateral action because they sought the path of least cost to themselves. In any case, the administration argued, the United States was a powerful, independent state that would not accept limits on its own freedom of action simply because others were weak willed.

The Bush administration's successful assertion of this vision of American identity in relationship to the identities of other actors in the international system created the political environment that allowed its neoconservative ideological agenda, and the war in Iraq in particular, to be carried out. But while this vision of the world may have been articulated for the immediate purpose of orienting and mobilizing public opinion, this book has argued that its assumptions were to a large extent sincerely believed within the administration and are responsible for creating erroneous expectations about the nature of the international environment, the threats faced by the United States, the efficacy of U.S. power, and the likely consequences of U.S. policy in the minds of President Bush and his circle of advisors. That the Ba'athist government of Iraq was concealing weapons of mass destruction, that the Iraqi regime had links with al Qaeda, that American forces would be greeted as liberators by grateful Iraqis, and that the international community would eventually rally behind American leadership in Iraq are conclusions that follow logically and coherently from the set of beliefs and assumptions that the administration elaborated as it constructed its vision of the world after September 11. The administration's understanding of American identity and the identities of other international actors, and the neoconservative ideology connected to these identity beliefs, led it to draw conclusions about the need for war and the likely effects of its policies that proved dramatically inconsistent with the realities of the conflict in Iraq.

The administration's worldview gave rise to what amounted to a web of interlocking assumptions about the United States and Iraq, each supporting the others. Neoconservative ideology held that the Arab peoples of the Middle East had suffered too long under oppressive regimes and would welcome liberation and democracy; the neoconservatives also believed that the United States was a benevolent force in international politics more generally, and held that American power could be effective in solving a wide range of international problems. These assumptions supported the conclusion that the war in Iraq would be marked by a rapid, decisive victory over Saddam Hussein's military forces, followed by a quick return to peace and a short occupation during which American forces would be welcomed by grateful Iraqis. These views dovetailed perfectly with the doctrine of military transformation promoted by Donald Rumsfeld, which held that only a small number of troops would be necessary to overthrow the Ba'athist regime. A large-scale occupation amid a hostile population would require greater numbers of more traditional forces, so the assumption that this would not be the situation in Iraq was critical for maintaining coherence in the administration's ideational framework because it allowed the premises of the military transformation doctrine to remain intact. Similarly, neoconservative ideology asserted that dependence on international organizations was unnecessary and even dangerous, so the Bush administration's assumption that the United States was capable of achieving its goals in Iraq without United Nations approval or broad international support was consistent with a principled unilateralism and hostility to the U.N. The administration was firmly opposed to the use of the U.S. military for "nation building;" therefore, it simply assumed that the United Nations or other international organizations would play this role, and that the emergence of democratic stability in Iraq would occur so rapidly that only a minimal postwar role for outside forces would be necessary in any case. The neoliberal and neoconservative idea that democracy was a universally applicable principle and would produce peace and political stability in any cultural context reinforced the administration's expectations of a short war, an appreciative reception by the Iraqi population, and a brief occupation. The view that the United States was locked in a struggle on behalf of civilization against terrorists and barbarians supported the conclusion that Iraqis would be happy to be rid of Saddam Hussein, who certainly fell into the latter category. That Saddam was a brutal, evil dictator was consistent with the idea that he must be concealing weapons of mass destruction in order to challenge the United States with them or give them to others to use against America or its allies. When conflict surged after Saddam's fall, the administration adapted its expectations slightly but not its underlying assumptions; it simply reasoned that it must be fighting against "terrorists" and Islamic extremists, since it had identified those groups as its enemies before the war began.

In retrospect, all of these assumptions were either badly mistaken or, at a minimum, reflected a very simplistic understanding of the reality of Iraq and the predictable consequences of U.S. policy there. All of these beliefs were enabled by a deeper failure of the Bush administration to confront the cognitive and cultural subjectivity of its own worldview, to consider the ways in which its perspective might not be shared by other international actors, and the implications of these differences for its consciousness of the nature of the threats and opportunities facing it and the likely results of its policy choices.

The administration underestimated the significance of United Nations, approval and international support more generally for the effectiveness of its policies in Iraq. The absence of significant U.N. involvement in the war adversely affected the coalition's efforts to restore social and economic stability after the fall of Saddam Hussein's government. It also deprived the occupation of a source of international legitimacy that might have diminished the sense in Iraq and elsewhere that the invasion was an act of U.S imperialism. In both of these ways the lack of U.N. approval helped to engender discontent and hostility toward coalition forces in occupied Iraq. The Iraqi population did not uniformly see the United States as America saw itself, and the U.S. military found that it faced an insurgency that was not made up solely of Islamic radicals but was in fact highly diverse and to a significant extent motivated by nationalism. Democratic elections did not put a quick end to the bloodshed in Iraq as the administration had hoped they would, and in general politics in Iraq after the fall of the Ba'athist government tended to reflect the schisms of Iraqi social and political life rather than the ideological and issue-based divisions that tend to characterize politics in Western democracies. In short, the administration made policy choices on the basis of a set of identity constructions and ideological principles that proved to be misguided, and the policies that resulted met with unintended and destructive consequences.

The Bush administration consistently advocated a vision of the appropriate ends of U.S. foreign policy heavily influenced by Wilsonian liberalism. The arguments made by the president and his advisors that global peace is indivisible, that democracy is morally superior to other political systems and universally viable across cultures, and that defending and supporting human rights should be an important goal of policy, all represent significant elements of Wilsonianism in the administration's rhetoric. Also consistent with Wilsonianism were Bush's arguments that technological change had made the world more interdependent and increased the significance of distant events for the United States, and that the promotion of democracy and human rights were not merely ethical concerns but also served practical U.S. interests. Strong religious overtones were also clear in the thinking of both Wilson and Bush.

But within Wilsonian liberalism as a body of thought, universal ideals as foreign policy goals are necessarily and intrinsically connected to international law and institutions as means. The reason is that Wilson was first an American political scientist and constitutional scholar, whose philosophy regarding international politics was based on an application of what he saw as the principles and experience of the American founding to the international system as a whole. He believed that even in an environment where the common interests of all were clear, they could easily be subsumed to the particular interests of individuals or factions unless accompanied by structures of governance that recognized and represented the perspectives of distinct communities. Without institutional structures that acknowledge the legal equality of subsidiary units in any political system, any principle asserted by the strong, no matter how just, would be regarded by others as a subjective rationale for the interests of those advocating it; a fair and equitable system of governance was required for those within it to be able to perceive their overarching common interests. Cognizance of common or even universal interests was thus not enough to create effective international order, for Wilson. Also necessary was the recognition of a *community* of states based on these common interests. This community could in turn form the basis on which those states would agree to submit themselves to some degree of common authority, allowing their sense of kinship to develop further over time.

The Bush administration, for its part, not only ignored this connection between universal ideals and international institutions, but actively sought to dismantle and degrade multilateral agreements and organizations in a wide range of cases. This was particularly true with regard to policy toward global security structures and agreements. While the most notable case of this was the administration's decision to go to war in Iraq in the absence of U.N. Security Council approval, its abandonment of the Kyoto climate change treaty process, its withdrawal from the Anti-Ballistic Missile Treaty, and its active hostility toward the International Criminal Court also indicated a pattern of unilateralism starkly inconsistent with Wilsonian philosophy. The Bush administration's attempts to defend liberal principles through illiberal means in its foreign policy ignored the fact, as John B. Judis has put it, that "the key to America's long-standing leadership has been its willingness to subordinate its singular will to that of international organizations and alliances."[1]

With regard to the process of policy making, the leaders of the Bush administration became, in effect, prisoners of their own ideology and cognitive constructions of the world. Among the president and his advisors, there was a culture of rigid adherence to this ideational framework, and expressions of doubt about these core ideas were taken as signs of weakness or disloyalty. The orthodox worldview that held sway within the administration was reinforced and protected by a decision-making process that did not admit dissenting opinions, introspection, or real debate over the fundamental premises of policy. Even as it became clear that some of the group's key assumptions were in error, the tendency of the president and those around him was to protect their fixed beliefs by rejecting discordant information and becoming even more determined to defend the choices made on the basis of these assumptions, in the name of showing "resolve." Thus, it was not simply the Bush administration's ideas that led to dysfunctional policies, but also a decision-making process that emphasized ideological coherence over critical thinking and firmness over adaptability.[2]

Constructing Twenty-First Century U.S. Foreign Policy: Theory and Practice

Throughout its history, the development of international relations theory has both influenced and been influenced by change in the international system itself. The emergence of liberal internationalism as a body of thought cannot be separated from its elaboration as the policy of Woodrow Wilson during and after World War I, for example, just as realism and neorealism, emphasizing enduring structural conflict, became the dominant strands of IR theory during the cold war. These theories gained credence because they seemed well matched to the global realities of their times and in turn shaped the course of history by providing coherent intellectual rationales for state policy. It should thus come as no surprise that the collapse of the dominant policy paradigm of the last half-century—cold war bipolarity—has been accompanied by a decline in the influence of neorealism in IR theory. More surprising is the failure of a new body of theory to emerge to fill this void, to offer an intellectual framework to address the complexities of the new international system. It is therefore high time that constructivism, the most important body of post–cold war IR theory, be considered for its implications for the practice of foreign policy as well as for its theoretical significance.

The implications of constructivist theory for the conduct of international politics can and should be more fully explored. As a body of theory, constructivism suggests the importance of understanding the culturally subjective contexts within which the perceptions and preferences of actors in the international system are created and employed. Since the 9/11 attacks, the Bush administration has pursued a series of policies that have consistently failed to recognize the cultural and historical positions from which other actors view the international system. This approach has been the primary cause of the most notable failures in recent U.S. foreign policy and the marked decline in American influence in the world. There is thus a critical need for wider understanding of the intersubjective, intercultural, and socially constructed nature of international politics in the making of U.S. foreign policy at this moment in history.

For the purposes of foreign policy analysis, national identity must be understood as being constructed at the international, societal, and policy-elite level. There is a political imperative for national leaders to frame their choices within the rhetorical boundaries of national identity. They are also the inheritors of the values and norms of their societies, no more free than any other individual to shed the cultural baggage that they have acquired throughout their lives. But unlike most individuals, national leaders have some capacity to shape societal interpretation of national identity and to a certain extent to shape national identity itself. Social constructions of identity structure the political preferences of members of society, but they are also subject to evolution over time; they do not tend to change quickly, but neither are they entirely rigid or fixed throughout history. Policy elites have some leverage by which they can affect this process—by avoiding or being in contact with external Others, for example, they can increase or decrease the exposure of their societies to those Others, and thus encourage change in broader social understandings of the set of acceptable and appropriate relationships with those Others.

Jeffery Legro has argued that constructivist theory can play a more formative role in advising policy makers by calling attention to the perspectives of other actors in the international system, the particular ways in which they understand themselves, the international environment, and their relationships within it. Legro writes that it "makes sense in the conduct of foreign policy to (1) pay attention to the ideas of nations and transnational groups, (2) anticipate changes in those ideas, and (3) help shape such notions when possible."[3] Understanding an Other's culture and mind-set, experience of recent history, and the set of sociocultural facts that lead that Other to particular perceptions of the world will not tell state leaders what their counterparts in another society are about to do. But it will help to suggest a likely range of intentions and their underlying causes, and provide the basis for influencing those intentions by creating conditions that increase or decrease insecurity or otherwise alter the intersubjective relationship between those societies and groups of leaders as seen by the Other. To understand that Iranian political culture is informed by a sense of history marked by tension between Islamic identity and the Judeo-Christian West, but also between the Shia/Persian and Sunni/Arab worlds and secular and religious traditions and ethnic identities within Iranian society, will not predict how the Iranian government will act. But it will suggest a piece of the cultural framework through which the Iranian government is likely to imagine the range of potential policy choices before it and understand the actions of others. And critically, it can inform the choices of U.S. leaders about strategies to shape those perceptions and thus influence Iran's actions. As Jervis suggests, "What matters in sending a message is not how you would understand it, but how others will understand it . . . if an actor does not understand others' beliefs about IR and about the actor, he is not apt to be able to see what inferences others are drawing from his behavior."[4] It may be that the United States and Iran will still have conflicting interests, but the ways in which they each understand what these interests are, and the array of appropriate means to addressing them, can be powerfully affected by a self-conscious mutual understanding of their intersubjective identities vis-à-vis one another.

Constructivist theory suggests that state foreign policies built on this kind of cognizance of the perspectives of other actors in the international system hold the promise of changing the intersubjective identity relationships that comprise the environment in which international politics occur. When deep social and political change take place, it is generally a result of a shift in a society's understanding of the appropriate categorization of people. Germany and Japan went from being enemies to being friends of the United States, and the Soviet Union went from ally to opponent, because the leaders of these societies and their populations came to conceptualize and group each other differently as the We and They of World War II were replaced by the We and They of the cold war. To the extent that they have been effective at creating political change within societies and internationally, human rights movements have done so by demanding a reevaluation of the dominant ways in which people are categorized, in effect arguing, do not see us as we have been seen, but instead recognize us as part of that group of fully legitimate humans in which you see yourself. The evolution of the relationship between Germany and France after World War II provides an example of the ways in which the intentional renegotiation of social identity can have profound effects on the substance of interstate relations as well, and the extent to which individual leaders can foster change in collective social identity. Two leaders in particular, Charles de Gaulle of France and Konrad Adenauer of Germany, consciously sought to work together to change the relationship between their societies by constructing a new identity for each in relation to the other. Among the critical elements in this process were explicit, ongoing, and public efforts on the parts of both governments to construct a new social narrative of the history of conflict between them, and of the future. Both governments acknowledged past wrongdoing and began to talk about the other in ways that shed the prior emphasis on competition, insecurity, and traditional stereotypes and stressed instead the virtues of the other society, their shared goals, and their common identity as parts of a single Europe.

There are many examples of this kind of change within individual societies and between them in the last century. Constructivist theory suggests that state foreign policy making, if animated by a consciousness of the possibilities for radical revision of the practices and relationships of the past through the reinterpretation of national identity, and of the agency that governments and individual leaders can have in this process, need not remain a prisoner of its own history.[5] This book has made a case about the causes of American policy in recent years, but it suggests a prescriptive argument for the future as well. The ideational basis of American identity is very broad, rooted in a set of beliefs that are relatively consistent over the nation's history but general enough to support very diverse interpretations and thus very different policies over the course of time. Change in the foreign policies of states and in the nature of international politics more generally is possible, but requires recognition that national identity does not constitute a solid chain that binds the actors of the present to a particular future. It comprises the social reality within which policy makers must act, but history demonstrates that new, even radical interpretations of identity are sometimes possible within these boundaries—that for those who can reimagine and recast it, identity can be a powerful tool for leadership and change.

NOTES

INTRODUCTION

1. Yosef Lapid, "Culture's Ship: Returns and Departures in International Relations Theory," in *The Return of Culture and Identity in IR Theory,* eds. Yosef Lapid and Friedrich Kratochwil (Boulder: Lynne Rienner Publisher, 1996), 3.
2. John Kurt Jacobsen, "Much Ado about Ideas: The Cognitive Factor in Economic Policy," *World Politics* 47 (1995): 283.
3. Jack Snyder, "One World, Rival Theories," *Foreign Policy* 145 (Nov–Dec 2004): 60.
4. Alexander Wendt, "Identity and Structural Change in International Politics," in *The Return of Culture and Identity in IR Theory,* eds. Yosef Lapid and Friedrich Kratochwil (Boulder: Lynne Rienner Publisher, 1996), 47–64.
5. Ted Hopf, *Social Construction of International Politics: Identities and Foreign Policies, Moscow, 1955 and 1999* (Ithaca: Cornell University Press, 2002), 16–17.
6. Robert Osgood, *Ideals and Self-Interest in America's Foreign Relations* (Chicago: University of Chicago Press, 1953), 5, 15–16.
7. Jeffrey W. Legro, *Rethinking the World: Great Power Strategies and International Order* (Ithaca: Cornell University Press, 2005), 11.
8. Kenneth Waltz, *Theory of International Politics* (New York: Random House, 1979).
9. Richard Ned Lebow and Thomas Risse-Kappen, eds., *International Relations Theory and the End of the Cold War* (New York: Columbia University Press, 1995), 2.
10. Friedrich Kratochwil, "The Embarrassment of Changes: Neorealism as the Science of Realpolitik without Politics," *Review of International Studies* 19 (1993): 63. Jutta Weldes, Mark Laffey, Hugh Gusterson, and Raymond Duvall, "Introduction: Constructing Insecurity," in *Cultures of Insecurity: States, Communities, and the Production of Danger* , eds. Jutta Weldes, Mark Laffey, Hugh Gusterson, and Raymond Duvall (Minneapolis: University of Minnesota Press, 1999), 4.
11. For example, Judith Goldstein and Robert Keohane, eds., *Ideas and Foreign Policy: Beliefs, Institutions, and Political Change* (Ithaca: Cornell University Press, 1993).

12. Peter Haas, ed., "Knowledge, Power, and International Policy Coordination," *Special Issue of International Organization* 46 (1992).
13. For example, Alistair Iain Johnston, "Thinking about Strategic Culture," *International Security* 19 (1995): 32–64.
14. For example, Peter Katzenstein, ed., *The Culture of National Security: Identity and Norms in World Politics* (New York: Columbia University Press, 1996).
15. Previous cognitive approaches to IR have tended to treat ideas as an intervening variable between systemic cause and policy effect, rather than understanding ideas as elemental to structure and focusing attention on the ways in which they are created and evolve. In such approaches, ideas become significant in policy when they become entrenched in organizational rules and procedures or when they are used as political "weapons" to legitimize policy choices (see Albert S. Yee, "The Causal Effects of Ideas on Policies," *International Organization* 50 [1996]: 71–82; Jacobsen, 298–300). Such approaches do not run counter to the positivism of mainstream rational-actor IR, but instead offer to refine them by claiming that "an ideas approach is always a valuable supplement to interest-based, rational actor models." Jacobsen, 285. Mark Laffey and Jutta Weldes among other have critiqued the willingness of these approaches to accept the neorealist notion of ideas and interests as separable. Weldes and Laffey argue that cognitive approaches treat ideas as tools "which are used by policy-makers to manipulate various audiences, such as international elites, domestic publics or bureaucracies," a practice that "reinforces the notion that 'ideas' are distinct from interests and that their role, in practice, is limited to manipulation; and it obscures the constitutive function of 'ideas.'" Mark Laffey and Jutta Weldes, "Beyond Belief: Ideas and Symbolic Technologies in the Study of International Relations," *European Journal of International Relations* 3 (1997): 200, 207. See also Andreas Bieler, "Questioning Cognitivism and Constructivism in IR Theory: Reflections on the Material Structure of Ideas," *Politics* 21 (2001): 93–100; Ernst B. Haas, "Why Collaborate? Issue-linkage and International Regimes," *World Politics* 32 (1980): 357–405; Jacobsen, 283–310; and Yee, 69–108.
16. Emmanuel Adler, "Seizing the Middle Ground: Constructivism in World Politics," *European Journal of International Relations* 3 (1997): 322.
17. Hopf, *Social Construction*, xi.
18. Alexander Wendt, "Constructing International Politics," *International Security* 21 (Summer 1995): 71–81.
19. Wendt, "Identity and Structural Change," 47–64.
20. Ted Hopf, "The Promise of Constructivism in International Relations Theory," *International Security* 23 (Summer 1998): 171–200.
21. Wendt, "Constructing International Politics," 74.

22. David Campbell, *Writing Security: United States Foreign Policy and the Politics of Identity* (Minneapolis: University of Minnesota Press, 1992), 1.
23. Weldes, Laffey, and Gusterson, 10. They suggest that "to refer to something as socially constructed is not at all the same as saying that it does not exist . . . our constructivism is interested in how one gets from here to such widely shared propositions as these: that the United States is threatened by Russian, but not British, nuclear weapons; that Third World states are more likely to use their nuclear weapons than Western countries; that Iraq's nuclear potential is more threatening than the United States' nuclear arsenal; and that the United States is safer with nuclear weapons than it would be without them." Weldes, Laffey, and Gusterson, 12. Tuathail and Agnew ask, "Who actually articulates these 'discourses of danger' and produces particular insecurities? In statist societies, the primary site for the production of insecurity is the institution or bundle of practices that we know as the state . . . those individuals who inhabit offices in the state play a central role in constructing insecurities . . . It is state officials who are granted the right, who have the authority, to define security and insecurity—to identify threats and dangers and to determine the best solution to them, although they are often assisted by what have been called 'intellectuals of statecraft' (Gearóid Ó Tuathail and John Agnew, 'Geopolitics and Discourse: Practical Geopolitical Reasoning and American Foreign Policy,' *Political Geography* 11 [1992]: 193) . . . Beyond the state narrowly defined, discourses of insecurity are also produced and circulate through what Gramsci called the extended state (Antonio Gramsci, *Selections from the Prison Notebooks*, edited and translated by Quintin Hoare and Geoffrey Nowell Smith (New York: International Publishers, 1971), 257–264 and passim)—schools, churches, the media, and other institutions of civil society that regulate populations." Weldes, Laffey, and Gusterson, 19.
24. Stefan Halper and Jonathan Clarke, *America Alone: The Neo-Conservatives and The Global Order* (New York: Cambridge, 2004), 206–207.
25. Campbell, 6, emphasis in the original.
26. Hayden White, *Tropics of Discourse: Essays in Cultural Criticism* (Baltimore: Johns Hopkins University Press, 1978), 3.
27. Walter L. Hixson, *The Myth of American Diplomacy* (New Haven: Yale University Press, 2008), 310; Michel Foucault, *Madness and Civilization: A History of Insanity in the Age of Reason* (New York: Pantheon Books, 1967).
28. Legro, *Rethinking the World*, 13.
29. Wendt, "Constructing International Politics," 72.
30. Ibid., 77. Emphasis in the original.
31. The most important constructivist statement on the significance of the anarchy of the international system remains Alexander Wendt,

"Anarchy Is What States Make of It: The Social Construction of Power Politics," *International Organization* 46 (1992): 396–397, in which Wendt argues that actors "act towards objects, including other actors, on the basis of the *meanings* that the objects have for them."

32. Henry Nau, *At Home Abroad: Identity and Power in American Foreign Policy* (Ithaca: Cornell University Press, 2002), 41–42.
33. Ibid., 18.
34. See J. Samuel Barkin, "Realist Constructivism," *International Studies Review* 5 (Fall 2003); Patrick Thaddeus Jackson, ed., "Bridging the Gap: Toward a Realist-Constructivist Dialogue," *International Studies Review* 6 (Summer 2004).
35. Samuel P. Huntington, "The Erosion of American National Interests," *Foreign Affairs* 76 (1997): 28. See also Jeffrey W. Legro and Andrew Moravcsik, "Is Anybody Still a Realist?" *International Security* 24 (1999): 5–56.
36. See Alexander Wendt, *Social Theory of International Politics* (Cambridge: Cambridge University Press, 2007), 16.
37. Zbigniew Brzezinski, "A Geostrategy for Eurasia," *Foreign Affairs* 76 (1997): 56; Henry Kissinger, *Diplomacy* (New York: Simon and Schuster, 1994), 533; Henry Kissinger, *Does American Need a Foreign Policy: American Foreign Policy in the Twenty-First Century* (New York: Simon and Schuster, 2001), 20. A number of classical realists suggest in places that culture and social understandings between actors can have important effects in international politics. Morgenthau, for example, says that "when we speak of power, we mean man's control over the minds and actions of other men . . . Political power is a psychological relation between those who exercise it and those over whom it is exercised. It gives the former control over certain actions of the latter through the impact which the former exert on the latter's minds. That impact derives from three sources: the expectation of benefits, the fear of disadvantages, the respect or love for men or institutions." He argues as well that "the political objective of war itself is not per se the conquest of territory and the annihilation of enemy armies, but a change in the mind of the enemy which will make him yield to the will of the victor." Hans Morgenthau and Kenneth W. Thompson, *Politics among Nations: The Struggle for Power and Peace*, Sixth Edition (New York: McGraw-Hill, 1985), 32, 36. For the classical realist Thomas Hobbes, among the major causes of human conflict are the desire for "glory" and defense of "reputation"—non-material, socially determined ends. "For every man looks that his companion should value him at the same rate he sets upon himself," Hobbes argues, "and upon all signs of contempt or undervaluing naturally endeavors, as far as he dares . . . to extort a greater value from his condemners by damage and from others by the example." Hobbes thus suggests that the dynamics of the state of nature, which are so much a focus of his inquiry, are to some extent

subjective and socially determined. Thomas Hobbes, *Leviathan*, Part I, Chapter 13.

38. Wendt, "Constructing International Politics," 73.
39. David Dessler, "Constructivism within a Positivist Social Science," *Review of International Studies* 25 (1999): 124.

CHAPTER 1

1. Ngaire Woods, "Economic Ideas and International Relations: Beyond Rational Neglect," *International Studies Quarterly*, 39 (1995):61.
2. Ted Hopf, *Social Construction of International Politics: Identities and Foreign Policies, Moscow, 1955 and 1999* (Ithaca: Cornell University Press, 2002), xi.
3. Ibid., 4; Iver Neuman has divided the scholarly consideration of identity into four major paths, which are the ethnographic, examining the constitution of ethnic and national groups; the psychological, focusing on the ways in which individuals and groups distinguish themselves from others cognitively; the Contintental philosophical, typified by Jurgen Habermas and others, elaborating the differentitation of self and other in the Western tradition; and the "Eastern Excursion," focusing on the non-Western alternative approaches to understanding identity typified by Edward Said and others. Mark B. Salter, *Barbarians and Civilization in International Relations* (London: Pluto Press, 2002), 11; Iver B. Neumann, *Uses of Others: "The East" in European Identity Formation* (Minneapolis: University of Minnesota Press, 1999), 5.
4. Hopf, *Social Construction*, 5, 7–8; Peter Berger and Thomas Luckmann, *Social Construction of Reality: A Treatise in the Sociology of Knowledge* (Garden City: Anchor, 1967); Clifford Geertz, *The Interpretation of Cultures* (New York: Basic Books, 1973); Michel Foucault, *The Archaeology of Knowledge and the Discourse on Language* (New York: Pantheon, 1982).
5. See Serge Moscovici, "The Phenomenon of Social Representations" in *Social Representations*, eds. R.M. Farr and S. Moscovici (Cambridge: Cambridge University Press, 1984), 3–69.
6. Charles Taylor, *Modern Social Imaginaries* (Durham: Duke University Press, 2004), 23–24.
7. Mark Neufeld, "*The Restructuring of International Relations Theory*, (Cambridge: Cambridge University Press, 1995), 76–77.
8. Hopf, *Social Construction*, 6.
9. To suggest that community categories such as race, ethnicity, and nation are socially constructed is not to suggest that there is no biological meaning to them. Of course my children are going to tend to be physiologically like me, and my extended family—my cousins and cousins' cousins, and so forth—will be more genetically similar to one

another than to an extended family of people on the other side of the globe from whom my family branched off much longer ago. But our group identity only derives from a shared culture, a social understanding between us that those genetic similarities mean something more than that our eyes or noses are the same shape. If as infants all the members of my extended family and I were scattered throughout the world and raised in different cultures and if we encountered one another later, we would not immediately feel any sense of kinship just because we looked similar (in fact, differences in dress and behavior might well cause us to fail to see the genetic similarity between us). It is only because we are raised in a common cultural tradition that we imagine genetic similarity to form the foundation of a kinship community. So categories like "race," "ethnicity," and "nation" must be understood as socially constructed, as is evidenced by their fungibility over time and space. They are politically significant not because of any underlying genetic facts but because of the way they are socially understood. The political significance of human groups derives from their social power rather than their material basis. As David Berreby puts it, "Human-kind categories don't need a logical or factual basis to be used in day-to-day life. They just need to be convincing to the mind, and nothing is more convincing than practical, lived experience." "Asking if race is real," he adds, "is like asking if money is real." The answer in both cases is yes, but that each is only significant due to the way it is socially understood. A dollar bill is "real" in the sense that it is a physical object, but the way in which it is generally thought of derives from a social understanding of its symbolic meaning—without this it would only be a piece of paper. "Race" and "nation" are much the same; one does not have to conclude that there are no physical differences between genetically related people to conclude that the practical importance of these similarities is overwhelmingly in their social interpretation rather than inherent in the differences themselves. David Berreby, *Us and Them: Understanding Your Tribal Mind* (New York: Little, Brown, and Company, 2005), 84.

10. Stuart Hall suggests that "identities are constructed through, not outside, difference . . . it is only through the relation to the Other, the relation to what it is not, to precisely what it lacks, to what has been called its constitutive outside that the 'positive' meaning of any term—and thus its 'identity' can be constructed." Or as William Connolly has put it, "Difference requires identity and identity requires difference . . . doubts about self identity are posed and resolved by the constitution of an other against which that identity may define itself." Stuart Hall, "Introduction: Who Needs 'Identity?'" in *Questions of Cultural Identity*, ed. Stuart Hall (London: Sage, 1996), 4; William E. Connolly, *Identity/Difference: Democratic Negotiations of Political Paradox* (Ithaca: Cornell University Press, 1991), x.

11. Hopf, *Social Construction*, 7.
12. David Campbell argues that identity, "whether personal or collective—is not fixed by nature . . . Whether we are talking of 'the body' or 'the state,' or particular bodies and states, the identity of each is performatively constituted. Moreover, the constitution of identity is achieved through the inscription of boundaries which serve to demarcate an 'inside' from an 'outside,' a 'self' from an 'other,' a 'domestic' from a 'foreign." David Campbell, *Writing Security: United States Foreign Policy and the Politics of Identity* (Minneapolis: University of Minnesota Press, 1992), 8. Jerome Barkow, Leda Cosmides, and John Tooby have argued that evolution has shaped human beings as a species to think not strictly about individual self-interest but about collective interests and ideas as well. Jerome Barkow, Leda Cosmides, and John Tooby, eds., *The Adapted Mind: Evolutionary Psychology and the Generation of Culture* (New York, Oxford University Press, 1992).
13. Berreby, 149.
14. The term "international imaginary" is used by both Said and Shapiro to connote this framework of meanings that constitutes the social understanding of the state and its purposes in international affairs within a give society. Edward Said, *Culture and Imperialism* (New York: Random House, 1993), 14; Salter, 310; Michael J. Shapiro, "Introduction to Part I," in *Challenging Boundaries: Global Flows, Territorial Identities*, eds. Michael J. Shapiro and Hayward Alker (Minneapolis: University of Minnesota Press, 1996), 3.
15. Robert Jervis, *Perception and Misperception in International Politics* (Princeton: Princeton University Press, 1976), 366.
16. Berreby, 209.
17. Rodney Bruce Hall, *National Collective Identity: Social Constructs and International Systems* (New York: Columbia University Press, 1999), 299.
18. Group identity and a proclivity for intergroup violence might be argued to be part of "human nature," but this conclusion is both too broad and too narrow. It is too broad because it does not do justice to the multiplicity of kinds of identity that human beings are capable of creating, and the fact that they are capable of creating them at all—that is, unlike animals, human beings generate ideological communities, groups based on shared interests and values, as well as perceived innate or biological identity. It is too narrow because in fact there is nothing uniquely human about group identity. As Berreby notes, "Many creatures, from mice and pigeons to lions and dolphins, know a member of 'our group' from a stranger . . . and the pattern is clear: fights within the group are limited . . . but fights between groups end in deaths . . . lions, gorillas, chimpanzees, hyenas, are happy to kill their own. The victim just can't be a member of their little band." Berreby, 17.

19. Mark L. Haas, *The Ideological Origins of Great Power Politics, 1789–1989* (Ithaca: Cornell University Press, 2005), 10.
20. Berreby, 216.
21. Kelman writes that "insofar as a group of people have come to see themselves as constituting a unique, identifiable entity with a claim to continuity over time, to unity across geographical distance, and to the right to various forms of self-expression, we can say that they have acquired a sense of national identity. National identity is the group definition of itself as a group—its conception of its enduring characteristics and basic values; its strengths and weaknesses, its hopes and fears; its reputation and conditions of existence; its institutions and traditions; and its past history, current purposes, and future prospects." Anthony D. Smith has defined the characteristics of a nation to include "1. the growth of myths and memories of common ancestry and history of the cultural unit of population; 2. the formation of a shared public culture based on an indigenous resource (language, religion, etc.); 3. the delimitation of compact historic territory, or homeland; 4. the unification of local economic units into a single socioeconomic unit based on a single culture and homeland; 5. the growth of common codes and institutions of a single legal order, with common rights and duties for all members." Hall, 9–10; H.C. Kelman, "The Role of National Identity in Conflict Resolution," in *Social Identity, Intergroup Conflict, and Conflict Reduction*, eds. R.D. Ashmore, L. Jussim, and D. Wilder(Oxford; Oxford University Press, 2001), 191; Anthony D. Smith, "The Problem of National Identity: Ancient, Medieval, and Modern?" *Ethnic and Racial Studies* 17 (July, 1994), 381; see also Roxanne Lynn Doty, "Sovereignty and the nation: Constructing the Boundaries of National Identity," in *State Sovereignty as a Social Construct*, eds. Thomas Biersteker and Cynthia Weber (Cambridge: Cambridge University Press, 1996).
22. Benedict Anderson, *Imagined Communities: Reflections on the Origin and Spread of Nationalism* (London: Verso, 1991), 5.
23. Peter J. Katzenstein, ed., *The Culture of National Security: Norms and Identity in World Politics* (Columbia University Press, 1996), 59. See also Latha Varadarajan, "Constructivism, Identity, and Neoliberal (In)security," *Review of International Studies*, 30 (2004), 323–324.
24. Alexander Wendt, *Social Theory of International Politics* (Cambridge: Cambridge University Press, 2007), 235–237. A critique of this conception of identity can be found in Maja Zehfuss, "Constructivism and Identity: A Dangerous Liaison, *European Journal of International Relations*, 7 (2001), 315–348.
25. Wendt, *Social Theory*, 229, 300–305.
26. Hopf, *Social Construction*, 287.
27. Christian Reus-Smit argues that systemic constructivists such as Wendt "bracket the corporate sources of state identity and interests, and concentrate entirely on the constitutive role of international

social interaction, exploring how structural contexts, systemic processes, and strategic practices produce and reproduce state identities." Chrisitain Reus-Smit, *The Moral Purpose of the State* (Princeton: Princeton University Press, 1996), 166. It might be added that there are and presumably will remain differences of perspective among elites as to where on this ideational continuum the world system currently is—some see an increasingly Kantian world, others a still fundamentally Hobbesian one—and so long as there is an uneven distribution of power between states in the system, domestic political change within powerful states will be able to affect the dynamics of the system as a whole. It can be argued that much of the negative response around the globe to the Bush administration's war in Iraq resulted from the pursuit of an essentially Hobbesian foreign policy in an environment of Lockean and increasingly Kantian norms. But it is too soon to dismiss these events as aberrations on the road toward a Kantian future; because these ideational structures depend on belief and perception, it must be acknowledged that the Bush administration's perceptions were as much part of the international social fabric as anyone else's and that the Bush administration, by seeing a Hobbesian world and acting consistent with this perception, to some extent made it real.

28. Hopf, *Social Construction*, 289; Steve Smith, "Wendt's World," *Review of International Studies*, 26 (January 2000), 161. Henry Nau attempts to compensate for this perceived weakness of Wendtian constructivism by asserting parallel concepts of identity: "national identity at the domestic level, and the structure of relative national identity at the international level. Nau defines identity "in terms of both a liberal (autonomous or internal) and a social (interrelated or external) dimension. The liberal or internal dimension captures the relative priority citizens assign to ideological, cultural, ethnic, religious, and other factors in establishing the rules for the legitimate use of force at home. The external dimension captures the history and experience of associations among countries that influence their inclination to use force against one another." Henry Nau, At *Home Abroad: Identity and Power in American Foreign Policy* (Ithaca: Cornell University Press, 2002), 10, 19–20.
29. Wendt, *Social Theory*, 147; Chaim D. Kaufman and Robert A. Pape, "Explaining Costly International Moral Action: Britain's Sixty-Year Campaign against the Atlantic Slave Trade," *International Organization*, 53 (Autumn, 1999); Hopf, *Social Construction*, 278–280.
30. Hopf, *Social Construction*, 289.
31. Nau, 20. Similarly, Korostelina distinguishes between "ethnic," "multicultural," and "civic" concepts of nationalism, but these distinctions may overshadow underlying similarities between the ways in which nationalism acts within communities in different cultural and historical contexts. To suggest that American nationalism is primarily a "civic" nationalism, for example, in which individuals

understand national identity to be rooted in a set of ideas about the rights and obligations of citizens to the government and vice versa, is to overlook the fact that other cultural traits also characterize Americans' sense of what binds them together and makes their society distinct from others, and the fact that other "ethnic" nationalisms are also in fact communities of ideas—that ethnic identity itself is in fact an idea, a shared belief. Karina V. Korostelina, *Social Identity and Conflict: Structures, Dynamics, and Implications* (New York: Palgrave Macmillan, 2007), 186.

32. Nau, 6.
33. Ibid.
34. Ibid.
35. On the importance of perceptions of intentions, see Thomas J. Christensen, "Perceptions and Alliances in Europe, 1865–1940," *International Organization,* 51 (1997), 65–69; William C. Wohlforth, *The Elusive Balance: Power and Perceptions During the Cold War* (Ithaca: Cornell University Press, 1993); and James Goldgeier and Philip Tetlock, "Psychology and International Relations Theory," *Annual Review of Political Science* 22 (2001), 67–92.
36. Hopf, *Social Construction,* 16–17.
37. Nau, 24, 16.
38. Vamik Volkan applies a psychodynamic understanding to large group identity, which he describes as "tens of thousands, or millions, of people—most of whom will never meet one another in their life times—sharing a permanent sense of sameness." Volkan describes large group identity as akin to a canvas tent that shelters many individuals within it, protecting them and creating a kinship bond akin to a family relationship between them. Most of the time, individuals do not pay much conscious attention to the tent, but when its structure is disturbed or undermined, those within it become actively concerned with sustaining and shoring it up. Among the pillars of large group identity Volkan identifies are "chosen traumas and glories" from history, mythologized events that create a narrative describing who a people is as a function of what it has accomplished or suffered, and in relationships with specific external Others. Associated with this history are what Volkan refers to as "suitable targets of externalization," objects or practices to which is attached a symbolic meaning of significance to group identity—such as flags, songs, foods, animals, religious symbols or icons, or images of individuals of importance to national collective memory. Volkan suggests that such targets of externalization may be either positive or negative, associated with either trauma or triumph. Holland and Lave similarly argue that memories of historical conflicts are "crucibles for forging identities." Vamik D. Volkan, *Killing in the Name of Identity: A Study of Bloody Conflicts* (Charlottesville: Pitchstone, 2006), 15; D. Holland and J. Lave, *History in Person: Enduring Struggles, Contentious Practice,*

Intimate Identities (Santa Fe: School of American Research Press, 2001), 3.

39. Walter L. Hixson, *The Myth of American Diplomacy* (New Haven: Yale University Press, 2008), 8; Michael Kammen, *Mystic Chords of Memory: The Transformation of Tradition in American Culture* (New York: Vintage Books, 1993), 3.
40. Hixson, 10.
41. Jervis, *Perception and Misperception*, 262.
42. Thomas Risse-Kappen, "Collective Identity in a Democratic Community: The Case of NATO," in Katzenstein, ed., *Culture of National Security*, 367.
43. Berreby, 218.
44. Julius Wishner, "Reanalysis of 'Impressions of Personality," *Psychological Review* 67 (1960), 96–112; Jervis, *Perception and Misperception*, 120.
45. William Scott, "Psychological and Social Correlates of International Images," in *International Behavior*, ed. Herbert Kelman (New York: Hold, Rinehart, and Winston, 1965), 100; Jervis, 121.
46. Jervis, *Perception and Misperception*, 286.
47. Nau, 22.
48. Korostelina, for example, points to the historical flexibility of social identity depending on political circumstances, saying of ethnic, national, and religious identities that "the salience, meaning, and content of these identities are exposed to changes. In some countries, such as Afghanistan, Iran, Turkey, Pakistan, and the Republics of Central Asia (during the Soviet period), national identity began to develop after borders of the counties had been established. In Central Asia, nineteenth-century populations and dialects blended into one another, making the most salient identification in the region tribal and clan based. . . . During the Soviet period, each ethnic group became more rooted in and committed to its Soviet-demarcated territory and indigenous Central Asians gradually came to dominate their republics demographically, linguistically, and politically. Iran, Turkey, and Pakistan also achieved statehood before acquiring a coherent sense of national identity." Korostelina, 64.
49. Campbell, 11.
50. Jutta Weldes, Mark Laffey, Hugh Gusterson, and Raymond Duvall, "Introduction: Constructing Insecurity," in *Cultures of Insecurity: States, Communities, and the Production of Danger*, eds. Jutta Weldes, Mark Laffey, Hugh Gusterson, and Raymond Duvall (Minneapolis: University of Minnesota Press, 1999), 14–15.
51. Charles Tilly, *Capital, Coercion, and European States, A.D. 990–1992* (New York: Wiley-Blackwell, 2007).
52. Hall, 6–7.
53. Before constructivists focused on the evolving forms of identity as significant factors to be understood in international politics, classical realists such as Hans Morgenthau had already acknowledged that

such facts were important in at least some circumstances. Morgenthau suggests, for example, that "communities of interest" exist among states and explores when and why such communities sometimes form the basis for interstate alliances. While he holds that alliances are primarily means to serve the interests of the states that join them, he does suggest that ideology sometimes plays a role in shaping perceptions of those interests. For instance, he argues that "the pure type of an ideological alliance is presented by the Treaty of the Holy Alliance of 1815 and the Atlantic Charter of 1941. Both documents laid down general principles to which the signatories pledged their adherence, and general objectives whose realization they pledged themselves to seek. . . . The ideological factor also manifests itself in the official interpretation of an alliance, based upon material interests, in terms of an ideological solidarity transcending the limitations material interests. The conception of the Anglo-American alliance. . . [as] based upon common culture, political institutions, and ideals, is a case in point." Morgenthau argues that the nineteenth-century Concert of Europe was in fact an ideational community of states and that a commitment to maintaining the balance of power in Europe was in itself an operational political value that motivated concerted action among like-minded states. "The great political writers of that age were aware of this intellectual and moral unity," he argues, "upon whose foundations the balance of power reposes and which makes its beneficial operations possible. . . In the declaration of February 5, 1814, from which the Concert of Europe is generally dated, the representatives of Austria, Great Britain, Prussia, and Russia stated that they did not speak solely in the name of their respective countries, 'but in the name of Europe which forms but a single whole.'" Though Morgenthau suggests that the deeper roots of alliances are in material interests, he does acknowledge that ideological elements can play some role in motivating them. Morgenthau, 202–204, 235–237. The realist scholar Stephen Walt also argues that there is a place for ideology in defining state interest. He suggests that changes in the dominant ideology within a state can create new conceptions of state interest and thus increase leader's sense of threat and generally recasting leaders' understanding of themselves and the world in which they are acting. Stephen Walt, *Revolution and War*, (Ithaca: Cornell University Press, 1997), Chapter 2.

54. G. John Ikenberry, *After Victory: Institutions, Strategic Restraint, and the building of Order after Major Wars* (Princeton: Princeton University Press, 2001).
55. Haas, *Ideological Origins*, 11; John M. Owen, "Transnational Liberalism and U.S. Primacy," *International Security* 26 (2001/02): 123.
56. H.C. Kelman, "Negotiating National Identity and Self-Determination in Ethnic Conflicts: The Choice between Pluralism and Ethnic Cleansing," *Negotiation Journal*, 13 (1997), 338. Korostelina also

notes the role the political actors can play in the intentional "negotiation of identities . . . [as] part of the process developing peaceful coexistence between former adversaries. Conflictual identities have to be redefined to accept a new type of intergroup relations and to accept multiple meanings of the events." Korostelina, 235–236.

57. Campbell, 33.
58. Martin Seliger, *Ideology and Politics* (London: George Allen and Unwin, 1976).
59. Walter Carlsnaes, *The Concept of Ideology and Political Analysis* (Westport: Greenwood Press, 1981).
60. Among the most significant scholarship regarding the role of collective ideas related to the notion of ideology as it is defined here are Max Weber, *The Protestant Ethic and the Spirit of Capitalism* (New York: Scribner, 1976); Emile Durkheim, *The Rules of Sociological Method* (New York: Free Press, 1966); Margaret Gilbert, "Modelling Collective Beliefs," *Synthese* 73 (1987); John R. Seale, *The Construction of Social Reality* (New York: Free Press, 1995). Haas defines ideology as "the principles upon which a particular leadership group attempts to legitimate its claim to rule and the primary institutional, economic, and social goals to which it swears allegiance. Ideologies are, in short, particular visions for ordering domestic politics." Haas, *Ideological Origins*, 5. A related concept is "strategic culture," which Alastair Iain Johnston has referred to as a set of preferences for certain policy options. Charles Kupchan uses the same term to describe commonly held understandings of the relationship between national security and empire. And Judith Goldstein examines "beliefs about the efficacy of particular strategies for obtaining objectives." Legro, *Rethinking the World*, 8; Alastair Iain Johnston, *Cultural Realism: Strategic Culture and Grand Strategy in Chinese History* (Princeton: Princeton University Press, 1998); Charles Kupchan, *The Vulnerability of Empire* (Ithaca: Cornell University Press, 1996); Judith Goldstein, *Ideas, Interests, and American Trade Policy* (Ithaca: Cornell University Press, 1994). Judith Goldstein and Robert Keohane distinguish between "principled beliefs," which convey "criteria for distinguishing right from wrong, and just from unjust," "causal beliefs," which structure expectations about cause and effect, and "worldviews" which determine "the universe of possibilities for action." According to these authors, ideas exert influence on policy when 1. "the principled or causal beliefs they embody provide road maps that increase actors' clarity about goals or ends-means relationships"; 2. when they serve as "focal points that define cooperative solutions or act as coalitional glue"; and 3. when they come to be reflected in political institutions. Judith Goldstein and Robert Keohane, "Ideas and Foreign Policy: An Analytical Framework," in *Ideas and Foreign Policy: Beliefs, Institutions, and Political Change*, eds. Judith Goldstein and Robert O. Keohane (Ithaca: Cornell University Press, 1993), 8.

61. Legro, *Rethinking the World*, 5, 20–21, 42. Legro suggests that nations and states possess organizational culture. "To act coherently," Legro notes, "large organizations require dominant themes for reasons of efficiency and identity. Culture provides a set of principles regarding collective identity and appropriate behavior, and by doing so it produces more coherent coordinated behavior among the many individuals involved in the planning and conduct of, say, foreign policy . . . nations require ideas that signify to their members what they stand for; as large organizations they require ideas to guide them in their interactions in the international arena. Ideas are not so much mental as symbolic and organizational; they are embedded not only in human brains but also in the 'collective memories,' government procedures, educational systems, and the rhetoric of statecraft. To stress the collective nature of ideas should not imply that they are unrelated to human reflection and action. States do not have brains and inherent cognitive capacity, people do. People guide states (and social groups) and likewise struggle over collective ideas. . . . As Marx famously noted, 'Men make their own history, but they do not make it just as they please . . . but under circumstances transmitted from the past. The tradition of all dead generations weighs like a nightmare on the brain of the living.'" Legro, *Rethinking the World*, 6. Karl Marx, "The Eighteenth Brumaire of Louis Bonaparte," in *The Marx-Engels Reader*, 2nd ed., ed. Robert Tucker (New York: Norton, 1978), 595.
62. Legro, 15, 16.
63. Ibid., 6.
64. The predominant thinking in IR scholarship in recent decades has tended to view ideology as entirely distinct from rational security seeking as motivations in world affairs. Leaders who were ideological motivated were behaving irrationally, and there was perhaps an air of emotion or fanaticism about such leaders. Jack Snyder, *Myths of Empire: Domestic Politics and International Ambition* (Ithaca: Cornell University Press, 1991); Alan Castles, *Ideology and International Relations in the Modern World* (New York: Routledge, 1996); Stephen M. Walt, *The Origins of Alliances* (Ithaca: Cornell University Press, 1987).
65. Haas, *Ideological Origins*, 13; letter of November 16, 1961, Foreign Relations of the United States, 1961–1963, Kennedy–Khruschev Exchanges, vol. 6, virtual archive, 56. http://www.law.uh.edu / cdrom/USFAC/FRUS/Frus_V06.pdf. A variety of scholarship has also demonstrated that ideological differences between actors tend to make communication more difficult. Jervis, *Perception and Misperception*, chaps. 4–5; Albert Mehrabian and Henry Reed, "Some Determinants of Communication Accuracy," *Psychological Bulletin* 70 (November 1968): 366, 373, 378. "Barriers to effective communication among ideological rivals will more often than not lead to increases rather than decreases in threat perceptions. Ideological rivals will tend

to interpret one another's words and deed in the worst possible light. As a result, these decision makers are likely both to perceive conflicts of interest with one another even when none exist, and to magnify the severity of existing disputes." Haas, *Ideological Origins*, 14.

66. Haas, *Ideological Origins*, 1–2.
67. Emanuel Adler and Michael Barnett, eds., *Security Communities* (Cambridge: Cambridge University Press, 1998).
68. Haas, *Ideological Origins*, 32.
69. Ibid., 4.
70. Michael Hunt, *Ideology and U. S. Foreign Policy* (New Haven: Yale University Press, 1987), 12, 14.
71. Richard Kerry, *The Star Spangled Mirror* (New York: Rowman and Littlefield, 1990).
72. Stanley Hoffmann, *Gulliver's Troubles* (New York: McGraw Hill, 1967), 212.
73. Ibid., 87–89. Andrew Levine defines the political liberalism derived from Locke and Mill and faith in free markets derived from Adam Smith as an American ideology. For Levine American ideology combines the belief in the rationality and efficiency of free markets advocated by Smith with the individual rights liberalism of Mill and Lock, that over time came to encompass social tolerance as well as individual freedom from the coercive power of the state in the American context. Rationality, efficiency, and deliberativeness are central aspects of this ideology as Levine sees it. Andrew Levine, *The American Ideology: A Critique* (New York: Routledge, 2004), 96–97.
74. George Kennan, "On America's Principles," *Foreign Affairs*; 74 (March–April 1995), 116–126. Other works on the role of culture in international politics have included Peter J. Katzenstein, ed. *The Culture of National Security: Norms and Identity in World Politics* (New York: Columbia University Press, 1996); Michael C. Desch, "Culture Clash: Assessing the Importance of Ideas in Security Studies," *International Security*, 17 (Summer 1998), 141–170; Alastair Iain Johnston, "Thinking about Strategic Culture," *International Security*, 19, 4 (Spring 1994), 32–64; Jeffrey W. Legro, "Culture and Preference in the International Cooperation Two-Step," *American Political Science Review*, 90, 1(March 1996); and Legro, *Rethinking the World*, 118–137.
75. Nau, 43–59.
76. Ibid., 63.
77. Seymour Martin Lipset, *American Exceptionalism: A Double-Edged Sword* (New York: W.W. Norton, 1996), 46. See also Roger M. Smith, "The 'American Creed' and American Identity: The Limits of Liberal Citizenship in the United States," *Western Political Quarterly*, 41 (1988), 229–230; Roger M. Smith, *Civic Ideals: Conflicting Visions of Citizenship in U.S. History* (New Haven: Yale University Press, 1997). American identity is rooted in an ideology of individualism

over collectivism. In that respect it is firmly rooted in one of two major social orientations described by sociologists, the other being a collectivist orientation in which the dominant assumption within society is that group interests are primary and individual interests secondary. Korostelina, 41.

78. John Gerard Ruggie, *Winning the Peace* (New York: Columbia University Press, 1998); Nau, 25.
79. Hixson, 8; Louis Hartz, *The Liberal Tradition in America* (New York: Harcourt Brace, 1955).
80. Hixson, 7–8.
81. The history of U.S. foreign relations in the last century suggests that it would be overly simplistic to argue that these definitions of military security are derived from definitions of economic security—or vice versa. Certainly, Liberal economic theory supports the conclusion that global security is interconnected because it holds that global economics are interconnected—and economic nationalists consistently argue that these conclusions about both economic and security interests are incorrect. But it does not follow that national leaders define security on the basis of their conclusions regarding economics; rather, it seems that for most leaders, all good things—and all bad things—go together with surprising consistency. The reasons for this seem likely to be rooted in both political expediency and individual psychology, but in any event, national leaders often assert conclusions about the domestic and international environments which allow them to support their policy choices unambiguously. Congressional isolationists before World War II, for example, concluded not only that the nation's well-being was not closely tied to European trade and investment and that war would not threaten American security but also that war on the Continent was not likely and that the United States did not have the means to prevent it or change the outcome if it occurred.
82. Tony Smith, *A Pact with the Devil: Washington's Bid for World Supremacy and the Betrayal of the American Promise* (New York: Routledge, 2007), 196.
83. Campbell, 134, 136; Albert J. Harkness, "Americanism and Jenkins' Ear," *Mississippi Valley Historical Review* XXXVII (1950): 89.
84. Hixson argues that gender was also central to the emerging American identity from the start, that "gendered discourse powerfully influenced foreign policy . . . through conceptions of honor, get tough policies, manly intervention, upholding credibility, drawing lines in the sand, and vowing to never cut and run." Hixson, 12. Linda Boose argues that "ambiguities and doubts belong to the feminine." Christina Jarvis claims that a "hegemonic militarized masculinity" shapes U.S. culture and the American approach to international affairs. Susan Jeffords asserts that it is not possible to understand "war and its place in American culture without an understanding of its gendered

relations." Hixson, 12; Amy Kaplan and Donald E. Pease, *Cultures of United States Imperialism* (Durham: Duke University Press, 1993), 610; Christina S. Jarvis, *The Male Body at War: American Masculinity During World War II* (DeKalb: Northern Illinois University Press, 2004), 8; Susan Jeffords, *The Remasculinazation of America: Gender and the Vietnam War* (Bloomington: Indiana University Press, 1989), 182.

85. Campbell, 122, 131, 136. On cultural identity and the history of U.S. foreign policy, see also: David Ryan, *U.S. Foreign Policy in World History* (London: Routledge, 2000); Neil Renwick, *America's World Identity: The Politics of Exclusion* (New York: St. Martin's Press, 2000); Anders Stephanson, *Manifest Destiny: American Expansion and the Empire of Right* (New York: Hill and Wang, 1995); Anatol Lieven, *America Right or Wrong: An Anatomy of American Nationalism* (New York: Oxford University Press, 2004); Ernest Lee Tuveson, *Redeemer Nation: The Idea of America's Millennial Role* (Chicago: University of Chicago Press, 1968); John Fousek, *To Lead the Free World: American Nationalism and the Cultural Roots of the Cold War* (Chapel Hill: University of North Carolina Press, 2000); Frank Ninkovich, *Modernity and Power: A History of the Domino Theory in the Twentieth Century* (Chicago: University of Chicago Press, 1994).
86. Hixson, 35.
87. Ibid., 36.
88. Ibid., 36, 38.
89. Ibid., 37; Conrad Cherry, *God's New Israel: Religious Interpretations of American Destiny* (Chapel Hill: University of North Carolina Press, 1998), 327; Weeks, "Foreign Relations of the Early Republic," *Journal of the Early Republic* (Winter 1994), 460.
90. Hixson, 13; Conrad Cherry, *God's New Israel: Religious Interpretations of American Destiny* (Chapel Hill: University of North Carolina Press, 1998), 7, 19.
91. Hixson, 13, 20–21.
92. Smith, *A Pact with the Devil,* 60.
93. Hixson, 37.
94. Pauline Maier, *American Scripture: Making the Declaration of Independence* (New York: Alfred A. Knopf, 1997).
95. George Washington, Farewell Address.
96. Hunt, 22.
97. Hixson, 56.
98. Ibid., 75.
99. Ibid., 97–98.
100. Ibid., 103–104.
101. Ibid., 102–103.
102. Jean-Baptiste Duroselle, *From Wilson to Roosevelt: Foreign Policy of the United States, 1913–1945* (Cambridge: Harvard University Press, 1963), 68.

103. Legro, *Rethinking the World*, 82–83.
104. Irving L. Janis, *Groupthink: Psychological Studies of Policy Decisions and Fiascoes* (Boston: Houghton Mifflin, 1982), 84.
105. Ibid., 109.
106. Secretary of State Dean Acheson, "Testimony before the Senate Appropriations Committee," *Supplemental Appropriations for 1951*, p. 272, quoted in Jervis, *Perception and Misperception*, 50.
107. Janis 58.
108. Ibid., 59, 61.
109. Campbell, 159, 195.
110. Jutta Weldes emphasizes the importance of this social process of naming within politics; in Cuba, what became known as the "October Crisis" acquired a meaning connected to nationalistic narratives about state sovereignty, independence, and anti-imperialism. "For the Soviets, in contrast, these events were the 'Caribbean crisis'. . . This situation was one of imminent U.S. aggression against Cuba. The time frame is much longer and includes not only the 1961 Bay of Pigs invasion but also a prolonged history of U.S. aggression against Cuba. The issue was U.S. imperialism and the threat it presented to socialism in general and to the socialist experiment in Cuba in particular. . . . The identity for which these events were the 'Carribean crisis' is a subject—the Soviet Union—defined as the leader of the socialist bloc pledged to support socialist states and surrounded by a hostile other—the aggressive, nuclear-armed, global capitalist alliance led by the United States. . . . This crisis also provided the Soviet Union with the opportunity—ostensibly realized in the U.S. pledge not to invade Cuba—to reaffirm its identity as the leader of the global socialist movement. . . . The 'Cuban missile crisis' . . . was a crisis for the subject 'the United States,' while the 'Caribbean crisis' was a crisis for the subject 'the Soviet Union,' and the 'October crisis' was one for 'Cuba.' Defining a crisis thus depends on the discursively constituted identity of the state." Jutta Weldes, "The Cultural Production of Crises: U.S. Identity and Missiles in Cuba," in *Cultures of Insecurity: States, Communities, and the Production of Danger*, eds. Jutta Weldes, Mark Laffey, Hugh Gusterson, and Raymond Duvall (Minneapolis: University of Minnesota Press, 1999), 38, 58.
111. U.S. National Security Council; 1950, 390; 1948, 165.
112. Weldes, "Cultural Production," 41; Arthur M. Schlesinger, *A Thousand Days: John F. Kennedy in the White House* (Boston: Houghton Mifflin, 1965), 806–807.
113. Legro, *Rethinking the World*, 170.
114. Ibid, 4, 11.
115. The term "punctuated equilibrium" is borrowed from Jerel A. Rosati, who borrows it in turn from the field of evolutionary biology. Jerel A. Rosati, "Cycles of Foreign Policy Restructuring: The Politics of Continuity and Change in U.S. Foreign Policy, in *Foreign Policy*

Restructuring: How Governments Respond to Global Change, eds. Jerel A. Rosati, Joe D. Hagan, and Martin W. Sampson (Columbia: University of South Carolina Press, 1994), 224. See also Albert Somit and Steven A. Peterson, *The Dynamics of Evolution: The Punctuated Equilibrium Debate in the Natural and Social Sciences*, (Ithaca: Cornell University Press, 1992).

116. Legro, *Rethinking the World*, 80.
117. Ibid, 81.

CHAPTER 2

1. Hopf, *Social Construction*, 22.
2. Jutta Weldes, *Constructing National Interests: The United States and the Cuban Missile Crisis* (University of Minnesota Press, 1999), 9.
3. Hopf, *Social Construction*, 290.
4. Legro, *Rethinking the World*, 183, 184.
5. Hopf, *Social Construction*, 22–23.
6. Legro points to State of the Union Addresses as particularly useful representations of dominant ideas within presidential administrations, sources of the "discourse that reflect intersubjective belief." "These speeches tend to be highly symbolic and are rightly seen as efforts to capture the character, thought, and direction of the nation." Presidents use them "to rally support and legitimacy through appeal to societal traditions and norms . . . These speeches are much more than simply the views of the individual leaders that present them . . . the uniform context and format makes it a useful point of comparison with previous State of the Union speeches." Legro, *Rethinking the World*, 52. On the use of State of the Union addresses as sources, see: Frank Klingberg, "The Historical Alternation of Moods in American Foreign Policy," *World Politics* 4 (1952); Ernest R. May, "National Security in American History," in *Rethinking America's Security: Beyond the Cold War to New World Order*, eds. Graham Allison and Gregory Treverton (New York: Norton, 1992).
7. Legro, *Rethinking the World*, 27.
8. Robert Draper, *Dead Certain: The Presidency of George W. Bush* (New York: Free Press, 2007), 154–155; Bob Woodward, *Bush at War* (New York: Simon and Schuster, 2002), 30.
9. For discussion of Wilsonian liberalism and the foreign policy of the Bush administration see Lloyd E. Ambrosius, "Woodrow Wilson and George W. Bush: Historical Comparisons of Ends and Means in Their Foreign Policies," *Diplomatic History* 30 (2006): 509–543; Max Boot, "George Wilson Bush," *Wall Street Journal*, July 1, 2002, Editorial Page; Robert Cooper, "Imperial Liberalism," *The National Interest* 79 (2005): 25–34; David M. Kennedy, "What 'W' Owes to 'WW,'" *The Atlantic*, 295 (March 2005); Melvyn P. Leffler, "9/11 and American Foreign Policy," *Diplomatic History* 29 (June 2005): 395–396; John

B. Judis, *The Folly of Empire: What George W. Bush Could Learn from Theodore Roosevelt and Woodrow Wilson* (Oxford: Oxford University Press, 2004); and John Lewis Gaddis, *Surprise, Security, and the American Experience* (Cambridge: Harvard University Press, 2005).

10. Robert Jervis, *American Foreign Policy in a New Era.* (London: Routledge, 2005), 80–83.
11. Snyder, 54.
12. Ibid., 58.
13. For a more thorough explication of Wilsonianism in rhetoric and practice, see Karl K. Schonberg, *Pursuing the National Interest: Moments of Transition in American Foreign Policy.* (Westport: Praeger, 2003), 13–98.
14. Ross Gregory, *Origins of American Intervention in the First World War.* (New York: Norton, 1971): 144, 146.
15. Osgood, 174.
16. Ibid., 178.
17. Ibid., 176.
18. Arthur S. Link et al, eds., *Papers of Woodrow Wilson*, LXII. (Princeton: Princeton University Press, 1985), 217.
19. Arthur S. Link, *Wilson the Diplomatist.* (New York: Quadrangle Books, 1963), 145.
20. Osgood, 187.
21. Gregory, 144.
22. Ibid., 144.
23. Osgood, 189.
24. Harley Notter, *The Origins of the Foreign Policy of Woodrow Wilson.* (Baltimore: Johns Hopkins University Press, 1937), 43, 331.
25. John Chalmers Vinson, *Referendum for Isolation: Defeat of Article Ten of the League of Nations Covenant.* (Athens: University of Georgia Press, 1961), 31.
26. Ibid., 96.
27. Ibid., 99.
28. Smith, *Pact with the Devil*, 21, 22, 109; Natan Sharansky with Ron Dermer, *The Case for Democracy: The Power of Freedom to Overcome Tyranny and Terror* (New York: Public Affairs, 2004), 88.
29. Smith, 80–81.
30. Ibid., 20, 111.
31. Ibid., 111–112.
32. Ibid., 113.
33. Taylor, 24.
34. James C. Thomson, Jr., "How Could Vietnam Happen: An Autopsy," *The Atlantic Monthly*, April, 1968, reprinted in G. John Ikenberry, ed., *American Foreign Policy: Theoretical Essays*, 4th ed. (New York: Longman, 2002), 463.
35. Thomas Ricks, Fiasco: *The American Military Adventure in Iraq*, (New York: Penguin, 2006), 8.

36. David L. Altheide and Jennifer N. Grimes, "War Programming: The Propaganda Project and the Iraq War," *The Sociological Quarterly* 46 (2005): 617–643. On the history and substance of "neoconservatism," see: Sam Tanenhaus, "Bush's Brain Trust," *Vanity Fair* 515 (2003); Gary Dorrien, *Imperial Designs: Neoconservatism and the New Pax Americana* (London: Routledge, 2004); James Atlas, "What it Takes to Be a Neo-Neoconservative," *New York Times*, October 19, 2003, 12; Stefan Halper and Jonathan Clarke, *America Alone: The Neo-Conservatives and the Global Order* (Cambridge: Cambridge University Press, 2004); G. John Ikenberry, "The End of the Neo-Conservative Moment," *Survival*, 46 (2004): 7–22; Irwin Stelzer, ed., *The Neocon Reader* (Grove Press, 2004); Irving Kristol, *Neoconservatism: The Autobiography of an Idea* (New York: Free Press, 1995); Anne Norton, *Leo Strauss and the Politics of American Empire*, (New Haven: Yale University Press, 2004).
37. Jeffrey Record, *Dark Victory: America's Second War Against Iraq* (Annapolis: Naval Institute Press, 2004), 22.
38. Smith, *Pact with the Devil*, 27; Gary Dorrien, *Imperial Designs: Neoconservatism and the New Pax Americana* (New York: Routledge, 2004), 153.
39. "Statement of Principles," Project for a New American Century, June 3, 1997. *http://www.newamericancentury.org/statementofprinciples.htm* (accessed September 10, 2008).
40. Halper and Clarke, 11–12.
41. Steven Mufson, "Bush Urged to Champion Human Rights: Conservatives Call on President to Promote Democracy, Freedom in Foreign Policy," *Washington Post*, January 26, 2001, A5.
42. Robert J. Lieber, "The Folly of Containment," *Commentary*, April 2003, 15–21.
43. Norman Podhoretz, "Oslo: The Peacemongers Return," *Commentary*, October 2001, 21–33.
44. Record, 20; Robert Kagan and William Kristol, "National Interest and Global Responsibility," in *Present Dangers: Crisis and Opportunity in American Foreign and Defense Policy*, eds. Robert Kagan and William Kristol (San Francisco: Encounter Books, 2000), 4.
45. William Kristol and Robert Kagan, "Toward a Neo-Reaganite Foreign Policy," *Foreign Affairs* (1996).
46. Smith, *Pact with the Devil*, 8, 12–13.
47. Record, 21; Robert Kagan and William Kristol, "National Interest and Global Responsibility," in *Present Dangers: Crisis and Opportunity in American Foreign and Defense Policy*, eds. Robert Kagan and William Kristol (San Francisco: Encounter Books, 2000), 6–7.
48. Record, 21; Kagan and Kristol, "National Interest and Global Responsibility," 9, 13–14, 16–18, 23–24.
49. Smith, *Pact with the Devil*, 35.
50. Ibid., 38.

51. Record, 23; Lawrence F. Kaplan and William Kristol, *The War over Iraq: Saddam's Tyranny and America's Mission* (San Francisco: Encounter Books, 2003), 37.
52. George Packer, *The Assassins' Gate: America in Iraq* (New York: Farrar, Strauss and Giroux, 2005), 51, 58; Bernard Lewis, *What Went Wrong? The Clash Between Islam and Modernity in the Middle East* (New York: Harper Perennial, 2003); Fouad Ajami, *Dream Palace of the Arabs: A Generation's Odyssey* (New York: Vintage, 1999).
53. Packer, 32.
54. Ibid., 64–65.
55. Smith, *Pact with the Devil*, 31.
56. Packer, 20.
57. Ibid., 18–19.
58. Ibid., 54.
59. Leo Strauss, *Liberalism Ancient and Modern* (New York: Basic Books, 1968), 4; Packer, 55.
60. Smith, *Pact with the Devil*, 29; Halper and Clarke, 65.
61. Packer, 106–107.
62. Ibid., 65; Smith, *Pact with the Devil*, 29; Halper and Clarke, 65.
63. Packer, 22–23, 56.
64. Ibid., 56–57.
65. Smith, *Pact with the Devil*, 28.
66. Packer, 56–57.
67. Ibid., 15, 29; Smith, *Pact with the Devil*, 28.
68. Packer, 15; Smith, *Pact with the Devil*, 28.
69. Jeanne Kirkpatrick, "American Power—What For?" *Commentary*, January 2000, 34.
70. Ronald Reagan, Address to Members of the British Parliament, June 8, 1982 (www.reagan.utexas.edu/archives/speeches/1982/60882a.htm). Accessed July 18, 2008.
71. Packer, 17.
72. Smith, *Pact with the Devil*, 28.
73. Packer, 13.
74. Smith, *Pact with the Devil*, 5.
75. Packer, 25.
76. Ibid., 26.
77. David L. Phillips, *Losing Iraq: Inside the Postwar Reconstruction Fiasco* (Boulder: Westview Press, 2004), 60.
78. Smith, *Pact with the Devil*, 146; Jeffrey Goldberg, "Breaking Ranks," *New Yorker*, October 31, 2005.
79. Record, 21–22; Paul Wolfowitz, "Statesmanship in the New Century," in *Present Dangers: Crisis and Opportunity in American Foreign and Defense Policy*, eds. Kagan and Kristol (San Francisco: Encounter Books, 2000), 319–320, 325.
80. Mark Bowden, "Wolfowitz: The Exit Interviews," *Atlantic Monthly*, July–August 2005.

81. Smith, *Pact with the Devil*, 146; Bill Keller, "The Sunshine Warrior," *New York Times*, September 22, 2002.
82. Colin Dueck, "Ideas and Alternatives in American Grand Strategy, 2000-2004," *Review of International Studies* 30 (2004): 511–535; Paul Lyons, "George W. Bush's City on a Hill," *The Journal of the Historical Society* 6 (2006): 119–131; Sandra Silberstein, *War of Words: Language, Politics, and 9/11* (London: Routledge, 2002).
83. Stanley A. Renshon and Peter Suedfeld, eds., *Understanding the Bush Doctrine: Psychology and Strategy in an Age of Terrorism* (London: Routledge, 2007).
84. *National Security Strategy of the United States*, The White House, 2002.
85. *National Security Strategy*, 1, iii, 15; "Text of the President's Speech at West Point," *New York Times*, June 1, 2002.
86. *National Security Strategy of the United States.*
87. Jackson Diehl, "Rice Produces a Brilliant Synthesis," *The Washington Post*, October 1, 2002, B3.
88. Condoleezza Rice, "The Promise of Democratic Peace: Why Promoting Freedom Is the Only Realistic Path to Security," *The Washington Post*, December 11, 2005, B7.
89. G. John Ikenberry, "Are Bush and Rice the New Liberal Internationalists?" *TPM Café*, http://www.tpmcafe.com/story/2006/1/22/204815/880 (accessed January 20, 2007).
90. Rice, "Promise of Democratic Peace," B7.
91. George W. Bush, 2002 State of the Union Address, January 29, 2002. http://www.whitehouse.gov/news/releases/2002/01/20020129-11.html (accessed August 25, 2008).
92. Ibid.
93. Ibid.
94. George W. Bush, 2003 State of the Union Address, January 28, 2003. http://www.whitehouse.gov/news/releases/2003/01/20030128-19.html (accessed August 25, 2008).
95. George W. Bush, 2004 State of the Union Address, January 20, 2004. http://www.whitehouse.gov/news/releases/2004/01/20040120-7.html. (Accessed August 25, 2008).
96. Ibid.
97. Lloyd E. Ambrosius, "Woodrow Wilson and George W. Bush: Historical Comparisons of Ends and Means in Their Foreign Policies," *Diplomatic History* 30 (2006): 509, 542–543.
98. Jonathan Monten, "The Roots of the Bush Doctrine," *International Security* 29 (2005).
99. Smith, *Pact with the Devil*, 45; Kaplan and Kristol, Chapter 6; Paul Berman, "What Lincoln Knew about War," *New Republic*, March 3, 2003.
100. Smith, *Pact with the Devil*, 48, 54.

101. Melvyn P. Leffler, "9/11 and American Foreign Policy," *Diplomatic History* 29 (June 2005): 395–96. See also Melvyn P. Leffler, "9/11 and the Past and Future of American Foreign Policy, *International Affairs* 79 (2003): 1045–1063.
102. Arnold A. Offner, "Rogue President, Rogue Nation: Bush and U.S. National Security," *Diplomatic History* 29 (2005): 433–435.
103. Adam Quinn, "'The Deal': The Balance of Power, Military Strength, and Liberal Internationalism in the Bush National Security Strategy," *International Studies Perspectives* 9 (2008): 40.
104. Halper and Clarke, 35–36.
105. Lloyd E. Ambrosius, "Woodrow Wilson and George W. Bush: Historical Comparisons of Ends and Means in Their Foreign Policies," *Diplomatic History* 30 (2006): 509, 520.
106. Chris J. Dolan, "The Bush Doctrine and U.S. Interventionism," *American Diplomacy*, IX, 2, 2004, http://www.unc.edu/depts/diplomat (accessed September 9, 2006); see also: Richard Falk, "The New Bush Doctrine," *The Nation*, July, 15, 2002; Stewart Patrick, "Don't Fence Me In: A Restless America Seeks Room to Roam," *World Policy Journal*, XVIII; Stewart Patrick, "Multilateralism and Its Discontents: Causes and Consequences of U.S. Ambivalence," in *Multilateralism and U.S. Foreign Policy*, eds. Patrick and Shephard Forman (Boulder: Lynne Rienner, 2002).
107. Ikenberry," Are Bush and Rice the New Liberal Internationalists?"
108. Ibid.

CHAPTER 3

1. Stuart Croft, *Culture, Crisis and America's War on Terror* (Cambridge: Cambridge University Press, 2006); Susan Willis, *Portents of the Real: A Primer for Post-9/11 America* (New York: Verson, 2005). François Debrix has described an institutional structure of ideology formation including not only the administration but also intellectuals in think tanks and academia who help to shape and reinforce the administration's consensus worldview and convey it to the wider public. The works of authors such as Robert Kaplan, Victor Davis Hanson, and Michael Ledeen in Debrix' view "encourage the USA's political and military leadership to embrace terror and violence and to be continuously at war against alleged American enemies . . . require[ing] their readers to be one with hatred and destruction, and to violently reject anything that appears to be un-American." While such works are "immensely influential in post-9/11 American national security circles," Debrix suggests, they also address a wider audience, seeking to "prepare and condition American citizens for years of ongoing violence, war and possibly terror." François Debrix, "Discourses of War, Geographies of Abjection: Reading Contemporary American Ideologies of Terror," *Third World Quarterly*, 26 (2005): 1157–1172.

2. Woodward, *Bush at War*, 17–19.
3. "A Day of Terror: Bush's Remarks to the Nation on the Terrorist Attacks," *The New York Times*, September 12, 2001, A4.
4. Woodward, *Bush at War*, 45.
5. Ibid., 94.
6. Ibid., 43.
7. Walt, 40.
8. Berreby points out that an association with death or illness is one of the most powerful negative stigmas that can be attached to an out-group. He cites the work of the psychologist Jamie Arndt, who placed two groups of volunteers at computers and showed pictures of foreigners and other out-group members, but in one group flashed a word associated with death among the photographs too rapidly to be seen. The groups who had been unconsciously exposed to this association with death had much more hostile reactions to foreigners thereafter. Arndt and others performed similar studies in five nations and found similar results across national boundaries. The association of one's political enemies with death is thus a very potent rhetorical strategy, as Berreby notes. Berreby, 233–234, 245.
9. Salter, 24.
10. R.B.J. Walker, *Inside/Outside: International Relations as Political Theory* (Cambridge: Cambridge University Press, 1993), 49.
11. Salter, 38; V.G. Kiernan, *The Lords of Human Kind: Black Man, Yellow Man, and White Man in an Age of Empire* (New York: Columbia University Press, 1986), 28.
12. Salter, 163.
13. Ibid., 17; Gerrit W. Gong, *The Standard of "Civilization" in International Society* (Oxford: Clarendon Press, 1984), 23, 29–30. The term "barbarian" traces its origins to ancient Greece and initially referred to those who could not speak Greek, who were unintelligible to Greeks and thus incapable of participation in the polis. Euripedes suggests that the term from early on implied both an inability to understand and be understood by Greeks, and also foreignness with an implication of inferiority. Aristotle indicates that "barbarism" was in itself a justification for domination, that "barbarians" were "slaves by nature." Kristeva has argued that the etymology of the term suggests that its meaning was also gendered from very early on. Salter, 18; Helen H. Bacon, *Barbarians in Greek Tragedy* (New Haven: Yale University Press, 1961), 10, n. 8.; Julia Kristeva, *Strangers to Ourselves* (New York: Columbia University Press, 1991), 51; Aristotle, "Politics," in *Basic Works of Aristotle*, ed. Richard McKeown (New York: Random House, 1941), Book I, 1128. Edward Said suggests that in the Western imagination the "barbarian" is understood to be vulgar, course, immoral, a violent threat to the "civilized" world. Edward Said, *Orientalism* (New York: Vintage, 1978), Salter, 54. Salter argues that "the space of the barbarian illustrates the limits of

the political community—the figure of the barbarian—either alone or in a horde—acts as the 'constitutive outside' of the polis . . . Barbarians are most often the locus of anxiety. The lack of restraint which they are represented as possessing in the sexual, political, and military realms is assumed to endow them with more power than the restraint of the Europeans." Salter, 4, 25.

14. Robert L. Ivie, "Savagery in Democracy's Empire," *Third World Quarterly* 26 (2005): 55.
15. Ikechi Mgbeoji, "The Civilised Self and the Barbaric Other: Imperial Delusions of Order and the Challenges of Human Security," *Third World Quarterly* 27 (2006): 855–869.
16. "A Nation Challenged: President Bush's Address on Terrorism Before a Joint Meeting of Congress," *The New York Times*, September 21, 2001, B4.
17. Ibid.
18. Ibid.
19. Ibid.
20. Ibid.
21. Bush, 2002 State of the Union Address.
22. Ibid.
23. Ibid.
24. Ibid.
25. Ibid.
26. Bob Woodward, *Plan of Attack* (New York: Simon and Schuster, 2004), 346, 178.
27. Michael Sherry, "Dead or Alive: American Vengeance Goes Global," *Review of International Studies* 31 (2005), 245–263.
28. Wyn Rees and Richard J. Aldrich, "Contending Cultures of Counterterrorism: Transatlantic Divergence or Convergence?" *International Affairs* 81 (2005): 905–923.
29. Bush, 2002 State of the Union Address.
30. Within the administration, Afghan society was conceived of as a confused array of tribal, national, and ethnic groups, each with its own interests and rivalries and each willing to sell its loyalty to the highest bidder. Tenet described Afghan Pashtuns as he saw them in a Principals' meeting on October 11, 2001. "The Pashtuns are anti-Northern Alliance—they could be anti-Taliban," he said. "They're not anti-U.S." He suggested that their allegiances like those of many if not all of the Afghan parties in the conflict could be bought. The United States needed to "incentivize them," he said. "They only want to control their shura," he noted, referencing the Islamic idea of self-governance. "Some of them are into vision and some of them are into money," he said. "We need to administer to both." Such was the administration's sense of the shifting loyalties of Afghan militias and tribes that the running joke in Bush's war cabinet was "you can't buy an Afghan but you can rent one." Woodward, *Bush at War*, 230, 232, 253.

31. Ibid., 131.
32. Ibid., 185, 192.
33. Bush, 2002 State of the Union Address.
34. Ibid.
35. Ibid.
36. Ibid.
37. Ibid.
38. Regarding the Bush administration's construction of Iran in particular, Arshin Adib-Moghaddam has outlined the "invented narratives, institutions, norms and other ideational factors" that have defined Iran in the "neo-conservative imagination," driving post-9/11 U.S. foreign policy toward Iran. ArshinAdib-Moghaddam, "Manufacturing War: Iran in the Neo-conservative Imagination," *Third World Quarterly* 28 (2007): 635–653.
39. Bush, 2003 State of the Union Address.
40. Ibid.
41. Ibid.
42. Bush, 2004 State of the Union Address.
43. Michael V. Bhatia, "Fighting Words: Naming Terrorists, Bandits, Rebels and Other Violent Actors," *Third World Quarterly* 26 (2005): 5–22.
44. Bush, 2004 State of the Union Address.
45. Ibid.
46. George W. Bush, 2005 State of the Union Address, February 2, 2005. http://www.whitehouse.gov/news/releases/2004/01/2004 0120-7.html (accessed August 25, 2008).
47. Bush, 2005 State of the Union Address.
48. Ibid.
49. Bush, 2005 State of the Union Address.
50. "State of the Union: We Strive to Be a Compassionate, Decent, Hopeful Society," *The New York Times,* February 1, 2006, A18.
51. George W. Bush, 2006 State of the Union Address, January 31, 2006. http://www.whitehouse.gov/stateoftheunion/2006/index.html (accessed August 25, 2008).
52. Ibid.
53. Ibid.
54. Smith, *Pact with the Devil,* 147; Condoleezza Rice, speech at Princeton University, Woodrow Wilson School of Public and International Affairs, September 30, 2005 *www.state.gov/secretary/rm/2005/54176.htm* (accessed June 18, 2008).
55. Smith, *Pact with the Devil,* 148.
56. Ibid.
57. Draper, 289.
58. Smith, *Pact with the Devil,* 149.
59. Woodward, *Plan of Attack,* 88–89.
60. Condoleezza Rice, "Promoting the National Interest," *Foreign Affairs* (2000): 47–48.

61. Woodward, *Plan of Attack*, 307–309.
62. Draper, 181.
63. Ibid., 179.
64. Ibid., 183.
65. David Frum, *The Right Man: The Surprise Presidency of George W. Bush* (New York: Random House, 2003), 196.
66. Woodward, *Plan of Attack*, 188–189.
67. Ibid., 119–120.
68. Draper, 185–186.
69. Record, 53; "'We're Calling for a Vote' at the U.N., Says Bush," *Washington Post*, March 7, 2003.
70. Ibid., 55–57.
71. Remarks by the president on Iraq, Cincinnati Museum Center—Cincinnati Union Terminal Cincinnati, Ohio, October 7, 2002. Accessed July 10, 2007; http://www.whitehouse.gov/news/releases/2002/10/20021007-8.html.
72. Ibid.
73. Ibid.; Woodward, *Plan of Attack*, 241. David Berreby argues that identifying individuals or groups as cheaters, ungoverned by the norms of ethical behavior, is a powerful political tool because of its deep significance within the human psyche. The human mind has evolved to judge the actions of others by unstated and often unconscious rules of justice and equity, Berreby suggests, and to be on the lookout for individuals who are evading those rules. "By stigmatizing certain people as unworthy of taking parts in exchanges, these techniques make us feel that those people are not, somehow, fully human." Berreby, 234.
74. Remarks by the president on Iraq, Cincinnati, October 7, 2002.
75. Ibid.
76. Mike Allen, "Bush: Hussein, Al Qaeda Linked," *Washington Post*, September 26, 2002.
77. Record, 51; Robert Harvey, *Global Disorder, America, and the Threat of World Conflict* (New York: Carroll and Graf, 2003), 67.
78. Record, 59; James Risen, "Captives Deny Qaeda Worked with Baghdad," *New York Times*, June 9, 2003.
79. Remarks by the president on Iraq, Cincinnati, October 7, 2002.
80. Ibid.
81. Ibid.
82. Ibid.
83. Ibid.
84. Bob Woodward, *State of Denial* (New York: Simon and Schuster), 393, 415, 418.
85. Draper, 173.
86. Berreby, 237.
87. Remarks by the President on Iraq, Cincinnati, October 7, 2002.
88. Ibid.

89. Andrew Flibbert, "The Road to Baghdad: Ideas and Intellectuals in Explanations of the Iraq War," *Security Studies* 15 (2006): 345.
90. Record, 24, 118; Condoleezza Rice, "Transforming the Middle East," *Washington Post*, August 7, 2003; Trudy Rubin, "Bush Never Made Serious Postwar Plans" *Philadelphia Inquirer*, June 26, 2003; Woodward, *Bush at War*, 37.
91. Record, 86; "In the President's Words: 'Free People Will Keep the Peace of the World.'" Transcript of President Bush's Speech to the American Enterprise Institute, Washington, D.C., February 26, 2003, *New York Times*, February 27, 2003.
92. Record 79, 99; Ali A. Allawi, *The Occupation of Iraq: Winning the War, Losing the Peace* (New Haven: Yale University Press, 2007), 148–149.
93. Smith, *Pact with the Devil*, 155–157.
94. James Webb, "Heading for Trouble," *Washington Post*, September 4, 2002.
95. Smith, *Pact with the Devil*, 155–157.
96. Draper, 166.
97. Record, 41, 44; Scott Sagan, "The Perils of Proliferation: Organization Theory, Deterrence Theory, and the Spread of Nuclear Weapons," *International Security* 8 (1994), 77–81; Allen Rankin, "U.S. Could Wipe Out Red A-Nests in a Week, General Anderson Asserts," *Montgomery Advertiser*, September 1, 1950.
98. Packer, 116.
99. Woodward, *Plan of Attack*, 76.
100. Record, 97; Phillips, 8; Michael R. Gordon and General Bernard E. Trainor, *Cobra II: The Inside Story of the Invasion and Occupation of Iraq* (New York: Pantheon Books, 2006), 498.
101. Thomson, 462–63; Record, 79; Jack Snyder, "Imperial Temptations," *National Interest*, 71 (Spring 2003), 39.
102. Flibbert, 311–312, 351.
103. "America After 9/11: Public Opinion on The War on Terrorism, The War with Iraq, and America's Place in the World" http://www.aei.org/publications/pubID.16974/pub_detail.asp (accessed May 30, 2008).
104. "America after 9/11."
105. "America after 9/11."
106. Douglas Kellner, *From 9/11 to Terror War* (Lanham, MD: Rowman and Littlefield, 2003), 54–55.
107. Kellner, 77.
108. Kathleen Hall Jamieson and Paul Waldman, *The Press Effect: Politicians, Journalists, and the Stories that Shape the Political World* (New York: Oxford University Press, 2003), 151-152; see also Pippa Norris, Montague Kern, and Marion Just, eds., *Framing Terrorism: The News Media, the Government, and the Public* (New York: Routledge, 2003).
109. Smith, *Pact with the Devil*, xxv.

110. Thomas Friedman, *New York Times*, March 3, 2006; January 8, 2004.
111. Smith, *Pact with the Devil*, 163.
112. Ibid., 91.
113. Ibid., 130–131, 145.
114. Moises Naim, "Bush's Willing Enablers," *Foreign Policy* 143 (2004): 95–96.

CHAPTER 4

1. Gordon and Trainor, 497–498.
2. Legro, *Rethinking the World*, 2, 19, 26; 't Hart, Stern, and Sundelius, 26–28; Vertzberger, 293.
3. Woodward, *Bush at War*, 46; Jervis, *Perception and Misperception*, 240.
4. Woodward, *Bush at War*, 32, 33, 53.
5. Ibid., 65, 168; Draper, 148.
6. Woodward, *Plan of Attack*, 25.
7. Packer, 40–41.
8. Woodward, *Plan of Attack*, 26.
9. Dan Balz, Bob Woodward, and Jeff Himmelman, "Afghan Campaign's Blueprint Emerges," *Washington Post*, January 29, 2002, A11.
10. Woodward, *Plan of Attack*, 49.
11. Jervis, *Perception and Misperception*, 203, 215; Woodward, *Plan of Attack*, 11.
12. Jervis, *Perception and Misperception*, 143; Ole Holsti, "Cognitive Dynamics and Images of the Enemy: Dulles and Russia," in *Enemies in Politics*, eds. David Finlay, Ole Holsti, and Richard Fagen (Chicago: Rand McNally, 1967), 86.
13. Jervis, *Perception and Misperception*, 146.
14. Ibid., 154, 172.
15. Ibid., 181.
16. Record, 146; Kosterlitz, "The Neoconservative Moment," *National Journal*, May 17, 2003, 1540-46; Robert Jervis, "The Compulsive Empire," *Foreign Policy*, (July-August 2003), 83.
17. Woodward, *Bush at War*, 257, 259.
18. Ibid., 340, 341.
19. Ibid., 321.
20. Draper, 165, 176, 286.
21. Ibid., 357.
22. Ibid., 386.
23. Ibid., 358, 387.
24. Ibid., 360–361.
25. Janis, 9, 11.
26. 't Hart, Stern, and Sundelius, 18–19, 21–22.
27. Janis, 13.
28. Woodward, *Bush at War*, 281, 282; Draper, xii.

29. Draper, 418–419; Packer, 391.
30. Janis, 35, 174–175; Vertzberger, 300.
31. Woodward, *Plan of Attack*, 379; Hixson, 292. On the influence of his Christian evangelical faith on George W. Bush, see Ira Chernus, *Monsters to Destroy: The Neoconservative War on Terror and Sin* (Boulder: Paradigm Publishers, 2006), 69–84.
32. Hixson, 292; Janis, 35.
33. Jervis, *Perception and Misperception,* 390, 396; Draper, 393.
34. Janis, 36–37.
35. Woodward, *Plan of Attack*, 76.
36. Ibid., 80–81.
37. Ibid., 81, 343.
38. Gordon and Trainor, 105.
39. Ibid., 142.
40. Draper, 209.
41. Jervis, *Perception and Misperception*, 382. Leon Festinger, *A Theory of Cognitive Dissonance* (Palo Alto: Stanford University Press, 1957), 13, 31.
42. Jervis, *Perception and Misperception,* 387, 404.
43. Packer, 148.
44. Ibid., 148, 390.
45. Jervis, *Perception and Misperception,* 196; Woodward, *Plan of Attack*, 415.
46. Thomson, 461.
47. Ibid., 456, 457.
48. Ibid., 460.
49. Woodward, *Bush at War*, 38–39, 96, 123; Woodward, *Plan of Attack*, 377.
50. Woodward, *Plan of Attack*, 262; Woodward, *Bush at War*, 215; Thomson, 461.
51. Woodward, *Plan of Attack*, 248–249.
52. Berreby, 6.
53. Woodward, *Plan of Attack*, 52, 61, 64, 75; Record, 109; "Sounding the Drums for War," *Washington Post*, August 10, 2003.
54. Draper, 174; Woodward, *Plan of Attack*, 87, 292, 429; Woodward, *Bush at War*, 137.
55. Woodward, *Plan of Attack*, 298, 311.
56. Jervis, *Perception and Misperception,* 319.
57. Ibid., 310.
58. Ibid., 323.
59. Gordon and Trainor, 65–66.
60. Ibid., 118–119, 134.
61. Gordon and Trainor, 58.
62. Ibid., 120, 124; Allawi, 174.
63. Woodward, *Bush at War*, 215, 218, 224.
64. Woodward, *Plan of Attack*, 206.

65. Paul L. Bremer with Malcolm McConnell, *My Year in Iraq: The Struggle to Build a Future of Hope* (New York: Simon and Shuster, 2006), 12.
66. Gordon and Trainor, 18.
67. Phillips, 71; Jane Mayer, "The Manipulator," *New Yorker*, June 7, 2004, 58.
68. Phillips, 68.
69. Packer, 74.
70. Phillips, 37.
71. Ibid., 164; Evan Thomas and Mark Hosenball, "The Rise and Fall of Chalabi: Bush's Mr. Wrong," *Newsweek*, May 31, 2004, 22.
72. Phillips, 61.
73. Ibid., 73, 7.
74. Ibid., 49.
75. Woodward, *Plan of Attack*, 258–260.
76. Draper, 187–189.
77. Packer, 147.
78. Woodward, *Plan of Attack*, 282–284.
79. Phillips, 126; Katherine McIntire Peters, "Blind Ambition," *www.govexec.com* (accessed July 1, 2004).
80. Gordon and Trainor, 127.
81. Phillips, 61; David Rieff, "Blueprint for a Mess," *New York Times Magazine*, November 2, 2003.
82. Draper, 281, 283, 284, 285.
83. Gordon and Trainor, 39.
84. Phillips, 63.
85. Woodward, *Plan of Attack*, 411.
86. Woodward, *Bush at War*, 342.
87. Gordon and Trainor, 103–104.
88. Bremer, 10.
89. Gordon and Trainor, 565, 567.
90. Draper, 178.
91. Woodward, *Plan of Attack*, 370; Record, 69, 96, 98, 100. 119; Susan Page, "Prewar Predictions Coming Back to Bite," *USA Today*, April 1, 2003; Record, 96; Rowan Scarborough, "War in Iraq Seen as Quick Win," *Washington Times*, September 8, 2002; Dan Balz, "Conduct of War Defended," *Washington Post*, March 26, 2003; Woodward, *Plan of Attack*, 325–326.
92. Bob Drogin and Greg Miller, "Plan's Defect: No Defectors," *Los Angeles Times*, March 28, 2003; Matt Kelley, "Pentagon's Wolfowitz Admits U.S. Erred in Iraq," *Associated Press*, July 24, 2003.
93. George Kennan, *Soviet-American Relations, 1917–1920* (New York: Atheneum, 1967), 12; Jervis, *Perception and Misperception,* 75, 76–77; Janis, 37.
94. Francis Fukuyama, "US vs. Them," *Washington Post*, September 11, 2002.
95. Record, 40.

CHAPTER 5

1. Flibbert, 312.
2. David Hastings Dunn, "Myths, Motivations, and 'Misunderestimations': The Bush Administration and Iraq," *International Affairs* 79 (2003): 279–297.
3. Woodward, *Bush at War*, 99; Richard Clarke, *Against All Enemies: Inside America's War on Terror* (New York: Free Press, 2004), 30–33; Flibbert, 338.
4. Jervis, *Perception and Misperception*, 319–42.
5. Dick Cheney, "Vice President Honors Veterans of the Korean War," August 29, 2002 (http://georgewbush-whitehouse.archives.gov/news/releases/2002/08/20020829-5.html) accessed February 19, 2009.
6. Woodward, *State of Denial*, 151.
7. Ricks, 96.
8. Ibid., 4–5.
9. Woodward, *State of Denial*, 279.
10. Ricks, 13.
11. Chris J. Dolan, "The Bush Doctrine and U.S. Interventionism," *American Diplomacy*, IX, 2, 2004, http://www.unc.edu/depts/diplomat (accessed September 9, 2006).
12. Bob Woodward, *Plan of Attack* (New York: Simon and Schuster, 2004), 360.
13. Gordon and Trainor, 23, 503–504.
14. Woodward, *State of Denial*, 122.
15. Jervis, *Perception and Misperception*, 128.
16. Gordon and Trainor, 5–6, 8.
17. Ricks, 34–38.
18. Gordon and Trainor, 4.
19. Ibid., 25.
20. Ibid., 103.
21. Ibid, 95–96; Joseph L. Galloway, "Risks of Iraqi War Emerging," *Philadelphia Inquirer*, March 25, 2003; "General Tommy Franks Discusses Conducting the War in Iraq," *Knight Ridder Washington Bureau*, June 19, 2003.
22. Gordon and Trainor, 95–96, 461.
23. Ibid.
24. Record, 119; Michael Gordon with Eric Schmitt, "U.S. Plans to Reduce Forces in Iraq with Help of Allies," *New York Times*, May 3, 2003; Michael Gordon, "How Much is Enough?" *New York Times*, May 30, 2003.
25. Woodward, *Bush at War*, 339–340.
26. Flibbert, 310–352, 343–344.
27. Reuel Marc Gerecht, "Crushing al Qaeda is Only a Start," *Wall Street Journal*, December 19, 2001.
28. Flibbert, 332.

29. Woodward, *State of Denial*, 370–71, 381–82.
30. Ibid., 376, 447.
31. Ibid., 247–248.
32. Ibid., 247–248.
33. Phillips, 201; Office of the White House Press Secretary, "Remarks Made By President George W. Bush at the White House," April 14, 2004.
34. Bremer, 198; John F. Burns, "The Long Shadow of a Mob," *New York Times*, April 4, 2004, Week in Review.
35. Gordon and Trainor, 259.
36. Ibid., 62.
37. Phillips, 201; James Risen, "Account of Broad Shiite Revolt Contradicts White House Stand," *New York Times*, April 8, 2004, A1; Christine Hauser, "Iraqi Uprising Spreads," *New York Times*, April 8, 2001, A1.
38. Ibid., 159; Briefing with Defense Secretary Donald Rumsfeld, U.S. Department of Defense, July 24, 2003.
39. Allawi, 180–181.
40. Hixson, 298.
41. Allawi, 243; Scott Johnson, "Inside an Enemy Cell," *Newsweek*, August 18, 2003; Zaki Chehab, "Inside the Resistance," *Guardian* (London), October 13, 2003.
42. Bremer, 121, 122.
43. Ibid., 129.
44. Phillips, 198.
45. Allawi, 137.
46. Ibid., 11.
47. Ibid., 176, 177.
48. Ibid., 186.
49. Ibid., 457.
50. Ibid., 187; Warren K. Strobel and Jonathan S. Landay, "Intelligence Agencies Warned About Growing Local Insurgency in Late 2003," *Knight Ridder Newspapers*, February 28, 2006.
51. Gareth Stansfield, "Divide and Heal," *Prospect Magazine* 122 (2006).
52. See Tareq Y. Ismael and Jacqueline S. Ismael, "Whither Iraq? Beyond Saddam, Sanctions and Occupation," *Third World Quarterly* 26 (2005): 609–629.
53. Feisal Amin Rasoul Al-Istrabadi, "Rebuilding a Nation: Myths, Realities, and Solutions in Iraq," *Harvard International Review* (2007): 14–19.
54. Allawi, 12, 20.
55. Nimrod Raphaeli, "Culture in Post-Saddam Iraq, *Middle East Quarterly* 14 (2007).
56. Ibid.
57. Allawi, 13–15.
58. Phillips, 131; Eric Schmitt and David E. Sanger, "Looting Disrupts Detailed U.S. Plan to Restore Iraq," *New York Times*, May 19, 2003, A10.

59. David Rieff, "Blueprint for a Mess," *New York Times Magazine*, November 2, 2003.
60. Phillips, 228.
61. Ibid., 131.
62. Gordon and Trainor, 575.
63. Phillips, 134–135, 155.
64. Thomas Friedman, "Bad Planning," *New York Times*, June 25, 2003.
65. Bremer, 17.
66. Ricks, 158–64.
67. Bremer, 45.
68. Phillips, 146, 148.
69. Ibid., 149, 152.
70. Allawi, 155–156, 157.
71. Ismael and Ismael.
72. Larry Diamond, What Went Wrong in Iraq?" *Foreign Affairs* 83 (2004): 43.
73. Packer, 198; *Newsweek*, September 20, 2004; Allawi, 372.
74. Phillips, 145.
75. Draper, 192.
76. Phillips, 170; Pratap Chaterjee, "Iraq: Selections Not Elections," *CorpWatch*, July 1, 2004.
77. Phillips, 172, 173.
78. Anthony Zinni, "Making Vietnam's Mistakes All Over Again," *New Perspectives Quarterly* (2004): 24–28.
79. Ricks, 192.
80. Ibid., 251.
81. Allawi, 186.
82. Packer, 236.
83. Ibid., 238.
84. Woodward, *State of Denial*, 248–249.
85. Bremer, 35.
86. Ibid., 58, 71.
87. Ibid., 326.
88. Ibid., 137.
89. Ricks, 375–376.
90. Woodward, *State of Denial*, 235–238, 259–260.
91. Ibid., 266–67.
92. Ibid., 325.
93. Ibid., 328–329.
94. Ibid., 325–326.
95. Ibid., 219–226.

CONCLUSION

1. John B. Judis, *The Folly of Empire: What George W. Bush Could Learn from Theodore Roosevelt and Woodrow Wilson* (New York:

Oxford University Press, 2004): 7–9; see also John B. Judis, "What Woodrow Wilson Can Teach Today's Imperialists," *New Republic* 228 (June 9, 2003), 19–23.

2. Identifying similar problems in earlier presidential administrations, Robert Jervis suggested that decision makers should "adopt safeguards to decrease their unwarranted confidence in prevailing beliefs, make them more sensitive to alternative explanations and images, and thus decrease the amount of discrepant information needed to make them reexamine their views . . . the actor must try to see the world as the other sees it. Or, rather, on those frequent occasions when the actor cannot be sure what the other's perspective is, he must examine the world through a variety of possible perspectives." Irving Janis suggested a variety of related prescriptions for avoiding groupthink, focusing on structuring the organizational process of decisionmaking in such a way that the tendency toward conformity around a policy based in untested assumptions is avoided. The practices Janis recommended included creating multiple groups under distinct leaders to discuss a given problem, care on the part of leaders to avoid biasing the process by expressing their own views or preferences too early or too strongly, the employment of outside experts and internal "devil's advocates" within the process, and time devoted to imagining alternative explanations for the behavior of international adversaries. Jervis, *Perception and Misperception*, 409; Janis, 262–271.
3. Legro, *Rethinking the World*, 183.
4. Jervis, *Perception and Misperception*, 187.
5. For constructivist approaches suggesting the possibility of changing policy by creating ideational change, see: Peter M. Haas," Introduction: Epistemic Communities and International Policy Coordination," *International Organization* 46 (1992); Martha Finnemore, *National Interests in International Society* (Ithaca: Cornell University Press, 1996); Richard Price, "Transnatioanal Civil Society Targets Land Mines," *International Organization* 52 (1998); Thomas Risse, "Let's Argue! Communicative Action in World Politics," *International Organization* 54 (2000); Frank Schimmelfeining, "The Community Trap: Liberal Norms, Rhetorical Action, and the Eastern Enlargement of the European Union," *International Organization* 55 (2001); Jeffrey T. Checkel, "Social Learning and European Identity Change," *International Organization* 55 (2001); Rodger Payne, "Persuasion, Frames, and Norm Construction," *European Journal of International Relations* 7 (2001); Neta Crawford, *Argument and Change in World Politics: Ethics, Decolonization, and Humanitarian Intervention* (Cambridge: Cambridge University Press, 2002).

Bibliography

Adib-Moghaddam, Arshin. "Manufacturing War: Iran in the Neo-conservative Imagination." *Third World Quarterly* 28 (2007): 635–653.

Adler, Emanuel and Barnett, Michael, eds. *Security Communities.* Cambridge: Cambridge University Press, 1998.

Adler, Emanuel. "Constructivism in International Relations." In *Handbook of International Relations,* edited by Walter Carlsnaes, Thomas Risse, and Beth A. Simmons, 95–118. London: Sage Publications, 2002.

———. *Communitarian International Relations: The Epistemic Foundations of International Relations.* New York: Routledge, 2005.

———. "Seizing the Middle Ground: Constructivism in World Politics." *European Journal of International Relations* 3 (1997): 319–363.

Ajami, Fouad. *Dream Palace of the Arabs: A Generation's Odyssey.* New York: Vintage, 1999.

Al-Istrabadi, Feisal Amin Rasoul. "Rebuilding a Nation: Myths, Realities, and Solutions in Iraq." *Harvard International Review* 29 (2007): 14–19.

Allawi, Ali A. *The Occupation of Iraq: Winning the War, Losing the Peace.* New Haven: Yale University Press, 2007.

Allen, Mike. "Bush: Hussein, Al Qaeda Linked." *The Washington Post,* September 26, 2002.

Altheide, David L. and Grimes, Jennifer N. "War Programming: The Propaganda Project and the Iraq War." *The Sociological Quarterly* 46 (2005): 617–643.

Ambrosius, Lloyd E. "Woodrow Wilson and George W. Bush: Historical Comparisons of Ends and Means in Their Foreign Policies." *Diplomatic History* 30 (2006): 509–543.

American Enterprise Institute. "America After 9/11: Public Opinion on the War on Terrorism, the War with Iraq, and America's Place in the World., *http://www.aei.org/publications/pubID.16974/pub_detail.asp* (accessed May 30, 2008).

Anderson, Benedict. *Imagined Communities: Reflections on the Origin and Spread of Nationalism.* London: Verso, 1991.

Aristotle. "Politics." In *Basic Works of Aristotle,* edited by Richard McKeown, 1127–1316. New York: Random House, 1941.

Atlas, James. "What it Takes to Be a Neo-Neoconservative." *New York Times,* October 19, 2003.

Bacon, Helen H. *Barbarians in Greek Tragedy.* New Haven: Yale University Press, 1961.

Balz, Dan. "Conduct of War Defended." *The Washington Post*, March 26, 2003.

Balz, Dan, Woodward, Bob, and Himmelman, Jeff. "Afghan Campaign's Blueprint Emerges." *The Washington Post*, January 29, 2002, A11.

Barakat, Sultan. "Post-Saddam Iraq: Deconstructing a Regime, Reconstructing a Nation." *Third World Quarterly* 26 (2005): 571–591.

Barkin, J. Samuel. "Realist Constructivism." *International Studies Review* 5 (2003): 325–342.

Barkow, Jerome, Cosmides, Leda, and Tooby, John, eds. *The Adapted Mind: Evolutionary Psychology and the Generation of Culture.* New York: Oxford University Press, 1992.

Barnett, Michael, and Martha Finnemore. *Rules for the World: International Organizations in Global Politics.* Ithaca: Cornell, 2004.

Barton, Frederick D., and Bathsheba Crocker. "Winning the Peace in Iraq,." *Washington Quarterly* (2003): 7–22.

Berger, Peter L., and Thomas Luckmann. *The Social Construction of Reality: A Treatise in the Sociology of Knowledge.* New York: Penguin, 1991.

Berman, Paul. "What Lincoln Knew about War." *New Republic*, March 3, 2003.

Berreby, David. *Us and Them: Understanding Your Tribal Mind.* New York: Little, Brown, and Company, 2005.

Bhatia, Michael V. "Fighting Words: Naming Terrorists, Bandits, Rebels and Other Violent Actors." *Third World Quarterly* 26 (2005): 5–22.

Bially-Mattern, Janice. "Power in Realist-Constructivist Research." *International Studies Review* 6 (2004): 343–346.

Bieler, Andreas. "Questioning Cognitivism and Constructivism in IR Theory: Reflections on the Material Structure of Ideas." *Politics* 21 (2001): 93–100.

Boot, Max. "George Wilson Bush." *Wall Street Journal*, July 1, 2002, editorial page.

Bowden, Mark. "Wolfowitz: The Exit Interviews." *Atlantic Monthly* 299 (2005): 110–122.

Bremer, Paul L., and Malcolm McConnell. *My Year in Iraq: The Struggle to Build a Future of Hope.* New York: Simon and Shuster, 2006.

Brzezinski, Zbigniew. "A Geostrategy for Eurasia." *Foreign Affairs* 76 (1997): 50–64.

Brysk, Alison, Craig Parsons, and Wayne Sandholtz. "After Empire: National Identity and Post-colonial Families of Nations." *European Journal of International Relations* 8 (2002): 267–305.

Burns, John F. "The Long Shadow of a Mob." *New York Times*, April 4, 2004, Week in Review.

Campbell, David. Writing *Security: United States Foreign Policy and the Politics of Identity.* Minneapolis: University of Minnesota Press, 1992.

Carlsnaes, Walter. *The Concept of Ideology and Political Analysis.* Westport: Greenwood Press, 1981.

Cassels, Alan. *Ideology and International Relations in the Modern World.* New York: Routledge, 1996.

Chandrasekaran, Rajiv. *Imperial Life in the Emerald City: Inside Iraq's Green Zone.* New York: Alfred A. Knopf, 2006.

Chaterjee, Pratap. "Iraq: Selections Not Elections." *CorpWatch*, July 1, 2004.

Checkel, Jeffery T. "Social Learning and European Identity Change." *International Organization* 55 (2001): 553–588.

———. "Social Constructivisms in Global and European Politics: A Review Essay." *Review of International Studies* 30 (2004): 229–244.

Chehab, Zaki. "Inside the Resistance." *Guardian* (London), October 13, 2003.

Cherry, Conrad. *God's New Israel: Religious Interpretations of American Destiny.* Chapel Hill: University of North Carolina Press, 1998.

Chernus, Ira. Monsters *to Destroy: The Neoconservative War on Terror and Sin.* Boulder: Paradigm Publishers, 2006.

Christensen, Thomas J. "Perceptions and Alliances in Europe, 1865-1940," *International Organization* 51 (1997): 65–69.

Clarke, Richard. *Against All Enemies: Inside America's War on Terror.* New York: Free Press, 2004.

Connolly, William E. *Identity/Difference: Democratic Negotiations of Political Paradox.* Ithaca: Cornell University Press, 1991.

Cooper, Robert. "Imperial Liberalism." *The National Interest* 79 (2005): 25–34.

Crawford, Neta. *Argument and Change in World Politics: Ethics, Decolonization, and Humanitarian Intervention.* Cambridge: Cambridge University Press, 2002.

Croft, Stuart. *Culture, Crisis and America's War on Terror.* Cambridge: Cambridge University Press, 2006.

Croucher, S.L. "Perpetual Imagining: Nationhood in a Global Era." *The International Studies Review* 5 (2003): 1–24.

Cumings, Bruce, Abrahamian, Ervand, and Ma'oz, Moshe. *Inventing the Axis of Evil: The Truth about North Korea, Iran, and Syria.* New York: New Press, 2004.

Debrix, François. "Discourses of War, Geographies of Abjection: Reading Contemporary American Ideologies of Terror." *Third World Quarterly* 26 (2005): 1157–1172.

———. "US Ideology and the War in Iraq." *The International Studies Review* 7 (2005): 90–92.

Desch, Michael C. "Culture Clash: Assessing the Importance of Ideas in Security Studies." *International Security* 17 (1998): 141–170.

Dessler, David. "Constructivism within a Positivist Social Science." *Review of International Studies* 25 (1999): 123–138.

Diamond, Larry. "What Went Wrong in Iraq." *Foreign Affairs* 83 (2004): 34–56.

———. *Squandered Victory: The American Occupation and the Bungled Effort to Bring Democracy to Iraq*. New York: Holt Paperbacks, 2006.

Diehl, Jackson. "Rice Produces a Brilliant Synthesis." *The Washington Post*, October 1, 2002, B3.

Dolan, Chris J. "The Bush Doctrine and U.S. Interventionism." *American Diplomacy*, IX, 2, 2004. *http://www.unc.edu/depts/diplomat* (accessed September 9, 2006).

Dolan, Chris J., and David B. Cohen. "The War about the War: Iraq and the Politics of National Security Advising in the G.W. Bush Administration's First Term." *Politics and Policy* 34 (2006): 30–64.

Dorrien, Gary. *Imperial Designs: Neoconservatism and the New Pax Americana*. London: Routledge, 2004.

Doty, Roxanne Lynn. "Sovereignty and the Nation: Constructing the Boundaries of National Identity." In *State Sovereignty as a Social Construct*, edited by Thomas Biersteker and Cynthia Weber, 121–147. Cambridge: Cambridge University Press, 1996.

Draper, Robert. *Dead Certain: The Presidency of George W. Bush*. New York: Free Press, 2007.

Drogin, Bob, and Greg Miller. "Plan's Defect: No Defectors." *Los Angeles Times*, March 28, 2003.

Dueck, Colin. "Hegemony on the Cheap: Liberal Internationalism from Wilson to Bush." *World Policy Journal* 20 (2003/04) 1–11.

———. "Ideas and Alternatives in American Grand Strategy, 2000–2004." *Review of International Studies* 30 (2004): 511–535.

———. "Realism, Culture and Grand Strategy: Explaining America's Peculiar Path to World Power." *Security Studies* 14 (2005): 195–231.

Dunn, David Hastings. "Myths, Motivations, and 'Misunderestimations': The Bush Administration and Iraq." *International Affairs* 79 (2003): 279–297.

Durkheim, Emile. *The Rules of Sociological Method*. New York: Free Press, 1966.

Duroselle, Jean-Baptiste. *From Wilson to Roosevelt: Foreign Policy of the United States, 1913–1945*. Cambridge: Harvard University Press, 1963.

Falk, Richard. "The New Bush Doctrine." *The Nation*, July 15, 2002.

Festinger, Leon. *A Theory of Cognitive Dissonance*. Stanford: Stanford University Press, 1957.

Finnemore, Martha, and Kathryn Sikkink. "Taking Stock: The Constructivist Research Program in International Relations and Comparative Politics." *Annual Review of Political Science* 4 (2001): 391–416.

Finnemore, Martha. *National Interests in International Society*. Ithaca: Cornell University Press, 1996.

———. *The Purpose of Intervention: Changing Beliefs about the Use of Force*. Ithaca: Cornell University Press, 2003.

Flibbert, Andrew. "The Road to Baghdad: Ideas and Intellectuals in Explanations of the Iraq War." *Security Studies* 15 (2006): 310–352.

Flint, Colin, and Falah Ghazi-Walid. "How the United States Justified Its War on Terrorism: Prime Morality and the Construction of a 'Just War'." *Third World Quarterly* 25 (2004): 1379–1399.

Foucault, Michel. *Madness and Civilization: A History of Insanity in the Age of Reason*. New York: Pantheon Books, 1967.

———. *The Archaeology of Knowledge and the Discourse on Language*. New York: Pantheon Books, 1982.

Fousek, John. *To Lead the Free World: American Nationalism and the Cultural Roots of the Cold War.* Chapel Hill: University of North Carolina Press, 2000.

Frederking, Brian. "Constructing Post-Cold War Collective Security." *American Political Science Review* 97 (2003): 363–378.

Friedman, Thomas. "Bad Planning." *New York Times*, June 25, 2003.

———. "Brave, Young, and Muslim." *New York Times*, March 3, 2005.

———. "War of Ideas, Part 1." *New York Times*, January 8, 2004.

Frum, David. *The Right Man: The Surprise Presidency of George W. Bush*. New York: Random House, 2003.

Fukuyama, Francis. "US vs. Them." *The Washington Post*, September 11, 2002.

Gaddis, John Lewis. *Surprise, Security, and the American Experience*. Cambridge: Harvard University Press, 2005.

Galbraith, Peter W. *The End of Iraq: How American Incompetence Created a War without End*. New York: Simon & Schuster, 2006.

Galloway, Joseph L. "Risks of Iraqi War Emerging." *Philadelphia Inquirer*, March 25, 2003.

Gartzke, Erik, and Kristian Skrede Gleditsch. "Identity and Conflict: Ties that Bind and Differences that Divide." *European Journal of International Relations* 12 (2006): 53–87.

Gavrilis, James A. "The Mayor of Ar Rutbah." *Foreign Policy* 151 (2005): 28–35.

Geertz, Clifford. *The Interpretation of Cultures.* New York: Basic Books, 1973.

"General Tommy Franks Discusses Conducting the War in Iraq." *Knight Ridder Washington Bureau*, June 19, 2003.

Gerecht, Reuel Marc. "Crushing al Qaeda is Only a Start." *Wall Street Journal*, December 19, 2001, editorial page.

Giddens, Anthony. *Modernity and Self-Identity*. Palo Alto: Stanford University Press, 1991.

Gilbert, Margaret. "Modelling Collective Beliefs." *Synthese* 73 (1987): 185–204.

Goddard, Stacie E., and Daniel H. Nexon. "Paradigm Lost? Reassessing Theory of International Politics." *European Journal of International Relations* 11 (2005): 9–61.

Goldberg, Jeffrey. "Breaking Ranks." *New Yorker*, October 31, 2005.

Goldgeier, James, and Philip Tetlock. "Psychology and International Relations Theory." *Annual Review of Political Science* 22 (2001): 67–92.

Goldstein Judith, and Keohane, Robert. "Ideas and Foreign Policy: An Analytical Framework." In *Ideas and Foreign Policy: Beliefs, Institutions, and Political Change,* edited by Judith Goldstein and Robert O. Keohane, 3–30. Ithaca: Cornell University Press, 1993.

———, eds. *Ideas and Foreign Policy: Beliefs, Institutions, and Political Change.* Ithaca: Cornell University Press, 1993.

Goldstein, Judith. *Ideas, Interests, and American Trade Policy.* Ithaca: Cornell University Press, 1994.

Gong, Gerrit W. *The Standard of "Civilization" in International Society.* Oxford: Clarendon Press, 1984.

Gordon, Michael R., and General Bernard E. Trainor. *Cobra II: The Inside Story of the Invasion and Occupation of Iraq.* New York: Pantheon Books, 2006.

Gordon, Michael R. "How Much is Enough?" *New York Times,* May 30, 2003.

Gordon, Michael R., and Eric Schmitt. "U.S. Plans to Reduce Forces in Iraq with Help of Allies." *New York Times,* May 3, 2003.

Gregory, Ross. *Origins of American Intervention in the First World War.* New York: Norton, 1971.

Guzzini, Stefano, and Anna Leander, eds. *Constructivism in International Relations: Alexander Wendt and His Critics.* London: Routledge, 2006.

Haas, Ernst B. "Why Collaborate? Issue-linkage and International Regimes." *World Politics* 32 (1980): 357–405.

Haas, Mark L. "The United States and the End of the Cold War: Reactions to Shifts in Soviet Power, Policies, or Domestic Politics?" *International Organization* 61 (2007): 145–179.

———. *The Ideological Origins of Great Power Politics, 1789–1989.* Ithaca: Cornell University Press, 2005.

Haas, Peter M. "Introduction: Epistemic Communities and International Policy Coordination." *International Organization* 46 (1992): 1–35.

Hall, Rodney Bruce. *National Collective Identity: Social Constructs and International Systems.* New York: Columbia University Press, 1999.

Hall, Stuart. "Introduction: Who Needs 'Identity?'" In *Questions of Cultural Identity,* edited by Stuart Hall, 1–17. London: Sage, 1996.

Halper, Stefan, and Jonathan Clarke. *America Alone: The Neo-Conservatives and the Global Order.* Cambridge: Cambridge University Press, 2004.

Hamlet, L. "Rethinking Realism with a Constructivist Twist." *The International Studies Review* 5 (2003): 284–286.

Harkness, Albert J. "Americanism and Jenkins' Ear." *Mississippi Valley Historical Review* XXXVII (1950): 61–90.

Hartz, Louis. *The Liberal Tradition in America.* New York: Harcourt Brace, 1955.

Harvey, Robert. *Global Disorder, America, and the Threat of World Conflict.* New York: Carroll and Graf, 2003.

Hixson, Walter L. *The Myth of American Diplomacy.* New Haven: Yale University Press, 2008.

Hobbes, Thomas. *Leviathan*, edited by Richard E. Flathman and David Johnston. New York: W.W. Norton, 1996.

Hoffmann, Stanley. *Gulliver's Troubles*. New York: McGraw Hill, 1967.

Holland D., and J. Lave. *History in Person: Enduring Struggles, Contentious Practice, Intimate Identities*. Santa Fe: School of American Research Press, 2001.

Holsti, Ole. "Cognitive Dynamics and Images of the Enemy: Dulles and Russia." In *Enemies in Politics*, edited by David Finlay, Ole Holsti, and Richard Fagen, 25–96. Chicago: Rand McNally, 1967.

Hopf, Ted. "The Promise of Constructivism in International Relations Theory." *International Security* 23 (1998): 171–200.

———. *Social Construction of International Politics: Identities & Foreign Policies, Moscow, 1955 and 1999*. Ithaca: Cornell, 2002.

Houghton, David Patrick. "Reinvigorating the Study of Foreign Policy Decision Making: Toward a Constructivist Approach." *Foreign Policy Analysis* 3 (2007): 24–45.

Hunt, Michael. *Ideology and U. S. Foreign Policy*. New Haven: Yale University Press, 1987.

Huntington, Samuel P. "The Erosion of American National Interests." *Foreign Affairs* 76 (1997): 28–49.

Ikenberry, G. John "Are Bush and Rice the New Liberal Internationalists?" *TPM Café. http://www.tpmcafe.com/story/2006/1/22/204815/880* (accessed January 20, 2007).

———. "The End of the Neo-Conservative Moment." *Survival* 46 (2004): 7–22.

———. *After Victory: Institutions, Strategic Restraint, and the Building of Order after Major Wars*. Princeton: Princeton University Press, 2001.

Ismael, Tareq Y., and Jacqueline S. Ismael. "Whither Iraq? Beyond Saddam, Sanctions and Occupation." *Third World Quarterly* 26 (2005): 609–629.

Ivie, Robert L. "Savagery in Democracy's Empire." *Third World Quarterly* 26 (2005): 55–65.

Jackson, Patrick Thaddeus, and Daniel H. Nexon. "Constructivist Realism or Realist-Constructivism?" *International Studies Review* 6 (2004): 337–341.

Jackson, Patrick Thaddeus, ed. "Bridging the Gap: Toward a Realist-Constructivist Dialogue." *International Studies Review* 6 (2004): 337–352.

Jacobsen, John Kurt. "Much Ado about Ideas: The Cognitive Factor in Economic Policy." *World Politics* 47 (1995): 39–60.

Jamieson, Kathleen Hall, and Paul Waldman. *The Press Effect: Politicians, Journalists, and the Stories That Shape the Political World*. New York: Oxford University Press, 2003.

Janis, Irving L. *Groupthink: Psychological Studies of Policy Decisions and Fiascoes*. Boston: Houghton Mifflin, 1982.

Jarvis, Christina S. *The Male Body at War: American Masculinity During World War II*. DeKalb: Northern Illinois University Press, 2004.

Jeffords, Susan. *The Remasculinazation of America: Gender and the Vietnam War.* Bloomington: Indiana University Press, 1989.

Jervis, Robert. "The Compulsive Empire." *Foreign Policy* 137 (2003): 83–89.

———. "Understanding the Bush Doctrine." *Political Science Quarterly* 118 (2003): 365–388.

———. "Why the Bush Doctrine Cannot Be Sustained." *Political Science Quarterly* 120 (2005): 351–377.

———. *American Foreign Policy in a New Era.* London: Routledge, 2005.

———. *Perception and Misperception in International Politics.* Princeton: Princeton University Press, 1976.

Johnson, Scott. "Inside an Enemy Cell." *Newsweek*, August 18, 2003.

Johnston, Alastair Iain. "Thinking about Strategic Culture." *International Security* 19 (1994): 32–64.

———. *Cultural Realism: Strategic Culture and Grand Strategy in Chinese History.* Princeton: Princeton University Press, 1998.

Judis, John B. "What Woodrow Wilson Can Teach Today's Imperialists." *New Republic* 228 (2003): 19.

———. *The Folly of Empire: What George W. Bush Could Learn from Theodore Roosevelt and Woodrow Wilson.* Oxford: Oxford University Press, 2004.

Kagan Robert, and William Kristol. "National Interest and Global Responsibility." In *Present Dangers: Crisis and Opportunity in American Foreign and Defense Policy,* edited by Robert Kagan and William Kristol, 3–24. San Francisco: Encounter Books, 2000.

Kammen, Michael. *Mystic Chords of Memory: The Transformation of Tradition in American Culture.* New York: Vintage Books, 1993.

Kaplan, Amy, and Donald E. Pease. *Cultures of United States Imperialism.* Durham: Duke University Press, 1993.

Kaplan, Lawrence F., and William Kristol. *The War over Iraq: Saddam's Tyranny and America's Mission.* San Francisco: Encounter Books, 2003.

Katzenstein, Peter J., ed. *The Culture of National Security: Norms and Identity in World Politics.* New York: Columbia University Press, 1996.

Kaufmann, Chaim D., and Robert A. Pape. "Explaining Costly International Moral Action: Britain's Sixty Year Campaign against the Atlantic Slave Trade." *International Organization* 53 (1999): 631–668.

Kaufmann, Chaim. "Threat Inflation and the Failure of the Marketplace of Ideas: The Selling of the Iraq War." *International Security* 29 (2004): 5–48.

Keller, Bill. "The Sunshine Warrior." *New York Times*, September 22, 2002.

Kelley, Matt. "Pentagon's Wolfowitz Admits U.S. Erred in Iraq." *Associated Press*, July 24, 2003.

Kellner, Douglas. *From 9/11 to Terror War.* Lanham, MD: Rowman and Littlefield, 2003.

Kelman, H.C. "Negotiating National Identity and Self-Determination in Ethnic Conflicts: The Choice between Pluralism and Ethnic Cleansing." *Negotiation Journal* 13 (1997): 327–340.

———. "The Role of National Identity in Conflict Resolution." In *Social Identity, Intergroup Conflict, and Conflict Reduction,* edited by R.D. Ashmore, L. Jussim, and D. Wilder, 187–212. Oxford: Oxford University Press, 2001.

Kennan, George. "On American Principles." *Foreign Affairs* 74 (1995): 116–126.

———. *Soviet-American Relations, 1917–1920.* New York: Atheneum, 1967.

Kennedy, David M. "What 'W' Owes to 'WW'". *The Atlantic* 295 (2005): 36–40.

Kerry, Richard. *The Star Spangled Mirror.* New York: Rowman and Littlefield, 1990.

Kiernan, V.G. *The Lords of Human Kind: Black Man, Yellow Man, and White Man in an Age of Empire.* New York: Columbia University Press, 1986.

Kirkpatrick, Jeanne. "American Power—What For?" *Commentary,* January 2000.

Kissinger, Henry. *Diplomacy.* New York: Simon and Schuster, 1994.

———. *Does America Need a Foreign Policy: American Foreign Policy in the Twenty-First Century.* New York: Simon and Schuster, 2001.

Klingberg, Frank. "The Historical Alternation of Moods in American Foreign Policy." *World Politics* 4 (1952): 239–273.

Korostelina, Karina V. *Social Identity and Conflict: Structures, Dynamics, and Implications.* New York: Palgrave Macmillan, 2007.

Kosterlitz, Julie. "The Neoconservative Moment." *National Journal,* May 17, 2003, 1540–1546.

Kratochwil, Friedrich. "Constructing a New Orthodoxy? Wendt's 'Social Theory of International Politics' and the Constructivist Challenge." *Millennium: Journal of International Studies* 29 (2000): 73–101.

———. "The Embarrassment of Changes: Neorealism as the Science of Realpolitik without Politics." *Review of International Studies* 19 (1993).

Kristeva, Julia. *Strangers to Ourselves.* New York: Columbia University Press, 1991.

Kristol, William, and Robert Kagan. "Toward a Neo-Reaganite Foreign Policy." *Foreign Affairs* (1996): 18–32.

Kristol, Irving. *Neoconservatism: The Autobiography of an Idea.* New York: Free Press, 1995.

Kubalkova, Vendulka. *Foreign Policy in a Constructed World.* Armonk, New York: M.E. Sharpe, 2001.

Kupchan, Charles. *The Vulnerability of Empire.* Ithaca: Cornell University Press, 1996.

Laffey, Mark. and Jutta Weldes. "Beyond Belief: Ideas and Symbolic Technologies in the Study of International Relations." *European Journal of International Relations* 3 (1997): 193–237.

Lantis, J.S. "Strategic Culture and National Security Policy." *The International Studies Review* 4 (2002): 87–113.

Lapid, Yosef. "Culture's Ship: Returns and Departures in International Relations Theory." In *The Return of Culture and Identity in IR Theory*, edited by Yosef Lapid and Friedrich Kratochwil, 3–20. New York: Lynne Rienner Publisher, 1996.

Lebow, Richard Ned, and Thomas Risse-Kappen, eds. *International Relations Theory and the End of the Cold War.* New York: Columbia University Press, 1995.

Leffler, Melvyn P. "9/11 and American Foreign Policy." *Diplomatic History* 29 (2005): 395–396.

———. "9/11 and the Past and Future of American Foreign Policy." *International Affairs* 79 (2003): 1045–1063.

Legro, Jeffrey W. "Culture and Preference in the International Cooperation Two-Step." *American Political Science Review* 90 (1996): 118–137.

———. *Rethinking the World: Great Power Strategies and International Order.* Ithaca: Cornell University Press, 2005.

Legro, Jeffrey W., and Andrew Moravcsik. "Is Anybody Still a Realist?" *International Security* 24 (1999): 5–56.

Levine, Andrew. *The American Ideology: A Critique.* London: Routledge, 2004.

Lewis, Bernard. *What Went Wrong? The Clash between Islam and Modernity in the Middle East.* New York: Harper Perennial, 2003.

Lieber, Robert J. "The Folly of Containment." *Commentary*, April 2003.

Lieven, Anatol. *America Right or Wrong: An Anatomy of American Nationalism.* New York: Oxford University Press, 2004.

Link, Arthur S. et al., eds. *Papers of Woodrow Wilson*, LXII. Princeton: Princeton University Press, 1985.

———. *Wilson the Diplomatist.* New York: Quadrangle Books, 1963.

Lipset, Seymour Martin. *American Exceptionalism: A Double-Edged Sword.* New York: W.W. Norton, 1996.

Lott, Anthony D. *Creating Insecurity: Realism, Constructivism, and U.S. Security* Policy. New York: Ashgate, 2004.

Lyons, Paul. "George W. Bush's City on a Hill." *The Journal of the Historical Society* 6 (2006): 119–131.

Maier, Pauline. *American Scripture: Making the Declaration of Independence.* New York: Alfred A. Knopf, 1997.

Marx, Karl. "The Eighteenth Brumaire of Louis Bonaparte." In *The Marx-Engels Reader*, 2nd ed., edited by Robert Tucker, 594–617. New York: Norton, 1978.

May, Ernest R. "National Security in American History." In *Rethinking America's Security: Beyond the Cold War to New World Order*, edited by Graham Allison and Gregory Treverton, 94–117. New York: Norton, 1992.

Mayer, Jane. "The Manipulator." *New Yorker*, June 7, 2004, 58.

Mearsheimer, John. *The Tragedy of Great Power Politics.* New York: Norton, 2001.

Mehrabian, Albert, and Henry Reed. "Some Determinants of Communication Accuracy." *Psychological Bulletin* 70 (1968): 365–381.

Meyer, Karl E. "America Unlimited: The Radical Sources of the Bush Doctrine." *World Policy Journal* 21 (2004): 1–13.

Mgbeoji, Ikechi. "The Civilised Self and the Barbaric Other: Imperial Delusions of Order and the Challenges of Human Security." *Third World Quarterly* 27 (2006): 855–869.

Monten, Jonathan. "The Roots of the Bush Doctrine: Power, Nationalism, and Democracy Promotion in U.S. Strategy." *International Security* 29 (2005): 112–156.

Morgenthau, Hans, and Kenneth W. Thompson. *Politics among Nations: The Struggle for Power and Peace*, Sixth Edition. New York: McGraw-Hill, 1985.

Moscovici, Serge. "The Phenomenon of Social Representations." In *Social Representations,* edited by Robert M. Farr and Serge Moscovici, 3–69. Cambridge: Cambridge University Press, 1984.

Mufson, Steven. "Bush Urged to Champion Human Rights: Conservatives Call on President to Promote Democracy, Freedom in Foreign Policy." *The Washington Post*, January 26, 2001, A5.

Naim, Moises. "Bush's Willing Enablers." *Foreign Policy* 143 (2004): 96.

Nau, Henry. *At Home Abroad: Identity and Power in American Foreign Policy.* Ithaca: Cornell University Press, 2002.

Neufeld, Mark. "*The Restructuring of International Relations Theory.* Cambridge: Cambridge University Press, 1995.

Neumann, Iver B. *Uses of Others: "The East" in European Identity Formation.* Minneapolis: University of Minnesota Press, 1999.

Ninkovich, Frank. *Modernity and Power: A History of the Domino Theory in the Twentieth Century.* Chicago: University of Chicago Press, 1994.

Norris, Pippa, Montague Kern, and Marion Just, eds. *Framing Terrorism: The News Media, the Government, and the Public.* London: Routledge, 2003.

Norton, Anne. *Leo Strauss and the Politics of American Empire.* New Haven: Yale University Press, 2004.

Notter, Harley. *The Origins of the Foreign Policy of Woodrow Wilson.* Baltimore: Johns Hopkins University Press, 1937.

Offner, Arnold A. "Rogue President, Rogue Nation: Bush and U.S. National Security." *Diplomatic History* 29 (2005): 433–435.

Onuf, Nicholas. "Constructivism: A User's Manual." In *International Relations in a Constructed World,* edited by Vendulka Kubalkova, Nicholas Onuf, and Paul Kowert, 58–78. Armonk: M.E. Sharpe, 1998.

Oren, Ido. Our Enemies and U.S.: America's Rivalries and the Making of Political Science. Ithaca: Cornell University Press, 2002.

Osgood, Robert. *Ideals and Self-Interest in America's Foreign Relations.* Chicago: University of Chicago Press, 1953.

Owen, John M., "Transnational Liberalism and U.S. Primacy." *International Security* 26 (2001/02): 117–152.

———. "When Do Ideologies Produce Alliances?: The Holy Roman Empire, 1517–1555." *International Studies Quarterly* 49 (2005): 73–99.

Packer, George. *The Assassins' Gate: America in Iraq*. New York: Farrar, Strauss and Giroux, 2005.

Page, Susan. "Prewar Predictions Coming Back to Bite." *USA Today*, April 1, 2003.

Patrick, Stewart. "Don't Fence Me In: A Restless America Seeks Room to Roam." *World Policy Journal* XVIII (2002): 2–14.

———. "Multilateralism and Its Discontents: Causes and Consequences of U.S. Ambivalence." In *Multilateralism and U.S. Foreign Policy: Ambivalent Engagement*, edited by Stewart Patrick and Shepard Forman, 1–46. Boulder: Lynne Rienner, 2002.

Payne, Rodger. "Persuasion, Frames, and Norm Construction." *European Journal of International Relations* 7 (2001): 37–61.

Peters, Katherine McIntire. "Blind Ambition." *www.govexec.com* (accessed July 1, 2004).

Phillips, David L. *Losing Iraq: Inside the Postwar Reconstruction Fiasco*. Boulder: Westview Press, 2004.

Podhoretz, Norman. "Oslo: The Peacemongers Return." *Commentary* 112 (2001): 21–33.

Price, Richard. "Transnatioanal Civil Society Targets Land Mines." *International Organization* 52 (1998): 613–644.

Quinn, Adam. "'The Deal': The Balance of Power, Military Strength, and Liberal Internationalism in the Bush National Security Strategy." *International Studies Perspectives* 9 (2008): 40–56.

Rankin, Allen. "U.S. Could Wipe Out Red A-Nests in a Week, General Anderson Asserts." *Montgomery Advertiser*, September 1, 1950.

Raphaeli, Nimrod. "Culture in Post-Saddam Iraq." *Middle East Quarterly* 14 (2007): 33–42.

Record, Jeffrey. *Dark Victory: America's Second War against Iraq*. Annapolis: Naval Institute Press, 2004.

Rees, Wyn, and Richard J. Aldrich. "Contending Cultures of Counterterrorism: Transatlantic Divergence or Convergence?" *International Affairs* 81(2005): 905–923.

Renshon, Stanley A., and Peter Suedfeld, eds. *Understanding the Bush Doctrine: Psychology and Strategy in an Age of Terrorism*. London: Routledge, 2007.

Renwick, Neil. *America's World Identity: The Politics of Exclusion*. New York: St. Martin's Press, 2000.

Reus-Smit, Christian. *The Moral Purpose of the State: Culture, Social Identity, and Institutional Rationality in International Relations*. Princeton: Princeton University Press, 1999.

Rice, Condoleezza. "Promoting the National Interest." *Foreign Affairs* 79 (2000): 47–48.

———. "The Promise of Democratic Peace: Why Promoting Freedom Is the Only Realistic Path to Security." *The Washington Post*, December 11, 2005, B7.

———. "Transforming the Middle East." *The Washington Post*, August 7, 2003.

Ricks, Thomas E. *Fiasco: The American Military Adventure in Iraq*. New York: Penguin, 2006.

Rieff, David. "Blueprint for a Mess." *New York Times Magazine*, November 2, 2003.

Risen, James. "Captives Deny Qaeda Worked with Baghdad." *New York Times*, June 9, 2003.

Risse, Thomas. "Let's Argue! Communicative Action in World Politics." *International Organization* 54 (2000): 1–39.

Risse-Kappen, Thomas. "Collective Identity in a Democratic Community: The Case of NATO." In *The Culture of National Security: Norms and Identity in World Politics*, edited by Peter J. Katzenstein, 357–399. New York: Columbia University Press, 1996.

Rosati, Jerel A. "Cycles in Foreign Policy Restructuring: The Politics of Continuity and Change in U.S. Foreign Policy." In *Foreign Policy Restructuring: How Governments Respond to Global Change*, edited by Jerel A. Rosati, Joe D. Hagan, and Martin W. Sampson, 221–264. Columbia: University of South Carolina Press, 1994.

Rubin, Trudy. "Bush Never Made Serious Postwar Plans." *Philadelphia Inquirer*, June 26, 2003.

Ruggie, John Gerard. *Multilateralism Matters: The Theory and Praxis of an Institutional Form*. New York: Columbia University Press, 1993.

———. *Winning the Peace*. New York: Columbia University Press, 1998.

———. *Constructing the World Polity: Essays on International Institutionalization*. London: Routledge, 1998.

Ryan, David. *U.S. Foreign Policy in World History*. London: Routledge, 2000.

Sagan, Scott. "The Perils of Proliferation: Organization Theory, Deterrence Theory, and the Spread of Nuclear Weapons." *International Security* 8 (1994): 66–107.

Said, Edward. *Culture and Imperialism*. New York: Random House, 1993.

———. *Orientalism*. New York: Vintage, 1978.

Salter, Mark B. *Barbarians and Civilization in International Relations*. London: Pluto Press, 2002.

Scarborough, Rowan. "War in Iraq Seen as Quick Win." *Washington Times*, September 8, 2002.

Scheuer, Michael. *Imperial Hubris: Why the West Is Losing the War on Terror*. Washington, D.C.: Potomac Books, 2005.

Schimmelfennig, Frank. "The Community Trap: Liberal Norms, Rhetorical Action, and the Eastern Enlargement of the European Union." *International Organization* 55 (2001): 47–80.

Schlesinger, Arthur M. *A Thousand Days: John F. Kennedy in the White House.* Boston: Houghton Mifflin, 1965.

Schmitt, Eric, and David E. Sanger. "Looting Disrupts Detailed U.S. Plan to Restore Iraq." *New York Times,* May 19, 2003, A10.

Schonberg, Karl K. *Pursuing the National Interest: Moments of Transition in American Foreign Policy.* Westport: Praeger, 2003.

Scott, William. "Psychological and Social Correlates of International Images." In *International Behavior: A Social-Psychological Analysis,* edited by Herbert Kelman, 70–103. New York: Holt, Rinehart, and Winston, 1965.

Seale, John R. *The Construction of Social Reality.* New York: Free Press, 1995.

Seliger, Martin. *Ideology and Politics.* London: George Allen and Unwin, 1976.

Shapiro, Michael J. "Introduction to Part I." In *Challenging Boundaries: Global Flows, Territorial Identities,* edited by Michael J. Shapiro and Hayward Alker, 3–4. Minneapolis: University of Minnesota Press, 1996.

Sharansky, Natan, and Ron Dermer. *The Case for Democracy: The Power of Freedom to Overcome Tyranny and Terror.* New York: Public Affairs, 2004.

Sherry, Michael. "Dead or Alive: American Vengeance Goes Global." *Review of International Studies* 31 (2005): 245–263.

Silberstein, Sandra. *War of Words: Language, Politics, and 9/11.* London: Routledge, 2002.

Smith, Anthony D. "The Problem of National Identity: Ancient, Medieval, and Modern?" *Ethnic and Racial Studies* 17 (1994): 375–399.

Smith, Rogers M. "The 'American Creed' and American Identity: The Limits of Liberal Citizenship in the United States." *Western Political Quarterly* 41 (1988): 225–251.

———. *Civic Ideals: Conflicting Visions of Citizenship in U.S. History.* New Haven: Yale University Press, 1997.

Smith, Steve. "Wendt's World." *Review of International Studies* 26 (2000): 151–163.

Smith, Tony. *A Pact with the Devil: Washington's Bid for World Supremacy and the Betrayal of the American Promise.* London: Routledge, 2007.

Snyder, Jack. "Anarchy and Culture: Insights from the Anthropology of War." *International Organization* 56 (2002): 7–45.

———. "Imperial Temptations." *National Interest* 71 (2003): 29–40.

———. "One World, Rival Theories." *Foreign Policy* 145 (2004): 83–92.

———. *Myths of Empire: Domestic Politics and International Ambition.* Ithaca: Cornell University Press, 1991.

Somit, Albert, and Steven A. Peterson. *The Dynamics of Evolution: The Punctuated Equilibrium Debate in the Natural and Social Sciences.* Ithaca: Cornell University Press, 1992.

"Sounding the Drums for War." *The Washington Post,* August 10, 2003.

Stansfield, Gareth S. "Divide and Heal." *Prospect Magazine* 122 (2006): 22–27.

Statement of Principles, Project for a New American Century, June 3, 1997. *http://www.newamericancentury.org/statementofprinciples.htm* (accessed September 10, 2008).

Stelzer, Irwin, ed. *The Neocon Reader.* New York: Grove Press, 2004.

Stephanson, Anders. *Manifest Destiny: American Expansion and the Empire of Right.* New York: Hill and Wang, 1995.

Strauss, Leo. *Liberalism Ancient and Modern.* New York: Basic Books, 1968.

Strobel, Warren K., and Jonathan S. Landay. "Intelligence Agencies Warned about Growing Local Insurgency in Late 2003." *Knight Ridder Newspapers*, February 28, 2006.

Susskind, Ron. *The One Percent Doctrine.* New York: Simon and Schuster, 2006.

't Hart, Paul, Erik K. Stern, and Bengt Sundelius. "Foreign Policy-making at the Top: Political Group Dynamics." In *Beyond Groupthink: Political Group Dynamics and Foreign Policy-making*, edited by Paul 't Hart, Eric K. Stern, and Bengt Sundelius, 3–34. Ann Arbor: University of Michigan Press, 2000.

Tanenhaus, Sam. "Bush's Brain Trust" *Vanity Fair* 515 (2003): 114–119.

Taylor, Charles. *Modern Social Imaginaries.* Durham: Duke University Press, 2004.

Telhami, Shibley, and Michael Barnett, eds. *Identity and Foreign Policy in the Middle East.* Ithaca: Cornell University Press, 2002.

Theiler, Tobias. "Societal Security and Social Psychology." *Review of International Studies* 29 (2003): 249–268.

Thomas, Evan, and Mark Hosenball. "The Rise and Fall of Chalabi: Bush's Mr. Wrong." *Newsweek*, May 31, 2004, 22.

Thomson, Jr., James C. "How Could Vietnam Happen: An Autopsy." *The Atlantic Monthly*, April, 1968. Reprinted in *American Foreign Policy: Theoretical Essays*, 4th ed., edited by G. John Ikenberry, 454–463. New York: Longman, 2002.

Tilly, Charles. *Capital, Coercion, and European States, A.D. 990–1992.* New York: Wiley-Blackwell, 2007.

Tuathail, Gearóid Ó., and John Agnew. "Geopolitics and Discourse: Practical Geopolitical Reasoning and American Foreign Policy." *Political Geography* 11 (1992): 190–204.

Tuveson, Ernest Lee. *Redeemer Nation: The Idea of America's Millennial Role.* Chicago: University of Chicago Press, 1968.

Varadarajan, Latha. "Constructivism, Identity, and Neoliberal (In)security." *Review of International Studies* 30 (2004): 319–341.

Vertzberger, Yaacov Y.I. "Collective Risk Taking: The Decision-making Group." In *Beyond Groupthink: Political Group Dynamics and Foreign Policy-making*, edited by Paul 't Hart, Eric K. Stern, and Bengt Sundelius. Ann Arbor: University of Michigan Press, 2000.

Vinson, John Chalmers. *Referendum for Isolation: Defeat of Article Ten of the League of Nations Covenant.* Athens: University of Georgia Press, 1961.

Volkan, Vamik D. *Killing in the Name of Identity: A Study of Bloody Conflicts.* Charlottesville: Pitchstone, 2006.

Walker, R.B.J. "East Wind, West Wind: Civilizations, Hegemonies, and World Orders." In *Culture, Ideology, and World Order,* edited by R.B.J. Walker, 2–23. Boulder: Westview Press, 1984.

———. *Inside/Outside: International Relations as Political Theory.* Cambridge: Cambridge University Press, 1993.

Walt, Stephen M. *The Origins of Alliances.* Ithaca: Cornell University Press, 1987.

———. *Revolution and War.* Ithaca: Cornell University Press, 1997.

Waltz, Kenneth. *Theory of International Politics.* New York: Random House, 1979.

Webb, James. "Heading for Trouble." *The Washington Post,* September 4, 2002.

Weber, Max. *The Protestant Ethic and the Spirit of Capitalism.* New York: Scribner, 1976.

Weeks, William Earl. "Foreign Relations of the Early Republic." *Journal of the Early Republic* (1994): 460.

Weldes, Jutta. "The Cultural Production of Crises: U.S. Identity and Missiles in Cuba." In *Cultures of Insecurity: States, Communities, and the Production of Danger,* edited by Jutta Weldes, Mark Laffey, Hugh Gusterson, and Raymond Duvall, 35–62. Minneapolis: University of Minnesota Press, 1999.

———. *Constructing National Interests: The United States and the Cuban Missile Crisis.* Minneapolis: University of Minnesota Press, 1999.

Weldes, Jutta, Mark Laffey, Hugh Gusterson, and Raymond Duvall. "Introduction: Constructing Insecurity." In *Cultures of Insecurity: States, Communities, and the Production of Danger,* edited by Jutta Weldes, Mark Laffey, Hugh Gusterson, and Raymond Duvall, 1–34. Minneapolis: University of Minnesota Press, 1999.

Wendt, Alexander. "Anarchy Is What States Make of It: The Social Construction of Power Politics." *International Organization* 46 (1992): 391–425.

———. "Constructing International Politics." *International Security* 21 (1995): 71–81.

———. "Identity and Structural Change in International Politics." In *The Return of Culture and Identity in IR Theory,* edited by Yosef Lapid and Friedrich Kratochwil, 47–64. Boulder: Lynne Rienner, 1996.

———. "Social Theory as Cartesian Science: An Auto-Critique from a Quantum Perspective." In *Constructivism and International Relations: Alexander Wendt and His Critics,* edited by Stefano Guzzini and Anna Leander, 181–219. London: Routledge, 2006.

———. *Social Theory of International Politics.* Cambridge: Cambridge University Press, 2004.

White, Hayden. *Tropics of Discourse: Essays in Cultural Criticism*. Baltimore: Johns Hopkins University Press, 1978, 3.

White House, *National Security Strategy of the United States*, 2002.

Willis, Susan. *Portents of the Real: A Primer for Post-9/11 America*. New York: Verson, 2005.

Wishner, Julius. "Reanalysis of 'Impressions of Personality.'" *Psychological Review* 67 (1960): 96–112.

Wohlforth, William C. *The Elusive Balance: Power and Perceptions During the Cold War*. Ithaca: Cornell University Press, 1993.

Wolfowitz, Paul. "Statesmanship in the New Century." In *Present Dangers: Crisis and Opportunity in American Foreign and Defense Policy*, edited by Robert Kagan and William Kristol, 307–336. San Francisco: Encounter Books, 2000.

Woods, Ngaire. "Economic Ideas and International Relations: Beyond Rational Neglect." *International Studies Quarterly* 39 (1995): 161–180.

Woodward, Bob. *Bush at War*. New York: Simon and Schuster, 2002.

———. *Plan of Attack*. New York: Simon and Schuster, 2004.

———. *State of Denial*. New York: Simon and Schuster, 2006.

Yee, Albert S. "The Causal Effects of Ideas on Policies" *International Organization* 50 (1996): 69–108.

Zehfuss, Maja. "Constructivism and Identity: A Dangerous Liaison." *European Journal of International Relations* 7 (2001): 315–348.

———. *Constructivism in International Relations: The Politics of Reality*. Cambridge: Cambridge University Press, 2002.

Zinni, Anthony. "Making Vietnam's Mistakes All over Again." *New Perspectives Quarterly* (2004): 24–28.

Index

Lightning Source UK Ltd.
Milton Keynes UK
UKOW06n0625200116

266715UK00014B/317/P